D0554491

JEFFERSON DAVIS AND HIS CABINET

Jefferson Davis
and his cabinet

REMBERT W. PATRICK

LOUISIANA STATE UNIVERSITY PRESS

Baton Rouge : 1944

MANUFACTURED IN THE UNITED STATES OF AMERICA
BY THE VAIL-BALLOU PRESS, INC., BINGHAMTON, N. Y.

IN MEMORY OF MY

MOTHER

Preface

THE attempt to tell the story of the Confederate Cabinet is an ambitious one. Although the materials for a study of the Confederacy are voluminous, there are few intimate accounts of the chief officers of the civil administration. Jefferson Davis's history of the Confederacy is disappointing in this respect. Only two of the Cabinet members, John H. Reagan and Stephen R. Mallory, left memoirs of value. Diaries, letters, and memoirs of contemporaries leave many questions unanswered. The dearth of personal records has resulted in the neglect of the former Confederate secretaries. Five of them have been the subject of biographies. Most of these studies, however, fail to exhaust the possibilities of the Cabinet member in his relations with his colleagues and the President. In 1938 Alfred Jackson Hanna's *Flight Into Oblivion* portrayed the flight of the Confederate Cabinet after the fall of Richmond. The following year Burton J. Hendrick's *Statesmen of the Lost Cause: Jefferson Davis and His Cabinet* brought to life several of the former secretaries. But the Confederate Cabinet has not been adequately treated as a unit. A reasonably accurate picture of the Confederate Cabinet can be drawn from the sources available. The definitive account of the Southern administration must await the publication of monographs on the men who held office in the Cabinet.

This study was begun in 1936 as a doctoral dissertation at the suggestion of Fletcher M. Green of the University of North Carolina. As it progressed under his direction he gave unsparingly of his time and made many valuable suggestions in regard to both historical accuracy and composition. His friendly advice and constant encouragement as the manuscript was enlarged and revised in the passing years remain a pleasant memory.

The author is also indebted to the following persons for

valuable comments on the manuscript: Howard K. Beale, James Miller Leake, William F. Woods, Ralph B. Flanders, Matthew Page Andrews, and Alfred Jackson Hanna who also gave free access to materials in his possession. Mr. William Alexander Montgomery allowed the use of an unpublished manuscript on the Confederacy by his father, the late Justice of the North Carolina Supreme Court. Mr. Joseph Grégoire de Roulhac Hamilton aided in the search for materials in the Southern Collection of the University of North Carolina. Miss Susan B. Harrison made available the newspapers and manuscripts in the Confederate Museum. The staffs of the following institutions were generous in meeting requests and making available the facilities of their respective libraries: the Alabama Department of Archives and History, the Confederate Museum, the Congressional Library, the Duke University Library, the Florida Historical Society, the University of Florida Library, the National Archives, the New York Public Library, the University of North Carolina Library, and the Virginia State Library. The author also is obligated to Dr. Marcus M. Wilkerson, Director of the Louisiana State University Press, and to Mrs. Leta Book Triche, editorial associate of that Press, for their part in making possible the publication of this book.

In 1940 the manuscript was awarded a Jefferson Davis prize by the United Daughters of the Confederacy. The author gratefully acknowledges this honor and appreciates the interest of Mrs. Livingston Rowe Schuyler and Mrs. Charles E. Bolling of the United Daughters of the Confederacy.

REMBERT W. PATRICK

GAINESVILLE, FLORIDA
MAY, 1944

Contents

Deep Fears and High Hopes

Political revolutions are motivated to some extent by fears that develop from the outlook upon the future. A people may revolt because of dread of danger that inheres in an old association as well as from a desire to reform an existing situation. This was the South's state of mind in 1861. The United States government was largely the handiwork of men of the South, whose representation in executive, legislative, and judicial departments of the Federal government had been disproportionately greater than that of the North. Southern congressmen, with few exceptions, had voted for the general governmental policies that had been adopted. Most of the people of slaveholding states considered the Union beneficial to them only if its Constitution were interpreted in the spirit of James Madison and Thomas Jefferson. Now that the men of the South saw the growth of a new interpretation, alien to what the founding fathers intended, they began to fear the consequences once the sponsors of the new interpretation were in the ascendancy.

The Republican party was a sectional party and, in the Southern view, its fundamental aim was the destruction of the Southern way of life. It had sponsored state "personal liberty laws," and it neither venerated the Constitution of the fathers nor felt an obligation to enforce such laws of the Union as protected slavery. Right was more sacred than law to the Republican, but he and the slaveholder failed to agree on a definition of right. The idea of the higher law, implicit in the Republican definition, doomed the institution of slavery and presaged the uprooting of Southern society.

The South, its leaders feared, would be relegated to the position of a minority region whose rights would be disregarded and trampled upon by a ruthless majority; one part of the Union, the South, would be exploited for the benefit of the other, the North. As long as the Republican party limited its influence to Northern states, the South, though protesting, would keep its compact of union. Once the Republicans gained control of the Federal government, the South was determined to leave the Union. The Southern politicians, fearing that the Northern states under a government controlled by Republicans, would transform the Union into a centralized despotism, warned that the election of a "Black Republican" to the presidency would be deemed sufficient cause for secession.

Abraham Lincoln's election, from the point of view of the South, capped a long series of insults and injuries. The South knew little and cared less about Lincoln. He was unimportant, himself, but the circumstances of his election and the issues raised in the campaign, together with antecedent wrongs, imposed upon the Southern states the duty to reassume the powers delegated to the Federal government and to use their full sovereignty for the protection of their citizens and their rights. Lincoln was the symbol, Roger Atkinson Pryor thought, of a pledge to put Southern rights and property in the course of ultimate extinction.[1] Lincoln represented

. . . that party which overrides all constitutional barriers, ignores the obligation of official oaths, and acknowledges allegiance to a higher law than the Constitution, striking down the sovereignty and equality of the States, and resting its claims to popular favor upon one dogma—the equality of the races, white and black.[2]

The accession of the Republican party to power was not a mere change of administration, but, as the South saw it, an all-embracing revolution that inaugurated new principles and theories of government utterly at variance with the Constitution. Lincoln's

[1] Roger Atkinson Pryor, *Speech on the Resolution Reported by the Committee of Thirty-three, Independence of the South* (Washington, 1861), 6.

[2] Stephen F. Hale (Commissioner from Alabama) to Beriah Magoffin (Governor of Kentucky), December 27, 1860, in *The War of the Rebellion: A Compilation of the Official Records of the Union and Confederate Armies* (Washington, 1880–1901), Ser. IV, Vol. I, 8. Cited hereafter as *Official Records*.

election was characterized by one Southerner, Stephen Hale, as
an open declaration of war in support of a political theory that

. . . destroys the property of the South, lays waste her fields, and
inaugurates all the horrors of a San[to] Domingo servile insurrection,
consigning her citizens to assassinations and her wives and daughters
to pollution and violation to gratify the lust of half-civilized Afri-
cans.[3]

Few thoughtful men of the South would have agreed with this
extreme point of view, but the sentiment was pronounced and
general that the South needed protection from the despotism
that eventually would follow upon Republican victory.

The Southern orator and publicist sought to divine the future.
What would be the position of the South in the Union under a
Republican regime? What advantages would be derived from
separation from the Union? Answers to these questions were
formulated only infrequently from thoughtful reasoning. The
possibility of the election of a Republican President had been
foreseen with dread by the conservative; it had been eagerly
awaited by the radical. "My man for the Presidency," wrote
William M. Lawton, "is the most ultra-Black Republican abolitionist to be found, hoping that in the event of his election, the
southern states may be forced or kicked into an organization of
such a government, as I wish to see established." [4] Lawton and
other radicals saw their opportunity in the Republican victory
of 1860. What of our position in the Union under the Republicans? Southerners asked. It was the question of the day, and the
propagandists answered it in terms of bitterness.

The political position of the South was manifest. Its people
were permanently and increasingly a minority in a government
controlled by a party, one wing of which had

. . . sent, and now are sending among our people fire, and murder,
and the sword, and rape, and poison, to desolate our land; whilst
the other wing is preparing and perfecting measures by the Govern-

---

[3] *Ibid.*
[4] Lawton to William Porcher Miles, May 6, 1860, in William Porcher Miles
Papers, University of North Carolina.

ment, to effect legally, and constitutionally, the "entire extinction of slavery in all the States." [5]

Its hold upon Congress gone and the presidency lost to it forever, the South furthermore must contemplate the time when its control of the Supreme Court would be wrested from it and Northern interpretation of the Constitution should prevail. Northern sympathizers would fill Federal offices in the South, as more and more the South's control was weakened. Stephen R. Mallory of Florida, later Confederate Secretary of the Navy, admitted the truth of William H. Seward's assertion that the South had ruled but would rule no longer. The Floridian neither deplored this loss of power nor feared the consequences, for Southern men had built a republic that was the wonder of the world; but he warned the North that it was assuming a great responsibility. [6]

Others, less complacent than Mallory and unwilling that the North should have the chance to show its political virtues, demanded that the South be protected from the rule of a sectional despotism. The radicals admitted that there were many conservative friends of the South in the free states, but they argued that the outcome of the election of 1860 proved that they were powerless to aid the South. These friends, it was contended, would veer with the political wind and join the enemies of the South.

> They wire in and wire out,
> And leave a body still in doubt,
> Whether the snake that made the tract,
> Is going South or coming back.

Radical fears, as they voiced them, were not based solely upon the attacks on slavery. That institution had suffered, it was true, from the overthrow of constitutional guarantees by the will of a despotic majority; but once oppressive principles were established, no interest would be secure and chance alone would determine what further rights would be marked for destruction.

[5] John Townsend, *The Doom of Slavery in the Union: Its Safety Out of It* (Charleston, 1860), 7.

[6] Occie Clubbs, "Stephen Russell Mallory, The Elder" (unpublished Master's Thesis, University of Florida, 1936), 142.

In the sacred cause of civil liberty, they urged, the South should declare its independence.[7]

That Lincoln's election spelled the abolition of slavery was the Southern radical's firm belief. Far from undermining the institution, Lincoln might make a friendly President, but "The danger to the South will be in exact proportion to his goodness."[8] Submission to a just and generous administration was but the first step, although a long one, in the shrewdly planned campaign of the abolitionists to kill slavery by constitutional means, for no doubts were expressed that abolition was the ultimate purpose of the Republican party. Southern leaders thought they could foretell the progressive steps by which this would be accomplished. Through the control of the Federal patronage the South gradually would be opened to a flood of abolitionist pamphlets and workers in the cause. The unity of Southern opinion could then be broken by boring from within; eventually a majority of good Southern men would be brought to favor freedom for the slaves and, duped by false promises, they would vote away their salvation.

Slavery could never be abolished, however, if the South withdrew from the Union. A union of the slaveholding states would constitute a nation that could dictate terms to the world. The Northern abolition movement would crumble before a threat to withhold cotton from the mills of the North. To save their industries, the free states would suppress every abolitionist society within their borders. The Southern nation could exact from the free states pledges of the return of all fugitive slaves by withholding a commercial treaty, and the threat of terminating the treaty would ensure a complete observance of its promises by the North. The relationship of an independent South to the North would be like that existing between Cuba and the United States. As Cuba was not in the Union, the abolitionist felt no responsibility for slavery there and did not interfere with it. Furthermore, no Northern foe of slavery took advantage of opportunities afforded by commercial intercourse to tamper with slavery in Cuba, being restrained by fear of retaliatory restrictions on

7 Pryor, *Speech on the Resolution*, 6.
8 "Editorial," *Southern Literary Messenger*, XXXI (1860), 472.

Northern trade. Interference with slavery in the South was due to the abolitionist's sense of responsibility for the country as a whole. Once the South established its independence, thus freeing the Puritan conscience of its scruples, the abolitionist movement would die. If a few persisted in interfering, they would be silenced by their own people for the sake of the North's economic interests. If the South remained in the Union it would eventually be overwhelmed by the North and slavery would be destroyed; as an independent confederation, it need have no fear of the abolition of its peculiar institution. Submission to the "Black Republican" party would be a disaster that ultimately would affect all elements of the South's people, for the ensuing emancipation of slaves would bring about the social and political equality of the black and white races. One propagandist asked:

What Southern man, be he slaveholder or non-slave-holder, can without indignation and horror contemplate the triumph of negro equality, and see his own sons and daughters in the not distant future associating with free negroes upon terms of political and social equality, and the white man stripped by the heaven-daring hand of fanaticism of that title to superiority over the black race which God himself has bestowed? [9]

No such problem existed in the North. One Southern publicist declared that it was possible to hold the few free Negroes of the North in check, but that the great numbers of Negroes in the South could be controlled only by the methods established under slavery. Northern fanatics, by their efforts to submerge the white man and give supremacy to the black man, would continue to add to the problem of Negro control in the South. Already the abolitionists had sent their agents to the South to foment insurrections, inciting slaves to fall upon peaceful families in the dead of night, massacre mothers, daughters, and wives, and in one thrust plunge the South into ruin, bloodshed, and rapine.[10] John Brown's raid was cited as an illustration of the woes that Northern abolitionist sentiment and ideals would inflict upon the South. Yet not a few Northern people, some even

[9] Stephen F. Hale to Beriah Magoffin, December 27, 1860, in *Official Records*, Ser. IV, Vol. I, 9.

[10] Cyrus Q. Lemmonds, *Speech on the Convention Bill Delivered in the House of Commons on Thursday, January 17, 1861* (Raleigh, 1861), 10.

partners in his crimes, declared he had made the gallows more glorious than the Cross. Cyrus Q. Lemmonds of North Carolina declared that at an abolitionist meeting in the North one speaker, a Mr. Knight, "said that the people of the North now looked upon Jesus Christ as a dead failure, and hereafter would put their faith in John Brown. . . ."[11] For the South to accept a "Black Republican" President, it was asserted, would mean its enslavement. Nor would it be a slavery that would benefit the moral, physical, and intellectual state of one race while giving wealth and leisure to the other. Rather, it would be an enslavement of intellect to lust, and barbarism would supplant civilization.[12]

The South warned that no reliance could be placed upon the pledges of Northern men. The North had already violated the spirit and destroyed the vitality of the Constitution, the most solemn and sacred compact that could be formulated. No bond could hold a people who ignored the Bible and nullified laws, and yet pharisaically called upon God to support their infamous course.[13] The Union at best would be fatal to the South, for it had long since become a union "of the lust of lucre—a bestial, adulterous and unholy alliance," impossible to preserve, and it was "sinful to try or even wish to save it."[14] The triumph of the Republican party would mean abolition, free Negroes, and social equality. "A drunken and licentious soldiery would hardly be as bad," Lawrence Keitt wrote to his friend William Porcher Miles.[15] The unwelcome prospect impressed even the nonslaveholder. Though perhaps he would not give his life to uphold property in slaves, he was determined to maintain the supremacy and social control over the Negro exercised by the brotherhood of white men.[16]

---

11 *Ibid.*

12 Hale to Magoffin, December 27, 1860, in *Official Records*, Ser. IV, Vol. I, 9.

13 Ambrose R. Wright (Commissioner from Georgia) to Thomas Holliday Hicks (Governor of Maryland), February 25, 1861, *ibid.*, 156.

14 "Editorial," *Southern Literary Messenger*, XXXI (1860), 472.

15 Keitt to Miles, October 3, 1860, in Miles Papers.

16 James Dunwoody Brownson De Bow, *The Interest in Slavery of the Southern Non-Slaveholder* (Charleston, 1860), 8-12; Ulrich Bonnell Phillips, "The Central Theme of Southern History," *American Historical Review*, XXIV (1928–1929), 30–43; id., "The Literary Movement for Secession," *Studies in Southern History and Politics, Inscribed to William Archibald Dunning,* . . . (New York, 1914), 59.

Few secessionists neglected to emphasize the assertion that the North had derived greater material benefit from the Union than had the South. Why did the North, despising the slave states as it did, desire to continue the Union? Because, wrote Edward A. Pollard, one of the editors of the *Richmond Examiner*, the people of the North lived in great part by taxing, cheating, and swindling the South through the Federal government.[17] Efforts were made to estimate the amount the Southern states contributed annually to Northern support. Thomas Prentice Kettell's conclusion that the annual drain from the South was $231,-500,000,[18] was accepted by Southern nationalists as a true statement of the sum. Other economists in the South put the annual loss at $105,000,000, but this would amount in twenty years to the vast total of $2,100,000,000. Southerners were convinced, according to William Howard Russell, that secession would save $47,000,000 a year,[19] ten millions of which was represented by advances, interest, and exchange on a two-hundred-million-dollar cotton crop handled by Northern traders. A reduction of the tariff would account for the remaining thirty-seven million dollars of the annual saving. While admitting that the Union provided the protection of a navy and the services of a postal system and gave well-paid offices to Southern gentlemen of leisure, Captain Meagher, a radical, told Russell that for all this the South paid more than its share.[20] When a sectional President, to add to the South's burdens, threatened to abolish forced labor,

[17] *Daily Richmond Examiner,* April 17, 1861.
[18] The estimates were as follows:

Bounties to fisheries, per annum ....$	500,000
Customs, per annum, disbursed at the North	40,000,000
Profits of Manufacturers	30,000,000
Profits of Importers	16,000,000
Profits of Shipping, Imports and Exports	40,000,000
Profits on Travelers	60,000,000
Profits of Teachers and others sent South	5,000,000
Profits of Agents, Brokers, etc.	10,000,000
Capital drawn from the South	30,000,000
Total from these sources	$231,500,000

Thomas Prentice Kettell, *Southern Wealth and Northern Profits;* . . . (New York, 1860), 127.

[19] William Howard Russell, *Pictures of Southern Life, Social, Political and Military* (New York, 1861), 14.

[20] *Ibid.*, 31.

which was the basis of Southern prosperity, the South would be compelled to declare the Federal compact annulled forever. The Anglo-Saxon people of the South in the nineteenth century, James H. Hammond asserted, paid from thirty to sixty million dollars a year "in *Dane-gelt* to these Northern pirates, and like the Anglo-Saxons of the ninth century, [we] have failed to buy our peace."[21]

Southern nationalists were convinced that the Federal government, from the first organization of the Union, had played favorites with Northern business. Why should a cold and barren North have forged ahead of the South with its mild climate and rich soil? asked Thomas Hill Watts, Confederate Attorney General. He answered his own question. It was, he said, because Congressional legislation had concentrated the large bulk of commerce and capital of the country in the North, despoiled the South of its wealth and commerce, and reduced it to a position little better than that of a tributary to Northern commercial powers.[22] Burdens that were legitimately those of Northern business were thrown upon the public treasury. Even the owners of fishing smacks received bounties for pursuing their own business; millions of dollars were expended for lighthouses and harbor developments; and Northern mail steamers and business, because of reduced postage, received a seven-million-dollar gift, as shown by the United States postal deficits.[23] The prosperity of the North, in great part, was dependent upon Federal largesse; that of the South, not at all. Three fourths of the nation's foreign trade was Southern, Duff Green pointed out, and yet the state of New York possessed more capital than the entire South.[24] He denied that this striking difference in financial resources could be attributed to the circumstance that one section was agricultural and the other commercial; the true explanation was that the financial system was organized in deference to the busi-

[21] Troup [Isaac William Hayne], *To the People of the South, Senator Hammond and the Tribune* (Charleston, 1860), 16.

[22] Inaugural address of Governor Thomas Hill Watts of Alabama, December 1, 1863, in *Representative Men of the South* (Philadelphia, 1880), 46.

[23] From the Georgia Ordinance of Secession, in *Official Records*, Ser. IV, Vol. I, 82.

[24] Duff Green, *Facts and Suggestions on the Subjects of Currency and Direct Trade* (Macon, 1861), 5–6.

ness of the North, and this system was not suited to the needs of the agrarian South. The planter needed long-term credit, while the merchants and the manufacturers required short-term loans. Green believed a financial system that would meet the planters' needs could be evolved. He used the experience of the railroads to illustrate the South's financial bondage. Mile for mile, they could be constructed at less expense in the South than in the North. In the South, too, the roads were assured of heavy traffic because that region had three times the value of exports of the North. Yet the North could borrow money for railroad construction at 5 per cent and even less, whereas the best Southern roads could not get money at less than 10 per cent. "Is not the answer to be found," he asked, "in the fact that the North has been the financial agent of the South?" [25]

Independence was the magic that Southern men counted on to wipe out all sectional inequalities. The course for the South, George Fitzhugh wrote early in 1860, was "Disunion Within the Union." [26] Total cessation of trade with any Northern state that did not respect slave property would at once lead to direct trade with Europe, would encourage Southern commerce, manufactures, agriculture, and education, and would enrich the South and make it economically independent. The abolitionists would thus be brought to immediate terms, for they could not live without slave products and a slaveholding market for their manufactured goods. "The Union is *ours*," Fitzhugh prophesied, "if we choose to use it and, hence, the abolitionists denounce it." But by 1861 ardent nationalists were certain that only secession could bring the desired advantages to the South. Withdrawal from the Union in any circumstances was opposed by only a few in the South; others were for giving Lincoln a chance and seeking to reach a compromise; and others still would delay secession until the South should be more prepared to act as a unit to defend itself, if necessary, by force of arms. The wisest policy, and at the same time the natural remedy, Benjamin H. Hill believed, was to demand the unconditional observance of the Constitution by every state, and to enforce compliance even to the extent of

[25] *Ibid.*, 10.
[26] George Fitzhugh, "Disunion Within the Union," *De Bow's Review*, XXVIII (1860), 1–7.

employing the armed force of the Federal government against recusant states.[27] While remaining in the Union the South would gain time to prepare for secession. Even if secession were peacefully accomplished, the South had no ships to transport its produce, no commercial treaties, no postal system; if secession brought war, it had no navy, no forts or arsenals, no munitions, and no armament except miscellaneous small arms. The South, while seeking the redress of wrongs within the Union, could prepare to withdraw from it, should that become necessary. Failure to obtain redress within the Union would itself unite the people of the cotton states and bring in other states, not then ready for secession, when they were forced to abandon all hope of security within the Union. Should only a few states secede by separate action, war would most likely result. Prepared beforehand, cooperative secession of the slave states would be accomplished peacefully. So ran the many and various reasonings of Southern men.

Preparation and cooperation were favored by most of the wealthy Southern politicians of national prominence. Few among the men who later held executive positions in the Confederacy would have counseled rushing headlong into secession. Leaders in South Carolina had foreseen the need for cooperation, and in the early months of 1860 they had sought to bring about the unity of the Southern people. It was especially important that Virginia's adherence be assured, and Christopher G. Memminger was packed off from Charleston to lobby in Richmond for a general conference. His efforts were unproductive, for he found sentiment in Virginia against a movement for a conference, and he was convinced that, should a convention be called, no strong measure could be adopted there.[28] Memminger left Richmond disgusted with a South that, weakened by internal differences, could not plan for the future.

The failure of South Carolina's scheme for a Southern convention served to intensify the activities and agitations of the radicals. The newspapers of the South teemed with articles devoted to the idea of secession. Wild harangues by crossroads

[27] Benjamin Harvey Hill, Jr., *Senator Benjamin H. Hill of Georgia. His Life, Speeches and Writings* (Atlanta, 1893), 247.

[28] Memminger to Miles, November 23, 1860, in Miles Papers.

orators and political hacks who portrayed a tyrannical North found a greater response than calm and reasoned discourses on current relations. "My own countrymen here in South Carolina are distempered to a degree that makes them to a calm and impartial observer real objects of pity," wrote James Louis Petigru, a staunch old Unionist.[29] Flag raisings and musters were ideal occasions for promoting the spirit of independence. When Miles was asked to make a speech at a muster in Charleston he was told: "We do not ask you to go to any trouble in preparing an elaborate speech but simply to give us a little heart-stirring appeal for the good of the cause, such as you can so well make." [30] The minor speakers took their cue from the utterances of the nationally known politicians who were out-and-out secessionists. An aggressive minority had become a majority by the fall of 1860, and few men of importance had the hardihood to come out openly against separation from the Union. A willingness for ultimate secession had to be avowed by the opposition before they would be heard on their plans for compromise or delay. Southern radicals feared and denounced the despotic Northern majority, but a foreign journalist on the spot recorded his impression of an irresponsible and cruel tyranny of the majority in the South.[31] This observer, writing after the Confederacy had been formed, declared that the minority had bowed to the will of the mass and was hastening to lick the feet of the conqueror. He could see no tolerance on the question whether the South had the right to secede or had acted wisely in doing so. If indeed an opposition existed, it was hiding in holes and corners, sitting in darkness, silent, fearful, and perhaps hopeless.[32]

Life in an independent South was alluringly pictured by propagandists both before and after secession. They envisioned an ideal state founded by a simplicity-loving agricultural people. Cotton, corn, sugar, and rice would be raised by faithful Negroes. With its agricultural products untaxed and freed of the tribute paid in Northern commissions, the South could buy all she de-

[29] Petigru to Edward Everett, October 28, 1860, quoted in James Petigru Carson, *Life, Letters and Speeches of James Louis Petigru: The Union Man of South Carolina* (Washington, 1920), 360.

[30] George H. Walter to Miles, November 23, 1860, in Miles Papers.

[31] Russell, *Pictures of Southern Life*, 33.

[32] *Ibid.*

sired and accumulate money besides. As its fields yielded bounteous crops of cotton, the nations of the world would prostrate
themselves before the throne of King Cotton, crying, "Cotton,
More Cotton! That is all we ask!" [33] In the train of independence
would come economic and cultural freedom from the North.
The South would wax prosperous through cultivation by slave
labor of staple crops for which there would be direct trade in the
markets of Europe. A financial system of the South's own devising would supply the needs of planters and provide capital for
transportation lines and small manufacturers. Its economic security established, the South would rapidly develop its own distinct culture. Magazines, newspapers, and books no longer would
be allowed to enter from the North. The South would have
written "finis" to that period of its history during which the
North had imposed its culture upon it in the form of abolitionist publications, hypocritical parsons, and ranting school-
teachers. The time would have passed when Southern planters
spent their vacations in places above Mason and Dixon's line,
to the considerable profit of Northern merchants and innkeepers.
The separation of North and South would be complete, for the
South would have nothing to do with the North, in part because
of its dislike of Yankee meddlers and their distorted ideas; but
chiefly for the reason that Southern culture would far surpass
that of the North. A new golden age, based on a sound and
equitable economy and transcending that of Augustan Rome,
would arise in the independent South.[34]

The crowning glory of the new golden age would be the government established by an independent South. Its leaders had
long believed that changes were needed in the Constitution of
the United States. They viewed the Constitution, in the main,
as an inspired work of the fathers, a document to be revered and
obeyed. They would not destroy a single essential feature in it.
Only certain sections, which had been erroneously interpreted
by Northern fanatics, should be altered for the sake of clarity.
Secession would not destroy the Constitution, rather it would
preserve it as it had been conceived. "We are not revolution-

---

[33] William Howard Russell, *My Diary North and South* (New York, 1863), 100.
[34] "The Future of Our Confederation," *De Bow's Review*, XXXI (1861), 40.

ists—" the Southerner declared; "we are resisting revolution. We are upholding the true doctrines of the Federal Constitution. We are conservative." [35]

This was a situation which, viewed from every salient, convinced Southerners that the Union must be dissolved. South Carolina led the way. The union existing between it and the other states under the name of the United States was declared dissolved on December 20, 1860, by unanimous vote of the delegates of a specially called state convention. South Carolina's action was followed by state conventions in Mississippi, Florida, Alabama, Georgia, Louisiana, and Texas. By February 1, 1861, seven states had left the Union. The Alabama convention on January 11 invited the slaveholding states to send delegates to a Southern convention to be held at Montgomery, Alabama, on February 4, 1861.

Every seceding state accepted the invitation.[36] The provisional Constitution was drawn up in four days by the delegates who had met in convention on the appointed date. A temporary government consisting of a provisional Congress of one house, which was charged with the election of provisional officers of government, was provided by the Constitution. Jefferson Davis was elected President, and Alexander H. Stephens, Vice-President by the Congress on February 9. In the following weeks the provisional Congress framed a permanent Constitution for the Confederate States of America, and on March 11 the document was submitted to the states for ratification. Before the end of April, 1861, all the seceding states had returned their acceptances of the Constitution. The permanent government, as provided for by the Constitution, was to be established on February 22, 1862, on which date the term of office of the Executive of the provisional government would expire.

[35] "Our Danger and Our Duty," *ibid.*, XXXIII (1862), 44.

[36] The delegates from Texas did not arrive at Montgomery until February 15, 1861. The Confederate States of America was enlarged by the admission of the following states: Texas, March 2; Virginia, May 7; North Carolina and Tennessee, May 16; Arkansas, May 18; the secession governments of Missouri and Kentucky were recognized and the states admitted to the Confederacy on August 19 and December 9, 1861. *Journal of the Congress of the Confederate States of America* (Washington, 1904–1905), I, 1, 54, 97, 193, 234, 235, 244, 370, 546, 547. Cited hereafter as *Journal of Congress*.

The delegates at the Montgomery convention in framing the Constitution for the Confederate States adopted, with only slight modifications, the Constitution of the United States, for which they retained a deep regard because they considered it the creation of men who were their spiritual fathers. "The Constitution framed by our fathers is that of these Confederate States . . . ," [37] Davis declared in his inaugural address. Stephens insisted that the Montgomery convention limit its alterations of the old Constitution to those changes necessary to safeguard the institution of slavery, protect state rights, and improve the machinery of government. His refusal to sanction any other important changes was supported by an overwhelming majority of the delegates. Stephens in the end believed that the Confederacy, by copying the Constitution of the United States and placing it in the hands of a people who would interpret it in the spirit of the fathers, had rescued that document from utter annihilation.

News of the organization of the Confederate government moved the editor of the *Southern Literary Messenger* to rhapsodical superlatives. "Civil liberty," he wrote, "has found a house of refuge, a home, safe forever alike from the tyranny of kings and from the despotism of agrarian mobs and lawless democracies!" [38] The Confederacy appeared to this ardent writer a grand achievement—a mighty revolution! All humanity would be exalted by the action of Southern men, and the name of the South henceforth would be synonymous with liberty. The bravest blood, the highest spirits, the most cultured intellects on the continent would repair to this haven of civilization and political freedom. "For high minded independent people, for fertile soil, for genial climate, for magnificent destiny, the peer of this youthful nation will not be found in all the world." [39]

Other advantages of which the new nation had a right to be proud were enumerated by ardent nationalists. There would be no need for an army or navy. Nor would the South need a mer-

[37] James D. Richardson (ed.), *A Compilation of the Messages and Papers of the Confederacy, Including the Diplomatic Correspondence, 1861–1865* (Nashville, 1905), I, 36.
[38] "Editorial," *Southern Literary Messenger*, XXXII (1861), 240.
[39] *Ibid.*

chant marine, for the world would come to the South begging
cotton. As for war, the South itself would never dream of it, nor
was there danger that another country would attack the South,
for no sane nation would make war on cotton. By cutting off the
cotton crop the South could bring the world to her feet without
firing a shot or drawing a sword.[40] Thus relieved of the expensive
burden of maintaining an army and navy, the cost of government would be comparatively small. All that a Southern Confederacy would need in the way of revenue would be from ten
to twenty million dollars, and this amount could be provided by
a 5 per cent tariff duty. No other taxes need ever be considered.
The entire cost of government would fall far short of the total
amount embraced by tariff duties paid by the South to the Federal government plus money spent in the North by Southerners.[41] The tariff in the agrarian South would be limited to the
purpose of revenue only, and the duties would be low. There
would be no question of internal improvements or subsidies
from the central treasury to private business. These, the Southern
nationalists declared, were things of the past.

Some foresaw the destiny of the Confederacy as a tropical
empire—in which Cuba figured prominently—expanded by the
acquisition of lands to the southward. Others, rejecting imperial-
ism, maintained that the true interests of the South did not lie
in expansion. George Fitzhugh opposed the idea that the Confederacy should acquire Cuba.[42] Spain, Brazil, and the South
were the only slaveholding nations, and for the Confederacy to
take Cuba would be to forfeit Spanish friendship. The annexa-
tion of one island in the Caribbean would require the annexa-
tion of all. Any attempt at the conquest of Cuba would probably
be attended by the emancipation of the slaves on the island. The
South should, therefore, make a commercial treaty with Spain
and cultivate the friendship of the Cuban people, rather than
annex Cuba. "This Cuban project is of Northern birth and
Northern nursing; we fear the Greeks and their presents." [43]
Whatever sentiment had existed for acquiring the territory of

40 Troup, *To the People of the South*, 11.   41 *Ibid.*
42 George Fitzhugh, "Cuba: The March of Empire and the Course of Trade,"
De Bow's Review, XXX (1861), 30–42.
43 "Southern Trade," *ibid.*, 570.

neighbors became virtually nonexistent by the time secession had become a fact and the Confederacy organized. The South was satisfied to remain within her own boundaries. After all, the slaveholding states and the Indian Territory were a splendid empire in themselves.

It pleased the Southern propagandist to contrast the idyllic prosperity in store for the South with the dismal prospect before the North. "That magic word, Secession," the editor of the *Richmond Examiner* gloated, "transferred thousands of millions of wealth from the North to the South." [44] Secession had left the North facing bankruptcy, he believed, and its people were confronted with the alternative of migrating to the West or starving. The census of 1860 would show, the editor was confident, that the sterile soils of the New England states, New York, and Pennsylvania could not produce enough to feed their own people. Nor had they commodities to sell in exchange for food. Their manufactures could sell only in the market of the Northwest, and at that they would be the cheapest and coarsest goods. Northern participation in a world market would be prevented by the increased price of cotton. The principal trade of New York City had been with the South, the argument ran. Southern gold had enriched that city's merchants, dividends from Southern stocks had created its millionaires, and Southern produce had filled its warehouses and the holds of the ships that sailed from its harbor. [45] Secession had wrought a change. The Northern metropolis had now lost the source of its livelihood.

. . . the silent streets, the deserted hotels, the closed places of amusement and recreation, every place and everything witnesses that the glory of the once-proud metropolis is gone, gone too, forever, for the trade of the South will never return. [46]

New York City's plight, wrote Pollard, was typical of the situation of the entire North. Four hundred million dollars would not cover the losses the United States had already suffered from secession, said Stephens in May, 1861. "They are now like leeches that have been shaken from a horse's legs," he said, "and

---

44 *Daily Richmond Examiner,* May 3, 1861.
45 *Ibid.,* June 4, 1861.   46 *Ibid.*

are beginning to find out what it was that fattened them. We are the horse; and what they are determined to do is to get the horse back again." [47]

Those who believed the North rich and the South poor were laughed to scorn by the *Examiner*. Pollard thought it was no exaggeration to say that the South was one of the wealthiest countries in the world and the United States one of the poorest. Sixty-eight bankruptcies in Boston within one week were convincing evidence for the editor that the Northeast was as poor as a pauper. Southern trade had been the basis of Northern wealth, and now that the North was cut off from that trade and from raw cotton the vaunted Northeastern capital had become valueless. Northern financiers who pretended to lend funds to their government would soon find themselves bankrupt, for their stocks and fixed capital had lost value at the very moment of secession. All the available specie of the North would be needed for ordinary circulation, and a government which had no visible means of repayment could not hope to obtain foreign loans. It would be easier for the "poor South" to raise a defensive army of two hundred thousand men, Pollard concluded, than for the wealthy North to maintain an invading army of fifty thousand men. [48] In terms of prophecy made familiar by a President of the United States seventy years later, Pollard foretold the fate that awaited the North. So confident was he of the economic collapse of the United States that he predicted that grass would be growing in the streets of its principal cities. The *Richmond Examiner* reprinted an article, "Grass in Their Streets," [49] from the *Louisville Courier* that must have warmed the hearts of patriotic Southerners. The article told of a reputable businessman of New York who had sent a friend in Louisville a parcel of grass he had plucked in a main street of his city. The editor of the *Selma Reporter* related that he had found a young man exhibiting a weed that had sprung up in a New York City street where none had grown before in forty years, and the newspaper represented the city as being on the brink of ruin. "New York

[47] Richard Malcolm Johnston and William Hand Browne, *Life of Alexander H. Stephens* (Philadelphia, 1878), 404.
[48] *Daily Richmond Examiner*, May 15, 1861.   [49] *Ibid.*, June 4, 1861.

has seen her brightest day," the editor pronounced; "Gotham must fall." [50]

The political future of the United States, as viewed by the ardent Southern nationalist in 1861, was as hopeless as the economic future. Only the plunder of the South had held the North together in a common bond; with that source of unity removed, the North would split into two or more sections. Within these separated parts dissensions would arise. The people had been promised plunder but were instead famine-stricken; the cold, naked, and starving masses would turn upon their leaders. [51] To add to the chaos, a fearful conflict eventually would ensue between the Northern capitalists and the exploited labor of the mills. That the United States would lapse into complete anarchy was an eventuality of which Stephens had little doubt. Another Southern propagandist predicted that when the United States could no longer, vampire-like, suck the blood from a compliant South; when atheism, fanaticism, and socialism had done their work among a crowded population, then taxation, misery of the masses, standing armies, despotism, and revolution would result. [52] A fitting epitaph for the North then would be: "Here lies a people, who, in attempting to liberate the negro, lost their own freedom." [53] In such dismal terms did Southern radicals picture the hopeless future that lay ahead of the Union.

Those in the South who feared that secession would bring war were reassured by the too-confident nationalists, who asserted that the North would not for a moment consider the possibility of a war whose aim was the destruction of the fundamental rights of statehood. [54] Its people could not be induced

---

[50] Ibid., July 16, 1861, quoting the Selma Reporter.

[51] George Fitzhugh, "The Message, the Constitution, and the Times," De Bow's Review, XXX (1861), 164.

[52] Wm. H. Holcombe, "The Alternative: A Separate Nationality, or the Africanization of the South," Southern Literary Messenger, XXXII (1861), 85.

[53] Ibid.

[54] The South failed to realize that the North believed secession would destroy the fundamental concept of the American Republic. An illustration of the Northern point of view is found in a letter of D. Clapp, a former resident of North Carolina, to William Alexander Graham. Writing from his adopted home, Danville, Illinois, on May 7, 1861, Clapp said, "Can the president save the Republic by acknowledging the right of secession? Certainly not! Admit this, and at once you destroy our Government. If South Carolina has the right to secede, so has Illinois. . . . The right of rebellion none deny. But in case of rebellion, what is the duty

to support war for such a purpose. Secession was a perfectly constitutional recourse, for the Northern states had broken the compact and had released the Southern states from their allegiance.
The individual state within the Union retained its sovereignty,
and in withdrawing from it, the Southern states were reassum-
ing certain definite powers which they had conditionally given
an agent, the Federal government. A state had the moral and
legal right, just as an individual had, to disavow an agent whose
course of action had run counter to the implicit instructions of
his contract. This concept of the original Union was fundamental and, as attested by history, had been so recognized. For
during the War of 1812 representatives of the New England
states had considered exercising the right of secession from the
Union. War, then, was unlikely to result from similar action by
the South. A few fanatics in the North would vote for war to
free the Negro, but their influence would be negligible, for the
meddling Puritan would never fight and he could find few willing to give up their lives for the Negro. By such arguments
Southern nationalists sought to lull the fears of the timorous
in the South.

Should the United States be so foolish as to contemplate a war
of conquest, however, the South had one trump—cotton. Hammond had said: ". . . you dare not make war on cotton. No
power on earth dares to make war upon it." [55] The South could
topple England into decay, and with her the entire civilized
world, by ceasing cotton production for three years, or by withholding it from the market. "Cotton is King," Hammond had
proclaimed, and thousands echoed him. Secession was bound to
be peacefully accomplished because England, France, and the
rest of commercial Europe required that it should be. [56] England
would sweep away the first attempt at a blockade of the South.
"Look out there," a Charlestonian told Russell, pointing to
cotton piled on a wharf. "There's the key will open all our

of the Government? . . . And one of the questions now to be tried and tested is,
whether a republican form of government can sustain itself or not. . . . The
North is a *unit in support of the Constitution and the enforcement of the laws.*"
William Alexander Graham Papers, University of North Carolina.

[55] Troup, *To the People of the South,* 12.

[56] W. H. Chase, "The Secession of the Cotton States: Its Status, Its Advantages
and Its Power," *De Bow's Review,* XXX (1861), 93.

ports, and put us into John Bull's strong box as well." [57] There were few in the deep South who did not accept this general belief in the omnipotence of cotton.

Mingled amusement and pity must have been the sensations of the witty and thoughtful Petigru as he contemplated the antics of his fellow countrymen. The Confederacy was formed, he wrote, on hollow and rotten principles, on the visionary concept that all nations would bend the knee to cotton.[58] The Constitution, he had always believed, was the South's greatest interest, but "unfortunately for me," he wrote, "my countrymen have in the course of the last 50 years, taken up the idea that it was a mistake and that cotton is our greatest interest." [59] The amiable old lawyer was beloved by most Charlestonians, but they paid scant heed to his "unsound" ideas. Whoever questioned the kingship of cotton, though he might support his opinion with sound reasoning, usually was looked upon as a "crack-brain," or, worse, a traitor to his section.[60] To accept the puissance of cotton was to rule out the possibility of war. Among the many statements made by ardent Southerners as to this impossibility of war was one by Leroy Pope Walker. He told a friend in later years that he had canvassed the state of Alabama counseling secession and had declared that with his pocket handkerchief he would wipe up all the blood shed as a result of the South's withdrawal from the Union.[61] All over the South utterances on a par with this were common. Robert M. T. Hunter, even though more restrained and cautious in his language, believed that war would never be attempted.[62] Howell Cobb, as late as January, 1861, did not expect war, but he advised that the South prepare for the worst and get a government functioning as speedily as possible. [63]

[57] Russell, *My Diary North and South,* 52.
[58] Petrigru to William Carson, March 2, 1861, quoted in Carson, *Letters and Speeches of Petigru,* 372.
[59] *Id.* to Reverdy Johnson, April 16, 1861, *ibid.,* 379.
[60] Thomas Cooper DeLeon, *Belles, Beaux and Brains of the 60's* (New York, 1909), 50.
[61] Pierce Butler, *Judah P. Benjamin* (Philadelphia, 1907), 234.
[62] Hunter to James Micou and others, December 10, 1860, in Charles Henry Ambler (ed.), *Correspondence of Robert M. T. Hunter, 1826–1876,* American Historical Association, *Annual Report,* 1916, Vol. II (Washington, 1918), 340.
[63] Howell Cobb to Miles, January 10, 1860 [1861], in Miles Papers.

The cheering belief that the South would be allowed to depart in peace was not held universally, however. Daniel H. Hamilton was as certain that secession would be attended by bloodshed as that the sun would rise the next day.[64] He had been educated in the North and wrote with some understanding. He believed that the events of the day might check the Northerners, but that they would never turn back until either their adversaries or they themselves were destroyed. The South, he declared, could not give way before such foes; it must stand and face them prepared, with knowledge that the fight was against an enemy without mercy. Davis saw little hope for peaceful secession, and predicted a bloody civil war,[65] an opinion in which most thoughtful Southern leaders agreed. In truth, men of intelligence who had some acquaintance with the attitudes of Northerners had little hope that the simple expedient of secession would effect a peaceful solution of all sectional problems, notwithstanding all the optimistic utterances retailed for popular consumption. Whatever the hazard, secession was justified, many believed, by the very fact that the North had refused either to concede to the South its constitutional rights in the Union or to allow it to withdraw from the Union in peace. "I would be an equal or a corpse," a correspondent wrote to Clement C. Clay.[66] War was probable, but the Southerner would not become a slave to "Black Republicanism" without an effort to retain his freedom.

And what if war should come? It would be a short one, hardly more than a glorified muster. The South could wage a successful campaign, for she had cotton, material supplies, and hardy men, trained to outdoor life and handy with the rifle. Among her sons were the great military minds of the Union. Had not a Southern man written the military tactics then in use by the United States? [67] What the South lacked in the way of a fleet or military

[64] Hamilton to *id.*, January 23, 1861, *ibid.*

[65] Davis to Francis Wilkinson Pickens, January 13, 1861; *id.* to George W. Jones, January 20, 1861, in Dunbar Rowland (ed.), *Jefferson Davis, Constitutionalist. His Letters, Papers, and Speeches* (Jackson, 1923), V, 36–39.

[66] David Clopton to Clay, December 13, 1860, in Clement Claiborne Clay Papers, Duke University.

[67] *Hardee's Infantry Tactics.* Evans and Cogswell, Charleston publishers, had several editions of the *Tactics* in preparation to meet the great demand, only to find that Colonel William Joseph Hardee held a copyright from the Confederacy.

supplies would be made up for by the intelligence and courage of her people. Had not the colonies, weaker far than the South and possessing less material wealth, defeated England, a nation greatly superior in strength to the North? All that the Confederacy need do would be to stand on the defensive, win a few victories, and the war would be over. Should the United States fatuously wish to consider a continuation of the struggle, European intervention would come swiftly and decisively.

Great financial advantages in war were envisioned by the *Daily Richmond Examiner,* always a blatant voice of good things to come.[68] Virginia's bane, the editor wrote, had been her purchase in the North of a thousand and one things that could easily be produced at home. By doing without unnecessary articles of Northern production, the state would save more than the actual expenses of the war. Thus the costs of the war would be defrayed at the enemy's expense, and Virginia would be enriched. There was danger of war, the editor admitted, but a premature peace was more to be feared; [69] for an early peace, followed by amicable relations, might result in Southern dependence on the North. On the other hand, a sanguinary fight would be insurance against Yankee teachers, parsons, drummers, merchants, and industrial products. The South must cross the red sea of blood, but she would not wander forty years in the desert. War would make the Confederacy great, the editor wrote in the glow of rosy prophecy, and soon visitors from the ends of the earth would come to witness the splendor of her building, the beauty of her cities, and the wealth of her land.[70]

War was welcomed by some Southerners as a spiritual force. Despite all the condemnation of war, they declared it had always been the favorite and most honored activity of man; and the women and children glorified it far more than the men.[71] An

---

Benjamin F. Evans wrote Miles that "The book is an *exact* translation from the French done by the order of the U.S. War Department and is no more the property of Colonel Hardee than it is of any other officer in the U.S. service. I have compared it with the original and it is word for word a *translation* and nothing but a *translation.*" Evans to Miles, May 20, 1861, in Miles Papers.

[68] See particularly the issue of April 30, 1861.

[69] *Daily Richmond Examiner,* May 10, 1861.   [70] *Ibid.,* April 30, 1861.

[71] The *Petersburg Daily Express* on September 3, 1861, printed the following letter from a young woman of Raleigh, North Carolina, to her grandmother in

association of soldiers who daily faced common danger would knit society together and cement friendships for half a century.[72] One panegyrist of war wrote, " 'To love one's neighbor as one's self' is the sum and essence of human morality. War tends to make men perform this duty; peace estranges men from each other." [73] Henry A. Wise, former governor of Virginia, rejoiced in war because it purified man, as the Lord demanded, by fire and blood.[74] He exhorted Southern men, called to the altar of baptism, not to turn aside though the path led through a river of blood. Another believer in the efficacy of such a purge was George William Bagby, the editor of the *Southern Literary Messenger*. He gave up his editorial position to become a common soldier and believed that only hard-fought battles would let out the bad blood in the veins of each section.[75] Out of conflict would come that respect for each other that would enable the North and the South to make peace and to found a friendship on the basis of mutual respect and wholesome fear.

In retrospect, the confidence and the flamboyant prophecies prevalent in the South are amazing. Though it is apparent that not everyone succumbed to the current propaganda, there was a remarkable degree of unanimity as to the purposes of war and its ultimate outcome. Utterances almost as absurd and bombastic as those in the South came from Northern nationalist speakers, writers, and newspaper editors. Propagandists were responsible for the war hysteria that seems inevitable whenever a people face the prospect of an armed conflict. The leaders seek to prepare the people for war by propaganda, often of a sort that appears crude and indefensible to posterity. The South was conforming

---

Petersburg: "O, what a heavy load must rest on the conscience of Lincoln and his Cabinet. He *may* bring sorrow and suffering, but he CANNOT, CANNOT *conquer* us. We will not be ruled by *tyrants*. We, who were born to breathe the pure air of liberty, shall we be *slaves?* Shall *we* be ruled by that black-hearted traitor, Lincoln? Never! From the lips of every true-hearted southern woman will come these words, with heartrending emphasis, and if, they think it necessary they will fight for the 'Sunny South.' I know I would. I, who have never handled a gun, would be one of the first to pull the trigger on the 'pet lambs.' "

[72] "The Times and the War," *De Bow's Review*, XXXI (1861), 8.

[73] *Ibid.*, 9.

[74] Edward A. Pollard, *Echoes from the South: Comprising the Most Important Speeches, Proclamations, and Public Acts Emanating from the South During the Late War* (New York, 1866), 151.

[75] "Editorial," *Southern Literary Messenger*, XXXII (1861), 74.

to the general pattern of human action, whereby every nation seeks to find valid reason for a recourse to arms, whether it be against another country or a part of itself. Its reactions were those of any people similarly situated and facing like problems.

In this maze of secessionist propaganda a few fundamentals stand out in bold relief. Southerners until 1850 had been fairly well satisfied with the Federal government. It had been the action of individual states that aroused Southern fears and caused the South to protest against unconstitutional action. Despite their steadfast insistence on state rights, the Southerners would have favored strengthening the Federal government to the point where its power would be sufficient to compel individual states to comply with the agreements of the whole; with the reservation, however, that the interpretation of the Constitution must accord with Southern ideas. Lincoln's election to the presidency in 1860, as the South viewed it, was an indication that the radical and unconstitutional ideas of the Northern states would become the policy of the Federal government, that political theory in that section had suffered a revolution, and that the North purposed to break away from the Constitution of the fathers. The abolition of slavery and the destruction of the Southern social order would follow in the train of this revolution. Slavery was an important question, but it was by no means the only one that aroused fear in the South.

The Southern agrarian population, in which was ingrained a hostility to industrialism and a conviction that the farmer was the main producer of wealth, believed firmly that the people of the North lived in ease largely on the product of Southern labor. The enrichment of the North at the expense of the South, Southerners contended, had been brought about by governmental favors to the North, favors which, now that the South was reduced to a hopeless minority, would be increased tenfold, until in the end the North would hold the entire South in economic bondage. They did not doubt that Northern selfishness, through its control of capital that could be obtained in the South only at ruinous interest rates, also held in check the economic development of the South, retarding railway construction, direct trade, and manufacturing. The draining of capital from the South to the North would be continued by means of an increased tariff, in reality a tax on agriculture, which would be effected by the Northern revolution. As Southerners regarded the situation, the future held no hope for betterment in the Union, but every indication of additional hardships for the South.

Secession, then, and the formation of an independent nation, were considered to be the remedies for all these evils. By such action alone could the institution of slavery be made secure, the economic domination of the North be thrown off, and Southern civilization be assured of a glorious future. Secession, furthermore, was a legal and constitutional remedy; it was not revolution. The South would keep the Constitution, observing it in the spirit of the old compact, and the North would be free to build another government based upon revolutionary ideas. So far as the Confederacy was concerned, the two governments would live in harmony, side by side. The North would hardly oppose an orderly and legal withdrawal of powers from an agent who no longer observed the terms of his contract. But should war result, the South would be ready to win its freedom. The war would be short, the ruin of the North would be utter, for Cotton was King of the Universe.

So the South left the Union, motivated by fear of ruin engineered by its sectional enemies, and inspired by the vision of a glorious future as an independent people. A new nation was founded, but the United States, stirred by a wave of nationalism, refused to let the Southern states depart in peace. Only the future could tell whether or not the new nation would endure. "We have piped and they would not dance," wrote Jefferson Davis, "and now the devil may care." [76]

[76] Davis to Clement C. Clay, January 19, 1861, in Clay Papers.

II

The Man and His Men

A MESSENGER from the provisional Congress in session at Montgomery, Alabama, bearing the notification of the election of Jefferson Davis to the presidency of the Confederate States of America, found the designate in his garden at Brierfield plantation, February 10, 1861. The notification, Mrs. Davis wrote, seemed to disturb her husband.[1] The magnitude of the task ahead depressed him, but he had no thought of refusing the honor. He made a touching farewell speech to his quickly assembled slaves, who responded with expressions of devotion, and after hurried preparations Davis left the plantation for the capital city on February 11.

Davis would have preferred to command the Southern army. His inclination was for a military career, and his predilection for military life had been strengthened by his training at West Point, his taste of glory in the War with Mexico, and his tenure as Secretary of War under President Pierce. In accordance with his preference, he had accepted the command of the Mississippi state forces after resigning his seat in the United States Senate, and he had disclaimed all political aspirations in the newly declared Confederacy.

Davis had made a brilliant record in politics and his election to the presidency probably came as no surprise. While his career at times had seemed somewhat aimless, he had consistently supported the interests of the South and after the death of John C.

[1] Varina Howell Davis, *Jefferson Davis, Ex-President of the Confederate States of America, A Memoir by His Wife* (New York, 1890), II, 19.

Calhoun he had become the outstanding champion of its cause. Conservative in his advocacy of secession, he had won for himself a position of almost undisputed leadership among the South's ablest men. For this leadership he was eminently fitted by reason of his military training and experience, his knowledge of and active participation in government, the purity of his life, and his manliness and courage.[2]

The election of Davis to the presidency, however, was not without opposition. Robert Barnwell Rhett and William L. Yancey both aspired to the office. But even more serious contenders were the Georgia triumvirate, Robert Toombs, Alexander H. Stephens, and Howell Cobb. The suggestion of Stephens for President, according to William Henry Trescot, created general and unpleasant surprise in South Carolina.[3] The little Georgian, despite his protestations, ardently desired the place but had little support except among his close friends, and was glad to get the vice-presidency.[4] Stephens later said that of all the aspirants Toombs was by far best fitted for the position.[5] Toombs was receptive when approached on the matter and willingly agreed to accept the presidency if it should be bestowed upon him. A canvass, made on his suggestion, of the probable vote of the states disclosed that Alabama, Mississippi, and Florida were for Davis; Louisiana and Georgia, for Howell Cobb; and that South Carolina was divided between the two.[6] According to Stephens, Georgia proposed Toombs, but found that South Carolina, Louisiana, Florida, and Alabama had united upon Davis because of a rumor that Georgia would support Howell Cobb.[7] Another account has it that Alabama had agreed to support Toombs, but had turned to Davis at the re-

[2] Lawrence H. Gipson, "The Collapse of the Confederacy," *Mississippi Valley Historical Review*, IV (1917–1918), 441.

[3] Trescot to Miles, February 6, 1861, in Miles Papers.

[4] A. L. Hull (ed.), "Correspondence of Thomas Reade Rootes Cobb, 1860–1862," Southern History Association, *Publications*, XI (1907), 171–72.

[5] Alexander H. Stephens, *A Constitutional View of the Late War Between the States: . . .* (Philadelphia, 1868), II, 332.

[6] Hull (ed.), "Correspondence of Thomas Reade Rootes Cobb, 1860–1862," *loc. cit.*, 171.

[7] Alexander H. Stephens to Linton Stephens, February 23, 1861, in Johnston and Browne, *Life of Stephens*, 389–90.

quest of Virginia leaders.[8] Cobb himself did not want the presidency, believing that it would be a most undesirable position.[9] Toombs's repeated jests at the expense of Cobb had alienated this powerful figure of the Georgia delegation.[10] Aided by his brother, Thomas R. R., Howell Cobb prevented the nomination of Toombs by the Georgia delegation and threw its support to Davis.[11] Conflicting though these reports are, it seems clear that from the first Davis had the support of Mississippi and Florida, that Alabama soon came over to his side, and that Louisiana followed when Howell Cobb threw his support to Davis. Georgia was obtained for Davis by the two Cobbs, and the wavering South Carolina delegation was brought in through the efforts of Robert Barnwell. Toombs's candidacy suffered because of the fear that he was too radical, despite the assurances of his friends that, for all his blustering speech, he was thoughtful in action. A further handicap to his ambition was his known weakness for liquor. When the time came for a final choice, the six states elected Davis by a unanimous vote.

The election was a popular choice. The South as a whole desired the selection of Davis or Howell Cobb, but the election of Davis and Stephens was acclaimed throughout the Confederacy. The state conventions of Alabama, Louisiana, Georgia, and Texas (the delegates of Texas had not arrived in Montgomery in time to participate in the election) sent messages to Congress approving its choice.[12]

[8] F. M. Gilmer, "Memoir Concerning Organization of the Confederate Government," in Rowland (ed.), *Davis*, VIII, 462–63.

[9] Howell Cobb to his wife, February 6, 1861, in Ulrich Bonnell Phillips (ed.), *The Correspondence of Robert Toombs, Alexander H. Stephens, and Howell Cobb,* American Historical Association, *Annual Report,* 1911, Vol. II (Washington, 1913), 537.

[10] "Toombs never lets Cobb pass without giving him a lick. The other night, in high glee, he told him in company that he had done more for secession than any other man. He had deprived the enemy of the sinews of war, and left them without a dollar in the treasury. He did not even leave old 'Buck' two quarters to put on his eyes when he died. This is a sore point with Cobb; but Toombs seemed disposed to rub in the salt. Even when the skin was off, he applied it to the raw." Johnston and Browne, *Life of Stephens,* 386.

[11] Hull (ed.), "Correspondence of Thomas Reade Rootes Cobb, 1860–1862," *loc. cit.,* 171.

[12] *Journal of Congress,* I, 45, 77, 123, 173.

As he journeyed to Montgomery, Davis was received with general acclamation. At every stopping point, except in strong Unionist sections of Tennessee, bonfires, musket salvos, cheers, and shouted greetings evidenced the good will of the people. The President-elect responded warmly, expressing his hope that the separation from the Union might be permanent and that the new nation might enjoy a brilliant existence. His reception in Montgomery on February 17, 1861, was cordial, and to the enthusiastic throng assembled to greet him at the railroad station he declared that the time for compromise had passed, that "Our separation from the old Union is complete," [13] a sentiment that was reassuring to some of the ardent nationalists who feared that the President-elect's conservatism might lead him to attempt reconciliation with the Union. At the Exchange Hotel that night he sounded a call to unity, and declared that in war or peace heaven would prosper the Confederacy.[14] In his inaugural address, on February 18, 1861, he gave voice, perhaps unwittingly, to words that are a fitting commentary on his entire administration. "You will see many errors to forgive," he told his hearers on that occasion, "many deficiencies to tolerate; but you shall not find in me either want of zeal or fidelity to the cause that is to me the highest in hope, and of most enduring affection." [15] In any considered appraisal of Jefferson Davis, few will find him flawless, but none will deny his labors for and his devotion to the Confederacy.

As President, Davis undertook the complex task of organizing the government. He hoped for peace with the Union but, realizing that conflict was almost inevitable, he planned for war. His conduct of the administration at first gave general satisfaction. The *Richmond Examiner*, later to become his most virulent critic, declared that he was the man of the hour.[16] That news-

13 Rowland (ed.), *Davis*, V, 48, quoting the *Charleston Mercury*, February 19, 1861.

14 William L. Yancey introduced Jefferson Davis to the people of Montgomery on this occasion, declaring ."They [the people of the South] have found the man as well as the principles—a man in whom is combined in so eminent a degree the wisdom of the statesman, the skill of the soldier, and the incorruptibility of the patriot. The man and the hour have met." *Montgomery Weekly Advertiser*, February 20, 1861; *Montgomery Weekly Mail*, February 19, 1861.

15 Richardson (ed.), *Messages and Papers*, I, 36.

16 *Daily Richmond Examiner*, May 6, 1861.

paper implored him to come to Richmond where his very presence would be worth an army of fifty thousand men, such was
the confidence, order, and energy that he inspired at every point.
No power that Congress could give him and no discretion, however absolute, would be unwise, the *Examiner* asserted, for the
President realized his great personal responsibility and measured up fully to his position.[17] Davis worked industriously, but
"he wisely left details to his assistants, while he occupied himself especially with the more important questions of State and
defense of the country."[18] The South was sure to win in any
contest, the *Examiner* concluded, because of the statesmanship
and experience of Southern leaders, and the firmness of the Confederacy's government;[19] furthermore, the President would be
no more of a dictator in war than he could have been in peace.
Davis's election as permanent President of the Confederate
States was foreshadowed by the general satisfaction which the
provisional administration gave to the people.

The election of November, 1861, was marked, however, by
general apathy. The lack of interest in the election was caused,
said the *Charleston Courier,* by the unanimity of the people for
Davis.[20] Some opposition to him had developed, this correspondent admitted, but he characterized it as leaderless and he asserted that no one man among those who opposed Davis was able
to command the confidence of the others. One after another, the
newspapers declared for Davis and Stephens. Support of the
latter, however, was given rather grudgingly in at least one instance. The *Examiner* questioned the advisability of electing
Stephens Vice-President because of his lukewarm attitude and because he lacked the popular confidence that Davis had in such
great measure.[21] Stephens, in the opinion of this critic, had but
one distinguishing characteristic: he had a good opinion of himself. There was no organized movement to replace Stephens, however, and the provisional executives were elected to permanent
office.

17 *Ibid.,* May 8, 1861.
18 *Ibid.,* May 13, 1861; *Montgomery Daily Post,* May 28, 1861.
19 *Daily Richmond Examiner,* August 10, 1861.
20 *Charleston Daily Courier,* November 11, 1861.
21 *Daily Richmond Examiner,* September 18, 1861.

Davis had been actively engaged, long before election, in attempting to establish the independence of the Confederacy. It was no longer possible for the visitor to obtain easy access to the Executive's presence; one now had first to state his business to one of the six aides to the President. If the visitor's business was considered of sufficient importance, he was conducted to an inner office. There the caller would meet a President who knew the theory of administration and how to apply that theory in actual practice. Davis, it soon became apparent to the caller, was a hard-working Executive, willing to listen to rational ideas, slow to reach a fixed decision, but jealous of his own position. This jealousy, perhaps, was not that of an ambitious man, but rather of one whose sense of personal responsibility was overweening. He took the position that, having been elected by the people, he was primarily responsible to them. He could not approve anything that did not accord with his concept of duty and right. His duty, in normal circumstances, would have been partly to lead and direct, but in larger measure to effectuate the will of the people as it was expressed in the acts of Congress. Now, in the extraordinary circumstances of a nation at war, he conceived it to be his all-important task to win the war and to establish Confederate independence.

His immediate paramount duty, as Davis saw it, was the successful direction of military operations. Government just then was less a matter of executing the popular will than of winning battles. Had he consulted his own inclinations, he would have welcomed the opportunity to lead the army, so confident was he of his ability to lead it to victory. His own conviction of his military ability was strengthened by newspaper editors and correspondents who urged that Davis assume command of the army in the first years of the war. An ardent nationalist, Edmund Ruffin, pleaded with him, "For salvation of our cause come immediately and assume military command." [22] Various resolutions were introduced into Congress looking to the time when the President should assume personal command of the armies. He was, in fact, by virtue of constitutional powers, the commander in chief of all armed forces of the Confederacy. As

[22] Ruffin to Davis, May 16, 1861, in *Official Records*, Ser. I, Vol. LI, Pt. II, 727.

President, however, he decided that he had a wider duty of guidance; he heeded the dictates of his conscience and forbore to take personal command of the nation's armed forces, but he did supervise the general plan of military operations.

This retention of power in his own hands did not tempt Davis to dictate plans and policies. There were, indeed, times when he knew better what to do in a given situation than did the general in immediate command. This was true because, with the entire chessboard before him and with a vision enlarged by information readily available to him, his horizon was wider than that of the commanding officer in the field. Yet the President did not act solely on the compulsion of his own ideas. The formation of any important plan was preceded by lengthy conferences. He listened attentively to the frequently conflicting suggestions and opinions of commanders, advisers, and secretaries and then, after deliberation, chose one or a combination of suggestions. His decision seldom went counter to the majority opinion. Criticisms of his decisions were not lacking, yet the need for them was compelling. The important task of coordinating the military forces of the Confederacy would have been performed by some other man or agency if Davis had not undertaken it.

The President's visits to the battlefields, according to Pollard, a bitter enemy of the administration, caused trouble and disturbed the plans of the generals.[23] Actually, save for a few instances, the President never visited a battlefield except upon invitation of the commanding officer, and the army of General Robert E. Lee, most successful of all Confederate armies, was the one most frequently visited by Davis. General Pierre G. T. Beauregard, an uncompromising foe of Davis, wrote: "The President had never interfered with my authority by moving my troops from point to point without passing his orders through me, except when he ordered General Bragg to Vicksburg."[24] Adding that Executive orders by way of the Secretary of War had directed movements contrary to his (Beauregard's) wishes, the General conceded the sincerity of the President's ac-

[23] Edward A. Pollard, *The Lost Cause: A New History of the War of the Confederates* . . . (New York, 1866), 456.

[24] Beauregard to Felix G. De Fontaine, June 25, 1863, in *Official Records*, Ser. I, Vol. LI, Pt. II, 727.

tion. While Davis sometimes erred in judgment and made mistakes, his acts never created chaotic conditions in the army. His orders were transmitted through regular channels, and they were never so phrased nor their execution demanded in such manner as to discredit the commander in the eyes of his subordinates. The Confederacy needed a forceful director who, visualizing the conflict in broad perspective, would compel each army engaged in the struggle to conform to the general plan and to assume its proper place in the entire scheme. To ensure the success of the plan, the forces of one general at times should have been reduced and those of another, increased. Such a plan would have entailed abandoning large sections of Confederate territory and putting them to the risk of invasion and spoilation. Such a program would have required a leader of unlimited tact, with a courage deaf to the outcries of short-sighted patriots and uncooperative governors. Davis was not such a man. His inherent weakness as a commander in chief was the inability to intervene, with considered judgment, in the Confederacy's military affairs.

Davis was primarily a militarist but he was also a constitutionalist. He sought Congressional approval for every act about which he had any doubt, and he regretted the circumstance that made necessary any harsh law. He was, indeed, more fundamentally a constitutionalist than his critic, Stephens, who worshiped a constitution as the barbarian did his tribal god. Stephens placed the enjoyment of constitutional liberty above all else, believing that a government ruling under basic law would be showered with all the blessings of life. Davis as President of the Confederacy regarded the winning of independence for the newly born nation as his foremost duty; yet he never forgot that he was acting on a plane of limited powers granted by sovereign states. He made every effort to obtain the cooperation of the states for the good of the Confederacy. Yet in the conflicts between governors and President, the governors were victorious. This was a fundamental weakness in a revolutionary government; Davis recognized it but was unable to overcome it. In the fight for independence, Davis adhered so closely to the Constitution that the individual states remained stronger than the government of the whole. In doing so Davis belied his opponents' accusation that he was a dictator.

Notwithstanding his courtesy and generally admirable qualities, the President lacked finesse in the personal phases of administration. All visitors were received by him with cordiality and politeness, and none found him wanting in dignity. On occasion he could and did unbend so that the visitor sensed his warmth of nature, but more usually he maintained the rigid dignity of his high office, giving the impression of cold austerity. Pollard wrote that the President could receive a Congressional delegation with such well-bred grace and studied courtesy that the legislators gained the impression they were talking to a post.[25] Too often Davis did not inform his opponents in Congress of the necessity and the reasons for his actions. Davis was abnormally sensitive and he often viewed legitimate opposition as a personal affront. Although a shrewd judge of character, he was apt to let his admiration for the good qualities of his friends blind him to their obvious faults.[26] Conversely, he could permit a fault in an opponent to eclipse his undeniable excellences. Conscious that he himself was bending all his energies toward the achievement of final victory, the President failed to realize that others who opposed him might be acting from motives as lofty as his own. Davis was susceptible to flattery, but he did not respond to it to the extent that his contemporary critics imagined.

At times he was too caustic in his written answers to criticism. To one critic who complained of General Sterling Price, Davis quoted Talleyrand's definition of language as a means of concealing thought and implied that Price's critic had no thought at all.[27] To General Beauregard, whose report after the battle of Manassas displeased him, he wrote, ". . . it seemed to be an attempt to exalt yourself at my expense; . . ."[28] However deserving of rebuke General Joseph E. Johnston may have been, it is doubtful if any good was ever accomplished by the President's severe characterization of his letter, of which he wrote:

[25] Pollard, *The Lost Cause*, 656.
[26] V. Davis, *Jefferson Davis*, II, 919.
[27] Davis to W. P. Harris, December 13, 1861, in Rowland (ed.), *Davis*, V, 179.
[28] *Id.* to Beauregard, October 30, 1861, *ibid.*, 156–57.

"Its language is, as you say, unusual; its arguments and statements utterly one-sided, and its insinuations as unfounded as they are unbecoming." [29] Davis had an abiding sense of the dignity of his office and as President he demanded the respect and honor that of right belonged to the presidency. He could not allow any statement that he regarded as unfounded on fact to go unchallenged, nor could he permit any insubordination to remain unrebuked. As long as he was President, he would defend the prestige of his office and exact the respect due to him as the nation's Chief Executive.

It is difficult to account for Davis's sensitiveness and his occasional bitterness. Some acts for which he was justly criticized can be attributed to his ill-health. The caustic letter to General Johnston was written at a time when Davis was convalescing from a severe illness. Although there were but few days when he was not hard at work at his office, he never really enjoyed good health during all the time the war lasted. Late in 1864 it was reported that the President's death was imminent, and John Beauchamp Jones was amused to observe the changed attitude of the secretaries and bureau heads toward Stephens.[30] The task Davis faced would have been a severe test for even the most robust of men. When the President's state of health and the violent criticism to which he was subjected are considered, it is remarkable that he maintained the poise he did. To his critics he was belligerently sarcastic or stiffly polite, but among intimates or surrounded by admiring throngs, he could throw off formalism and charm his hearers with his ease of manner and his wit.

Davis must have realized his limitations and the defects of his administration, and sought strength and consolation in religion. This spiritual impulse was quickened as the Confederacy fought for its being, and the Chief Executive frequently invoked divine guidance. Days of prayer and fasting were proclaimed for the nation, but this pious gesture was criticized. Work was stopped and the departments were closed for prayer. This provoked the *Richmond Examiner* to comment that man received God's bless-

---

[29] *Id.* to Johnston, September 14, 1861, in *Official Records*, Ser. IV, Vol. I, 611.

[30] John Beauchamp Jones, *A Rebel War Clerk's Diary at the Confederate States Capital,* edited by Howard Swiggett (New York, 1935), II, 357.

ing by using the faculties given him and not by vain and affected supplication. Yet, the editor complained, the President stands in a corner telling his beads, and depends on a miracle to save the country.[31] Others believed more days of prayer were needed, as did an Alabamian who asked Davis, "Do you not believe in Prayer?"[32] The days set apart for national prayer, however, were fewer after the *Examiner*'s sneering comment; but the President's faith grew stronger as the need for divine aid became greater.

Almost from the first, Davis was the target for a fire of criticism. Opposition to him arose, Barnwell told a friend, before the President had even a chance to do anything wrong.[33] He was accused of lacking ability, of wanting to be a dictator, of showing favoritism. The man from upcountry hated him for being a radical Southerner, and the low-country man reviled him as being too much of a Union sympathizer.[34] Disappointed office seekers, disgruntled generals who felt that their ability was not sufficiently recognized, men who wanted peace, and men who demanded that a more aggressive war be waged, all laid at the door of the administration the blame for the ills they denounced.

Contemporary critics concentrated on the conduct of the military department. A belief developed among the people that the military authorities were arrogating powers to themselves. It seemed to those who opposed Davis that military usurpations were a step in his premeditated design to make himself a dictator. Any failure in the subsistence department was also blamed on the President, for he had appointed Colonel Lucius Northrop Commissary General of Subsistence and retained him in office against all opposition. The army officer from civilian life, ambitious for advancement, was vexed by the swift rise of the graduate of West Point. That institution, in the opinion of many critics, did not possess the virtue either of instilling courage or

[31] *Daily Richmond Examiner,* May 19, 1862.

[32] James Malone to Davis, October 25, 1864, in Jefferson Davis Papers, Duke University.

[33] Mary Boykin Chesnut, *A Diary from Dixie,* . . . , edited by Isabella D. Martin and Myrta Lockett Avary (New York, 1929), 104.

[34] *Ibid.,* 134.

of imparting common sense. Since West Pointers were regarded as men who by instinct and training exalted might above right, the appointment of trained military men was considered as further evidence of the President's desire for dictatorial power, besides indicating his favoritism.

His critics averred that the administration had failed to seize the opportune moment to invade the North and force peace. Even when the Confederacy's armies were unable to thrust back the country's invaders, the naïve critic believed the nation's armed strength sufficient to take the offensive in hostile territory. It was charged that the President had interfered with his generals and had prevented their forward movement. Louis T. Wigfall carried on a protracted correspondence with General Beauregard, trying to find evidence that Davis had, in the autumn of 1861, refused to heed pleas to carry the war into the enemy's country. Beauregard, in furtherance of the plan, asked General Gustavus W. Smith to send Wigfall the necessary information. He cautioned Smith, however, to keep everything quiet, "In other words, let D.[avis] commit himself first, and then fasten on him the lie."[35] Beyond the fact that the President had professed his inability to furnish sixty to seventy thousand troops for the generals and their refusal to take the offensive without reinforcements, Wigfall was unable to discover evidence to support his charge. But he continued to harp on imaginary faults of the administration, notwithstanding the lack of evidence.

The administration's foreign policy, as well as its domestic, was under attack, and the President was blamed for its failure. The inflamed patriots who had implicit faith in the omnipotence of cotton had plans that they were sure would save the country, and they pilloried Davis for his lack of vision in refusing to use King Cotton. Others rebuked him for retaining commissioners in Europe and for allowing foreign consuls to reside within the Confederacy.

As the President's critics grew bolder, Mrs. Davis came under their censure. They regarded her as one who ruled the country through a husband who in her hands was as plastic as clay in

[35] Beauregard to Smith, March 31, 1864, in *Official Records*, Ser. I, Vol. LI, Pt. II, 844.

the hands of the potter. Many believed that the road to rapid
official advancement lay in paying court to her and winning her
favor. As a corollary, they believed that an idle or derogatory
remark about Mrs. Davis passed in the woman's world by the
wife of a civil or military official was certain to bring swift de-
motion. These rumors were without basis in fact. On the contrary, Secretary of the Navy Mallory, whose wife and Mrs. Davis
were known not to be on cordial terms, was kept in office even
when he desired to retire. To say that Mrs. Davis was wholly
without influence on her husband would be as far from the truth
as was the contention of those who held that she was all-powerful.
Any wife who has the love and respect of her husband is bound
to exert an influence upon him, but there is no evidence to support the accusation that Mrs. Davis took advantage of her favored position to exert undue influence upon her husband. Whatever power she may have employed assuredly was the normal
power that any woman exercises over a husband to whom she is
devoted. Mrs. Davis's position was first that of a wife and mother,
to which her role as First Lady of the nation was subordinate.

Among the administration's foes the press was in the forefront,
and foremost among its journalistic critics were John Daniels
and Edward A. Pollard, editors of the *Richmond Examiner*. In
the beginning they were ardent supporters, but their ardor gradually cooled and gave way to a hatred that continued to increase
until the downfall of the Confederacy. Nothing the administration did was right in the view of the *Examiner;* nor was there any
personal matter too sacred to escape this newspaper's ridicule.
That the newspaper was often inconsistent in its attitude did
not disturb the editors, who went blithely on their censorious
ways. As the war continued, the savagery of their attacks and the
ruthlessness of their methods were intensified; Pollard's facile
pen indited volumes on the war and the conduct of the administration.[36] On reading *The Second Year of the War,* a contem-

---

[36] James T. Leach of North Carolina, member of the House of Representatives,
and opponent of the administration replied to an attack by the *Examiner:* "Now,
Mr. Speaker, I desire to say, without excitement, hatred, or ill will, that I regard
the *Richmond Examiner* as a low, pitiful, dirty, scurrilous sheet, and as a common
sewer of falsehood and infamy. I understand, sir, the President has had some
apprehensions for his personal safety. Now, let me say to that high functionary,

porary thought that Pollard had produced the greatest tissue of falsehood and misrepresentation in existence.[37] Yet it must be admitted that, however much he may be condemned, Pollard's influence upon the history of the Confederacy was tremendous. His were the first books in the field, and the Northern writer of history eagerly adopted the estimates and opinions of a Southern editor, whose methods fell far short of the objectivity of a real historian, and whose writings, moreover, were music to the ears of the Confederacy's foes. In truth, Pollard's access to authoritative information was limited; furthermore, near the end of the war he was confined in a Northern prison. Nevertheless, his works were accepted in some quarters as authentic history of the Confederate administration.

President Davis was noticeably affected by these harsh attacks upon himself, his family, and the members of his administration. Try as he would, he could not resist the impulse to defend himself. "That vile scavenger Pollard," [38] was Davis's characterization of him in after years. On one occasion he wrote to his wife, "I wish I could learn to let people alone who snap at me; in forbearance and charity to turn away. . . ." [39] At times his concern, however, was not so much that he would be belittled by the opposition, as it was that the Confederacy's future would be endangered thereby. As the war continued, the President developed a defensive shell within which he tended to withdraw. More and more he was content to let criticisms go unanswered, satisfied in his inner consciousness that his every effort was directed toward the goal of Southern independence. "You would not wish your husband," he wrote to a friend, "to escape the

through some kind friend, that if he will break up this sewer of falsehood, he need not have fears in the future. When I say this I do not mean to advise him to put the Editors in the army, for they might soon be found in a position more congenial to their disposition—giving aid and comfort to the enemy. When I say break them up, I mean hang them up with a cord of porcupine quills and lash them with a thong of scorpions, until they are dead, dead, dead—and then turn them over to their rightful owner, the father of lies." *North Carolina Weekly Standard,* December 7, 1864. Except for attempts to impress Confederate journals with the necessity for discretion in reporting military affairs, the newspapers were not molested.

37 Taylor Beatty, Diary, Southern Collection, University of North Carolina, I, 76.
38 Davis to W. T. Walthall, December 27, 1875, in Rowland (ed.), *Davis,* VII, 474.
39 *Id.* to V. Davis, May 16, 1862, *ibid.,* V, 246.

reviling of those who envy such as they cannot rival, and strive
to drag others down from heights to which they cannot rise." [40]
Once the victory was gained and independence achieved, Davis
expected that truth would vindicate his administration.

These newspapers were not alone in their violent antipathy
to him. Some political leaders shared the press's dislike of the
President and his administration, and the forces that sought
to embarrass him gathered about the wizened figure of Vice-
President Stephens, who, perhaps without intent, was the spokes-
man of a malcontent faction that was disorganized and somewhat
incoherent. The Vice-President at least was definite in his objections, and he specified acts of which he disapproved. The suspension of the writ of habeas corpus, conscription, impressment,
the increased power of the military, and the funding act, at
divers times were condemned by Stephens. His objections were
based on an academic ideal; not for a moment would he surrender an iota of individual liberty to achieve collective independence. That Stephens was more concerned with the maintenance of the constitutional rights of the people than with
winning the war is a fair conclusion from the evidence of his
speeches and writings.[41]

Stephens was a pathetic little figure, frail in physique yet
courageous and sincere in his desire for good government. His
criticisms never had the personal venom of the attacks by Henry
S. Foote or Louis T. Wigfall. The latter went so far as to suggest
that Davis was insane.[42] Benjamin H. Hill, concurring with the
administration's critics that "Eternal vigilance is the price of
liberty," denied "that eternal vigilance means perpetual snarl-
ing, snapping, fault-finding and complaining." [43] The President
realized the irreparable damage done to the Confederate cause
by faction, but he generously concluded that his enemies had
not intended such disastrous and unforeseen results.[44]

As against the element who saw hope for the Confederacy only

[40] *Id.* to Mrs. Clement C. Clay, August 31, 1864, in Clay Papers.
[41] Louis Pendleton, *Alexander H. Stephens* (Philadelphia, 1908), 293.
[42] Wigfall to Clement C. Clay, August 13, 1863, in Clay Papers.
[43] Hill, *Senator Benjamin H. Hill*, 268.
[44] Davis to Mrs. Howell Cobb, March 30, 1865, in Phillips (ed.), *Correspondence
of Toombs, Stephens, and Cobb*, 661.

in the replacement of the President, there were those who were steadfast in their support of him. In defense of the administration, the *Richmond Enquirer,* the *Richmond Sentinel,* and the *Charleston Courier* gave blow for blow to the *Richmond Examiner,* the *Richmond Whig,* and the *Charleston Mercury.* The President's editorial friends demanded that the opposition be more accurate and more concrete in its attack, for specific criticism could be more easily refuted. Contemporary charges against the administration were exceedingly vague. The critics pointed to failures, but seldom bothered to analyze or seek to find the reason for this or that reversal. Those who answered them showed what had been accomplished and asked how anyone in like circumstances could have prevented certain defeats.

Estimates of the character and ability of their elected superior by executive officials provide an interesting sidelight. Stephens, piqued by the President's coolness, wrote that Davis was neither a statesman nor a genius and that, while he was a man of good intentions, he was timid, peevish, and obstinate.[45] Later he even expressed doubt of Davis's good intentions. Toombs at one time wrote, "Davis's incapacity is lamentable. . . ."[46] But Toombs left the Cabinet retaining a warm friendship for the Chief Executive, and his harsh comment may be attributed to his failure to achieve renown on the battlefield rather than to any genuine conviction of the President's incapacity. Robert M. T. Hunter and George Wythe Randolph blew hot and cold, and other members of the Cabinet were quiet or loud in their praise, according to their several natures.

Three secretaries who served throughout his administration have left revealing estimates of their chief. The widely traveled Judah P. Benjamin declared he had never known a finer or more patriotic man than the President.[47] He wrote the *London Times* that he had never heard Davis express an unworthy thought or an ungenerous sentiment during his four years of close associa-

[45] Stephens to Herschel V. Johnson, April 8, 1864, in *Official Records,* Ser. IV, Vol. III, 279.

[46] Toombs to Stephens, May 17, 1862, in Phillips (ed.), *Correspondence of Toombs, Stephens, and Cobb,* 595.

[47] Benjamin to his sister, August 1, 1865, in Butler, *Benjamin,* 369.

tion with him.[48] John H. Reagan declared that he had known few men equal and none superior to the Confederate leader in special departments, and that Davis was the ablest man in character and general ability he had ever known.[49] On closer acquaintance, the sense of Davis's greatness grew rather than diminished with Reagan. Mallory recalled Davis as a man of will and energy, patience and industry, possessing a knowledge of men and public affairs and an analytical and comprehensive judgment, to all of which were added the prompt business habits of a merchant.[50] In summation, Mallory believed few men equal to the President could be found in all history. All testified to his humanity and forbearance toward his enemies and to his excellent relationship with trusted advisers.

In the testimony of friends and foes one may discern the real Jefferson Davis, and it is safe to enumerate certain characterizations that are indisputable. His patriotism and integrity were beyond question. He had one fixed purpose for which he considered he had been elected President, namely, the winning of Southern independence. He strove to achieve this Southern independence by the use of all the means within his power, but as a constitutionalist and state rights idealist he trod warily. His conscience was torn between the demand of military expedience and his duty to act within the Constitution. In the end he was often the victim of this divided allegiance, and the military strategist yielded to the constitutionalist. Far from being a dictator, he wanted little but peace, a peace with independence for his country; and he desired an end to the vituperation, slander, and libel directed at him personally. It is undeniable that he wished to be the savior of the Confederacy. When fate withheld from him that glory, unwisely and unfortunately for his place in history, he spent long years in efforts to vindicate himself.

Davis appreciated the weight of responsibility upon him and

[48] Judah P. Benjamin and B. F. Butler, "Two Witnesses on the 'Treatment of Prisoners,'" Southern Historical Society, Papers, VI (1878), 183–89.

[49] John H. Reagan, Memoirs with Special Reference to Secession and the Civil War, edited by Walker F. McCabel (New York, 1906), 252.

[50] Stephen R. Mallory, Diary, 148–49, quoted in footnote in Clubbs, "Stephen Russell Mallory," 251.

the importance of his position as the chosen leader of a powerful people. Duty was to him an unconditional command. The fact that he had a serious part to take in a momentous conflict was never wholly absent from his thoughts, and therefore he could not tolerate idle remarks or jesting acts. Had his been the rough humor and rugged character of Lincoln, he could have taken criticism in his stride and profited by it. But Davis was sensitive, supersensitive indeed, and the darts he received as the leader of his people's cause stung him to the quick. Unable to throw them off, he withdrew to the comforting circle of his intimate friends. In his treatment of the opposition he was at times tactless. His consciousness that he was right made him seem more obstinate than he was. Actually, he welcomed advice when offered in good faith or with the courtesy observed between gentlemen; it is possible to find many instances to support the opinion that he leaned too much on the counsel of others. He was firm, however, in refusing to allow a subordinate to excuse failure by laying the onus on the Executive. This resulted in bickerings and controversies with generals who were less tactful and far more selfseeking than the President.

When the people of the South became divided and grew lukewarm in their support of the war, Davis was lost and bewildered. Had he been so fortunate as to function during a time of peace, he would doubtless have been eminently successful as President. His conservative appeal, his desire by compromise to unify all factions, his firm belief in the political and economic ideals of his people, might have welded the Southern Confederacy into a strong federal union.

Davis's claim to conspicuous ability as a leader is incontestable. Undeterred by physical handicaps, he went steadily forward, holding his people together long after they had become too weak to continue the war effectively. His energy, will, determination, and knowledge did much to enable a nation possessed of little in resources and military effectives to hold off for four years an enemy vastly superior in wealth, material, and man power. The final defeat of the cause he led has dimmed Davis's reputation for leadership. A world that ever applauds success, too often, as in his case, fails to appreciate the quality of leadership that falls short of attaining the goal. The leader's errors and the defects and limitations of his character are magnified and stand out as do a few spots of ink on a sheet of white paper.

Comparisons of Davis with Lincoln are many; generally they have been to the disadvantage of the South's leader. The war in which they were on opposing sides was not won or lost by one man. The contest was not between two leaders or two administrations, but between two peoples. The Confederate President exercised great leadership at the head of his nation during the war, and so did the Chief Executive of the Union. If the man power and economic resources of the two nations be weighed, it will be seen that Jefferson Davis was able to get proportionately more from his people, resources of the South considered, than was Abraham Lincoln from his. The Confederacy chose as its President its most suitable citizen and he did everything in his power to establish its independence.

THE CABINET

Stephens and Toombs, among others, had hoped to incorporate into the scheme of government for the Confederacy a feature of the parliamentary system. They intended to combine with some features of the Constitution of the United States the English Cabinet system whereby department heads would have seats in Congress, or the President would be required by law to appoint only members of Congress to his Cabinet. Such a provision, however, was not included in the Confederate Constitution; indeed, the Constitution does not provide specifically for a Cabinet. It provides only for "Executive Departments," and "Heads of Departments." The document does provide, however, that ". . . Congress may, by law, grant to the principal officer in each of the Executive Departments a seat upon the floor of either House, with the privilege of discussing any measures appertaining to his Department." [51] But this power was never exercised by Congress under the permanent Constitution.

Cabinet members did enjoy the privilege of seats in the provisional Congress. Toombs, Memminger, Reagan, and Hunter

[51] *Confederate Constitution*, Art. I, Sec. 6, Par. 2.

were representatives in that body from their states at the same time that they were members of the Cabinet. After they had been appointed by the President to his Cabinet they retained their seats in the provisional Congress, and it does not appear that their dual capacities placed any limitation upon their legislative activities as regarded either discussion of pending measures or voting upon proposed legislation. But that there was some question of their rights to legislative status is evident in the fact that on February 25 Secretary Memminger introduced a resolution to admit the heads of the departments to secret and open sessions of Congress.[52] On Memminger's motion the resolution was referred to the Committee on Rules, whose chairman, Stephens, acting for the committee, reported it favorably. It was adopted March 4,[53] but questions continued to be raised as to the rights of a Cabinet officer not a member of Congress on the floor of that body. A resolution offered by Representative John Perkins, Jr., of Louisiana granting them the privilege of discussing any measure relating to their respective departments was adopted by a four to two vote.[54] The nonmember secretaries, however, so far as the *Journal of the Provisional Congress* reveals, took no part in its proceedings. On one occasion Attorney General Benjamin delivered a verbal message from the President relative to prisoners of war,[55] and representatives who were also departmental heads continued to exercise active leadership in the Congress.

After the government had been established under the permanent Constitution several efforts were made to give seats in Congress to Cabinet members. A bill with this purpose was introduced in January, 1863, by Senator Wigfall.[56] It was reported favorably by the Judiciary Committee, and debated on the Senate floor March 10 and 11.[57] A motion to strike out the clause "with the privilege of discussing any measures appertaining to his Department" was agreed to by a vote of fourteen to ten on the second day of the debate.[58] Thus stripped of any prospective value, even the administration supporters voted to postpone the meas-

[52] *Journal of Congress*, I, 82.   [53] *Ibid.*, 103.
[54] *Ibid.*, 182. The vote was by states. The Louisiana delegation was divided.
[55] *Ibid.*, 260.   [56] *Ibid.*, III, 24.
[57] *Ibid.*, 44, 146, 153.   [58] *Ibid.*, 153.

ure indefinitely. A bill to grant seats in both houses to Cabinet secretaries, introduced by Senator Waldo P. Johnson of Missouri in February, 1865, was referred after a second reading to the Judiciary Committee, where it died.[59] An almost identical procedure was followed in the House of Representatives, where bills were reported, referred to the Judiciary Committee, and either buried there or laid on the table by a vote of the House. One interesting possibility of the Confederate Constitution was therefore never developed.

Why Congress refused to give the Cabinet members seats in the Senate and House is somewhat obscure. Davis desired the privilege for his secretaries, and the administration had majority support in the national legislature. The President believed their presence there would do much to speed legislation and to obviate misunderstandings.[60] The *Richmond Enquirer*, which frequently reflected administration opinion, hoped that Congress would enact the needed legislation.[61] The pressing military situation undoubtedly prevented adequate consideration of the bill in 1862, for, with Richmond in extreme danger, Congress had little inclination to spend time on experimental legislation. Changes in the military situation likewise were largely responsible for delays when the measure later was under consideration.

Opposition to granting seats to Cabinet members, however, had arisen in Congress even before the permanent government was established. Many congressmen felt that Benjamin's appointment as Secretary of State had been forced upon them, and they did not relish the prospect of having that persuasive personality in their midst. Later, Secretary Memminger was to become the principal object of Congressional animosity. The administration's foes would not vote for any measure that might result in exerting influence on wavering members. Some of the administration supporters in Congress, on the other hand, believed themselves able to handle Congress without the aid of secretaries who perhaps would gain credit at the expense of deserving congressmen. It is difficult to imagine Cabinet members eagerly

[59] *Ibid.*, IV, 533.
[60] Jefferson Davis, *The Rise and Fall of the Confederate Government* (New York, 1881), I, 259–60.
[61] *Daily Richmond Enquirer*, December 7, 1863.

striving to gain admittance to a Congress where they would have to listen to members rant against the official acts of department heads. The secretaries had not exercised their right to seats in Congress under the provisional government unless they were accredited representatives of their respective states. Had they been granted admittance under the permanent government, they would have taken little or no advantage of it.

In a strictly legal sense there was no Confederate Cabinet, but the law gave the President the right to appoint six men to advise him and to direct the departments established by Congress. This group of appointed executives shared the burdens of the administration. Today they are little known, and their trials and errors, their successes and failures as administrative officials have attracted little interest. Even their names have been forgotten by most Southerners except those of the old school. Northern and Southern historians alike dismiss them with a few passing remarks, for the most part derogatory. This neglect may be due to the fact that investigators generally have thought of the Confederate Cabinet, with the single exception of Benjamin, as an inefficient group of mediocrities; or they have been passed over as unimportant simply because the cause in which they labored failed.[62]

The members of the Cabinet were an important group, however, and deserve greater attention than they have received. Politics was the special forte of the South and the South possessed men of great political ability. How then is the weakness of the Confederate Cabinet to be explained? Why did Davis select certain men? Why were so many changes made in the Cabinet? It is indeed unaccountable that investigators have been content to let the Confederate Cabinet remain in the obscurity to which historians have relegated it. In the lives and work of President Davis's official family are numerous questions that need to be answered. Many questions that come to the mind of an investigator must remain unanswered for lack of intimate personal records. Yet there is available material adequate for the purpose

[62] Burton J. Hendrick's *Statesmen of the Lost Cause: Jefferson Davis and His Cabinet* (New York, 1939), is primarily a study of the foreign affairs of the Confederacy.

of presenting a reasonably accurate picture of the men whom the President chose for his advisers.

Davis said that in selecting his Cabinet he did not encounter the difficulty that confronted the President of the United States; for in the Confederacy there were no sections and no parties, no promises to be kept, no friends to reward, and no enemies to punish.[63] Nothing could be further from the truth. There were seven states to placate, and the President surely realized it. There were friends to satisfy, men who had been in the forefront of secession, and a conservative element that could not be ignored. Unity had to be attained, and one way of achieving it was by adroit handling of patronage.

In a confederation the state is sovereign and should have, if possible, equal representation in the central government. Some of the seven Southern states had claims to preferential consideration. South Carolina had been the leader of the movement for independence. The omission of one of her citizens from the Cabinet was certain to be resented by his fellow citizens. Much the same was true of Alabama and Georgia. Next in importance were Louisiana and Mississippi. These five states, by every right, had prior claim to representation in the Cabinet. The atmosphere of tension called for compromise. A division of patronage among the states would do much to consolidate all the states of the South into a confederacy. This was one of the chief determining factors in Davis's selection of men, and he held consistently to it throughout the war. Of the eleven states that eventually composed the Confederacy, nine were represented in the Cabinet. Mississippi's representative refused to serve, but that state had the presidency. Only Tennessee and Arkansas were unrepresented, and in the case of the former, one of her outstanding men, Gustavus A. Henry, declined to be considered for a Cabinet post. Even the border state of Kentucky had a representative in John C. Breckinridge. By spreading the patronage widely the President hoped to knit the sovereign states into a closer unit. Most of the men appointed were those recommended by the congressmen from their respective states. This had the effect of

[63] Rowland (ed.), *Davis*, V, 48, quoting the *Charleston Mercury*, February 19, 1861.

securing the support of legislators for a desired administration program. The harmony that existed between the legislative and executive branches prior to the elections of 1864 certainly may be attributed in part to the influence of Cabinet officers on the delegations from their respective states. A former secretary, Thomas Bragg, was used in the attempt to bring recalcitrant officials of North Carolina into line, and from the same state George Davis was selected primarily to still the Unionist and other peace demonstrators there. How to create a strong central government out of independent and jealous commonwealths was a pressing domestic problem, and Davis sought to solve it by judicious selection of the members of his Cabinet.

The President owed political debts to certain men for his elevation to the chief magistracy. Barnwell had swung a divided South Carolina delegation to him; Clement C. Clay had been a power in influencing the support of Alabama's representation. Both deserved the President's consideration. More than any other, Howell Cobb had been instrumental in bringing about the election of Davis. None of these men desired a Cabinet appointment, and each declined to be considered for a portfolio; nevertheless, their opinions were to be consulted and their wishes heeded.

It was necessary also to give consideration to the various factions of Southern economic and political thought, if the President hoped to achieve national solidarity. While it was expedient that the support of men of wealth be assured, Davis had to avoid the mistake of appointing an undue number of men of great fortune. The old Whig and mild Unionist partisans could not safely be overlooked. The conservative and radical elements within the Democratic party must be recognized. Such men as Yancey of Alabama and Toombs of Georgia had followings to be reckoned with, but Rhett of South Carolina, once a power in his state, was now discredited and could be ignored with impunity. Truly, Cabinet-making was a complex task for the President.

In the selection of his secretaries, Davis appears to have followed a general pattern. First, he wanted men of ability. Then, the men selected ought to represent politically the divergent factions and the sovereign states. He relied heavily upon recom-

mendations, not only of Congressional delegations but also from
influential private citizens in the selection of specific men.
Occasionally, however, he made appointments against the wishes
of state delegations, as in the case of the Secretary of the Navy.
Davis insisted that Mallory, the man best fitted for the position,
be confirmed. Personal friendship and favoritism did not enter
into appointments. Only Henry T. Ellet and James A. Seddon
could be classed as intimate friends of Davis. Some of the others
were not known to him personally and were selected on the
recommendation of advisers in whom he had confidence. It is
entirely erroneous to believe that the President kept his own
counsel and consulted no one in selecting his secretaries.

The eventual personnel of the Cabinet would have been far
different had the appointments been accepted by those to whom
they originally were offered. Davis's first selections were: Robert
Barnwell, for Secretary of State; Robert Toombs, Secretary of
the Treasury; Braxton Bragg, or perhaps Clement C. Clay, Secretary of War; Stephen R. Mallory, Secretary of the Navy; Henry
T. Ellet, Postmaster General; William L. Yancey, Attorney General. Only two of this group eventually held posts in the Cabinet.
Barnwell declined, and he and a majority of the South Carolina
delegation recommended Christopher G. Memminger for the
Treasury portfolio.[64] Toombs became Secretary of State, although there is evidence that he probably had a choice between
the State and Treasury departments. Clay and Yancey declined
the appointments proffered them and urged the selection of
Leroy Pope Walker for Secretary of War. Ellet also declined, and
the Texas delegation recommended the appointment of John
H. Reagan. Judah P. Benjamin of Louisiana was made Attorney
General. Mallory's confirmation completed the make-up of the
provisional Cabinet. Except in the case of Mallory, the nominees
were quickly and apparently unanimously confirmed by the provisional Congress.

Davis's selection of his advisers gave general satisfaction.
Examination of contemporary newspaper comment discloses
that the Cabinet received nation-wide praise, approval being
expressed in the phrase "the right man for the right place,"

[64] For amplification of this controversial issue, see note 5, pp. 204-205.

monotonously repeated. It was not until months later that any
dissatisfaction with the choice of executive secretaries was reflected in newspaper comment. "The Cabinet is strong and gives
satisfaction," wrote Thomas R. R. Cobb; [65] and his opinion was
representative of those of his contemporaries who expressed their
convictions. Naturally, there were some who were keenly disappointed that they or their friends had failed of appointment.
". . . I had the folly to believe that there was great patriotism
in this movement," Cobb wrote, but ". . . it looks now as if it
was nothing but office seeking." [66]

Criticisms of the Cabinet, both by contemporaries and by
later writers, deserve reviewing. Herschel V. Johnson, against
whose appointment Confederate leaders had protested so vigorously that the President promised not to consider him, believed
the Cabinet was weak and that none of the changes from the beginning to the fall of the Confederacy strengthened it.[67] Pollard
called it a "ridiculous cipher" whose members never dared declare themselves on public questions, and who asserted their
existence only to the extent of certifying the will of the President.[68] Many of Davis's modern biographers, mindful of his
obvious desire to bring about harmony by means of the bestowal
of offices, have concluded that the appointments were ill-advised.
Allen Tate, a recent writer, believes that the President, far from
conciliating all parties, actually antagonized the powerful radicals.[69] Tate indicates that the Rhett faction, not the Barnwell
and Memminger group, was dominant in South Carolina. That
Rhett was discredited in his own state and with his fellow delegates at Montgomery is evident upon even a cursory survey of
the political situation then existing. His appointment to a Cabinet office would have been sheer political folly. Any sweeping
statement that Davis's selection of a Cabinet pleased none of the

[65] Hull (ed.), "Correspondence of Thomas Reade Rootes Cobb, 1860–1862,"
loc. cit., 238.

[66] Ibid., 234.

[67] "From the Autobiography of Herschel V. Johnson, 1856–1867," American
Historical Review, XXX (1924–1925), 329–33.

[68] Edward A. Pollard, Southern History of the War, Two Volumes in One (New
York, 1866), 636.

[69] Allen Tate, Jefferson Davis, His Rise and Fall. A Biographical Narrative (New
York, 1929), 87–88.

great Southern leaders is far from true.[70] The leaders, in fact, were largely instrumental in the selection of the secretaries. Most of those of real importance politically would have admitted that Davis selected men of ability and succeeded in getting a Cabinet as satisfactory, on the whole, as was possible. The Confederate Cabinet, indeed, was composed of men of tested ability, and it was not and never did become a collection of mere political hacks.

Dissatisfaction arose, however, as the war progressed, and Cabinet changes came frequently. Even before the seat of government was removed from Montgomery there were rumors of differences among the department heads. A correspondent of the *Charleston Courier* apologized to his readers for reporting such idle gossip, and stated that upon investigation he had found good feeling on all sides.[71] The real reason for the rumor was the proposal to reorganize the Cabinet in order to give representation to the four new states.[72] Virginia gained a place in it when Hunter replaced Toombs on July 25, 1861. Walker resigned on September 17, 1861, Benjamin was shifted to the War Department, and Bragg of North Carolina took over the Attorney General's office. The administration, in the opinion of the *New Orleans Picayune*, now presented an array of men of first ability, uniting sound opinions with practical knowledge of public affairs.[73] The reconstructed Cabinet, however, was not so satisfactory to some others. Opposition centered upon the War and Navy department heads. Benjamin was under fire because of military reverses, and Mallory was accused of being dilatory.

When the permanent government was established the President was advised by several newspapers to reconstitute his Cabinet. Hunter had announced his intention of resigning to run for a seat in the Senate, and it was rumored that Reagan also would leave. Should Benjamin and Mallory yield to popular clamor and surrender their posts, four places would thus be vacated. There was at that time no criticism of Memminger and Bragg.

[70] Harrison A. Trexler, "Jefferson Davis and the Confederate Patronage," *South Atlantic Quarterly*, XXVIII (1929), 45.
[71] *Charleston Daily Courier*, May 16, 1861.
[72] *Ibid.; Montgomery Daily Post*, May 16, 1861.
[73] *New Orleans Daily Picayune*, December 5, 1861.

The *Richmond Examiner,* while admitting that the South had no surplus of great men, averred that it had many of more ability than those in office. The editor warned the President that only a flatterer would deceive him by saying the Cabinet commanded the confidence of the South. He wrote that

Under the present regime the so-called secretaries are mere clerks. They are fit for nothing else. They are men of business in their various private professions; they may be tolerably familiar and adroit in the local politics of their cities and neighborhoods. But not one of them is a statesman of caliber equal to these or any other times.[74]

Continuing, the editor expressed the belief that the Cabinet had been selected on a regional basis, and declared that the South could not afford that kind of concession to office seekers, for the life and fortunes of the entire country depended upon the ability of the central government to direct its forces to success. Intellectual capacity, general public information, patriotism, activity, and courage should be the tests applied in selecting Cabinet material, the editor believed, and if the greatest men of the country were all inhabitants of one county that circumstance should not weigh a feather in the choice.[75] Seeking to explain Confederate reversals, the *Examiner* said the Yankees had outwitted the Confederacy at the point where it was supposed to be superior—the art of government. The editor concluded that the nation must get more talent into the Cabinet or be ruined; certainly new men must be obtained for the War and Navy departments. The ousting of Mallory, in particular, was demanded by the *New Orleans Crescent.*[76] The dropping of Benjamin, Mallory, and Reagan was urged by the *Savannah Republican:* "President Davis has an opportunity of instituting the necessary reform . . . , and if he fails to do it, he will be untrue both to the country and his own fame." [77] William Woods Holden's *North Carolina Standard* believed the whole country was against the appointment of Mallory and Benjamin.[78] Like the *Examiner,*

[74] *Daily Richmond Examiner,* February 22, 1862.
[75] *Ibid.,* February 24, 1862. The *Examiner* was insistent, however, that a Virginia man, as was Virginia's right, be placed in the Cabinet.
[76] *Charleston Mercury,* February 28, 1862, quoting the *New Orleans Crescent.*
[77] *Ibid.,* February 28, 1862, quoting the *Savannah Republican.*
[78] *North Carolina Weekly Standard,* March 1, 1862.

Holden opposed constructing a Cabinet with reference to the states.

That vicious principle has forced itself upon our institutions. It never was worthy for a moment of a wise man's regard. It had its origin in the ambition of petty men, who looked to locality to supply the defect of merit. It cannot be discarded too soon. The best, the ablest, the most patriotic, disinterested and energetic men should be selected, if they all come from the same house. . . . Wisdom in council, and vigor in action, are what we now want and we must have them, without regard to persons.[79]

The newspaper editors did not limit themselves to giving general advice; they proposed specific men for consideration as Cabinet members and conjectured as to the eventual selections. The *Savannah Republican* suggested William Cabell Rives of Virginia for the State Department and Solomon Cohen of Savannah for Postmaster General. The *Charleston Mercury's* suggestions, which were legion, included: John Buchanan Floyd, Beauregard, Toombs, Matthew Fontaine Maury, Rhett, Isham Green Harris, Yancey, Seddon, and Thomas S. Bocock. Both the *Mercury* and the *Richmond Examiner* thought strong pressure was being exerted upon the President to name Toombs Secretary of War. Floyd was the choice of the *Examiner,* which feared that the choice would fall to General Lee, "the despondent individual." [80] On February 27, the *Examiner* reported that the Cabinet under the permanent Constitution would be composed as follows: Benjamin, Secretary of State; Lee, Secretary of War; Randolph, Secretary of the Navy; Memminger, Secretary of the Treasury; Gustavus A. Henry, Postmaster General; and Herschel V. Johnson, Attorney General.

It was not until March 19, 1862, that the members of the first Cabinet of the permanent government became known. They were: Benjamin, Secretary of State; Randolph, Secretary of War; Mallory, Secretary of the Navy; Memminger, Secretary of the Treasury; Reagan, Postmaster General; and Thomas Hill Watts,

---

[79] *Ibid.,* March 5, 1862. An editorial in the *Standard,* March 26, 1862, however, objected to the permanent Cabinet on the ground that Davis had appointed no North Carolina man to a Cabinet post. See p. 56.

[80] *Charleston Daily Courier,* March 3, 1862, quoting the *Daily Richmond Examiner.*

Attorney General. The President had taken a long time to select his Cabinet. The two secretaries in the provisional Cabinet who were most criticized, Mallory and Benjamin, were the men he especially wished to retain in the new Cabinet. Mallory wished to resign but was persuaded to remain. The success of the iron-clad warship *Virginia* did much to soften criticism of him. It is probable that Davis held out for Benjamin to head the War Department until he became certain Benjamin could not be confirmed for that post, and that by a compromise he was named for the State Department. Randolph, who succeeded Benjamin as Secretary of War, was a young and able brigadier general, a member of an old Virginia family. The other newcomer, Watts of Alabama, who replaced Bragg as Attorney General, had been, prior to 1861, a strong Unionist. It was evident from the personnel of the reorganized Cabinet that the President had been but little affected by the newspaper agitation, instigated chiefly by the hostile *Examiner*.

Announcement of the new Cabinet's personnel brought immediate reaction from the country, as reflected in newspaper comment. In North Carolina the *Wilmington Journal* said the Cabinet was proof that Davis was above party spirit. Holden's *Standard* retorted that the opposite was true; all but one of the secretaries came from cotton states; and all but Watts had been original secessionists, and even Watts was not really representative of old Union men; North Carolina had been ignored; and the Cabinet smelled too strongly of cotton.[81] The Cabinet had been patched, the *Charleston Mercury* commented, but not mended. The *Examiner*, true to form, was most bitter in its criticism. It asserted that Davis had retained all those who did not want to leave, and that in consequence the changes were insignificant. "The representation of the Synagogue is not diminished; it remains full," this newspaper sneered. "The administration has now an opportunity of making some reputation; for nothing being expected of it, of course every success will be a clean gain."[82]

81 *North Carolina Weekly Standard*, March 26, 1862.
82 *Daily Richmond Examiner*, March 20, 1862.

But not all newspaper comment was in this vein. In fact, the reaction was generally favorable. Friendly editors quickly came to the President's support and commended the qualifications of the men he appointed. Some few private citizens wrote letters to the newspapers in praise of the President's selections. But the scarcity of references to the Cabinet in the correspondence, even of men in high political office, is revealing. The average citizen seemed to be little concerned about whom the President chose as his advisers and executives.

Only a few changes were ever made in the personnel of the permanent Cabinet. None occurred in the departments of State, Navy, and Post Office; there was one change each in the Treasury and Justice departments, and two in the War Department.[83] Randolph resigned his post in the War Department ostensibly because of a disagreement with the President, and Seddon was appointed to succeed him in 1862. Watts resigned the attorney-generalship late in 1863 to become governor of Alabama, and George Davis of North Carolina took his place. Memminger's and Seddon's withdrawals from the Treasury and War departments, respectively, were the result of Congressional opposition in 1864 and 1865. Their places were filled by George A. Trenholm of South Carolina and John C. Breckinridge of Kentucky. The most important members of the Cabinet were: Benjamin, Secretary of State; Seddon, Secretary of War; Memminger, Secretary of the Treasury; Mallory, Secretary of the Navy; Reagan, Postmaster General; and Watts, Attorney General.[84] These men

[83] There were three *ad interim* appointments.

[84] The appointments to the Confederate Cabinet were:

Secretary of State—Robert Toombs, February 21, 1861; Robert M. T. Hunter, July 25, 1861; William M. Browne, *ad interim, ca.* February 1, 1862; Judah P. Benjamin, March 18, 1862.

Secretary of War—Leroy Pope Walker, February 21, 1861; Judah P. Benjamin (Acting Secretary, September 17 to November 21, 1861), November 21, 1861; George Wythe Randolph, March 18, 1862; Gustavus W. Smith, *ad interim,* November 17, 1862; James A. Seddon, November 21, 1862; John C. Breckinridge, February 6, 1865.

Secretary of the Treasury—Christopher G. Memminger, February 21, 1861; George A. Trenholm, July 18, 1864.

Secretary of the Navy—Stephen R. Mallory, March 4, 1861.

Postmaster General—Henry T. Ellet, February 25, 1861 (refused to accept the appointment); John H. Reagan, March 6, 1861.

Attorney General—Judah P. Benjamin, February 25, 1861; Thomas Bragg,

remained in office long enough to leave their impress upon Confederate policy.

During a period of more than four years fourteen men occupied the six executive positions in the Cabinet.[85] Their ages at the time of their appointments ranged from forty-two years, for Reagan, to fifty-eight, for Memminger, and the average was forty-eight years. Three were foreign-born: Benjamin, Memminger, and Mallory. Mallory's parents, however, were citizens of the United States. Memminger's childhood had been spent in the care of a Charleston orphanage. The economic and social background of the group discounts the belief held in some quarters that only wealthy aristocrats could attain high place in the old South. Most of this group had attained security, and in some cases wealth, through their own efforts. Thirteen were lawyers; one, Trenholm, a merchant, and at one time or another all had been slaveholders and owners of plantations. Nine of them had college degrees and four had attended college for one or more years, but all had an education equivalent to a degree. All had had experience in state or national politics. Among their number was a former Vice-President of the United States and a Speaker of the House of Representatives. Six had been members of the United States Senate, and five had been in the House of Representatives. Numbered in the Confederate Cabinet were six former delegates to the Confederate Provisional Congress, one Confederate Senator, one governor, and four judges. Three religious creeds, Jewish, Catholic, and Protestant, were represented in the Cabinet's personnel. A varied group with contrasting personalities, they were trained men and, by the accepted standards of their day or this, were possessed of abilities above the average.

Why then, one wonders, was the Cabinet such an unstable body? The statement that Davis's manner was highhanded and that he reduced his Cabinet secretaries to the status of "mere clerks" is widely accepted. Investigators have been generally content to reiterate the more easily accessible judgments of Pol-

---

November 21, 1861; Thomas Hill Watts, March 18, 1862; Wade Keyes, *ad interim*, October 1, 1863; George Davis, January 2, 1864.

[85] Not including Henry T. Ellet and the three *ad interim* members.

lard and the *Richmond Examiner*. One of Davis's later-day
biographers accepts without question the statement that the
Cabinet members complained that they were "mere office
boys." [86] It would be interesting to know just how many of
the department heads either spoke or wrote such complaints.
Toombs implied as much but he did so, perhaps in pique, when
the military glory he craved had not materialized. He left the
Cabinet on most cordial terms with Davis and did not consider
his status that of an underling. Davis was accused of being arbitrary in his relations with Secretary Randolph. While surface
facts support this charge, there were extenuating circumstances
that lead one to discount hasty conclusions. The "chief clerk"
accusation is refuted by the testimony of other Cabinet members.

Davis regarded the War Department as his peculiar field.
There, his finger can be found in everything. Innumerable orders and reports were sent to him for approval. Through it all,
however, can be discerned evidence of his desire for unity of
action and purpose; he wanted to be sure that every part fitted
the whole. There is no valid reason for believing that he ever
limited or discouraged the initiative of a Secretary of War.
There was more than enough room for two executives in an
organization as big as the War Department, nor did their relationship have to be that of boss to handy man. John Beauchamp
Jones, the outspoken clerk of the department, was disgusted to
see even the Assistant Secretary of War, John Archibald Campbell, in possession of the power of decision in many matters.
The President's primary interest was in the development of
military plans, and he left the business details of the War Department to the various secretaries. Despite his keen interest in
this department, Davis wanted an aggressive secretary at its head
and not a rubber stamp.

In other departments the President's interference was slight
indeed. A few Toombs-Rhett trade plans were vetoed, but it was
the consensus of most of the Cabinet members that they should
be disapproved. Even with the aid of hindsight, one is puzzled
to see just what the Confederacy could have done that it did not
do (except win the war) to gain foreign recognition. Its State

[86] Tate, *Jefferson Davis*, 89.

Department was, in fact, a most unimportant branch of the government. So far as foreign affairs were concerned, the Secretary of State would have few duties until victory established the independence of the Confederacy. Davis's relationship with the departments of the Treasury, Navy, and Post Office was limited almost wholly to upholding the policies of the respective secretaries under attack by the administration's foes. Even when occasional differences between departments arose he did not assert an arbitrary rule. Instead, he referred the dispute to the Attorney General whose opinion he accepted as his guide to a final decision. It is straining credulity to believe the Cabinet was a group of timorous "office boys" dominated by a stern master, when we remember that the Cabinet, the President being absent and uninformed of their action, decided to expel foreign consuls from Confederate territory.

What, then, is the explanation of the brief tenure of Cabinet members? From the beginning of the Confederacy to its fall, ten men relinquished their seats in the Cabinet. In the cases of Benjamin, Memminger, and Seddon the changes were due to the opposition of Congress. Personal ambition was the impelling force behind the resignations of Toombs, Hunter,[87] and Watts. Toombs yearned for military laurels and the plaudits of an admiring populace. Hunter, severely stung by a United States Presidential bee, was not long in the Confederate government before his pet ambition returned to plague him. Watts not only considered the governorship of Alabama a higher honor than the Attorney General's office, but felt it his duty to accept the "mandate" of the people of his state. Benjamin left the Justice Department to become Secretary of War. Walker, overworked, ill, and disillusioned, was forced out by criticism and by the President's desire to replace him with a more capable official. Randolph did in truth resent what he regarded as interference by the President in his department, but he was also glad to obtain release from a taxing job. Why Bragg did not desire reappointment in 1862 is not certainly known, but obviously he did not quit the Cabinet because of hatred of the President. There were many factors

[87] Technically, Hunter did not resign. His term of office expired with the provisional government and he was not reappointed. This was also true of Bragg.

involved in each change in the Cabinet. One thing is certain—
there was no arbitrary domination by Davis that made strong
men resign and weak men remain.

Official Cabinet meetings were held regularly throughout the
life of the Confederacy. At these meetings general conversation
usually preceded the consideration of the business at hand.[88]
Davis would tell some anecdote or reminiscence, sometimes ap-
plying it to current situations. He was a good storyteller and possessed powers of mimicry that added to his effectiveness as a raconteur. The subjects discussed when the meeting got down to
business were gone into thoroughly and definite conclusions
were reached. Often a general would sit in with the official
family; at times a military aide would be called in to describe a
battle.[89] On at least one occasion a state Congressional delegation joined Davis, Lee, and the secretaries in a meeting at which
"there was a full and free interchange of opinion. . . ."[90] In
addition to official meetings, the President held informal Cabinet councils at his home.

Davis was censured, however, for not calling the Cabinet into
session more frequently. Mallory thought this criticism was
justified, believing that there should be more discussion especially of possible military appointees.[91] Seddon and Reagan
did not agree with Mallory, and Attorney General George Davis
asserted that military plans were discussed by the Cabinet, but
that the President gave orders and instructions privately after
the meeting.[92] The President himself, replying to one complainant, wrote:

You inform me that "the highest and most reputable authors" say
that I "have not had a cabinet council for more than four months."
I read your letter to a member and ex-member of my cabinet to-day;
they were surprised at the extravagance of the falsehood, and did not
believe that so much as a week had at any time occurred without a

[88] Stephen R. Mallory, "Last Days of the Confederate Government," *McClure's Magazine*, XVI (1900–1901), 240.

[89] Chesnut, *Diary*, 102.

[90] John Goode, "The Confederate Congress," *Conservative Review*, IV (1900), 112.

[91] Stephen R. Mallory, Diary, July 26, September 1, 1861, June 24, 1862, University of North Carolina.

[92] George Davis to Jefferson Davis, February 8, 1878, in Rowland (ed.), *Davis*, VI, 80–81.

cabinet consultation. I would like to know who the authors of such stories are. Your own estimate of me, I hope, assured you that I would not, as stated, treat the "Secretary of War as a mere clerk!" And if you know Mr. Benjamin you must realize the impossibility of his submitting to degradation at the hands of anyone. The opposition here complain that I cling too closely to my cabinet, not, as in your section, that they are disregarded; and the only contempt of the sentiments of Congress which is here alleged against me (so far as I have heard) is that their wish for the removal of two or more members of the cabinet has not been yielded to. Perhaps there might be added dissatisfaction on the part of a few at the promotion or appointment of military officers without consulting the members of Congress in relation to them. Against the unfounded story that I keep the Generals of the army in leading strings may be set the frequent complaint that I do not arraign them for what is regarded their failures or misdeeds, and do not respond to the popular clamor by displacing commanders upon irresponsible statements.[93]

Jones recorded that the President summoned the Cabinet to discuss the question of calling out conscripts when he might have issued the order without consulting the secretaries.[94] In view of Davis's sensitive nature, it is most probable that he was over-zealous in obtaining the opinions of known friends before making important decisions. According to Reagan, Davis was at all times receptive to suggestions from friends and political advisers, and despite criticisms to the contrary, he was thoughtful and deliberate in forming conclusions. Reagan has further refuted the assertion that there was a lack of discussion at Cabinet sessions, and that Davis expected his secretaries to be yes men. At the first meeting he attended, Reagan relates, the President told the secretaries he desired them to be frank with him as he would be with them. He asked for full and free discussion of his message to Congress, adding: "If a paper can't stand the criticism of its friends, it will be in a bad way when it gets into the hands of its enemies." [95] The Postmaster General (who asserted that he more than anyone else had opposed the President), fearing lest

93 Jefferson Davis to W. M. Brooks, March 13, 1862, *ibid.*, V, 217.
94 Jones, *Diary*, I, 257.
95 John W. Daniel (ed.), *Life and Reminiscences of Jefferson Davis, by Distinguished Men of His Time* (Baltimore, 1890), 260.

his attitude might perhaps embarrass his chief, offered to resign. Davis answered

. . . that he had been a member of a Cabinet himself; adding that if the Cabinet should accept without question the opinion of the President, he did not well see what their use would be as advisers of the President, and that he was far from being displeased with my course in this respect. He observed that the free interchange of opinions was the way of arriving at correct conclusions.[96]

The secretaries were unhampered in the selection of assistants for the transaction of the business of their departments. The President impressed upon them, however, that he would hold department heads responsible for the conduct and efficiency of their appointees. The only test for office should be loyalty to the Confederacy, honesty, and competence. Davis favored civil service reform and sought to have able and intelligent officials in his administration.

On occasion the President could and did go counter to the opinion of his advisers. Reagan cites the case in 1862 when Davis refused to act on the Cabinet's advice to interfere with General Joseph E. Johnston's command.[97] When Colonel Ulric Dahlgren's expedition against Richmond was repulsed, the people and the Cabinet did not favor treating the captured remnant of his band as prisoners of war. The secretaries urged that every tenth man of the prisoners be shot immediately.[98] The President opposed the suggestion, and the ensuing discussion was so heated as almost to create enmity between him and the Cabinet. At no other meeting of the Cabinet had there been such intensity of feeling or such great danger of a serious disagreement.[99] "To Jefferson Davis alone, and to his constancy of purpose, did these men owe their safety in spite of hostile public opinion and in opposition to two-thirds of the Cabinet." [100] Jones comments that the secretaries wanted to fight under the banner of a black flag, that is, he amended, to have others do the fighting.[101]

[96] Reagan, *Memoirs*, 162. [97] *Ibid.*, 137.
[98] *Ibid.*, 182. [99] *Ibid.*
[100] Benjamin and Butler, "Two Witnesses on the 'Treatment of Prisoners,'" *loc. cit.*, 187.
[101] Jones, *Diary*, II, 309.

The President and the Cabinet worked for the most part in reasonable harmony. What differences arose between them were such as naturally arise when men of pronounced individualities discuss subjects about which there can be conflicting opinions. In 1861 Mrs. Mary Boykin Chesnut heard of bitter dissensions among the secretaries and believed that only a match was needed to blow the Cabinet sky-high.[102] These rumored differences, a newspaper later hostile to the administration reported, were figments of the imagination of men eager to obtain secretaryships for border-state men.[103] Unquestionably there was a division of opinion as to the advisability of prosecuting the war along the lines of defense or offense. And, too, Reagan had serious tiffs with Memminger over post-office funds. Mallory had cause to complain of Seddon, and Seddon of Reagan. They were never a docile group, and it took a high degree of tact for an umpire to straighten out difficulties between departments. But, while there were clashes of opinion in the Cabinet, meetings were not marked by passion or strife.

Neither the historians of his own nor those of later periods have dealt kindly with Davis's choice of his advisers. From the time he nominated the secretaries for the provisional Cabinet down to the present, the wisdom of his selections has been questioned. Official opposition started when the appointment of Mallory went before the provisional Congress for confirmation. After a lull, Congressional disapprobation fell upon the heads of Benjamin and Memminger, in particular, and the entire Cabinet in general. It is worth while tracing the attitude of Congress toward the President's advisers.

Davis had little opposition from Congress once his Cabinet nominations had actually come to a vote on confirmation. Mallory's confirmation was fought by the Florida delegation in 1861, and his approval for a Cabinet post was delayed, only to receive a large majority in the end. There was strong opposition to him again when he was named Secretary of the Navy in the permanent Cabinet. The sentiment in Congress against Benjamin for

---

[102] Chesnut, *Diary*, 90, 108.
[103] *Charleston Mercury*, May 18, 1861. The *Montgomery Daily Post* and the *Charleston Daily Courier* reached the same conclusion. See note 72, *supra*.

Secretary of State found expression in 1862 in the close vote on a motion to reconsider his confirmation. Benjamin probably would have failed of confirmation as Secretary of War in 1862 even if the President had insisted upon nominating him. With the exception of these two men, the provisional Congress and, under the permanent government, the Senate acted quickly and favorably in confirming all nominations to Cabinet posts. More often than not the Senate confirmed a nominee without the formality of referring the nomination to the Committee on Appointments.

Congressional opposition to Cabinet members developed chiefly after the secretaries had taken office. Failure to attain the ideal was sufficient cause for many legislators to condemn a secretary as incompetent. Legislators did not trouble to discover fundamental causes of a failure. Even when an investigation gave proof that circumstances beyond an official's control were responsible for his lack of success, the die-hard opponent did not abate his condemnation. Much of the bitter criticism was directed at individual secretaries in the hope of goading them into resigning; at other times the President's foes were hitting at him over his secretaries' shoulders.

Three changes in the Cabinet resulted from attacks by Congress. Benjamin's continuance in office as Secretary of War was prevented in 1862. The blame for defeat in the Roanoke Island disaster was laid on him by a Congressional investigating committee, but the President succeeded in having the able Louisianian confirmed as Secretary of State. Opposition to Benjamin continued unabated throughout the war, and became especially bitter after his speech in the African Church in 1865. Benjamin seems to have had no intention of resigning, however, and certainly the President had no wish to have him do so. Memminger shared with Benjamin the concentrated fire of Congressional attack late in 1863. The movement to have him ousted from the Treasury Department reached its height under the leadership of Representative Henry S. Foote. The congressman declared that the Secretary was lacking in ability and denounced him for his failure to put into effect the financial program of Congress. Memminger resigned, although he was upheld by the

President. The appointment of Trenholm, who had been Memminger's adviser, was quickly confirmed by the Senate. The Charleston merchant prince was constantly praised for his abilities and official acts by Memminger's detractors, even though he continued his predecessor's policy. Seddon was the third and last Cabinet secretary to be forced out of office by Congress. Against the wishes of the President, the Secretary of War resigned in resentment of the request of most of the Virginia delegation that the Cabinet be reconstructed.

Hardly anything was left untried by Mallory's enemies to force him to quit the Cabinet. Had he followed his own inclinations, he probably would have resigned, but he had the unyielding support of the President and held his office to the last. Aside from the four members named above, the personnel of the Cabinet almost wholly escaped official criticism.

When their efforts to force Cabinet resignations failed, the opposition in Congress conceived the idea of limiting the terms of executive secretaries. Senator Robert W. Johnson of Arkansas introduced a bill on December 10, 1863, fixing at two years the tenure of office of heads of executive departments.[104] The committee to which this limitation bill was referred reported it favorably and the bill was debated intermittently until February 15, 1864.[105] The intent of the measure was that the term of each Cabinet member should expire upon the assembling of every new House of Representatives after the regular elections. The President could reappoint any or all of the secretaries, but as the Senate could refuse to confirm a nomination, an undesirable secretary could thus be forced out of office without resort to impeachment proceedings. Jones believed the measure was really aimed at Davis and, although he was convinced it would not be enacted, he feared it meant a declaration of war upon the President.[106] Some of the secretaries, Jones believed, would resign on February 18, 1864, but when the Confederacy entered upon its third year under the permanent Constitution no secretary resigned, and the measure was eventually dropped. It had no con

---

[104] *Journal of Congress*, III, 454–55; *Daily Richmond Examiner*, December 12, 1863.

[105] *Journal of Congress*, III, 606–607, 689–90, 732, 744–45.

[106] Jones, *Diary*, II, 132.

stitutional precedents back of it and never had a chance of passing the two houses of Congress.

The introduction of the measure was the occasion for the administration's friends and foes to give expression to their several views about the government. The *Richmond Examiner* saw in it a practical opportunity to curtail a reign of imbecility that had caused defeats and the conquest of half the area and population of the Confederate States. "The South began the struggle with resources nearly equal to the enemy but a poor administration had wasted half the original store. This law would reach the sources of incompetency and produce accountability and responsibility in the Executive Departments." There was much good in the proposal, the editorial concluded, and no objection to it, for a secretary of "proven . . . wisdom, energy, and integrity . . . will always be approved; and it is right that he, who is a load of stupidity, listlessness, or corruption, . . . should be put out." [107] In a later issue the editor declared that:

On the streets, along the highways of travel, at the private fireside, in public assemblies, everywhere, among all classes, the opinion may be heard, delivered in every form of words, that the first necessity of the Confederate cause is reform of the administration. The sentiment is universal, deliberate, dispassionate, unselfish. [108]

The editor claimed that the Senate bill had been brought up to relieve an unbearable situation. Only by this means could the country be rid of the "calamitous" and "disgraceful" administration of Secretary Mallory, or prevent the continuation of "Mr. Memminger's finances" for six years.

The Cabinet measure was hailed by the *Montgomery Mail* as the first ray of intelligence it had seen in the Senate. [109] The *Charleston Mercury* surpassed all other newspapers in praising the bill. The *Mercury* feared a life tenure for the Cabinet under the law as it then stood, for a secretary could pass on for an

107 *Daily Richmond Examiner*, December 12, 1863.

108 *Ibid.*, January 30, 1864. The editor was carried away by his own phrases. A minority only wanted changes. If the populace spent their days in talking reform of the Cabinet, an examination of thousands of personal letters of individuals in many walks of life shows at least that they did not put their thoughts in writing. Except for several references to Benjamin by military men, there are few derogatory references about any Cabinet member.

109 *Ibid.*, December 30, 1863, quoting the *Montgomery Daily Mail*.

indeterminate time from one President to another. Without the enactment of the Senate bill, or one similar, the Confederacy might be saddled with inefficient secretaries for years to come.[110] The opposition newspapers lined themselves up solidly with the Senate against the administration.

These attacks were answered by newspapers favorable to the administration. The *Richmond Enquirer* believed that a faction of the Senate, in an effort to force out of office a secretary not acceptable to it, would adopt a principle destructive of the fundamental idea of the government.[111] The bill would make the Senate more powerful than the House of Representatives, since the Senate would be enabled to control the Cabinet and to impose its wishes upon the President. Moreover, the secretaries would become the Senate's puppets, set up to spy upon and thwart the President, who under such a system would be forced to treat the Cabinet members as mere clerks and himself assume personal management of the departments. The *Enquirer* preferred a Cabinet selected by Davis to one chosen by the Senate. Recalling its repeated advice that the State Department be closed and Benjamin thus relieved of the arduous duties of doing nothing, the newspaper yet preferred him to some minion of the Senate. "With all due respect for the Senate," the *Enquirer*'s editorial sarcastically closed, "we must say that we are not disposed to increase its powers, since no provision is made in the law for an increase of its wisdom." [112]

Some time after the limitation bill had died in the Senate, the *Richmond Sentinel* reviewed the entire situation. When circumstance required removal of secretaries and the appointment of new ones, said the editorial, a President who had any regard for his dignity of character, his reputation, or the success of his administration, would resign rather than submit to dictation by the Senate. Above all, an executive must have moral firmness, and this was best illustrated by Davis's selection and treatment of his Cabinet. The executive secretaries were the President's advisers, and no President would select for so confidential and responsible a position a man whose past life had not furnished

110 *Charleston Mercury*, February 12, 1864.
111 *Daily Richmond Enquirer*, December 15, 1863.   112 *Ibid.*

evidence of wisdom, integrity, and unusual aptitude for the duties of office. A President's reputation was largely in the hands of his Cabinet and the success of his administration depended upon their wise counsel and earnest cooperation. No President would appoint other than the ablest and most trustworthy men to his Cabinet, nor would he remove them at the demand of un-informed idle clamor that preferred no distinct charges against them. The administration had been a success and in the absence of specific charges and proof of personal inefficiency there was actually no need to answer the epithets hurled at the members of the Cabinet. There was danger, however, that these accusa-tions, if unanswered, would undermine public confidence. De-struction of the administration through the undermining of its public support, the *Sentinel* concluded, was evidently the de-sire of the President's political foes.[113]

In the crafty Vice-President the enemies of Davis found an ally. Usually the ardent advocate of a strict adherence to the Constitution, Stephens now became a mere political opponent. He unreservedly approved the Senate limiting bill, declaring that "The Heads of Departments now hold their places . . . at the will and pleasure of Congress. . . ."[114] When an executive secretary or the President pursued a policy not approved by Congress, Stephens felt that it was the duty of the national legis-lature to show its disapproval and to compel a change in the Cabinet. Carried to its logical conclusion, Stephens's argument would have meant the resignation of a President of whom Con-gress had thus registered its disapproval. Stephens did not over-look the possibility that a vote of lack of confidence conceivably might not result in the resignation of the Cabinet member censured. In that event, he advised that Congress by withholding supplies could compel the President to meet its wishes. It is a sad commentary on the patriotism of the administration's foes that, with the country engaged in a life and death struggle, a faction could entertain the thought of cutting off supplies in order to win a technical victory over the President.

---

113 *Richmond Sentinel,* July 29, 1864.
114 Stephens to Thomas Jenkins Semmes, January 27, 1864, in Thomas Jenkins Semmes Papers, Duke University.

Davis and his administration rode out the storm with comparative ease. The opposition continued to snipe at the Cabinet, however, and Memminger retired later in the year. He stated in his letter of resignation that he could no longer conduct the Treasury, opposed at every step by an unfriendly Congress that forced him to work with unworkable financial ideas. Davis's critics were happy in the thought that they had forced the resignation of a Presidential appointee, but the President, having in Trenholm the man he wanted as Memminger's successor, must have enjoyed a quiet laugh at the opposition's continued laudation of the new Secretary.

A fresh wave of criticism arose in the fall of 1864 when the vigilant Representative Foote accused Secretary of War Seddon of profiteering by selling his wheat at an inflated price. As usual, Benjamin was included in the attack. The people had grown weary of the war and there were many who favored peace at any price rather than to continue to wage a struggle in which they had come to despair of victory. Many, too, sincerely believed that a reorganization of the Cabinet might possibly revive public confidence and prop a tottering Confederacy. Akin to this thought was the movement to make General Lee dictator of the sorely beset nation. Associated with the men of patriotic character who advocated these remedial measures were many self-seeking politicians whose main purpose was the glorification of themselves and the discrediting of the administration.

The opposition movement came to a head in late January and early February of 1865. Wholesale resignations and reform of the Cabinet were called for by almost the entire Virginia delegation, led by Representative Thomas S. Bocock who waited on the President to explain the action of the delegation. Bocock in a written statement on the next day, January 21, reiterated his position. In substance he said that public sentiment had been growing worse and that the government must do something to bolster confidence. The propriety of passing a resolution declaring that the country lacked confidence in the Cabinet as an administration had been discussed by members of Congress, at least three fourths of whom, Bocock assured the President, would vote for such a resolution if introduced. To save the President from embarrassment, his friends in the Virginia delegation thought it proper to advise him to forestall the introduction of such a resolution by making changes in the Cabinet.[113]

That Bocock greatly overestimated the support a vote of censure would have received in the House is the logical conclusion to be drawn from a consideration of the situation. It is hard to understand why, after Davis had thrown down the gauntlet in a stinging criticism of the action of the Virginia delegation in his letter to Seddon of February 1, 1865, the opposition did not counter by proposing a resolution of no confidence including the President as well as his Cabinet. If there had existed, before Davis wrote his letter, a three-fourths vote for reorganization of the Cabinet, certainly after it there would have been ample votes to censure the entire administration. Had success been certain, as Bocock asserted, there was a sufficient number of men who hated Davis to have initiated the move in Congress. A short time after this incident, the Senate was unable to pass a resolution of censure against Secretary Benjamin. Yet he was the most execrated member of the Cabinet and the opposition to him had grown because of his revolutionary ideas as expressed on a prior occasion at the meeting in the African Church. What the Senate was unable to do in the case of one man, it is improbable that the House could have done in the case of the whole Cabinet, for the intensity of House opposition was hardly greater than that of the Senate.

Seddon resigned his post as a result of the Virginia delegation's action. But Davis utilized the occasion to protest against interference with the prerogatives of the President. He said:

The relations between the President and the Heads of the Executive Departments are . . . of the closest and most intimate character; they imply mutual confidence and esteem and a general concurrence of opinion on Administrative policy; and it is not a Constitutional function of the Legislative Department to interfere with these relations, nor can it be assumed that a change of the Heads of Departments would alter the Administrative policy of the Government without also assuming as true the injurious supposition that the President

113 Bocock to Davis, January 21, 1864 [1865], in *Official Records*, Ser. I, Vol. XLVI, Pt. II, 1118.

has permitted them to pursue a policy at variance with his own, and has thus failed to do his own duty as Chief of the Executive Department.[116]

The Confederate government, the President's letter pointed out, was not similar to that of England, where the ministers were a part of the legislative branch. In the Confederacy the secretaries did not have the right of debate in Congress on matters relating directly to their departments, and the executive and legislative departments, the letter reminded the delegation, were distinct branches of government.

The Virginia delegation replied that they had acted from friendly motives. Fearing the development of a possible rift between Congress and the Executive as the outcome of the demand for a change in the Cabinet, they had sought to prevent it. They regarded the Cabinet as a group of counselors held responsible to public opinion.

Whatever may be the theory of our Government, it has not occurred to us before the publication of the correspondence now under consideration that, practically, a body so eminent in our political system could through dependence on the pleasure of the President, become so insignificant that a change of the heads of departments could not alter the administrative policy of the Government in any degree. It could not be presumed that a body of statesmen in our country, filling those high places, would contribute no independent advice, information or influence to the policy of the administration, or that they would long continue to hold office either in complete subserviency to a single mind or in defiance of the general sense of their countrymen.[117]

The President's outburst had provided the opportunity for the above cutting rejoinder. The essential purpose of his letter had been to show that the Confederate policy was the result of the joint efforts of the Executive and his advisers and that there could be no condemnation of the Cabinet that did not include the President. As President, Davis was willing to share or assume responsibility for the government policy; he upheld his Execu-

[116] Davis to Seddon, February 1, 1865, in Rowland (ed.), *Davis*, VI, 459.

[117] The statement of the Virginia delegation dated February 11, 1865, and signed Thos. S. Bocock is printed in the *Richmond Daily Dispatch*, February 16, 1865.

tive privileges and at the same time defended his aides. Unfortunately, his language was susceptible to a different interpretation; and the Virginia delegation seized the opportunity to place their own interpretation upon it, and to make it appear that the President treated his Cabinet members as so many convenient lay figures. The tone of their reply raises the question as to whether or not their original advice was motivated by the friendship they professed.

Each side in the controversy was at fault, but the onus was on the President. A more tactful man would have accepted the advice of the Virginia delegation with at least a show of grateful consideration. For the sake of harmony, Secretary Seddon's reference in his letter of resignation to the action of his fellow Virginians could have been passed over. The President, jealous of the dignity of his office, felt bound to defend himself and the Cabinet from unmerited attack. The demand for changes in the Cabinet personnel was growing, but the clamor for the dismissal of the secretaries was not justified by inefficiency or a lack of ability on the part of the incumbents. Public confidence in the government was being undermined and the will to repel invasion was being weakened. In desperation, many public men believed a change in several of the departments would improve the national situation. Justly or unjustly, the people desired a change, said the *Richmond Sentinel*.[118]

Davis knew that the cry for Cabinet changes arose from the desire to find a scapegoat for the disasters the Confederacy had suffered, and he was unwilling to sacrifice to popular clamor men who had served their country faithfully and well. The President was correct in his loyalty to the Cabinet, but he was tactless in his handling of the demand for its reorganization. He had every consideration of right and justice on his side, but long political service and four years of war had not taught him to bear patiently the annoyances incident to public office.

That Congressional interference with the Cabinet was open to criticism was admitted even by the *Richmond Examiner*. The newspaper believed, however, that there had to be some method of bringing home to the President the fact that there was long-

[118] *Richmond Sentinel*, January 24, February 4, 1865.

ing for new faces in the Cabinet. Arguments were unnecessary, for the problem was ". . . the safety of the Country, and not the techy dignity of this or that public functionary, or the courtesies due between coordinate departments of the government." [119] The advisability of the six-year Presidential term was questioned by the *Examiner,* since there was no real check on the Executive by impeachment, a political weapon that never reached an erring official. Other critics flatly proposed that Davis and Stephens resign and a clean sweep of the administration be made.[120]

To what extent the Confederacy was harmed by this opposition, is a question that is difficult to answer. Certainly, incessant sniping at administration officials did no good. Men like Stephens, Toombs, Johnston, Wigfall, and Foote had a considerable following, and their carping did much to impair the morale of the Southern people. By 1865, perhaps half of his countrymen had little use for Davis or his administration. It would be easy, however, to credit the opposition with too great influence. Victory more than words counted with the people. A Secretary of War, for instance, who had the luck to hold office during a period when the armies were winning battles was accepted as a brilliant official, though actually he might not be worth a tinker's dam. Conversely, an able secretary who directed the War Department at a time when military reverses abounded was forthwith pronounced a worthless specimen of humanity, utterly lacking in ability. Failure was the fundamental cause for public despondency, and the despairing feeling engendered by the Confederacy's woes was intensified by the opposition.

So far as the actual conduct of the government was concerned, opposition had few damaging effects. The President and his secretaries were embarrassed, of course, and two Cabinet members resigned in the face of criticism; but from first to last, the ad-

[119] *Daily Richmond Examiner,* February 9, 1865.

[120] State Senator John Collier of Virginia said in the Virginia Senate: "The civil administration has been so signal a failure, and is so dead in the popular affection, that I shall forbear to drag this lifeless Hector around the walls of Troy. The chief characteristic of that administration, is that it has separated the Government from the people, and has made more vigorous and effective war on the resources of the country than it has made on the public enemy." *Richmond Daily Dispatch,* February 28, 1865,

ministration of Davis remained strong. It was far stronger in the late months of the war than were the divided and discouraged people it represented. The administration had overcome Congressional opposition throughout the war, making occasional compromises but always steering a straight course toward the goal of Southern independence. This is not to say that the Confederate Congress was a time-serving body under the Executive thumb. On the contrary, the Senators and Representatives were men of aggressive temper, strong-minded, and tenacious of their opinions. History affords few examples of a nation at war where faction tried so much to hamper a ruler as did the Confederacy to hamper its President. Davis vetoed thirty-nine acts of Congress, not one of which could be passed over the veto.[121] The strength of the administration perhaps could not be more strikingly illustrated.

In their criticism of individual Cabinet members the opposition directed censure at the secretaries whose abilities were greatest. The Attorneys General escaped attack because the office was of negligible importance in comparison with the other departments. The consensus was that the postal service was inefficient, but that Postmaster General Reagan was accomplishing as much as could reasonably be expected of any man. The conduct of the State Department was censured because it was headed by the Jewish Benjamin, who had been unpopular as Secretary of War. The five outstanding members of the Cabinet—Benjamin, Mallory, Memminger, Seddon, and Reagan—were the more severely criticized. The reason that the attack centered on the best, rather than on the least worthy, is not obscure. Official opposition to the administration had never been organized into an effective fighting unit. Criticism was a hit-or-miss affair prompted by some incident or happening of the moment. The men most active in the government were most frequently objects of attack for the reason that the abler officials ventured more, and consequently were more shining targets than officials of less daring and ability.

In reality there was no opposition, in the sense of an organized group working in unison; rather it was a group of critics unable

[121] *Journal of Congress, passim.* See note 118, p. 241.

to agree among themselves. There was no man or policy that all of Davis's opponents could agree to support. They remained disorganized, harassing the administration, embarrassing it sometimes, and finally weakening the morale of the nation. Had they become unified, under an able leader with a definite policy, the administration might have been wrecked, and Davis forced out of the presidency.

III

Men of Ambition

JAMES LAWRENCE ORR, chairman of the House Committee on Foreign Relations, once said that the Confederacy never had any foreign policy.[1] This is far from being an accurate statement. The Confederacy indeed had a clearly defined foreign policy, but this policy never succeeded in attaining its objectives. The provisional Congress, even before the inauguration of Jefferson Davis as President, had resolved to appoint commissioners to Washington to obtain recognition of the South's independence, to agree upon a division of common property, and to work out a settlement of the common debt. One day later, February 13, the Congress agreed to the appointment of three commissioners to European countries. Their task, as seen by Robert Barnwell Rhett, would be to obtain recognition of the Confederacy on the basis of liberal commercial treaties negotiated for a twenty-year period and a guaranty that no tariff on imports would exceed 20 per cent. There was considerable sentiment in Congress for their appointment by the legislative body before the arrival of the President-elect. Davis was saved from possible embarrassment by the acceptance of wiser counsel. By the time the President took office Confederate policy was fairly well outlined. Stated in its simplest terms, this policy was that the South would seek peaceful separation from the Union, would negotiate for recognition of the Confederacy by the governments of Europe, and would cultivate friendly commercial relations with all countries.

The President accepted the suggestions made by Congress.

[1] James Morton Callahan, *The Diplomatic History of the Southern Confederacy* (Baltimore, 1901), 66.

Even before provision had been made for a State Department, he was considering the men available to represent the Confederacy in its negotiations with other nations, in Washington as well as abroad. As commissioners to Washington he named, on February 25, André Bienvenu Roman of Louisiana, Martin Jenkins Crawford of Georgia, and John Forsyth of Alabama. This action was substantially a continuation of the policy inaugurated by South Carolina. It was commonly believed in the South that a strong sentiment existed in the North for peaceable separation and an early establishment of diplomatic relations with the Confederacy in order that trade relations between the two countries might be continued. On February 27, the President nominated William L. Yancey, Pierre Adolphe Rost, and Ambrose D. Mann as envoys to the European countries. All the nominations had been fairly launched before the Secretary of State had time to organize his department. The credit for the formulation of policy belongs more to Congress than to the President, since it conformed generally to the ideas of a majority of the members of Congress.

ROBERT TOOMBS

Meanwhile, a Secretary of State had been appointed by the President. This position, at the moment considered as second only to the presidency in importance, had been first offered to Robert Barnwell, who had declined the honor and had suggested Howell Cobb or Robert Toombs of Georgia for the office. Cobb had refused to enter the Cabinet,[2] and the position of Secretary of State was then offered to Toombs. Davis, as he himself stated, had planned to invite Toombs to become Secretary of the Treasury, but Barnwell and the South Carolina delegation were actively supporting one of their own members for that office.[3] Toombs had hoped to be President of the Confederacy and many politicians predicted that he would decline an honor so far inferior to the one to which he aspired, but he accepted the appointment as Secretary of State with little hesitation.

[2] Howell Cobb to his wife, February 20, 1861, in Phillips (ed.), *Correspondence of Toombs, Stevens, and Cobb*, 544.

[3] Davis, *Rise and Fall*, I, 242.

Robert Toombs had served an early apprenticeship in politics and had received extensive training in public affairs. He was born in Wilkes County, Georgia, on July 2, 1810, attended secondary schools and Franklin College in his native state, was graduated from Union College, New York, and studied law at the University of Virginia. His preliminary training for public life was completed by his service in the Creek War and subsequently as a Whig member of the state legislature, after which, in 1844, he was elected Representative in Congress. Seven years later he was elected to the United States Senate as the candidate of the Constitutional Union party, and retained a seat in the Senate until his resignation in 1861.[4]

The Confederacy's first Secretary of State was not an ardent Southern radical; he had accepted the Compromise of 1850 in good faith and, with Howell Cobb and Stephens, he had striven to stem the rising tide of secession in Georgia. After 1852 Toombs, one-time Whig and anti-secessionist, drew closer to the Democratic party; by 1856, he had come to believe that John C. Frémont's election would be a cause of war. Those who were politically wise classed Toombs as a conservative in comparison with the young Benjamin H. Hill,[5] for all the Georgia Senator's blustering ways and rabble-rousing oratory. In a speech on John Brown's raid Toombs accused the Republican party of moral complicity in the Harpers Ferry foray, and declared that there was no peace, fraternity, or common country in the Union. When Lincoln was elected President, the Georgian took the ground that separation would ensue, but he willingly participated in the efforts made to save the Union. When the Crittenden resolutions failed, he advocated immediate secession and telegraphed his constituents:

All further looking to the North for security for your constitutional rights in the Union ought to be instantly abandoned. Secession by the 4th of March next should be thundered forth from the ballot box by

[4] The best biography of Toombs is that by Ulrich Bonnell Phillips, *The Life of Robert Toombs* (New York, 1913). An older but useful account is that by Pleasant A. Stovall, *Robert Toombs, Statesman, Speaker, Soldier, Sage . . .* (New York, 1892).

[5] A. E. Allenben, "A Pro-Slavery Statesman," *National Magazine*, XVI (1891), 306.

the united voice of Georgia. Such a voice will be your best guaranty for liberty, security, tranquillity and glory.[6]

Southern institutions and the social system of the South found a staunch supporter in Toombs. As the owner of a large and well-managed plantation, he naturally regarded abolitionists as fanatics who would destroy an institution valuable alike to slave and master. Political conditions of his time being what they were, he placed Southern honor, rights, and interests above national welfare. He was convinced that the South should leave the Union. He entered wholeheartedly into the secession movement in his state and was appointed a delegate to the Montgomery convention. Then he became a member of the committee on the permanent Constitution and chairman of the Finance Committee of the provisional Congress.

Toombs, tall of stature, burly of physique, hearty in manner, with flashing black eyes, combined in himself characteristics that were both lovable and repellent. He had a capacity for devoted friendship or relentless enmity. He was at his best in a company of congenial friends upon convivial occasions. The general estimate of him was that he was a braggadocio, but his friends credited him with sound judgment on important questions. The harsher assessment of his character, unfortunately for his place in Confederate history, was the correct one, as his record conclusively proves. His vagaries disgusted his colleague, Thomas R. R. Cobb. A telegram which went out over the nation's wires in February announcing free trade for all in the Confederacy was attributed by Cobb to Toombs who "was pretty high from wine."[7] Toombs was abundantly endowed with brains, but he often made poor use of them. Through his lack of self-control he largely negatived his qualities of generosity, courage, and frankness, and stood in his own light more often than did any other person. His forte lay in destructive attack, not in constructive statesmanship.

His duties as Secretary of State were cut out for him when he took office. He continued a plan inaugurated before he assumed

6 *Ibid.,* 309.
7 Hull (ed.), "Correspondence of Thomas Reade Rootes Cobb, 1860–1862," *loc. cit.,* 179.

office and was of little influence upon the spirit of Confederate policy in its dealings with the Union. Negotiations had already been opened with Washington, looking to peaceful separation and an amicable agreement as to the division of common property and the settlement of debts. The North was to be assured of the Confederacy's disposition to live with it on terms of political and commercial amity. The advantages of continued trade with the South were to be detailed as an incentive to recognition of its independence. At the same time, the Southern commissioners were instructed to draw attention to the disastrous consequences to the North that would attend the cutting off of the South's raw materials. The South generally pinned its faith completely on the power of King Cotton.

Toombs's first important instructions as Secretary of State were written on March 16, 1861, for the commissioners to Europe.[8] An able statement of the theory of secession was included in the letter of instruction, which also outlined the grievances of the South against the North. The commissioners were to assure the foreign governments that in no circumstances would the Southern people consider a reconstruction of the Union, and that there could be no doubt of the Confederacy's ability to maintain its independence if the need to defend itself arose. Virtual free trade and liberal navigation laws were to be held out as inducements to foreign countries to recognize the Confederacy. To England a gentle hint was to be thrown out in the reminder that the annual gross yield from its manufactures from cotton was nearly six hundred million dollars. What would happen to this cotton supply in a long war could readily be realized by the British. Toombs's second letter of instructions, written after the opening of hostilities, informed the commissioners that the President had invited applications for letters of marque. In it Toombs instructed the commissioners to assure foreign powers that there would be no interference with their commerce. Further instructions were sent the commissioners on May 18, May 21, and July 15.

The Secretary of State hoped to obtain speedy recognition of

[8] Toombs to Yancey, Rost, and Mann, March 16, 1861, in Richardson (ed.), *Messages and Papers*, II, 1–8.

the Confederacy from England and France. He succeeded only in obtaining an acknowledgment of belligerent rights. The Declaration of Paris was accepted by the Confederacy, except for the provision abolishing privateering. Toombs prevented the Southern privateers from being classed as pirates. This success and the acknowledgment of belligerent rights were the only diplomatic victories of the South over the United States. And they were the logical outcome of necessity.

Various official duties were performed by the Secretary of State. There were credentials to be issued for the commissioners sent by the Confederacy to the seven border states. A representative to the Mexican government was instructed to convey hints of a defensive and offensive alliance that might be effected between Mexico and the Confederacy. The matter of investigating applicants for letters of marque and issuing the papers also took up considerable time. Toombs was always ready to offer advice at the frequent Cabinet meetings held in the first few months of the newly formed government. Also, he regularly attended the legislative sessions and took an active part in the deliberations. It is evident that his duties as Secretary of State were not so onerous as to require his full time.

Whether or not Toombs was wholly in sympathy with Confederate foreign policy is open to conjecture. Several writers are inclined to believe that his ideas were rejected by Davis.[9] Had the direction of foreign policy been left to Toombs, many students of this period believe, he would have accepted Rhett's counsels and offered England and France commercial privileges and a minimum tariff for a term of years as the price of recognition. Toombs, however, never strongly supported such a plan. If, indeed, he favored it, he was quiet about it in Congress, so far at least as there is a record. The legend of Toombs's splendid intellectual originality in these few months is traceable to his biographer, Pleasant A. Stovall. It was after the war that the beautiful theories of what should have been done were developed and given currency by many Southern leaders. Confederate foreign policy, in fact, was not complex. It was predicated

[9] Callahan, *Diplomatic History*, 84–89; Tate, *Jefferson Davis*, 94; Hamilton J. Eckenrode, *Jefferson Davis: President of the South* (New York, 1923), 134–35.

upon the widely accepted theory that the South had a legal right to withdraw from the Union, and on the belief that cotton was king. It was not the policy solely of Davis, but of Congress and the Southern people. Aside from that, the plan for favorable commercial treaties which Rhett and Toombs were supposed to have advocated was not of extraordinary value. Study of the instructions sent the foreign commissioners shows that the South paved the way for commercial treaties of greater advantages in return for recognition than those Rhett had in mind.

Toombs and Davis had been contemporaries in the United States Senate, but they had never been intimate friends. Davis had been impressed by Toombs's knowledge of political economy, but the characters of the two men were antithetical. The Georgian had hoped to be the power in the Cabinet, if not the country's ruler, but he soon realized that he was but one of six secretaries. The President listened willingly to his ideas and counsel, as he did to those of other Cabinet members, but it was the consensus of the Cabinet that Davis considered in making his final decision. Toombs and Walker, the Secretary of War, were the only two secretaries who desired the adoption of an aggressive, warlike policy toward the United States.[10] The Secretary of State deprecated all delay, counseled immediate invasion of the North, and believed in making the war as terrible as possible. Other secretaries believed it impossible to invade the North, but were for rapid preparation for war. Toombs found himself in a minority of the Cabinet and became dissatisfied with his position.

Toombs's dissatisfaction arose from the nonacceptance of his ideas about the conduct of the war rather than from any feeling that he was being held in check on questions of foreign policy. One is inclined to doubt that Toombs, on the occasion when the Cabinet was discussing the advisability of attacking Fort Sumter, really uttered the melodramatic protest attributed to him by his biographer. Stovall quotes his hero as saying:

Mr. President, at this time, it is suicide, murder, and will lose us every friend at the North. You will wantonly strike a hornet's nest which

---

[10] Jones, *Diary,* I, 39–40.

extends from mountains to ocean, and legions, now quiet, will swarm out and sting us to death. It is unnecessary; it puts us in the wrong; it is fatal.[11]

Such counsel of caution is not consistent with the markedly aggressive character of the man's nature. On May 22, at least, he was complaining of the policy of standing on the defensive.[12] One searches in vain to discover complaints that he was held under the President's thumb and treated like a chief clerk of the State Department. Toombs, indeed, made some reference to "chief clerks" later, but only after he had experienced many disappointments and reverses as a military leader. As a member of the Cabinet, he and Davis never were on terms of close attachment but their relations nevertheless were those existing between friends.

It is not to be wondered at that Toombs did not become one of the President's intimates, for his official course was hardly conducive to the development of such relationship. He openly criticized the administration's war policy, and contended that, had the state authorities in Virginia taken the initiative, 25,000 men could have driven the Yankees far into Pennsylvania. Had he been President, he would have acted quickly and aggressively.[13] He seemed to take pleasure in intimating that the administration should assemble an army of 500,000 men. Yet he knew every effort was being exerted to recruit all the volunteers possible for the duration of the war. Even assuming that his plan of an aggressive war was superior to the administration's war policy, it is apparent that as a member of the administration he should have observed greater discretion in his speech. Toombs had one supreme ambition: to hold the highest office in the Confederacy. It was beyond his reach. Yet because he himself could not rule, he could not bring himself to cooperate wholeheartedly with the President. It followed that as Secretary of State he failed, as he was to fail later in another post.

In Toombs's view, the office of Secretary of State was relatively unimportant in the Confederacy's governmental setup. Until the South's independence should become an accomplished fact,

---

11 Stovall, *Robert Toombs*, 226.   12 Jones, *Diary*, I, 39.
13 *Ibid.*

the holder of that portfolio would have little opportunity to demonstrate his capacity for statesmanship. Recognition of the Confederacy depended upon military success rather than upon foreign policy, be it ever so brilliantly directed. Until the goal of independence should be attained, the Secretary of State could do little but twiddle his thumbs. When on one occasion Toombs was asked if he did not want more assistants in his department, he answered scornfully that he "carried the State department in his hat." [14] The retort gave rise to many variations on the popularly accepted theme that Toombs was restless and uneasy in an office whose duties were too few to keep him fully occupied. The impulsive Georgian, according to the often trivial Thomas Cooper DeLeon, was approached by thousands of place seekers. Toombs told one insistent applicant, the bearer of a letter of recommendation, "Perfectly useless, sir!" "But, Sir," the job hunter pleaded, "if you will only look at the letter . . . I think you can find something for me." "Can you get in here, sir?" roared the Secretary, taking off his hat and pointing into it. "That's the Department of State, sir!" and he sputtered out a volley of resounding oaths.[15]

The inactivity of his position plainly irked Toombs. His situation would have been more tolerable had his conception of war policy found favor with the President and the Cabinet; but since it evoked no support from them, Toombs reacted with all the vehemence of his turbulent nature. As disputatious as the missionary who disagreed with the cannibal who ate him, Toombs did not always agree with himself.[16] Because of his connection with the administration, he was restrained at times from public expression of his disagreement with the policy pursued by the Confederacy. He had so little to do in the State Department that he had ample time to swap yarns with congenial visitors. Nor did his duties as a member of Congress satisfy his restless spirit.

Toombs loved a good fight, and he saw an opportunity to satisfy his craving for belligerent action on the battle front. His

[14] *Daily Richmond Examiner,* May 15, 1861.
[15] Thomas Cooper DeLeon, *Four Years in Rebel Capitals: . . .* (Mobile, 1892), 33.
[16] *Id., Belles, Beaux and Brains of the 60's,* 83.

experience in actual warfare was limited to his service as a captain of militia in the Creek War, but he had no misgivings about his military ability. He was contemptuous of the trained graduate of West Point, for he believed that any man with common sense, unflinching courage, and the ability to inspire men could command troops successfully. His courage and his possession of the inspirational quality to lead troops were beyond question. More and more, as he compared his humdrum situation as Secretary with the action and glory of battle, his dissatisfaction grew. Toombs will not be with us long, Jones records, but will take the first opportunity to repair to the field.[17] At length the Secretary talked over the situation with the President. He was discontented with the inactivity of his position, perhaps a little jealous of the President, vexed because his advice was disregarded by the Cabinet, and very certainly lured by a vision of military glory. Toombs requested of the President an appointment as brigadier general in the regular army.

Davis, a trained soldier himself, hesitated to give a civilian an important military command. At the same time he realized that Toombs had an extensive personal following in the Confederacy and he wanted to keep the friendship of the blustering Georgian for the administration. The President weighed one consideration against the other; despite the meagerness of his military experience, Toombs deserved a reward for his past services.[18] Besides, to refuse his request would be to give ground to the repeated accusations of "partiality" toward men with West Point training. Davis granted Toombs's request and appointed Robert M. T. Hunter Secretary of State on July 24. Toombs turned over the office immediately to his successor, and his nomination as brigadier general was confirmed by the provisional Congress on August 2.

The first change in Cabinet personnel occasioned little notice. The *Richmond Enquirer* was sure that in the field Toombs would find ample scope for his ardor, patriotism, and gallantry.[19] An important civil post had lost the services of one of the abler

17 Jones, *Diary*, I, 40.
18 Davis to D. W. Lewis, September 21, 1863, in Rowland (ed.), *Davis*, VI, 43–44.
19 *Daily Richmond Enquirer*, July 27, 1861.

men in the Confederacy, the *Richmond Dispatch* commented, but his successor in office was a man of equal ability.[20] An editorial in the *Richmond Examiner* about two weeks later deprecated the general desire of congressmen and Cabinet members for military careers. It was a generous but nonetheless mistaken idea, the editor wrote, to abandon the highest and most indispensable civil duties for those of the camp. The editorial concluded:

There are men who cannot be spared from the councils of civil life, from the education and direction of public sentiment, and from offices of civil dignity, even for the war we are waging—at least not until that war reaches an extremity which it has not yet approached.[21]

Undeterred by this note of disapproval, Toombs entered joyously upon his new duties with the good wishes and Godspeed of his friends. He was destined to experience disappointment and to suffer near disgrace in his new field. He soon became as unhappy in the army and as intractable as he had been in the Cabinet. He did not hestitate to storm at his superior officers when crossed or to disobey direct orders occasionally, and his contumacy reached the point where he actually challenged his commander to a duel.[22] "Toombs is ready for another revolution," Mrs. Chesnut reported in June, 1862, "and curses freely everything Confederate from the President down to a horse boy." [23] After the battle of Sharpsburg (Antietam), Brigadier General Toombs resigned his commission, left the army and retired to his Georgia home at Washington. But he found little solace as a country squire in a country torn by war. He was denounced when he planted a full crop of cotton because the country's need was for food crops.

Whatever his disappointments and tribulations, however, the former brigadier general never wavered in his loyalty to the Confederacy and never favored reunion with the North. "When all else is lost," he wrote, "I prefer to unite with the thousands

20 *Richmond Daily Dispatch,* July 26, 1861.
21 *Daily Richmond Examiner,* August 7, 1861.
22 Gipson, "The Collapse of the Confederacy," *loc. cit.,* 451.
23 Chesnut, *Diary,* 171.

of our own countrymen who have found honorable deaths, if not graves, in the battlefields." [24]

In 1864 he resumed his military career by serving with the Georgia state troops. It was not long before Richmond was hearing rumors that Toombs had been arrested by General Beauregard. The events leading up to this action soon became known. Toombs's men, state troops mustered temporarily into Confederate service, when at Augusta, Georgia, had built fires in the railway box cars, whereupon the station agent refused to allow the train to proceed until the fires had been put out.

General Toombs coming up in the midst of the altercation between the agent and his men, declared the fires should not be extinguished, that the train should leave in spite of the agent, and after cursing and using much bitter language towards the latter had him arrested and kept in custody by a guard. He also threatened to have the agent cut in pieces and thrown into the engine for fuel, together with other direful calamities to his corporeal man. [25]

The matter of Toombs's arrest was hushed up, and again he retired to his home.

Although embittered toward Davis, Toombs was magnanimous and in May, 1865, he offered to call his personal followers together and assure the President a safe escape. [26] The offer was typical of the man. He was never underhanded or spiteful toward an antagonist. He was ruled by his emotions, and could never submit to discipline, whether self-imposed or at the hands of a superior. He was a man of brilliant parts who wasted much of the talent with which he was endowed.

Toombs's antipathy to the President did not develop until he had failed as an army officer. On September 1, 1861, he wrote

[24] "Letter to a Peace Democrat," *Atlantic Monthly*, XII (1863), 781.

[25] *Richmond Daily Dispatch*, February 13, 1864; *Daily Richmond Enquirer*, February 13, 1864, quoting the *Savannah Republican*. The above was the story as it actually happened, though perhaps colored. There were many variations. According to one, Toombs was put off the train for having no passport. Thereupon he gave vent to his feelings in treasonable language. "An old lady, who was returning from visiting her soldier sons, witnessed the arrest. 'Well, well, well!!' said the old lady, 'they have got Bob Toombs. I heard him say he'd swallow the blood of all Yankees that came South. Well, well, well! he can swallow all he sheds.'" *Daily Richmond Enquirer*, February 4, 1864.

[26] Reagan, *Memoirs*, 215.

Davis expressing sorrow at the news of his illness, and advised rest and relaxation for his chief. Of himself, the former Secretary wrote that he was pleased with the ease and repose of camp life.[27] It was a kind and friendly letter, hardly the sort a person of Toombs's frank nature would have written had he resigned from the Cabinet in resentment at what he considered the President's tyranny. The crumbling of his hopes for military glory wrought a change in his attitude toward Davis. The embittered Georgian then blamed the President for a multitude of things. Later Davis expressed regret over Toombs's estrangement from the administration, which he attributed to his disappointment at failure to win promotion in the army.[28]

In the Cabinet he was neither an able Secretary of State nor a competent adviser to the President. His state papers, on the whole, were of mediocre quality. The dispatches in his diplomatic correspondence, however, were tersely and clearly written, and occasionally couched in forceful language. Generally his sentences were long, a single sentence often taking up an entire paragraph, and his longer paragraphs lacked unity of subject. In handling the minutiae of the office he was almost a total failure. Because of his exuberant humor he could have lightened the decidedly somber atmosphere of the administration. His failure as an adviser was only natural, for his native spirit of independence could not brook rejection of his advice or suggestions. Either he must lead, or he would revert to insurgency. Toombs left the Cabinet on good, if not cordial, terms with the President and his fellow secretaries. The violent and open hatred of the administration that he later developed was unfortunate, but hardly preventable.

Davis and his Cabinet, always under criticism, could have profited by the support of Toombs and his followers; but the price they would have had to pay for it was too dear. Had the President promoted him to a full generalship, Toombs's powerful support might have been won; but the brigadier general's record did not justify the promotion; and Toombs's superior

---

[27] Toombs to Davis, September 1, 1861, in Robert Toombs Papers, Duke University.

[28] Davis to D. W. Lewis, September 21, 1863, in Rowland (ed.), *Davis*, VI, 43–44.

officers, having no reason to recommend him for advancement, did not do so. When he was denied what he considered his due, Toombs turned against the entire government. His resentment did not lead him to consider reconciliation with the Union, but it did cause him to make war upon the leaders of the Confederacy; and in becoming an independent opponent of the administration he found a vent for his surcharged emotions. He had no doubt of the constructiveness of his criticism, and he was convinced of the need for an aggressive war policy. He may have been right, yet his record in the Cabinet forces one to the conclusion that despite natural ability, he was among the least helpful and reliable, if not indeed the most inept, of Davis's secretaries.

ROBERT MERCER TALIAFERRO HUNTER

The question of selecting a successor to Robert Toombs was simplified for the President. A strong demand for reconstruction of the Cabinet had arisen because of the advisability of including in it men from the four states that joined the Confederacy after its organization. Virginia, the largest and most important of the four, deserved the honor of being represented in the administration at the first opportunity. Robert Mercer Taliaferro Hunter stood out above any other Virginia citizen in national reputation, and in national political circles Hunter, Davis, and Toombs were frequently mentioned as the "Southern Triumvirate." [29] Hunter had the support of his state delegation, especially of the influential Seddon, and his selection for the State Department post was certain.

Hunter was born in Essex County, Virginia, on April 21, 1809. He was tutored by his sisters, attended the neighborhood school, and eventually entered the University of Virginia. After two or three years of college work, he read law under Judge Henry St. George Tucker and was admitted to the bar. He bought a farm near the village of Lloyds and followed the life of a planter-lawyer. He was elected to the Virginia House of Delegates when only twenty-six years old. Thereafter political

[29] Ambler (ed.), *Correspondence of Robert M. T. Hunter*, 9.

promotion came rapidly. He was elected to the United States House of Representatives in 1837, and two years later became Speaker of that body. He entered the United States Senate in 1847 and continued in that office until he resigned in 1861. He prospered as a planter. The lands originally purchased had been greatly added to, and in 1862 he owned nearly one hundred able-bodied slaves.[30]

Hunter's political philosophy embraced state sovereignty and low tariff. He had early associated himself with the Whig party and in turn became a leader of the Calhoun following in Virginia. Though a sturdy champion of Southern interests, Hunter had been more liberal than many of his Southern colleagues, perhaps because he hoped to win national support of his aspirations to the presidency. After 1858, he led a conservative element in Virginia politics that advocated lessening the emphasis on the slavery issue. He was accused by his political foes, led by Henry A. Wise, of sacrificing the interests of the South in his endeavor to gain the Democratic nomination for the presidency in 1860. Hunter continued to evidence his desire for a compromise settlement of the issues between North and South, even after the election of Lincoln. He had no doubt whatever of the legal right of secession as a recourse against violations of the Constitution, but he did not consider Lincoln's election a just cause for the South's withdrawal from the Union. He favored holding a Southern convention that should propose constitutional amendments designed to give security to Southern rights and property. Such amendments he hoped would be accepted by the North. But as between the United States and the Confederacy, if it came to a choice, he would have Virginia associated with the Confederacy.[31] When Virginia seceded, Hunter represented his state in the provisional Congress at Montgomery. He served on the Finance Committee and actively supported the bill providing for the removal of the capital to Richmond.

Hunter's record entitled him to an appointment to the Cabinet, and his nomination by the President as Secretary of State

[30] For a full account of Hunter's life, see Henry Harrison Simms, *Life of Robert M. T. Hunter, A Study in Sectionalism and Secession* (Richmond, 1935).

[31] D. R. Anderson, "Robert Mercer Taliaferro Hunter," *John P. Branch Historical Papers of Randolph Macon College*, II (1905–1906), No. 2, 57.

was confirmed without question by the provisional Congress on July 24, 1861. He was regarded by Mrs. Chesnut as the sanest, if not the wisest, man in the newly born Confederacy.[32] The *Richmond Dispatch* endorsed his selection as that of "the right man for the right place." [33] His profound statesmanship, philosophic temper, and varied learning led the *Richmond Enquirer* to assure its readers that he would conduct the business of diplomacy with the same masterly ability that had marked his official acts during a long public career.[34] The Virginian's selection as Secretary of State was generally hailed as very satisfactory.

The new Secretary followed in general the foreign policy of his predecessor. In his first letter to the commissioners to Europe he wrote that he saw no reason for any change in their instructions, as the purposes of the government remained unchanged.[35] In notifying them of their appointment as a special commission to the Spanish government, he instructed them to put emphasis on the right of secession, to explain that the Confederacy had a working government that had taken up arms only in the defense of its territory, and that the Confederacy sought no favors for which it was not prepared to give something of value in return. Spain was to be assured that the Confederacy had no designs on Cuba; rather, it desired to be in closer association with Spain's colony because of the similarity of Cuba's social system to that of the Confederacy. Spain had more cause to fear aggression from the United States than from the Confederacy because a victorious Union would be a threat to Spanish colonial possessions.[36] By such instructions, Hunter hoped to banish Spain's fear that a powerful independent Confederacy would demand from it the cession of Cuba. It was natural that Spain should have misgivings for, before the secession from the Union, Southerners had attempted to acquire the island as a means of balancing power between the free and slaveholding states. This motive for acquisition disappeared, however, when the Confederacy had been established. Hunter's adroitly worded and clever

---

[32] Chesnut, *Diary*, 54.   [33] *Richmond Daily Dispatch*, July 26, 1861.

[34] *Daily Richmond Enquirer*, July 27, 1861.

[35] Hunter to Yancey, Rost, and Mann, July 29, 1861, in Richardson (ed.), *Messages and Papers*, II, 52.

[36] *Id.* to *id.*, August 24, 1861, *ibid.*, 72–76.

thesis failed to impress the Spanish government. But the Secretary of State still had profound faith in the power of cotton to influence England and France to a disposition favorable to the Confederacy.[37]

It had become increasingly clear to the administration that recognition of the Confederacy was not to be gained immediately. Hence the President and the Secretary of State felt that a permanent representative at each important European court would be of greater effect than a commission.[38] Yancey's resignation as a member of the commission provided Hunter with the opportunity to change the method of diplomatic representation. Mann was sent to Belgium and Rost to Spain to present the Confederacy's cause to the government of each of these states. James M. Mason and John Slidell were chosen for the important posts of envoy to England and France, respectively.

Hunter's instructions to Mason and Slidell ably defined the theory of secession and the policy of the Confederacy. The Confederacy, he showed by his analysis of the original Constitution, was not a coalition of rebellious states attempting to overthrow lawful authority, but a legally organized government possessing the strength and organization necessary for moral and political responsibility for all its actions. Step by step he reconstructed the evolution of secession and the efforts made by the South to achieve peaceful settlement with the United States. The Confederacy now asked recognition in the name of the sacred right of self-government. The advantages that a speedy recognition would bring to all nations were stated generally, after which the Secretary gave concrete examples of benefits which England and France would derive. Confederate exports of cotton, tobacco, naval stores, coal, and iron were estimated at $250,000,000

[37] The *Richmond Daily Dispatch*, August 10, 1861, said: "Of all the generals in the field, and all the rebels in the South, there is none whom the North has such reason to fear as King Cotton. Talk of rebels! Why, the rebellion of the North against King Cotton is the most suicidal and hopeless rebellion that men ever engaged in. Cotton is King—King of the North. . . ."

William L. Yancey had changed his mind as to the potency of King Cotton after a few months in England. ". . . important as cotton is," he wrote, "it is not King in Europe. . . ." Yancey to Samuel Reid, July 3, 1861, in William L. Yancey Papers, Alabama Department of Archives and History.

[38] Frank Lawrence Owsley, *King Cotton Diplomacy. Foreign Relations of the Confederate States of America* (Chicago, 1931), 77.

a year, making the South a source of raw material and a market for the manufactured products of English and French industry. Unlike the United States, the Confederacy had no desire to become the rival of England and France in commercial and industrial enterprises. It would open its ports freely and would tax imports so lightly as almost to become a free-trade nation. As illustrations of the Confederacy's commercial policy, Hunter's instructions cited Southern tariff legislation and liberal navigation laws. Furthermore, the nations of Europe need feel no uneasiness as to the Confederacy's political course, for it would be a nation devoted to peace and without aspirations to add to its already ample territory. Once, Southern leaders had demanded territorial expansion as a measure to maintain the balance of power in the old Union, but the necessity for this course disappeared when the South became independent of the Union. Nor did the Confederacy seek material aid from, or alliances with, any foreign country; it desired only the moral support that recognition would give it. A nation that refused to grant this support, the Secretary held, would have some responsibility for continued bloodshed, since the achievement of independence was inevitable and recognition was only a question of time.

In this cogent appeal for foreign support, Hunter followed, in general, the ideas expressed by his predecessor, and in some cases lifted whole sentences from the instructions Toombs had written for the commissioners. Hunter's papers, however, were clearer and better organized than those of his predecessor. His brief, plain, explicit statements give evidence of considerable orderly reasoning and a capacity for statecraft. The Confederacy's early position had been that no war would result from secession; it now had to formulate a policy requiring logical expositions of the reasons why the South could not lose the war that had resulted.

More definite conditions to which the Secretary could refer presented themselves as the war progressed. The ineffectiveness of the Federal blockade was emphasized in Hunter's instructions. He contended that the blockade contravened the principles of the Treaty of Paris of 1856, and collected data on the number of ships successfully entering and leaving Southern ports. The Confederacy's agents were instructed to use this information in support of the demand that England and France refuse to recognize the blockade. This policy was developed more and more by Hunter and his successor. England and France would respond to this plea, it was believed, for it was an argument that set forth the immediate interest of their merchantmen.

Hunter endeavored to get from Congress a statement of policy on the blockade. On July 30 he introduced a preamble and resolutions defining the Confederacy's position on points of maritime law enunciated by the Congress of Paris.[39] He succeeded, on August 13, in getting Congress to pass resolutions declaring the Confederacy's stand in respect of maritime law.[40] The resolutions asserted the right of privateering and the immunity of noncontraband neutral goods, and held that blockades to be binding must be effective, that is, maintained by sufficient force to prevent access to the coast of an enemy. This definite statement was needed to show the contrast between Confederate idealism and the threatening and arbitrary show of power by the United States in its treatment of foreign commerce. The South could well afford a liberal attitude because, lacking a navy, it had nothing to lose and a great deal to gain by such a policy.

Hunter's instructions explaining the basis upon which the Confederacy would be willing to make peace are noteworthy. The South, he stated, demanded independence for the eleven states comprising the Confederacy and the territories of New Mexico and Arizona. A plebiscite in the states of Maryland, Kentucky, and Missouri could decide whether they would join the Confederacy or remain in the Union. It would be a wise policy, however, for European nations to insist upon the inclusion of these border states in the Southern nation, as it would enable the South to balance the power of the North and would make the Confederacy wholly independent of the Union. It followed that the larger the South's territory, the greater the opportunities foreign nations would have for trade with it. The Confederacy's program, as stated by Hunter, was one of great scope.

[39] *Journal of Congress*, I, 294.   [40] *Ibid.*, 341.

It is impossible to say positively to what extent Hunter's state papers, in this or other cases, are the immediate reflection of the President's views rather than the Secretary's, for the record of the relations existing between these men is too meager. Hunter was more acceptable to the President than Toombs had been. For one thing, there was little likelihood that the reserved Virginian with his equable disposition would fly into a temper in the middle of a Cabinet meeting. "Hunter (milk and water)," was Thomas R. R. Cobb's unfriendly allusion to him.[41] Studious habit had encouraged the development of his calm and conciliatory nature, and when he had advice to offer, Davis undoubtedly heard him attentively. There are no indications that the two men became close friends, but there is no reason to conclude that they were not on friendly terms. Mrs. Davis, in her memoirs, written after the two men had quarreled, mentions her husband's attachment for Hunter. After his resignation from the Cabinet, the Virginian continued to be a consistent supporter and defender of the administration. Undoubtedly he urged the appointment of Seddon as Secretary of War, and he kept in close touch with the Cabinet. The President relied upon him to assist Memminger in planning the government's fiscal policy.

There is some evidence that Hunter was jealous of the President. The presidency of the United States had been the Secretary's dearest ambition. Secession was yet young when he forsook that vision of power in the Union for the one of being the candidate for the highest office in the Confederacy. Ambition ran wild within him, the unfriendly Jones recorded, for all his unassuming demeanor and his faithful devotion to a task, and the diarist believed that Hunter would have sacrificed everything for the Confederate presidency and Southern independence.[42] The Secretary's self-discipline was admirable, however, and his ambition was never allowed to become obtrusively evident, although the fact that it existed must have affected somewhat the relations between him and Davis. As a possible candidate for the presi-

---

41 Hull (ed.), "Correspondence of Thomas Reade Rootes Cobb, 1860–1862," *loc. cit.*, 313.
42 Jones, *Diary*, II, 225.

dency in 1868, Hunter could not afford to be identified either
as a wholehearted friend or as a foe of the administration of
Davis. A loyal Southerner with property interests at stake,
Hunter's paramount desire was for the independence of the
Confederacy; but he planned for the possible advancement of
his political fortunes which victory for the Confederacy would
make possible.

It was not long until the Secretary of State was expressing the
wish to serve in the Senate. His reasons for the change in office
are easily understandable. He found, as Toombs before him had
discovered, that the office he held was relatively unimportant.
While Montgomery was still the Confederate capital his friends
had urged his qualifications as the first President of the permanent government. When this hope faded away, Hunter and his
following believed that he should hold a more important office
than that of Secretary of State in which his success necessarily
could not be demonstrated except in the event of the triumph
of Confederate arms. "It is to be an obscure place," Jones wrote
of the Department of State in July, 1861, "and if he [Hunter]
were indolent, without ambition, it would be the very place for
him." [43] But Hunter was far from being indolent, especially in
seizing opportunities for promoting his political advancement.
An additional consideration was that with the end of the provisional government his term in Congress would expire. He had
been very active in that body and his work had served to ameli-
orate the tedium of his secretaryship and make the post more
bearable. Even if the Congress under the permanent government should allow heads of departments the privileges of the
legislative floor, they would have no vote and could discuss only
such measures as pertained to their respective departments.
When Hunter considered these prospects and contemplated the
sepulchral quiet and repose of the Department of State, the role
of a Confederate Senator appeared extremely attractive to him.
He had made his reputation as a United States Senator and his
experience assuredly would command for him a high standing
in the Confederate Senate.

Hunter's plan to resign and enter the Senate, Mrs. Davis be-

[43] *Ibid.*, I, 60.

lieved, was reluctantly assented to by the President. Davis thought, according to her account, that his Secretary of State was averse to sharing in the responsibility for possible failure of the administration.[44] Mrs. Davis repeats the idea that Hunter feared that to be closely identified with the President would hurt his chances of becoming Davis's successor. Yet it is entirely possible that Davis was in favor of Hunter's plan to enter the Senate, for the administration sorely needed a strong supporter in that body. Hunter's course in the Senate prompts the conclusion that the project of resigning had been worked out in close collaboration with the President. The Virginian was of more value to the administration in his capacity as an influential Senator than as an executive secretary in a comparatively minor post. The change would give Hunter more congenial tasks and afford him a vantage point from which to advance himself politically. The Secretary of State, at all events, did not resign his office until his election to the Senate was assured.

That outcome, however, was not accomplished without a spirited contest preceding the election in the Virginia legislature. The choice of Hunter for Senator was suggested in October, 1861, by the Athens, Georgia, *Southern Banner,* for the reason that experienced men would be needed in the first Congress.[45] The *Richmond Examiner* agreed that experienced legislators were needed, but was noncommittal on Hunter. This newspaper in the latter part of December and early January published many letters from readers who advocated Hunter's election to the Senate. The general tenor of the letters was that many men could fulfill the routine duties required of a Secretary of State, but none could be as satisfactory as Hunter in the Senate. The *Examiner,* in an editorial of January 8, opposed the election of Hunter, questioned his claim to greatness, and asserted that in seeking the senatorship he was actuated by selfish ambition and the hope of political reward. The *Examiner* by indirection threw its support to the candidacy of James A. Barbour, pointing out that his election would give Virginia two Senators and one Cabinet officer, whereas the election of Hunter would reduce the

[44] V. Davis, *Jefferson Davis,* II, 165.
[45] *Daily Richmond Examiner,* October 30, 1861, quoting the *Southern Banner.*

state's influence to that exercised by the Senators only. There was no possibility that both Hunter and Barbour would be elected because both came from eastern Virginia.

The activity of Hunter's supporters increased as the election date drew nearer. To offset the *Examiner*'s argument that by Hunter's election Virginia would lose a Cabinet member, they reminded the editor that his term as Secretary of State would end automatically on February 22. This point was not well taken, the *Examiner* replied, for the reappointment of a secretary would be only a formality unless he had deliberately shirked his duty and had placed himself in open hostility to the government.[46] Hunter's followers countered with the statement that their candidate positively would not remain in the Cabinet after February 22, whether or not he was elected Senator. Hunter's majority in the Virginia Senate twice were able to have the senatorial election postponed. Then Barbour withdrew, and Hunter was elected on January 23 by 140 to 24 votes.[47]

Hunter's short term of less than six months as Secretary of State was marked by able endeavor. He did not materially change the foreign policy he had inherited from his predecessor. He centered his activities upon efforts to induce foreign countries to break the blockade. He inaugurated the policy of having the Confederacy represented abroad by individual missions, and sent Henry Hotze to London to disseminate Confederacy propaganda. But when Mason and Slidell were captured, he failed to seize the opportunity to make capital of it, and in common with many men in the Confederacy, he expected God and England to fight the South's diplomatic battles.

[46] *Ibid.*, January 23, 1862.

[47] *Charleston Daily Courier*, January 28, 1862; *Charleston Mercury*, January 27, 1862. The administration supporting *Courier* stated that Hunter was sick of the inactive life of Secretary of State and anxious to return to the Senate chamber and conference room. Later Edward A. Pollard declared Hunter resigned because he was treated as a "chief clerk." "The truth was, there had been a disgraceful quarrel in the cabinet, and when Mr. Hunter offered some advice about the conduct of the war, Mr. Davis had said with a flushed and almost insolent manner: 'Mr. Hunter, you are Secretary of State, and when information is wanted of that particular department, it will be time for you to speak.' The spirited Virginian next day sent in his resignation." Edward A. Pollard, *The Life of Jefferson Davis* . . . (Atlanta, 1869), 150–51.

Evidently Pollard failed to recall the editorials of his own paper. Hunter's resignation did not come on the spur of the moment, but was planned.

Hunter had many admirable qualities as an executive. Unlike the tempestuous Toombs, he was always self-controlled, he exercised an efficient supervision over the routine of his department, and, by reason of his firm yet conciliatory nature, he was able to get the maximum service from his subordinates. His cultivated taste in literature and his interest in history were of advantage to him in giving him a broader grasp of public affairs and a riper judgment than Toombs possessed. His manner was unhurried, and the impression it gave of polite indolence was heightened by his short and portly build and his sleepy-looking dark brown eyes. "He is a man of high talent and fine acquirement," a friend wrote of him in 1865, "but wants activity, energy, and will to enable him to give shape or direction to great political movements." [48] When he had a task to do, Hunter fulfilled it with methodical thoroughness. His state papers are written in plain, direct, and effective language. They exhibit a pardonable pride in the success of Confederate arms and a firm optimism as to the outcome of the war. He and the President worked together in a fair degree of accord. Hunter, more than any other Confederate Secretary of State, used such terms as "by direction of the President," or "the President desires." This might seem to indicate that he was closely controlled by Davis, but more probably it was simply a formal expression Hunter had adopted. There is no reason to believe that the Secretary of State was not treated with respect or that the President slighted his advice.

There are points of similarity in the personal ambitions of Hunter and Toombs that operate against either distinguishing himself in the office of Secretary of State. Toombs yearned for military fame; Hunter desired the opportunity to acquire political eminence. He believed that as a Confederate Senator he had a better chance of realizing his ambition than he would have as Secretary of State. Neither Hunter nor Toombs displayed initiative in their conduct of the Department of State. Like their successor, Benjamin, they made no attempt to har-

[48] John B. Balwin to Governor Francis Harrison Pierpont, August 15, 1865, in *Calendar of Virginia State Papers and Other Manuscripts from January 1, 1863, to April 15, 1869*, edited by William P. Palmer, H. W. Flournoy, and Sherwin McRae (Richmond, 1893), XI, 451.

monize Confederate and state government. Unlike Benjamin, however, neither foresaw the opportunity that a Secretary of State had to become the general adviser of the President; nor had either the ability to act in so important a capacity. Toombs and Hunter gambled nothing and lost nothing. Their appointments to office were hailed with mild praise and their retirements elicited equally mild regret. Each man had his following, and the administration was fortunate in retaining Hunter's support as Senator.

The former Secretary of State was in a familiar atmosphere in the Confederate Senate. He was elected President pro-tem and placed on the important Finance Committee. He was a consistent supporter of the administration until the parting came over the bill to enlist Negro troops; and after the Hampton Roads Conference, Hunter's break with Davis was complete. He later refused to visit the President, believing that Davis had spread the report that Hunter favored submission of the South to Lincoln. Actually, Hunter did believe that the Confederate cause was doomed in 1865 and advised his friends that further resistance was futile.

WILLIAM M. BROWNE

Hunter resigned on February 22, 1862, as Jones noted, to take his seat in the Senate. The actual duties of the Department of State had been assumed before this date by William M. Browne. The Secretary of State *ad interim* was a native of England who had become naturalized. He had been the editor of the *Constitution* before the war, an organ of the Buchanan administration, and had adopted Georgia as his state. He was a strong believer in state rights and after merging his paper with the *Montgomery Advertiser* he became assistant to the Secretary of State in the Confederacy.[49] He had been commissioned acting secretary during Hunter's temporary absence at the death of R. M. T. Hunter, Jr.[50] Davis gave him the title of Secretary of

[49] He was commonly referred to as assistant Secretary of State. On February 26, 1861, the provisional Congress gave the Secretary the right to appoint an assistant. *Journal of Congress*, I, 87. It was not until January 15, 1862, that provision was made for an assistant Secretary of State. *Ibid.*, 672.

[50] *Daily Richmond Examiner*, December 5, 30, 1861.

State *ad interim* in a communication to the House of Representatives on March 7, 1862,[51] and Browne signed official correspondence as Secretary of State *ad interim*.

Browne headed the department for about one month, and in that time he signed some of the commissions of the men appointed members of the Cabinet in the permanent government.[52] When Benjamin was appointed Secretary of State on March 18, two days later he selected Browne as Assistant Secretary and the appointment was confirmed by the Senate. Benjamin continued to act as Secretary of War for several days after his appointment to the Department of State, and Browne continued in actual charge of the department.

Browne's was a varied career. After becoming a Presidential aide he was appointed a brigadier general in 1864, but the Senate demonstrated its prejudice against the English by refusing to confirm the nomination by a vote of 18 to 2. After the war he engaged in agriculture in Georgia, where he published *Farm and Home,* an agricultural journal. Later he became professor of history and political economy at the University of Georgia. He was a man of scholarly attainments, with a command of several languages and a broad knowledge of foreign affairs. His courtly manner and attractive personality endeared him to Davis. Browne was a capable but unimaginative Assistant Secretary of State and, in the shaping of Confederate policy, his part was a minor one.

51 *Journal of Congress,* V, 72.

52 Memminger's appointment, for instance, was signed by Browne on March 20, 1862. Christopher G. Memminger Papers, University of North Carolina.

IV

Men of War

THE leaders of the Southern Confederacy at first contemplated a small military organization. The ideal establishment envisioned by an economically minded South was a skeleton force to garrison forts and control the Indian territory, this force to be supplemented by a state militia. The Confederacy intended no aggression and anticipated no attack upon its territory. Even though the United States held forts within Southern borders it was generally believed that their peaceful surrender would be brought about by diplomatic negotiations or by a threat of force.

Nevertheless, the provisional Congress foresaw the need for some military establishment. Congress asked the Committee on Military Affairs on February 13, 1861, to report a bill providing for the organization of the army, and requested that a survey be made of the military establishment in the several states.[1] Two days later Congress resolved that immediate steps should be taken to seize Fort Sumter and Fort Pickens, and authorized the President to make all military preparations necessary to accomplish this purpose. The next day Christopher G. Memminger introduced a resolution in Congress looking to the establishment of an armory and the manufacture of gunpowder. Memminger's proposals were enlarged in the act of February 20, which authorized the President or the Secretary of War to make contracts for the purchase and manufacture of small arms, munitions, and machinery, and for the employment of artisans in munition factories.[2]

President Davis acted at once on these measures. In his first

---

[1] *Journal of Congress*, I, 49–50. [2] *Official Records*, Ser. IV, Vol. I, 106.

instructions, giving Raphael Semmes power to purchase and contract for munitions, the President was careful to state that all contracts must be sent to the Secretary of War and be formally approved by him.[3] Later, his critics cited the President's acts as proof that, from the very first, he had planned to direct every detail of the War Department, reducing the Secretary to a "chief clerk." Davis, in fact, acted for the good of the Confederacy, realizing the necessity of urgent military preparedness. A Secretary of War had not been appointed, nor had any provision been made for the organization of the War Department. Congress did not provide for a Secretary of War until February 20, 1861.[4]

LEROY POPE WALKER

It is uncertain whom the President would have selected as Secretary of War had he not felt obligated to political leaders. Braxton Bragg possibly might have been chosen. Mrs. Virginia Clay-Clopton reported that the post was offered to Clement C. Clay, who refused it because he had pledged his support to Leroy Pope Walker for the office.[5] Yancey also favored Walker for the post.[6] Both Walker and his friends were active in promoting his selection for some position in the Cabinet. The candidate received a letter from his brother, Richard W. Walker, on the morning of February 11, holding out hope that his chances for an executive appointment were excellent. Walker hastened to Montgomery provided with recommendations and sent word to Clement C. Clay requesting him to telegraph his endorsement of Walker to Davis.[7] An invitation to Walker to become Secretary of War was soon forthcoming. The President was not personally acquainted with him and selected him for the office solely on the recommendation of friends, and for the additional reason that he was the only Alabamian whose nomination to a Cabinet post was urged.[8]

3 Davis to Semmes, February 21, 1861, *ibid.*, 106–107.
4 *Journal of Congress*, I, 69.
5 Mrs. Virginia Clay-Clopton, "Clement Claiborne Clay," Alabama Historical Society, *Transactions*, II (1897–1898), 76–77.
6 Eckenrode, *Jefferson Davis*, 123.
7 Hugh Lawson Clay to Clement C. Clay, February 11, 1861, in Clay Papers.
8 Davis, *Rise and Fall*, I, 243.

Walker's appointment to the War Department was pronounced an excellent selection by the *Charleston Mercury*, and this ardent Southern nationalist organ regarded his record as a Southern leader as especially impressive.[9] Walker was born in 1817 near Huntsville, Alabama, and was educated by private tutors and at the universities of Alabama and Virginia. He was admitted to the bar before he had reached the age of twenty-one years, and politics soon attracted him. He had held many state offices when in 1853 he resigned as Judge of the Circuit Court in order to give his entire attention to his growing law practice. He soon became the leading lawyer in North Alabama and, next to Clement C. Clay, the most influential member of the Democratic party in that section.[10] He resumed an active participation in politics in 1860 when, as a delegate to the Democratic national convention at Charleston, he was a prime mover in the withdrawal of the Alabama delegation. He was active in advocating the rights of the South and in promoting secession, both as a delegate to the Richmond convention and as a commissioner from his state to Tennessee in January, 1861. The fact that he resided in a pro-Union section of Alabama operated to check somewhat the realization of his political ambition, for as a "fire-eating" Southerner he failed to be selected as a delegate to the provisional Congress at Montgomery. His younger brother, Richard W. Walker, however, headed the Alabama delegation in the Congress and undoubtedly was instrumental in bringing about that body's recommendation for the appointment of a straight-out secessionist, Leroy Pope Walker, to a Cabinet membership.

The Confederacy's first Secretary of War was a man of energy. William Howard Russell described him as the kind of man usually represented as the "Yankee"—tall, lean, angular, straight-haired, with fiery eyes and impulsive manner.[11] He was addicted to tobacco, which he chewed with evident relish and to the ac-

---

[9] *Charleston Mercury*, February 23, 1861. An editorial in the *Montgomery Weekly Mail*, March 8, 1861, said of Walker: "We have known him long and intimately, and always regarded him as one of the giant intellects of the South. His perceptions are clear and exact, and his reflective faculties, vigorous and reliable. His mind is strong and compact. . . . When joined in battle he is ardent, bold, daring, and often merciless."

[10] *Harper's Weekly*, V (1861), 341.

[11] Russell, *My Diary North and South*, 70.

companiment of unusually profuse spitting. He had had no military training and was not a soldier, but he had held a commission
as brigadier general in the Alabama militia. Unquestionably,
he was ardently devoted to the Confederacy and supremely confident of its success.

Walker attacked the problem of obtaining war supplies, once
he had disposed of the preliminary work of organizing the War
Department. His early correspondence clearly indicates that he
did not expect war. Nevertheless, he worked assiduously from
late February to early April, pushing operations to ensure a supply of war materials in the event that a peaceful agreement with
the United States could not be reached. Agents were dispatched
to the North and to various Southern states, and provision was
made for the sending of a mission abroad to purchase arms and
equipment. Letters had been arriving daily offering to sell
the Confederacy manufacturing plants, guns, and powder, but
Walker tended to haggle over what he considered the excessive
prices demanded. As late as March 29, the War Department was
satisfied that the supply of shot and shell was ample.[12] Efforts
were expedited on other fronts to obtain rifles and powder. Apparently, the Confederacy had adopted a policy of "watchful
waiting" for an indication of the North's intentions. The South
hoped for peace and had no desire to present a picture of feverish
preparation for war.

When it became evident that negotiations with the United
States would fail, Walker became more active. By April 8, he
became convinced that the United States intended to resort to
coercion of the South.[13] Where before he had haggled over costs,
he now willingly and without question agreed to the prices demanded for war material. Heretofore he had requested the states
to equip a definite number of troops and transport them to a
given point; now he demanded that each state drill, equip, and
hold troops in instant readiness for service in the Confederate
army. Almost immediately difficulties arose over the acceptance

[12] Johnson Hooper to James Roberts Gilmore, March 29, 1861, in *Official Records*, Ser. IV, Vol. I, 194.

[13] Walker to the Governors of South Carolina, Alabama, Florida, Georgia, Louisiana, Mississippi, and Texas, April 8, 1861, *ibid.*, 211.

and organization of state troops. Walker, in the belief that he was correctly interpreting the intent of Congressional statutes, wanted the states to equip the troops, for whose care and pay the Confederate government would assume responsibility as soon as they were mustered into the general service. Questions concerning transportation, the appointment of officers, and the requirements as to full companies arose at once. Many companies had their full officer personnel but only a skeleton force of men in the ranks. Walker fully realized the difficulty of bringing the companies up to their full quota of enlisted men, but refused to accept the incomplete units. He engaged in a heated correspondence with Governor Joseph E. Brown of Georgia concerning that state's troops. Toombs, who was in Georgia because of an illness in his family, late in March wrote to the Secretary urging him to settle the difference with Governor Brown, and in the end an arrangement was made that satisfied the Governor.

Congress on March 6, 1861, authorized the President to accept up to 100,000 volunteers to serve for twelve months, unless sooner discharged.[14] Davis claimed that the passage of a bill calling for sixty-day enlistments was prevented (late in February) by his personal efforts.[15] Reagan said that the Committee on Military Affairs proposed a six-month enlistment, believing that the rapid enlistment of men would discourage the United States from starting a war, but that the President proposed enlistment for a term of three years, or for the duration of the war.[16] The best the administration was able to get, however, was the twelve-month enlistment. After the fall of Fort Sumter, when war became certain, pressure was again put on Congress to lengthen the term of army service; and on May 8, an act was passed empowering the President to call additional volunteers for service throughout the war unless sooner discharged.[17] That the administration demanded the longer enlistment term is indicated by Walker's readiness to seize the opportunity. The day before the act was passed, confident that it would be enacted, he had

[14] James M. Matthews (ed.), *Statutes at Large of the Provisional Government of the Confederate States of America* (Richmond, 1864), 45.
[15] Jefferson Davis, *Rise and Fall*, 304.
[16] Reagan, *Memoirs*, 117.   [17] Matthews (ed.), *Statutes at Large*, 104.

written that enlistments must be for the duration of the war.[18]
From this date emphasis was placed on long-term enlistments,
but not without a deluge of protests and objections from governors and from private citizens. One person wrote that the policy had played havoc with the "poor hillman" who owned no
slaves and had been persuaded to enlist for twelve months.[19]
Walker eventually adopted a policy of accepting for a twelve-
month term troops that were fully armed, but volunteers who
looked to the government for equipment were accepted only for
the duration of the war.

The War Department was flooded with offers of companies in
return for an officer's commission to the person making the offer.
Investigation of these offers revealed that in many cases the "patriots" making them had nothing more than visionary companies, but had hoped that commissions would enable them to
recruit men for their commands. Many of the offers were genuine, but all were declined. Two reasons were given: one, that
acceptance would interfere with the arrangements by which governors could meet requisitions for quotas of troops from their
states; the other, that the principle of state sovereignty was involved, since Walker held that the Confederate government had
no control over state militia except as it was exercised through
the governors of states. Despite the War Department's repeated
explanations of its policy, offers of troops continued to come in
from unofficial sources. Requests to recruit Negro troops were
refused even as early as August 2, 1861.[20] The Confederacy did
not lack men willing to serve as officers or in the ranks on short
terms of enlistment. Its problem was to obtain volunteers on
the basis of the War Department's policy.

Arms, not men, was the real problem, however. Walker declared on July 24, that 200,000 volunteers could be enlisted
within two months, but that arms were not available for them.[21]
He urged his agents in Europe to obtain arms, for "The neces-

18 Walker to Joseph E. Brown, May 7, 1861, in *Official Records,* Ser. IV, Vol. I,
295.
19 W. M. Brooks to Davis, May 13, 1861, *ibid.,* 318–19.
20 Albert T. Bledsoe to William S. Turner, August 2, 1861, *ibid.,* 529.
21 Walker to Davis, July 24, 1861, Letter Book of Official Correspondence, War
Department, Confederate States of America, February 21–September 15, 1861,
Manuscripts Division, Library of Congress, 192.

sities of the Government are such as to require the utmost expedition and industry. . . ."[22] Jones recorded late in June, 1861, that the army at Manassas did not have enough ammunition to engage in a respectable skirmish. This statement was an exaggeration, but conditions were unquestionably bad. The responsibility for this situation was due largely to the unwillingness of state executives to permit the war materials under their control to leave their states.[23]

Efforts of agents of the War Department to tap the state reservoirs met with little success, and early in May wide authority was given agents to make purchases, the department promising to take all arms, brass cannon, and materials of war obtainable. Those who would undertake to ship materials into the Confederacy were assured of good prices, with transportation costs paid by the buyer, and insurance provided against losses at sea or from capture by the enemy.[24] The Confederacy's agents were sent to Cuba and Mexico for available materials, and domestic manufacture of arms was encouraged. Contracts for 61,200 stands of small arms were made in July, 1861, and large advance orders encouraged the munitions industry. Armories at Richmond, Virginia, and Fayetteville, North Carolina, were ready to begin production.[25] Walker was elated over the Confederate victory in July, and hoped that thinking men would redouble their efforts to supply munitions. He wrote the Confederacy's agents in Europe to increase their operations, to depart at their discretion from their original instructions, and to spare no expense to obtain supplies.[26] The Secretary was not content to rest on an early victory; he pushed his work all the harder, for by this time he foresaw a long war.

Any comprehensive account of the War Department's work would itself run to the length of a book. In briefest summary, Secretary of War Walker directed its military side to the point where the Confederacy's forces were able to repel early invasion

22 Walker to Charles Green, July 1, 1861, *ibid.*, 154.
23 The standard work on Confederate and state controversies is that of Frank Lawrence Owsley, *State Rights in the Confederacy* (Chicago, 1931).
24 Walker to W. H. Aymar, May 3, 1861, in *Official Records*, Ser. IV, Vol. I, 275.
25 Walker to Davis, July 24, 1861, *ibid.*, 496-97.
26 Walker to Cabel Huse and Edward C. Anderson, July 22, 1861, *ibid.*, 493-94.

of its territory; under his conduct of the department both the provisional army and the regular army were equipped as fighting units. The success that attended his efforts and, too, the weaknesses in the South's military organization are well worth study, but our interest is primarily concerned with the man himself, his working methods, and his relations with the President.

Walker was an industrious worker, but much of his effort was misdirected. His professional training as a lawyer, in which he was eminently successful, had not accustomed him to adopt methods by which he could save himself avoidable labor. His keen sense of personal responsibility for the conduct of the War Department led him to devote far too much time to details that should have been left to subordinates. It ran counter to his courteous nature to send brief replies to inquiries. The *Richmond Examiner* on May 13 reported Walker "worn and fagged with his arduous duties." Hosts of callers ready to offer their services to their country, especially if service carried with it the dignity of wearing epaulettes, besieged his office.[27] He received them with all the courtesy of a gentleman, but it was, of course, impossible to please all, and the work of the department was seriously delayed by the inroads made on his time.

The strain on him told, and by the time the seat of government was removed, Walker, never too robust at best, was a sick man. He was absent from the department during a great part of June, and illness often obliged him to leave his office for short periods during the remainder of his term. As a result of these frequent absences, the work of the department piled up, and critics began to complain. Furthermore, the Secretary had a tendency to procrastinate, and this increased the volume of unanswered correspondence and incidental duties. "Mr. Walker is a man of capacity, and has a most extraordinary recollection of details," Jones conceded; but "I fear his nerves are too finely strung for the official treadmill. I heard him say yesterday, with a sigh, that no *gentleman* can be fit for office." [28] Although noted for his methodical habits as a lawyer, Walker used little system in his work as Secretary of War and threw his unanswered letters helter-skelter about his office. On one occasion the President

[27] *Daily Richmond Examiner*, May 13, 1861.   [28] Jones, *Diary*, I, 64.

found half a bushel of letters deposited in Walker's armchair.[29]

Walker's failure to answer letters promptly caused many state officials to write direct to the President in the hope of obtaining more considerate treatment than the Secretary gave them. He was criticized as being arbitrary and highhanded in his attitude toward state officials, yet he gave more respect to state rights than did any of his successors in the War Department. His conduct of the department frequently was marked by indecision, particularly in his instructions to commanders and purchasing agents. His letters contained sweeping statements about the ability of the Confederacy to triumph, but they were robbed of force and conviction by the interjection of qualifying clauses showing how victory depended upon a number of given actions.

Walker never doubted that the Confederate cause would triumph. His optimism and his desire to invade the North led him to make statements that caused unpleasant repercussions for him. He was reported to have prophesied that the Confederate flag would be flying from the Capitol in Washington, if not from Faneuil Hall in Boston. The *Charleston Courier* said the statement was made at a flag-raising on April 10, 1861. The *Richmond Enquirer* and the *Charleston Mercury* placed the date of the speech on April 12, when the Secretary, as these newspapers quoted him, said, ". . . the Confederate flag would soon wave over Fort Sumter; and that if the independence of the Confederate States was not acknowledged, it would soon float from the Capitol at Washington." [30] Another version puts the occasion after the fall of Sumter, when Jefferson Davis was being serenaded. The President refused to comply with calls for a speech, on the plea that he was too tired. Walker, however, animated by the spirit of the occasion, addressed the throng, and, as the *Richmond Examiner* reported, hoped "our flag, which now floats over the government building would, in three months, . . . be waving from the dome of the Capitol at Washington." [31]

Whatever the Secretary may have said, reports went out that the Confederacy planned an invasion of the North. A corre-

[29] *Ibid.*, 54.
[30] *Daily Richmond Enquirer*, April 15, 1861; *Charleston Mercury*, April 15, 1861; *Montgomery Weekly Advertiser*, April 17, 1861.
[31] *Daily Richmond Examiner*, April 17, 1861.

spondent wrote Benjamin H. Hill that many men in East Tennessee had rallied to the Union to defend Washington against the attack threatened in Walker's imprudent speech,[32] and Northern propagandists made capital of the reported utterance. Stephens doubted that Walker had made any such statement.[33] He surmised the Secretary's speech had been to the effect that the South would win her independence by armed force if not allowed the right of peaceful self-government. There was little reason to condemn Walker. Even the conservative Stephens was quoted as saying it would take seventy-five times seventy-five thousand men to intimidate the South.[34] It was a time of extravagant and intemperate talk, when men were proclaiming their ability to lick Yankees with cornstalks.

The Confederate administration was fully aware that an attack on Fort Sumter would precipitate war. The government wished to avoid a conflict as long as there remained any hope of peace, and the leaders of the Confederacy urged South Carolina to be patient. Walker became satisfied that war could not be avoided, notwithstanding assurance to the contrary. "Give little credit to rumors of an amicable adjustment," he wrote Beauregard on March 15. On April 2, 1861, he declared the government had never had any faith in the assurances coming from Washington. The people of the South, especially in South Carolina, were insistently demanding that Fort Sumter be seized. A correspondent of the *Richmond Dispatch* on April 9 informed his readers that a Cabinet meeting of grave character had been held at which serious decisions had been reached, that warlike orders had been issued, and that excited secretaries had remained in their departments until after midnight.[35] From this date until after the fall of Sumter, Cabinet meetings were held almost daily, the sessions lasting far into the night. The Cabinet, with the possible exception of Toombs, agreed that Fort Sumter should be attacked before reinforcements should arrive. This decision was reached in the full realization that war would follow, but the Confederate

[32] Robert M. Barton to Hill, January 23, 1863, in *Official Records*, Ser. IV, Vol. II, 367–70.
[33] Stephens, *Constitutional View*, II, 421.
[34] *Raleigh State Journal*, April 24, 1861.
[35] *Richmond Daily Dispatch*, April 13, 1861.

administration was convinced that war was inevitable however the Sumter incident might end. The actual decision finally was left to Beauregard, but the Cabinet admonished him not to bombard the fort unless it became necessary to do so.

Just what relationship existed between President Davis and Secretary Walker is not easy to determine. DeLeon's statement that "many declared that he [Walker] was only a man of straw, set up by Mr. Davis simply that he [Davis] might exercise his well-known love for military matters," [36] was unquestionably the product of imagination. Walker had come to the secretaryship with a proved reputation as a lawyer of unusual ability. He had been recommended to Davis in good faith by his friends. Even though the President liked to interest himself in military plans, he wanted an able man for Secretary of War. John Beauchamp Jones wrote that Walker had to submit completely to the President, but he added that Davis would soon be too busy to devote much attention to one department.[37] If we accept as true the War Department clerk's statement that Davis gave nine tenths of his time to minor details, such as the granting of passports and other matters of a like routine, it is hard to believe that the President had much time to interfere in the conduct of the War Department.

It is true, nevertheless, that Walker had little influence on the military strategy of the Confederacy. The President lacked confidence in his Secretary's ability to plan a general campaign. The Secretary's attempt to order military movements without acquainting the President of his action resulted in confusion. On July 26, Walker ordered two regiments from Bristol, Tennessee; on the same day General Samuel Cooper, by direction of the President, telegraphed the commander at Lynchburg to proceed to Bristol superseding the Secretary's orders. Walker knew nothing of the superseding telegram and sent further orders the next day, to which the bewildered commander at Lynchburg replied, "I do not know what to do." [38] The fault for this mix-up was largely General Cooper's since he failed to inform the Sec-

---

[36] DeLeon, *Belles, Beaux and Brains of the 60's*, 56.
[37] Jones, *Diary*, I, 38.
[38] S. R. Anderson to Walker, July 27, 1861, in *Official Records*, Ser. I, Vol. II, 1002.

retary of the change in plans. Davis would never intentionally embarrass his Secretary, however much he supervised the conduct of military operations. The President gave his Secretary every opportunity to present his views on these operations, but Davis was rarely influenced by this advice.

It was different, however, where the business transactions of the War Department were concerned. Here the President rarely interfered with Walker's duties or instructions. Letters written to the President concerning civil matters of the department were promptly referred to the Secretary. This procedure was followed even in cases where governors had written to the President direct.

Davis did not question Walker's ability as a lawyer, but he doubted his fitness as Secretary of War. When Mallory on September 4, 1861, tried to persuade the President to take a vacation of a few days, Davis was unwilling to do so as he felt that Walker could not manage the War Department. Mallory, Benjamin, and Memminger all doubted that Walker possessed the ability to conduct the War Department successfully. The President, while sharing this opinion, added that he did not believe any civilian could competently direct its affairs.[39]

Walker's misdirected efforts caused him to overwork himself and resulted in a physical breakdown. Davis, who stood by those in whom he had confidence, sympathized with his ill Secretary, but he did not defend him against criticism. The severity of the criticisms often caused the courtly and conservative Alabamian to wince. Fortunately for his sensitiveness, some harsh judgments, that of Mrs. Chesnut, for instance, came to light only after his retirement from office. This trenchant commentator described the Secretary as a "slow-coach," and doubted that he would even recognize another Napoleon should he apply for a commission in the Confederate army.[40] Hundreds of disappointed men and their friends berated the Secretary because he failed to recognize their military genius and reward it with officers' commissions. If all those who wished to become officers should enlist as privates, the Charleston Mercury said, the Confederacy would have another army as large as the one in the

---

39 Mallory, Diary, September 4, 1861.
40 Chesnut, Diary, 76, 86.

field.[41] So great was the pressure on him for appointment, that Walker became suspicious of even a friendly greeting from an important congressman.

Men of standing and of widely divergent character expressed lack of confidence in the Secretary. One of these, Vice-President Stephens, believed that Walker managed the War Department badly and was very inefficient. "He'll 'do and do and do,' and at last do nothing," he wrote. "He is like a man who in playing chess thinks and thinks and thinks before moving, and at last makes a foolish move. He is very rash in counsel, and lamentably irresolute and inefficient in action." [42] Thomas R. R. Cobb, Stephens's exact opposite in character, told his wife that the Secretary of War was "utterly unfit for his post." [43] Even more bluntly, a soldier in the field complained to his wife, "President Davis is a stubborn fool and as for Walker of the War Department, he is beneath criticism and contempt." [44] The belief that a more energetic secretary could have provided more war materials and men was at the bottom of most criticism from army sources.

The tremendous difficulties under which the Secretary worked were not always taken into consideration. Also Walker's high-minded refusal to grant official favors aroused opposition in Congress. Among the accusations directed against him was the claim that he was putty in the hands of congressmen. His letter books and other correspondence clearly disprove this; he was curt and none too cordial in his refusal to grant the numerous requests, whether made by persons in private or official station.

Condemnation of the Secretary's conduct of the War Department brought Congressional resolutions which from time to time demanded information from the Secretary on the hospital service, army organization, daily rations issued to the soldiers, and numerous other matters. At length, before Congress adjourned on August 31, 1861, a committee was appointed to investigate the

---

[41] *Charleston Mercury*, May 14, 1861.

[42] Johnston and Browne, *Life of Stephens*, 405.

[43] Hull (ed.), "Correspondence of Thomas Reade Rootes Cobb, 1860–1862," *loc. cit.*, 312.

[44] John Lawrence Manning to his wife, July 7, 1861, in Williams-Chesnut-Manning Papers, University of North Carolina.

organization and administration of the medical commissary, and
of the quartermaster's divisions of the department. Walker promised his full cooperation with the committee, and gave orders
which allowed the members to pass freely into the army lines and
encampments.[45] Before the committee had time to make a report
on its findings, Walker had relinquished his office.

Various motives for his withdrawal from the Cabinet have
been suggested. One, made by Jones, was that the Secretary
wanted an active military life; when the battle at Manassas was
raging, the diarist reports, Walker spent the evening damning
the office he filled.[46] Walker's real ambition was to be elected
to the Confederate Senate, and he asked for a military appointment only as a stopgap to enable him to keep in the public eye.[47]
One writer assigned as the cause, a serious difference between
the President and the Secretary over the amount of arms to be
imported and the number of men to be placed in camp in 1861.
Davis's refusal to allow Walker as many of both as he desired
caused the Secretary's resignation, according to this account.[48]
This, however, does not appear to be the true explanation.

Walker, in fact, was gently forced out of the Cabinet by Davis.
On August 19, 1861, Walker went to Orange Courthouse to
visit a friend who was wounded. In his absence the President,
because of pressing business in the department, and at Benja-

[45] Walker to Committee, September 4, 1861, in *Official Records,* Ser. IV, Vol. I,
598–99.

[46] Jones, *Diary,* I, 64.

[47] Walker to Davis, September 10, 1861, in *Official Records,* Ser. IV, Vol. I, 603.

[48] Robert Barnwell Rhett, Jr., "Civil Government of the Confederate States," in
R. U. Johnson and C. C. Buel (eds.), *Battles and Leaders of the Civil War, Being
for the Most Part Contributions by Union and Confederate Officers . . .* (New
York, 1887–1888), I, 104. Dr. Walker, writing of his ancestor, said: "The real cause
of General Walker's withdrawal from Mr. Davis's cabinet was a decided difference
of opinion as to the policy to be pursued in the conduct of the war office. The
position was fast becoming subordinated to a mere clerkship without latitude or
power—one mind dominating all. . . . General Walker was very strongly in favor
of accepting all the volunteers presenting themselves in 1861 but very many were
not accepted for lack of equipment and arms. He was urgent in his desire to
purchase . . . stores before the ports were closed.

"Many appointments which should have been made by the Secretary were made
over his head, so finding himself in an impossible position he was naturally compelled to retire." Walker to Michael L. Woods, January 18, 1906, in Judah P.
Benjamin, Braxton Bragg, Leroy Pope Walker Papers, Alabama Department of
Archives and History.

min's suggestion, appointed an acting Secretary of War.[49] When Walker returned he closeted himself in his office, and later Jones noted a letter to the President marked "immediate," and in the Secretary's own handwriting.[50] In the days that followed, Walker did not attend meetings of the Cabinet, and Davis wrote sharp criticisms on reports by the Secretary.[51] From Davis's letter to Walker on September 9, a prior conference between the two men may be reconstructed.[52] At the meeting they discussed the lack of confidence shown by Congress in the administration of the War Department, and Davis suggested that Walker accept an appointment as a representative of the Confederacy in Europe. This suggestion was not agreeable to Walker, who, however, expressed his desire to retire from the Cabinet. The letter of September 9 followed, when the President, feeling that immediate action was required, wrote asking Walker whether there was any other position to which he aspired. "To sever the relation which has so closely united us is so repugnant to my sentiment," the President wrote, "that only the conviction of a public necessity . . . could have reconciled me to the separation."[53] Before he received this communication Walker had submitted his resignation, to become effective September 16.

Walker's reply to the President's letter of the ninth was friendly in tone. ". . . I have often said of you," he wrote, "that you were the only man I had ever met whose greatness grew upon me the nearer I approached him, . . ."[54] He asked, in closing, to be assigned as commander of Mobile. The President appointed him a brigadier general and assigned him to the command of Alabama troops.

Glowing editorial praise of his work must have comforted the former Secretary. The *Richmond Examiner* closed its tribute of praise thus:

Upon the difficulties, the labours, the embarrassments, which lay, necessarily, in his path, upon the pure and lofty purpose with which

[49] Jones, *Diary*, I, 73.   [50] *Ibid.*, 74.

[51] *Ibid.* Davis wrote: ". . . when papers of such volume are sent to him [the President] for perusal, it is the business of the secretary to see that brief abstracts of their contents accompany them."

[52] Davis to Walker, September 9, 1861, in *Official Records*, Ser. IV, Vol. I, 600.

[53] *Ibid.*   [54] Walker to Davis, September 10, 1861, *ibid.*, 603.

he has addressed himself to public duty, upon the great success which has crowned his endeavours, upon the signal fact that, with a patronage of the most enormous character, the breath of suspicion has never once visited his reputation for integrity, public opinion will rest its verdict of "Well done, good and faithful servant!" [55]

The *Petersburg Express* referred with pride to the Confederate victories won under Walker's direction. The *Charleston Courier* declared that he went out of office unpopular enough to please his worst enemy, but added that time would bring him the acclaim of a grateful nation.

Walker was soon forgotten by the public and definitely mistreated by the War Department. He was appointed to the command of four Alabama regiments, but to a man they were unarmed. Benjamin, on October 26, asked him to come to Richmond with his entire brigade, as neither the War Department nor General Albert Sidney Johnston could arm the troops, but generals near Richmond could.[56] General Walker did not respond enthusiastically to this suggestion. When Benjamin ordered two of Walker's regiments to Manassas, a long correspondence between the two men ensued, and Walker eventually appealed to Davis. By February, 1862, Walker was at Mobile and had succeeded in arming one of his regiments and half of another, only to be ordered to North Alabama by General Bragg.[57] Resenting what he considered a slight by Bragg,[58] Walker soon resigned his commission. A correspondent of Clement C. Clay wrote that "it would be a pitty [sic] to have him

55 *Daily Richmond Examiner,* September 17, 1861.

56 Benjamin to Walker, October 26, 1861, in *Official Records,* Ser. I, Vol. LII, Pt. II, 186.

57 Bragg to Adjutant General C. S. Army, February 1, 1862, *ibid.,* Ser. I, Vol. VI, 820–21. General Bragg wrote: "To enable me to progress at all in my labors at Mobile it was necessary to dispose of Brigadier-General Walker, whose rank rendered him an incumbrance. You will see he was sent to Montgomery, to command the unarmed men [there]. . . . I have no idea he will be of any service; but he can do less harm there." *Ibid.*

Of this order the former Secretary wrote bitterly: "I am not only left without a command, to be ridiculed and laughed at . . . , but am sent into the interior . . . , safe from every danger, where the enemy would never think to go. . . . No honorable man would dare to hold such a position a day beyond your approval of this order." Walker to Benjamin, February 6, 1862, *ibid.,* Vol. LII, Pt. II, 264.

58 John Withers to Clay, March 30, 1862, in Clay Papers.

[Walker] picked up and bagged by the minions of Old Abe, yet should such evil come upon him, my curiosity would be excited to know which position he found most 'intolerable.' " [59] Why Davis allowed his former Secretary of War to be humiliated possibly may be explained by the Confederacy's inability to equip its soldiers. Perhaps to make amends, Walker was appointed presiding judge of the military court for North Alabama, and throughout the war he remained a steadfast supporter of the Davis administration.

While Walker was not a success as Secretary of War, there are many mitigating circumstances which help to explain his failure. His ill-health, the failure to obtain arms from Europe, the slowness in raising troops and issuing commissions, and petty jealousies hampered him in his work and caused criticism of his conduct of the War Department. He was not responsible for any of these shortcomings, except for his ill-health, which possibly was brought on by overwork as a result of improper organization of his efforts. He could not create munitions from thin air, work as he might; consequently he could not accept all who volunteered for service in the army. The failure in this respect was due to the inadequacies of Southern industry and the lack of foresight in Southern leaders. Walker became convinced of the certainty of war long before many other Confederate politicians did; once sure of his ground, he acted with energy.

Walker's lack of expedition in handling the business of the department is easily explained. So many applications for commissions in the army poured into the department that by the time he had gone through the day's mail, two or three times the original number of applications had arrived. Hundreds of business matters that required immediate attention drew him from other duties of almost equal importance. Moreover, at a time when applications for army service were at their highest the department was organized on the basis of peacetime operations, and Walker had less clerical help than any of his successors. Perhaps the Secretary's arduous labor shares the blame with any mismanagement of work for his physical breakdown.

[59] *Ibid.*

Even if one is unable to agree with the *Richmond Examiner*'s fulsome praise, already quoted,[60] the truth of much of George Fitzhugh's summary of Walker's accomplishments in office can be conceded.[61] Never in the history of the world, Fitzhugh asserted, had so large an army been recruited, assembled from distant points, provisioned, armed, and disciplined in so short a time. Starting without men, money, munitions, or a fully organized government, a fully equipped army of a quarter of a million men was created. The enemy was fought on Confederate soil because the Secretary of War and all the Cabinet knew no other course could be pursued. The Southern forces had been more successful than their enemy. The tremendous achievement of the Confederacy had been due to the ardor of its people and to the cooperation of the state executives. Without wise, prudent, practical, and vigorous administrative direction, the uprising of the people would have gone for naught. Fitzhugh's summary was a tribute to a public official who had unquestionably worked hard and who, despite obvious failings, had accomplished much. Though he had relinquished his post somewhat disillusioned, Walker remained firm in his faith in the righteousness of the Southern cause and confident that it would ultimately triumph.

GEORGE WYTHE RANDOLPH

The Richmond press indulged in much speculation concerning Walker's eventual successor. In the words of the *Richmond Examiner*, the former Secretary left "his empty detractors behind him, buzzing and flitting like bees about the street of Richmond, getting ready their honey of commendation for the Secretary that is to be, whoever he may be, and sharpening their stings

[60] See pp. 117–18. The *Daily Richmond Examiner* on September 10, 1861, said: "She [history] will describe the names and characters of the leaders of this great revolution, and among them will be that of the eloquent champion of southern honour who so prominently aided to place Alabama in line for independence, as also that of the warrior-statesman who, with a frame shattered in the public service, borrowed a strength from his own iron will, and stood forth in the fight like Richard the Lion Hearted, ever ready to do battle for the right and to strike down to earth the foul despotism which oppressed his country."

[61] Fitzhugh's article was published in the *Richmond Daily Dispatch,* September 30, 1861.

of calumny in event that his appreciation may not be responsive to their own." [62] The *Examiner* joined the buzzing detractors a short time thereafter, when Benjamin became Secretary of War, serving from September 17, 1861, to March 24, 1862. During his period of service the Confederacy not only lacked munitions; it experienced serious reverses in the military field. Benjamin's retention as Secretary under the permanent government was prevented by the opposition, and several men were suggested for the secretaryship in 1862. The office went to George Wythe Randolph who had been favored by some newspaper editors for Secretary of the Navy rather than for the War Department.

The new Secretary was a grandson of Thomas Jefferson and the bearer of the proudest name in Virginia.[63] He was born at Monticello on March 10, 1818, and after attending a private school in Cambridge, Massachusetts, served as a midshipman in the United States Navy from 1831 to 1837. He was graduated with a degree in law from the University of Virginia two years later, and began the practice of his profession in Richmond. He had interested himself in the local militia, commanded a company of the state troops at the time of John Brown's raid, and later served as the chairman of the commission to buy arms for Virginia. He was sent by the Virginia convention to try to persuade President-elect Lincoln not to use force in the dispute between the North and the South. Failing in his efforts, Randolph returned to his state to become a leading advocate of secession. In the Virginia convention he delivered a prepared speech favoring the union of Virginia with the Confederate states because of the economic advantages that would accrue to his state.[64]

When war came, Randolph raised a company of artillery and served in the state forces. General John Bankhead Magruder on September 13 asked permission of Governor John Letcher to combine companies of artillery and place them under Major

[62] *Daily Richmond Examiner,* September 21, 1861. For the account of Walker's successor, Benjamin, see pp. 162–81.

[63] Brief accounts of Randolph's life are in Allen Johnson and Dumas Malone (eds.), *Dictionary of American Biography* (New York, 1928–1936), XV, 358–59; Clement Anselm Evans (ed.), *Confederate Military History: . . .* (Atlanta, 1899), I, 607.

[64] Henry Thomas Shanks, *The Secession Movement in Virginia, 1847–1861* (Richmond, 1934), 167–68.

Randolph, of whom he said: ". . . in my judgment, no rank in the army, however great, could be conferred upon him, the duties of which he would not discharge in a manner eminently conducive to our success." [65] This letter was sent by Governor Letcher to Davis, who noted that the praise in it accorded with all that he had already heard of Randolph. Randolph at that time was in poor health and spent the month of November in Albemarle recovering from a severe illness.[66] He detested the war which took "me from my books, my home, and everything that I love, to swelter in the pestilent marshes of the Peninsula." [67] In February, 1862, he resigned his army commission to become candidate for the Confederate House of Representatives but failed of election.[68] Davis appointed him a brigadier general in the Confederate forces on February 12, 1862, and on March 17, 1862, nominated him Secretary of War.

Randolph's selection for the post had not been generally expected. His record prior to secession was undistinguished, nor had he accomplished anything outstanding as a military officer. In his own right he was deserving of respect, his ancestry was illustrious, and he was allied to the Adams family of Mississippi by his marriage to a wealthy widow, a member of that family. The circumstance that Virginia, his native state, was considered entitled to representation in the Cabinet, with the added circumstance of Randolph's distinguished family connections, were strong factors influencing his appointment. The Richmond correspondent of the *Charleston Mercury* reported that the Virginian's appointment came solely as the result of several reports, in particular one on coast defenses, which Randolph had submitted to the President.[69] Whatever the reasons behind his selection, the appointment was very popular with the newspapers.

[65] Magruder to Letcher, September 13, 1861, in *Calendar of Virginia State Papers*, XI, 195. Randolph, on August 26, 1861, defended Magruder against a charge of drunkenness, in *Official Records*, Ser. I, Vol. LI, Pt. II, 251.

[66] Randolph to Thompson Brown, November 20, 1861, in George Wythe Randolph Papers, Confederate Museum, Richmond.

[67] *Id.* to Albert T. Bledsoe, August 26, 1861, in *Official Records*, Ser. I, Vol. LII, Pt. II, 251.

[68] *Charleston Mercury*, February 6, 1862; *Charleston Daily Courier*, February 1, 19, 1862. The *Courier* reported that Randolph resigned from the army because of ill-health.

[69] *Charleston Mercury*, March 28, 1862.

The *Mercury* believed that as Secretary of War he would be an improvement over Benjamin, if his health would permit him to perform the arduous labor of the office; but the newspaper warned the President that Randolph could not be controlled like a puppet. The *Southern Literary Messenger* declared that Randolph was an incorruptible and irreproachable man who possessed neither the procrastination nor the pliancy of his predecessors.[70] To the accompaniment of such warm praise this politically untried scion of a prominent family entered upon his duties.

The new Secretary arrived in Richmond on Saturday, March 22, 1862, and took over his duties early in the next week.[71] Although Benjamin had been Secretary of State since March 18, he continued as active head of the War Department until Randolph had qualified, and remained the President's military adviser. It was thus that Benjamin, not his successor in the War Department, aided in the drafting of the conscription bill, and helped push it to enactment by Congress. Benjamin, too, had prepared a long list of recommendations for military promotions which was sent to the Senate on March 28. A new Secretary, unfamiliar with the details of his office, naturally required time to get his bearings.

It is difficult to determine what effect Randolph as Secretary had upon Confederate policy. More than any other Secretary, he sent the correspondence that came into his office to the President for his information and instructions, without at the same time giving his own opinion. This was especially true in the early months of his tenure. He had become more confident by late September and October, and he began to state his own ideas with greater freedom. His official orders were brief and direct, with little or no explanation. His correspondence appeared at times to be a parrot-like repetition of instructions received by him from his official superiors. The President regarded the conduct of the War Department as the major part of the Confederate government, and since he had a trusted adviser in General Lee,

70 "Editorial," *Southern Literary Messenger*, XXXIV–XXXVI (1862), 197. The editor characterized Randolph as, "An intrepid gentleman, he will neither give nor take a slight."

71 *Charleston Daily Courier*, March 28, 1862.

the Secretary of War was relegated to a minor position. Even
after General Lee had become commander of the Army of Northern Virginia, Randolph's relative power was not appreciably increased.

The passage and enforcement of the Conscription Act was perhaps the most important achievement during Randolph's term
of office. Some reports made him instrumental in obtaining the
passage of this act.[72] Actually, his influence in bringing about the
enactment of the law was negligible, but he did put the act into
effective operation. The law, as he explained it, superseded
the old system under which each state had been called on for a
definite quota of troops. The Confederacy, however, still accepted
state troops in full regiments. The purpose of the act was to retain all troops in service as of April 16, and to fill depleted
regiments with recruits. The operation of the draft did not put
an end to volunteering, but the government expected that it
would have the effect of inducing increased numbers of men to
offer their services rather than wait to be conscripted.[73] The act
required all men from eighteen to thirty-five years of age to
remain in army service ninety days, unless sooner relieved by new
enlistments. The Secretary wanted to interpret this clause so
as to require all volunteers to serve ninety days longer than their
terms of enlistment.[74] Attorney General Watts held that no soldier could leave the service earlier than ninety days after
April 16, no matter when his term of enlistment expired, but
that a discharge must be given on request to any soldier whose
term ended ninety days or longer after the April date. Randolph
objected to this interpretation and appealed to the President,
stating that he would disregard Watts's opinion unless the President directed otherwise. After studying the opinion, Davis upheld the Attorney General and wrote that, while an interpretation by the government's law officer might not change the
opinions of any department secretary, it should be relied on to
settle questions about which there was doubt. For the sake of
harmony, the President concluded, when the Attorney General

72 *Charleston Mercury*, April 3, 24, 1862.
73 Randolph to H. T. Clark, April 30, 1862, in *Official Records*, Ser. IV, Vol. I,
1105.
74 *Id.* to Davis, August 5, 1862, *ibid.*, Vol. II, 33–34.

upon request gave an opinion on law it should be accepted.[75]

Randolph's recommendation for the age limit that should be fixed in the second draft was accepted. After examining the census of 1850 he estimated that an extension of the age limit to forty years would give the Confederacy a total of 863,500 men. Three sevenths of this number, he calculated, would be exempted, leaving 493,500 men, or as large a force as the government could feed, clothe, and arm. This number, the Secretary concluded, amounted to 5 per cent of the Confederacy's total population and was a larger proportion of their population than European powers had placed in the field. Davis accepted his Secretary's views and limited the call to those between thirty-five and forty years of age, although he had suggested a thirty-five to forty-five age limit in a message in August to Congress.[76]

Randolph's attempts to enforce the Conscription Act with strict adherence to the letter led to clashes with state executives. He asked Governor Letcher of Virginia for his cooperation in preventing conflict between the state and the Confederacy, and intimated that the War Department would accept the decision of Virginia's supreme court in the dispute.[77] To Governor Joseph E. Brown of Georgia, he wrote: "I think we might as well drive out the common enemy before we make war on each other." [78] Eventually, all the disputes were settled amicably, but not before delays which weakened the service.

Conscription brought a host of attending problems, one of the most difficult of which was that of exemptions. Randolph followed the law governing them, but advised that Congress should change the law. The South's need for materials led to the practice of detailing conscripted soldiers to special nonmilitary duty. The Secretary recommended that a drafted man be allowed a substitute only in cases where the service of the principal was as useful at home as in the field,[79] for substitutes were often found to be unfit for military service and they frequently

[75] Davis to Randolph, August 9, 1862, *ibid.*, 41–42.
[76] Randolph to Davis, October 20, 1862, *ibid.*, 132.
[77] *Id.* to Letcher, October 16, 1862, *ibid.*, 123–24.
[78] *Id.* to Joseph E. Brown, June 18, 1862, in *Sumter Republican*, June 27, 1862.
[79] Report of the Secretary of War, August 12, 1862, in *Official Records*, Ser. IV, Vol. II, 45.

deserted. The department, in order to prevent other evils, refused to accept foreigners as substitutes. The Secretary also held that once a substitute became liable to conscription, his principal could then be forced into the service,[80] an interpretation that Congress eventually enacted as law. Desertions became a major problem of the department during Randolph's term. Courts martial, executions, rewards for information on deserters, and appeals to governors for aid were none too successful in reducing the number of desertions. How to curb desertions and return deserters to the ranks remained an unsolved problem from the summer of 1862 until the fall of the Confederacy. Yet, despite all the difficulties attending enforcement of the Conscription Act, the Secretary was convinced that it was essentially sound.

Randolph had little part in developing military plans. General Lee and President Davis took the responsibility for this duty. The Secretary, however, was present at meetings where plans were discussed. The President called a conference on April 4, 1862, to determine the strategy the Confederate forces should adopt in opposing General George B. McClellan. General Joseph E. Johnston wanted a concentration of forces near Richmond, but only Gustavus W. Smith of the conferees supported him. Randolph favored making an attempt to stop the Union forces at Yorktown, since a withdrawal of troops to Richmond would force the evacuation of Norfolk with the loss of naval vessels and the abandonment of all hope of creating a navy. General Lee held like opinions. A second conference was held, after which the President ordered Johnston to follow the plan favored by Lee and Randolph.[81] General Johnston gave in but executed the plan in such a manner that eventually the fighting was waged according to his original ideas.

The rebel war clerk not only believed that Randolph lacked initiative, but also considered him an inefficient Secretary of War. It was General Lee who possessed so much power that Randolph had little to do and it was Lee who made the War Department into "a second class bureau, of which the President himself

---

[80] Albert Burton Moore, *Conscription and Conflict in the Confederacy* (New York, 1924), 33–34, 44–45.

[81] For an account of the conferences, see Douglas Southall Freeman, *R. E. Lee, A Biography* (New York, 1934–1936), II, 21–22.

is the chief." [82] Randolph was truly "a mere clerk" and most of
the departmental correspondence was referred to the various
bureaus for action because the bureau heads knew much better
than Randolph what to do.[83] Randolph was too ready to yield to
protestations of subordinates, and his failure to keep the department running smoothly caused the President much embarrassment.[84] These sweeping condemnations were colored by the war
clerk's prejudice, and his conviction that Randolph's political
advancement was based upon his distinguished ancestry.

When General Henry A. Wise had been refused a new command, after the capture of his forces at Roanoke Island, he declared there was no Secretary of War. To the question of one of
his subordinates who asked, "What is Randolph?" the General
replied: "He is not Secretary of War; he is merely a *clerk*, an
underling, and cannot hold up his head in his humiliating position. He will never be able to hold up his head, sir." [85]

Another critic complained of Randolph's attitude toward visitors. The Secretary's office was a room, formerly used as a committee room, in a building on North Street. Too many officers
of high rank were treated with careless impertinence, according
to the critic, or even denied an interview with the Secretary, who
at times waited until he was in the mood before receiving a visitor in his office.[86]

Relations between the President and the Secretary of War
had been growing increasingly cooler. If, as the *Charleston Mercury* reported, Davis had been led to appoint Randolph because
of his admiration for the latter's reports on coastal defense, he
had expected to find in him a most capable official. He was disappointed. He found the Secretary indecisive. Randolph was
not physically equal to the taxing duties of the War Department,
and this may have contributed to the President's dissatisfaction
with the conduct of the department's affairs. Whatever the reason or reasons, it became increasingly clear that the two men did
not make a team. The issue between them came to a head in
November, 1862. Late in October, Randolph had ordered Lieu-

---

[82] Jones, *Diary*, I, 162.   [83] *Ibid.*, 142.
[84] *Ibid.*, 133–69.   [85] *Ibid.*, 142.
[86] Joseph Grégoire de Roulhac Hamilton (ed.), *The Papers of Randolph Abbott
Shotwell* (Raleigh, 1929–1936), I, 439.

tenant General Theophilus Holmes, whose forces were then stationed in Arkansas, to cross the Mississippi River at his discretion and direct the combined operations on the east bank.[87] The President objected to the order, and the Secretary modified his instructions to Holmes. Jones, commenting on this rebuke, expressed his amazement that Randolph, who had never before taken similar action without having first obtained the President's sanction, should have given an order of such gravity and importance without having consulted the President. The occurrence looked like a rupture to the war clerk, who wrote that "after acting some eight months merely in the humble capacity of clerk, Mr. Randolph has all at once essayed to act the PRESIDENT." [88] The break came on November 14. Davis on that day told Randolph that confusion and embarrassment would result unless all departmental orders were sent through the proper channel, the Bureau of Orders and Correspondence. The President further informed the Secretary that all matters relating to military strategy and the selection of commissioned officers should be referred to the Executive office before final action was taken.[89] The next day Randolph submitted his resignation and it was accepted immediately. Randolph's withdrawal was summary and, in one respect, unusual. He did not remain at his post until a successor was appointed, as was customary, but quit his office as soon as his resignation was accepted on Saturday, November 15. He left considerable unfinished business that might have been disposed of that day.[90]

Randolph's resignation took the country by surprise. He had taken over the War Department, the Richmond Dispatch recalled, and almost instantly turned defeat into victory. This newspaper expressed regret at Randolph's withdrawal and believed that his independence would be generally approved.[91] Editorials of a similar strain later appeared in the Richmond Examiner, the Richmond Whig, the North Carolina Standard,

[87] Randolph to Holmes, October 27, 1862, in Official Records, Ser. I, Vol. XIII, 906–907.
[88] Jones, Diary, I, 190.
[89] Davis to Randolph, November 14, 1862, in Rowland (ed.), Davis, V, 371–72.
[90] Mallory, Diary, November 15, 1862.
[91] Richmond Daily Dispatch, November 18, 1862.

and the *Charleston Mercury*. An Alabama paper expressed joy
that the country would know thereafter on whose shoulders the
blame for defeat or the praise for victory should rest. If the President claimed the right to be consulted on every detail, then his
was the responsibility.[92] The newspapers took advantage of the
Secretary's resignation to attack the President rather than to
praise Randolph's record.

All this verbal pother amused the cynical war clerk. He believed that Randolph had acted the part of a very foolish or
desperate man. Of the charge that no discretion had been allowed
the Secretary, Jones said that Randolph knew very well that the
latitude given him became greater and greater as he became more
and more familiar with the duties of his office. The Secretary
had, for a time, been content to be a nonentity but had suddenly
displayed a desire to become a ruler. Such action, Jones concluded, if "not a silly caprice, . . . was a deliberate purpose, to escape a cloud of odium he knew must sooner or later
burst around him." [93] A letter written by Randolph a few months
after his resignation indicates that there was considerable truth
in the last statement. In it he referred to the "gentlemanly ease
of private life" in contrast to the burdens he "grunted and
sweated" under as Secretary of War. Out of a sense of duty Randolph tendered his services in the field after relinquishing his
office. The War Department offered him a choice of the command of John Echols's brigade or of a new one in formation.
Randolph believed it would be unfair to supplant Echols, and
he had no desire to take the other command. In declining the
command, he stated somewhat insincerely: "I regret that I can
do nothing for the cause, but I have the satisfaction of knowing
that it is not my fault." [94]

When Mrs. Randolph's fortune was lost through carelessness

[92] *Mobile Advertiser and Register*, November 26, 1862.
[93] Jones, *Diary*, I, 191.
[94] Randolph to Thompson Brown, January 14, 1863, in Randolph Papers. The
above paragraph is based on this letter. Randolph accused the War Department
of trying to push him out of the service. The truth is that Randolph desired to
be relieved from service, but the War Department refused. Attorney General
Watts, on request of Seddon, held that Randolph, after resigning as Secretary
of War, was still a brigadier general and subject to the command of the War
Department.

on the part of a trustee, financial necessities obliged her husband to resume the practice of law. Randolph saw the possibilities of lucrative practice in defending men who claimed exemption from military service. In partnership with G. A. Meyers, he made a specialty of assisting foreign Jews and other aliens in their efforts to escape army service.[95] At the same time, however, he served the Confederacy by organizing the city volunteers for the defense of Richmond in case of emergency. Late in 1864 Randolph, accompanied by his family, left for Europe in the hope of restoring his health.

Randolph's record in office was praised or condemned in 1862 according as it was judged by a foe or a supporter of the Davis administration. Those who considered that Randolph had been a capable secretary contended that the President not only dictated the conduct of the department, but denied the Secretary any part in the selection of military officers or in the planning of strategy. It is true that the President reserved these two fields for himself, but it is unfair and incorrect to assert that he resented advice from his secretaries in such matters; on the contrary, he invited and welcomed their counsel. Every Secretary of War influenced the President's ideas to a greater or lesser degree. Randolph's place in the latter group was at the very bottom. He possessed neither the physical energy nor the forcefulness of character to win for himself an important place in Confederate councils. He gained high praise as a Secretary from the newspapers, but the causes of his popularity are to be found in the success of Southern arms during his term of office.

A consideration of the circumstances attending Randolph's resignation leads one to the conclusion that he was in the wrong. In sending an important order on his own responsibility and outside the customary channel of such communications, he violated a necessary rule. The President himself would not have ordered, without having first consulted his Cabinet or army advisers, a change in military plans so important as that order by Randolph. The Secretary, resigning after the President's rebuke, did so either because he was weary of his office and wished to

95 Hamilton (ed.), *The Shotwell Papers*, 439; Jones, *Diary*, I, 218-19.

retire, or else because he was egged on by the administration's foes. In any event, he was glad to return to the repose of civilian life, the enjoyment of books, and of social activities.

GUSTAVUS WOODSON SMITH

Randolph's hurried departure from the office of Secretary of War made necessary the immediate appointment of someone to keep the departmental machinery running. General Gustavus Woodson Smith was available and he received the appointment of Secretary of War *ad interim.* Smith was born in 1822 at Georgetown, Kentucky.[96] He was graduated from the United States Military Academy in 1842 and served in the army until 1854. In 1855 Smith accepted a position as engineer of Peter Hewitt's Trenton Iron Works, but soon gave up his job to become Street Commissioner of New York City. He returned to his native state in 1861. After the war began he was commissioned a major general in the Confederate army, and became acting commander of the Army of Northern Virginia when General Joseph E. Johnston was wounded in the battle of Seven Pines on May 31, 1862.

Smith's appointment to the War Department was a purely temporary one. It could hardly have been otherwise, for Smith was a friend of General Joseph E. Johnston and had little respect for General Lee.[97] Furthermore, the Kentucky officer was none too popular with either soldiers or civilians who, without adequate reason, questioned his loyalty to the South.[98] Someone was needed to fill in at the War Department until the President could select a suitable man for the post. Telegraphic reports, in the meantime, spread the rumor that Smith was to be appointed permanently, and the *Mobile Advertiser and Register* lauded him as "the right man in the right place." When it became clear that the President had no such purpose in mind, and when a

[96] For brief account of Smith, see Evans (ed.), *Confederate Military History,* I, 607–608; the introduction to the Gustavus W. Smith Papers, Duke University.

[97] Smith to Johnston, July 18, 1862, in *Official Records,* Ser. I, Vol. LI, Pt. II, 593–94.

[98] Hamilton (ed.), *The Shotwell Papers,* I, 225.

permanent Secretary of War was named, it was charged that Smith resigned because he refused to become a mere clerk under Davis.

Smith served only four days as Secretary *ad interim* but continued for a time in military duty. He soon resigned his commission to become superintendent of the Etowah iron works in Georgia. When General Sherman's army was nearing Georgia, Governor Brown put Smith in command of the state militia. Smith was arrested at Macon, Georgia, on April 20, 1865, by the Federal cavalry under command of Major General James H. Wilson, but was quickly released. After the war he was superintendent of the iron works at Chattanooga, Tennessee, and still later became insurance commissioner of Kentucky. He finally returned to New York City, where he resided until his death in 1896.

JAMES ALEXANDER SEDDON

Davis discussed with the members of his Cabinet the selection of a permanent Secretary of War to succeed Randolph. The President's own preference, according to Reagan, was James Alexander Seddon, with Joseph E. Johnston and Gustavus W. Smith next in the order named.[99] A former assistant secretary said that Seddon, although of undoubted patriotism and integrity of character, was not a worker either by nature or habit.[100] Objection was made to Seddon's appointment because of his frail health, but Davis never considered lack of physical stamina a bar to appointment to the War Department. Of the five war secretaries and one *ad interim* secretary, four were in feeble health. Seddon was appointed Secretary of War and took office on November 22, 1862.[101]

Seddon's appointment received considerable newspaper commendation. He was strongly endorsed by the *Richmond Examiner,* which had long been his supporter in Virginia; the *Charleston Mercury,* the *Richmond Enquirer,* and the *Charleston Courier* joined in the chorus of praise of the new Secretary.

99 Reagan, *Memoirs,* 161.
100 Albert T. Bledsoe to Davis, November 19, 1862, in Davis Papers.
101 *Daily Richmond Examiner,* November 22, 1862; Jones, *Diary,* I, 194.

On the other hand, doubts of his ability were expressed by the *Richmond Whig*, and the *North Carolina Standard*, while the *Petersburg Express* unhesitatingly pronounced him unqualified for the War Department.

Jones believed that the new Secretary would not long remain in office if he attempted to perform all its duties, but he was pleased with Seddon's manly appearance in comparison with that of his predecessor who, Jones said, looked like a monkey.[102] Seddon's physique, however, was none too robust. It was said that the rattle of his bones could be heard as he descended the stairways of the Spottswood Hotel. He was gaunt in frame; his complexion was a deathlike pallor; and he wore his hair long and straggling. His prominent nose and the skull cap he wore gave him the appearance of a rabbi. With characteristic over-statement, Jones wrote of him: "Mr. Secretary Seddon, who usually wears a sallow and cadaverous look, which, coupled with his emaciation, makes him resemble an exhumed corpse after a month's interment, looks to-day like a galvanized corpse which had been buried two months."[103] Seddon's sickly appearance was deceiving, for Jones on the same day gave testimony to the Secretary's vigor and industry.

Seddon was an accomplished politician. He had seen service in the state and national legislatures and had shone as a thinker and planner rather than as one who executed plans. His frail health imposed on him an inactive role in public life but, in the quiet of his Goochland plantation, he remained a power in the politics of Virginia.

He was born in Stafford County on July 13, 1815, and passed his early childhood in the home of an uncle.[104] Later, he joined his family at Fredericksburg. Illness delayed the completion of his college training, but he was graduated with first honors from the University of Virginia in 1835. He established himself in the practice of law at Richmond, and soon became active in the Calhoun wing of the Democratic party. In the House of Repre-sentatives, where he served two terms, he was noted for his grace-

102 Jones, *Diary*, I, 194.   103 *Ibid.*, 380.
104 For accounts of Seddon's life, see *Southern Illustrated News*, September 5, 1863; Johnson and Malone (eds.), *Dictionary of American Biography*, XVI, 545–46; Evans (ed.), *Confederate Military History*, I, 609.

ful and impressive manner as a speaker, as well as for the effective reasoning of his oratory. He retired from active political life in 1851, but ten years later re-entered it as a member of the Virginia Peace Convention. His experience in that meeting strengthened his already well-developed extremism on the question of secession and he strove earnestly to have Virginia join the Confederacy. He had little fear of war resulting, but promised the Northern invader "hospitable graves . . . six feet to each . . . and a few inches more to their leader, if he were taller." [105] Seddon was a member of his state's delegation in the Confederate Provisional Congress, and in 1862 sought election to a seat in the House of Representatives, but was soundly defeated, notwithstanding the *Richmond Examiner*'s support of his candidacy. Thereafter until his appointment as Secretary of War he remained in retirement from public life.

The new Secretary, slightly neurotic and semi-invalid, was a civilian with no experience whatever in military affairs. His appointment was welcomed for the moment by leaders in the South, in the belief that practical ability, more than technical knowledge, was needed in the conduct of the War Department. Also, because he was an intimate friend of Davis, it was expected that he would prove more satisfactory to, and of greater influence with, the President than any other available man. This belief proved to be correct. No other Secretary of War, not even Benjamin, influenced the South's military strategy to the same extent as did Seddon.

He had not long been in office before he became convinced that the weak spot in Confederate defense was in the West. He did not overlook the importance of the Virginia area of battle, but there the two opposing armies fought back and forth to no conclusive result. The Union forces meanwhile were cutting the roots of the Confederacy in the western zone of combat. Able generalship in combination with departmental planning had resulted in the victories of Lee in Virginia, and a plan, therefore, should be worked out along similar lines for the West. Because of the distance from Richmond, Seddon thought that the commander of the forces in the West should of necessity have freedom

[105] *Daily Wilmington Herald*, March 8, 1861.

of action in order to coordinate all agencies of defense. Only an able tactician and daring leader could hope to succeed. Seddon believed that General Joseph E. Johnston would measure up to these requirements, and recommended his appointment.[106]

General Johnston had been resting, with nothing of importance to occupy his time, since he was wounded in the battle of Seven Pines. The President had no very high opinion of Johnston's ability or of his willingness to work in harmony with others, and Benjamin vigorously opposed his appointment. Seddon, however, was insistent that Johnston be chosen for the important assignment, and he succeeded in winning over a majority of the Cabinet to the support of the General.[107] Davis himself yielded reluctantly and on November 24, 1862, he appointed Johnston to the command of the Confederate forces in the West. The new Secretary of War had won his first battle, but he continued to impress upon the President the necessity of giving Johnston full power of action. The weight of Seddon's influence upon Davis was evidenced by the President's action in giving General Johnston full power to direct the entire Western campaign and to assume personal command, at his discretion, of any of the armies engaged in it.

Seddon had hit upon a serious weakness of the Confederacy. The victories of General Lee had thrilled the nation to the point where the slow and continuous loss of ground in the West was getting little attention. Seddon's foresightedness now held out the hope of a general victory through the coordination of the scattered forces in the West. Louis T. Wigfall gave the Secretary full credit for the plan to develop a real Western policy and to put it into execution.[108]

The selection of Johnston was unfortunate. He delayed taking the command to which he had been appointed, giving as his reason the uncertainty of the powers and authority granted him. Repeatedly the Secretary explained to him that he had full authority to direct the entire military operations in the West and

106 Louis T. Wigfall to Clement C. Clay, December 11, 1862, in Clay Papers.
107 For an account of Seddon's part in the appointment of Johnston, see Eckenrode, *Jefferson Davis*, 194–95.
108 Wigfall to Clement C. Clay, December 11, 1862, in Clay Papers.

at his discretion could assume personal command of any army in the district. The President also, at Seddon's suggestion, wrote General Johnston confirming what the Secretary of War had told him. But Johnston refused to credit what he saw in writing. He continued to be querulous, and expressed fear that the position to which he had been assigned was such that he would receive all the blame for any defeats that might be suffered, and get no credit for victories he might win.[109]

Seddon had a poor opinion of Bragg's military ability and believed it would be advisable to have him removed from command of the Army of Tennessee. The Secretary accordingly instructed Johnston to investigate the Army of Tennessee and give him a full report on the command. Still protesting his lack of power, Johnston visited Bragg in response to Seddon's instructions. His report to the latter, however, was not what Seddon had expected, for Johnston described conditions in Bragg's command in glowing terms and paid tribute to the "great vigor and skill" of the commander. Despite this endorsement of Bragg, Seddon continued to press Johnston to take personal command of the Army of Tennessee, and to avail himself of Bragg's excellences as an organizer and disciplinarian. Seddon frankly expressed his wish to have General Bragg recalled, and urged Johnston, for the good of the Confederacy, to take command. In the end, the Secretary, despite Johnston's favorable reports, ordered him to send Bragg to Richmond for a conference. Johnston did not obey the order, and gave one excuse after another for his noncompliance with it. The Secretary became frantic. His plan was being checked by an overcautious, noncooperating general, who would neither take general direction of the district nor personally command the large Army of Tennessee. In May, Seddon ordered Johnston to proceed to Mississippi to assume command of the forces there. No implication appeared in this order that Johnston was thereby relieved from his duties as first officer of the Western district although Johnston later so interpreted it.

[109] This and the following paragraph are based on letters of Davis, Seddon, and Johnston, in *Official Records*, Ser. I, Vol. XXIII, Pt. II, 624–27, 632–33, 640–41, 658–59, 674, 698, 708, 741, 745–46, Ser. I, Vol. XXI, Pt. III, 835–36, 842–43, 856–57.

Doubts of Johnston began to be expressed by those who knew of Seddon's efforts with him and their fruitlessness. C. H. Lawson wrote Clement C. Clay that all Johnston's friends could not save the General from censure, and added: "It will not do for him to intrench himself behind the *Examiner's* Editorials—the ill-will and interference of the President." [110] The Secretary of War, although frustrated, remained convinced of the importance of the West in the scheme of war operations, and he began to strip the Atlantic seaboard of every man possible in order to reinforce the armies in the West. He was quickly checked in this, however, by the opposition of military leaders in the East, who feared that a reduction of their forces would invite Federal attack.

The Secretary saw only one other possibility. If a part of General Lee's army could be rushed to the West, an all-important victory might be won while Lee's depleted forces held the Federals in check. While Davis was confined to his home, in the second week of May, 1863, Seddon suggested to Lee that General George E. Pickett's division be sent to Johnston, but Lee objected to this move and was sustained by the President.[111] Davis, Seddon, and Lee on May 15 held a conference, at which Lee proposed an invasion of the North as a means of drawing General Ulysses S. Grant from Vicksburg. He convinced Davis and Seddon of the wisdom of the maneuver. The information that General John C. Pemberton's forces were shut up in Vicksburg, however, necessitated a re-examination of plans. In a momentous Cabinet meeting on May 26, the President questioned the advisability of Lee's proposal to penetrate the North and requested Seddon to state the arguments for it. Seddon, at this time, still supported Lee's plan. Reagan was the most vehement of the secretaries in the discussion; he argued forcefully and earnestly against a dependence on invasion to draw off Grant, and pleaded for direct and immediate aid to the beleaguered Pemberton. He spoke in vain, for Cabinet opinion was not with him. He was persistent in his opposition, however, and pressed Davis to reconsider. Only when Reagan found that

110 Lawson to Clay, May 31, 1863, in Clay Papers.
111 *Official Records,* Ser. I, Vol. XXV, Pt. II, 708–709, 713–14, 724–25, 790, 797.

he alone was in opposition and that he could not move his fellow secretaries, did the Postmaster General cease his efforts.[112]

Seddon's realization of the tremendous importance of the West to the Confederacy gives him a valid claim to greatness as an adviser in the South's military operations. General Johnston, to whom he had looked for the successful execution of his plan and who refused to carry it into execution, had been largely responsible for the lack of fruition of Seddon's efforts. Seddon was disappointed in Johnston, and saw no reason to expect decisive results from him in May, 1863, even though reinforcements from Lee's army were sent him. This uneasiness about Johnston, in addition to Lee's convincing reasons, turned Seddon from his original purpose.

Seddon's influence with Davis on military policy declined from the summer of 1863, but it never became negligible. After Bragg's disastrous defeat at the battle of Chattanooga in November, 1863, the President held a Cabinet meeting to decide on a new commander for the Army of Tennessee. Lieutenant General William Joseph Hardee was considered for the place, but he declared himself unqualified. Seddon proposed Johnston, but Benjamin objected on the ground that, while Johnston was a strategist on defense, he lacked the initiative requisite in a commander.[113] The President was inclined to agree with Benjamin. Most of the Cabinet members favored Seddon's choice and the President reluctantly assented and appointed Johnston on December 16, 1863. Hardly half a year had passed before the Cabinet again met to consider the removal of Johnston. This was after the General's forces had been pushed back to Atlanta. The War Department repeatedly had endeavored, without success, to obtain from Johnston information on his plan of campaign. The Cabinet believed that an offensive movement in Georgia was urgently needed. The secretaries unanimously agreed that Johnston should be removed and they urged Davis to act. Only after "slow deliberation, misgivings, and reluc-

[112] Account based on *ibid.;* Reagan, *Memoirs;* Eckenrode, *Jefferson Davis,* 218–35.
[113] Seddon to W. T. Walthall, February 10, 1879, in Rowland (ed.), *Davis,* VIII, 351.

tance," [114] did the President decide to remove him. On July 18, 1864, Davis appointed General John B. Hood to take command of the army defending Atlanta. General Braxton Bragg, at the time a military adviser to the President, has been blamed for General Johnston's removal. Undoubtedly he strongly favored it, but the entire Cabinet held a similar opinion.

Seddon, as we have seen, exerted a powerful influence on the President. Besides holding political views in common, the two men had a warm personal regard for each other. The frequent and long conferences of the Secretary and the President were recorded by Jones, who, at times, was disgusted with the noncommittal attitude of both. The Secretary would ask the President's advice, the President would request an expression of the Secretary's opinion, and in the end the President would agree to Seddon's proposed action.[115] The little Virginian had a considerable part in assigning minor officers to military commands,[116] but he relied upon the recommendations of commanding generals in preparing lists of men for promotions. This was specially true in General Lee's case. The President was frequently absent from his office because of physical indisposition, and on such occasions the Secretary ordered military movements and assigned commands on his own responsibility. When this happened he reported his action to the President, who only rarely countermanded the Secretary's instructions.

Seddon had put great reliance on his project for the rehabilitation of the Confederacy's forces in the West under Johnston's leadership. When this well-thought-out plan went amiss, doubts naturally arose in the President's mind. As time passed, Seddon's power in respect to military strategy waned. Late in February, 1864, Bragg came to Richmond, charged with the conduct of military operations. Seddon resented the General's appointment, for he retained the poor opinion of the General's capacity that had been in evidence in the past. A natural outcome of Bragg's appointment was the decline of the Secretary's influence in military councils. Jones thought Bragg outranked the Secretary

114 *Ibid.*, 349–50. 115 Jones, *Diary*, II, 26.
116 *Ibid.*, 140, 265.

in departmental affairs, and cited instances when the President followed Bragg's advice in preference to that of the Secretary of War.[117] Bragg's appointment was denounced by members of Congress and the press as an insult to Seddon.[118] The attacks on Bragg actually were directed at the President, a point that neither Seddon nor Davis missed.

There was some talk that Seddon would resign; indeed he considered doing so, although jealousy of Bragg entered only slightly into his contemplations. His health had grown worse in the summer of 1864, neuralgia frequently kept him from work; and in June he was absent from duty for an entire week. Though ill, tired, fearful of defeat, and desirous of resigning, he continued in office and, despite Bragg's appointment, remained a power in military affairs. The long conferences between the Secretary and the President continued to be held. Davis at times was his own Secretary of War, but Seddon never was relegated to a stultifying position or demoted to the status of a clerk.

An attempt was made in 1863 and 1864 to alienate Seddon from his support of the President. The war clerk Jones, noting long talks between the Secretary and Hunter and their walks together in the square, scented some sort of plot, or the hatching of a political scheme. Senator Wigfall, who occasionally joined them, would calm Hunter's fear of ultimate failure to defeat Grant, of which he said, ". . . . nothing was easier. The President would put the old folks and children to *praying* at 6 o'clock A. M.," and Grant would be routed very soon.[119] Wigfall urged Seddon to keep the President from making issues with Congress. The Senator accused the President of nourishing suspicions and miserable malignancy toward opponents of the administration in Congress, with a resultant loss of confidence by everyone whose opinion was of value.[120] Seddon made no reply to these accusations and Wigfall, in disgust, wrote, "The truth is Seddon is subjugated and has lost all manhood if he ever had any." [121]

---

117 *Ibid.,* 171, 184–85, 190.   118 *Ibid.,* 209.

119 *Ibid.,* 231. Jones believed that Hunter persuaded Seddon not to resign on several occasions and especially after Bragg became military adviser to the President. *Ibid.,* 117, 120–21, 127, 150, 317, 330, 332.

120 Wigfall to Clement C. Clay, August 13, 1863, in Clay Papers.

121 *Ibid.*

The Secretary was not conscious of having lost courage, nor did he feel beaten, and he paid scant heed to the criticism of his one-time intimate.

Transaction of the routine business of the War Department was trying to Seddon. His office, at one time used as a committee room, was entered through the clerk's office, and here the Secretary worked six hours daily, while from outside came the noise and confusion caused by callers impatient to see him. He was accused by some persons of being haughty and inaccessible, but in reality it was not difficult to gain admittance to his office, the entrance to which was guarded by a mere lad. To Seddon came all sorts of people on the most trivial, as well as the most important, business: to offer advice, to make applications for places for themselves, to seek favors for others. Seddon did not have the tact and ease that Benjamin displayed in receiving people; his decisions came more slowly than those of his predecessor; and the business of the department lagged. Thomas Hill Watts, former Attorney General and later governor of Alabama, complained in 1864 that two of his letters had remained unanswered.[122] Governor Zebulon B. Vance of North Carolina waited a month and a half for a reply to one of his letters. H. L. Clay reported to his brother that the administration of the department lacked energy; he compared the Secretary to a boy venturing timidly upon thin ice.[123] The delay was due to Seddon's absence from duty because of illness, as well as to his inability to work steadily for long periods. The derelictions of subordinates caused some of the complaints, and some were based upon inadequate facts. Seddon was not so business-like as Benjamin, but an English visitor saw an impressive flow of work, rather than signs of hesitation or confusion, in the War Department.[124]

Seddon recognized the need of delegating authority to his subordinates. He gave the Assistant Secretary, John A. Campbell, considerable responsibility, and Campbell not only issued orders without consulting his superior, but also wrote portions of War

122 Watts to Seddon, June 3, 1864, in *Official Records*, Ser. IV, Vol. III, 466.
123 H. L. Clay to Clement C. Clay, May 31, 1863, in Clay Papers.
124 An English Merchant, *Two Months in the Confederate States Including a Visit to New Orleans under the Domination of General Butler* (London, 1863), 163.

Department reports.[125] Campbell often used the phrase "by order of the Secretary of War," and occasionally forwarded letters endorsed by the President, without waiting for Seddon to read them.[126] Campbell favored leniency in interpreting the law governing exemptions, but he was a competent assistant in the War Department. Neither Seddon nor his successor could have afforded to lose the services of this former Justice of the United States Supreme Court.

Seddon adopted the policy of his predecessors in his efforts to obtain war materials. In his report of January 3, 1863, he noted that the blockade had caused an increase in the price of arms, but he asserted that the Confederacy was better supplied than at any other period in its history. To further the efforts made to speed imports, laws were enacted regulating the classes of goods a shipowner might bring in, and reserving for the Confederate government a part of each ship's cargo. The War Department eventually, in conjunction with the Treasury and Navy departments, took over control of the production and importation of specific commodities and materials.

The Confederate army reached its maximum strength in numbers and efficiency during Seddon's term of office. He relied firmly on the Conscription Act which "wrought our salvation from destruction or infamous thraldom." [127] He gave orders that the exemption law should be interpreted strictly, but he favored changes to mitigate its severity. The numerical strength of the Confederate army declined after the spring of 1863.[128] Desertions were so common that Seddon could truthfully state that from one third to one half of the enrolled men were absent without leave. Organized deserters roved over the country and resisted capture. Thus, when the Confederacy's forces needed all their

---

125 Jones, *Diary*, II, 308, 311.   126 *Ibid.*, I, 242.

127 *Report of the Secretary of War, January 3, 1863* (Richmond, 1863), 8.

128 The December 31, 1862, official Confederate returns listed 235,374 men in the army and present for duty out of a total enlistment of 449,439. The returns of December 31, 1863, however, listed only 215,860 present for duty of a total enlistment of 464,646. *Official Records*, Ser. IV, Vol. II, 278, 1073.

The enlisted men not present for duty included the ill, those on furlough, and deserters. In the last year of the war, there were over 100,000 deserters. The best studies of desertion in the Confederacy are Ella Lonn, *Desertion During the Civil War* (New York, 1928), and Georgia Lee Tatum, *Disloyalty in the Confederacy* (Chapel Hill, 1934).

strength to defend their own territory, its officers were obliged
to keep men from the front to protect lines of communication
and to protect its people from deserters. Most of the Southern
men fought from first to last, but many deserted the ranks and
either hid out or waged guerilla warfare against their own government. Vigorous efforts to effect the return of deserters met
with little success. Appeals for cooperation were made to state
executives, but they were so busy keeping their pet state militia
forces from being drafted into Confederate service that they were
of little real assistance. The Confederacy was unable to accomplish much in the face of such conditions.

Insufficiency in its military strength found a counterpart in
the lack of workers by which both industry and government
bureaus were handicapped. The low salary scale paid by the
government was not attractive to workers, unless it carried exemption from military duty. After conscription had been put
into effect, a system of detail was arranged by which soldiers were
assigned to duty in offices or at such work as was necessary for
the production of supplies or the maintenance of transportation
systems. This system was effective in obtaining laborers at low
cost, but the military authorities complained that it stripped
their commands of fighting men. General Lee believed that when
a man received a government contract he forthwith began to
work to get his friends out of the army on the representation that
he was unable to find other workmen. The General was willing
to honor all orders to detail men, but he gave warning in advance
that he would allow no man to leave the army on detail except
by specific order. Lee never assented to the system, but it continued until the collapse of the South became certain.

Seddon attributed the confused state of military affairs largely
to the Confederacy's monetary situation. Had there been a stable
currency, he believed, men would have been more willing to
take jobs, and supplies could have been more easily obtained.
Secretary Memminger, in an effort to restrict the issuance of
treasury notes, had ordered that a part of the purchase price of
commodities or services be paid in Confederate bonds. The result was that people regarded their goods as far more valuable
than paper money or vague promises to pay. Seddon in his re-

ports to the President repeatedly referred to the embarrassment
caused by a depreciated currency. Memminger did not submit in
silence to the attack on his management of the Treasury Department. His chance to reply came when in June, 1863, Major
Simeon Hart requested permission to seize cotton in Texas and
sell it in Mexico to raise funds for the purchase of army supplies.
Memminger wrote the President that cotton could be impressed
only for imperative and immediate military needs and added,
somewhat gratuitously, that, while it was natural for military
men to disregard the law, but few public benefits could result
from even an occasional violation of the law.[129] Seddon retorted
that there would be little occasion for extralegal methods, "provided the honorable Secretary of the Treasury can manage to
keep his notes at some fair relation or approximation to
specie . . . , even to obtain his notes in sufficient quantities and
in due time is found impracticable." [130] Until Memminger
managed his department better, the Secretary of War continued, he should keep his nose out of the affairs of other governmental agencies. But no solution for the monetary problem was
ever found, and Seddon worried along as best he could.

Another brake on the War Department's efficiency was inadequate transportation. "Of all the difficulties encountered by
the administrative bureaus," Seddon reported, "perhaps the
greatest has been the deficiency in transportation." [131] The railways lacked rails, few cars or engines were obtainable, and the
managements had not the means to keep the old equipment in
repair. Moreover, there was no uniformity in the gauges of the
series of independent lines in the Confederacy. The terminals of
the railroads were often widely separated in the towns and the
teamsters, out of self-interest, prevented a union of the roads
into a continuous system. Seddon, endeavoring to obtain a unified plan of transportation, in the spring of 1863 and again in
1864, called the presidents of the railroads to Richmond to work
out a scheme. Seddon proposed a solution which would have

---

[129] Memminger to Davis, June 30, 1863, in *Official Records*, Ser. I, Vol. LIII,
Supplement, 869.

[130] Endorsement of Seddon, July 15, 1863, *ibid.*, 870.

[131] Report of the Secretary of War, April 28, 1864, in *Official Records*, Ser. IV,
Vol. III, 339.

placed all the railroads under the control of one administrator, but the plan failed to win the President's support.[132] Limited power to exercise some supervision was given a military officer, but he was without real authority and the transportation question remained unsolved.

Seddon also faced the problem of making a decision on the very debatable policy of arming the slaves. The question of using slaves as fighting men had been considered in the first months of the war, and promptly rejected. Such use of Negroes continued to be urged unofficially at intervals, and late in 1864 the increasing desertions and the failure to obtain new enlistments of white men caused a prolonged effort to bring about the enlistment of slaves. Benjamin was the leader of the movement. Seddon did not doubt that Negroes would fight, but he contended that there was no necessity for calling on them, since there were enough white men for military duty if they could be brought into the service. On November 24, 1864, he backed up this opinion by refusing to consider the enlistment of Negro troops.[133] Evidently, administration pressure was brought to bear upon him, for before the end of the year he asked Howell Cobb's opinion about using slaves in the army, and whether or not freedom should be granted to them if they enlisted.[134] The Georgian regarded the proposal as "the most pernicious idea that has been suggested since the war began." [135] To make soldiers of slaves, he declared, would cut the foundation from the Southern theory of slavery and society. Hunter held the same view. Seddon agreed with Cobb and Hunter, and had no part in the later action of Congress providing for the enlistment of slaves. The Confederacy never used slave troops, however, for the war was over before the Negroes could be armed and put in the field.

Seddon resigned his office more than a month before the passage of the law permitting slave enlistments. He had become more and more pessimistic over the military situation, and longed for the serenity of Sabot Hill, his home in Goochland

[132] Eckenrode, *Jefferson Davis,* 348.
[133] Seddon to E. B. Briggs, November 24, 1864, in *Official Records,* Ser. IV, Vol. III, 846.
[134] Seddon to Howell Cobb, December 30, 1864, *ibid.,* 981.
[135] Howell Cobb to Seddon, January 8, 1865, *ibid.,* 1009.

County. He had been accused by Representative Foote in the fall of 1864 of impressing grain at nominal prices of seven to nine dollars a bushel, while selling his own grain to the government at forty dollars a bushel. Foote believed his charges caused Seddon's resignation. This was not true. Seddon was not dishonest and his resignation was not due to Foote's charges.[136] The immediate cause of his resignation was his resentment of the action of the Virginia delegation in the House of Representatives. The Virginia representatives met on January 16, 1865, to consider some means of bolstering Confederate morale. They decided that a reconstruction of the Cabinet was a prerequisite to the attainment of this purpose. They called on the President and requested that he make a clean sweep of the Cabinet. Two days later, Seddon was informed of the action of his fellow Virginians and immediately sent in his resignation. Three days later Thomas S. Bocock, a member of the delegation and former Speaker, wrote to the President setting forth the Virginia delegation's idea in such a manner that Davis interpreted the movement as a threat to force changes in the Cabinet.[137] Davis was angered by what he considered interference with the President's prerogatives, and he endeavored to dissuade Seddon from his decision to resign. Seddon had tired of the office, however, and could not be persuaded to reconsider his action.

The President, in accepting his resignation, wrote him a long friendly letter in which he took occasion to review his theory of Confederate government. Though he could not silently accept the interference with his Executive functions, he wrote, he recognized Seddon's right to a private opinion that the action of the Virginia delegation impaired his usefulness and made his position as Secretary of War distasteful. Davis expressed the hope that the personal relations between the retiring Secretary

[136] Foote claimed Seddon resigned immediately after the accusation. The Secretary possibly sold his grain for forty dollars a bushel. Government agents were busy buying food supplies whenever possible in the open market. Impressment at regulated prices was resorted to only when commodities or materials could be obtained in no other way. Seddon could have sold his grain in the Richmond market for more than forty dollars a bushel.

[137] Thomas S. Bocock to Davis, January 21, 1864 [1865], in *Official Records*, Ser. I, Vol. XLVI, Pt. II, 118.

and himself would be continued in the pleasant manner of the past. In terms of high praise, he continued:

That you have devoted yourself with entire singleness of purpose to the public welfare; that your labors have been incessant, your services important, and your counsels very valuable to myself and your colleagues, would be as readily attested by them as by myself. The regret that our official relations now end is relieved by the reflection that you will be near me, and by the assurance that I can ever call on you with confidence for any aid that you can render in private life.[138]

Seddon continued at the department until a successor was named, giving up his office over the weekend of February 5. He then retired to his country home in Virginia, where he remained until his arrest the following May at the order of Edwin M. Stanton, United States Secretary of War.

Seddon was subjected to almost incessant attacks upon his conduct of the War Department. Most of the criticism reflected the despair at the Confederacy's military reverses rather than any hostility to Seddon's conduct of his office. Foote and Pollard were among his bitterest assailants. The attacks by Foote and Pollard centered on Seddon's activities in obtaining men and supplies to carry on the war. Seddon, it was quite true, was zealous in executing the Conscription Act and also in the impressment of materials, but only when other means of obtaining troops and supplies had failed. The law was often ignored and injustice done in the execution of the Secretary's orders. Seddon regretted the necessity of harsh measures, but saw no alternative. Leniency in the treatment of deserters, on the other hand, was alleged against him by his opponents. They claimed that Seddon's leniency encouraged desertion and lax discipline among the troops. These charges were obviously false; the President alone could pardon deserters condemned to death. Had it been left

---

[138] Davis to Seddon, February 1, 1865, *ibid.*, Ser. IV, Vol. III, 1047–48. The Virginia delegation did not desire the resignation of Seddon, as illustrated by the following: "It would not have been proper to point out one man for partial action, least of all to single out the man from one state, as highly as we esteem him. . . . Seddon mistook the spirit of our advice. . . ." Statement by the Virginia Delegation, February 11, 1865, in *Richmond Daily Dispatch*, February 16, 1865.

to Seddon, who was of sterner stuff than the commander in chief, he would not have interfered with the decisions of military courts.

In Seddon's view there was no difference in kind between the enemy and the Southern slacker. His reports attest violent hatred of the North; in most of them Seddon refers to the Northern soldiers as plundering and ravishing barbarians. He often spoke of the "fanatic or insidious enemies," "Yankees and their allied hordes of miscreant foreigners," and "malignant foes." The Secretary would give no quarter to the destroyers of private property and the ravishers of women. His orders permitted Libby prison to be mined so that it might be blown up at the time of Colonel Ulric Dahlgren's raid when it was feared that Dahlgren might enter Richmond and release the Federal prisoners in Libby prison. Dahlgren's raid failed and some of his men were captured. Seddon advised that they be executed. Davis stood out against his Cabinet and saved the Northern prisoners from death. Similarly, whatever the praise or the blame for pardoning Confederate soldiers, it belongs to the President.

There was little truth in the Foote-Pollard assertion that the Secretary was a servile "pet" of Davis. At times the President overruled him but, on the whole, Seddon exerted a great influence on his chief and in many cases spurred the President from indecision to positive action. Cultivated gentleman and clear thinker that he was, Seddon dictated military policy to a far greater extent than any other secretary.

Jones's estimate of the Secretary was that he was an invalid scholar of refined and philosophical temperament, one more likely to imitate than to initiate. Seddon's appearance was deceiving. His vigor of action was in striking contrast to his frail body. He had natural talents in administrative affairs, and his fertile brain planned original schemes. He was receptive to suggestion and ready to hear complaints. He ordered that charges of deficiencies be investigated, and acted upon the findings either to correct an evil or to silence unfounded accusations. He was a man of resolute courage and determination, of whom the pro-administration *Richmond Sentinel* gave a fairly accurate picture in the following:

He was deemed the fittest man in the Confederacy for the station. He has rather exceeded than fallen short of public expectations. He has given renewed vigor to our arms. He occupies a station where great abilities have full opportunity for exercise and display . . . [and] whilst serving his country with industry, devotedness and success, has achieved a reputation that will place him on the pages of history along side of Davis and Lee.[139]

JOHN CABELL BRECKINRIDGE

Seddon's fall was the only Cabinet casualty of the movement in 1865 to limit the power of the President. Although Davis resisted Congressional interference, he determined to nominate for Secretary of War one who would be acceptable to Congress. In John Cabell Breckinridge he found the man. Breckinridge was one of the most famous men in the Confederacy and so popular with the Senate as to receive the privileges of the floor of that chamber. His name had been suggested as a possible successor to Secretary of War Walker in 1861.[140] Breckinridge was now willing to accept the appointment, and Davis sent in his name on February 6, 1865. The Senate immediately confirmed the nomination.

The new Secretary, then in his middle forties, had lived a full political life.[141] Born near Lexington, Kentucky, January 15, 1821, he was graduated from Centre College, practiced law, fought in the Mexican War, and settled down to a political career in 1849. Two years later he was elected to the United States House of Representatives, after serving in the lower house of the state legislature. In 1857 he was Vice-President of the United States, and four years later, a United States Senator. He worked for compromise at the outbreak of the war, but when that failed he retained his seat in the Senate to oppose President Lincoln. Late in 1861 he went to Richmond and was commissioned brigadier general and later was advanced to major generalship in the

[139] *Richmond Sentinel,* July 29, 1864.
[140] *Charleston Mercury,* October 28, 1861.
[141] For a full account of Breckinridge's life, see Lucille Stillwell, *John Cabell Breckinridge: Born to be a Statesman* (Caldwell, 1936).

Confederate army. His military career was distinguished by courage and bravery.

Breckinridge's career had an air of romantic adventure; his gallant appearance gave the impression of a man of the world, as indeed he was. He was tall, with a well-proportioned figure, shapely head, and pleasing features set off by a long, drooping mustache. He combined a keen sense of humor with frankness of nature. Few men could outdo him in cordiality of manner or chivalrous attitude toward women. He had few equals in his consumption of liquor and his ability at the same time to retain his sobriety. He was a queer combination of energy and indolence. He acted with vigor when thoroughly aroused, but he had to be spurred to action.[142]

Breckinridge was just the type of man Campbell was eager to have appointed Secretary of War. The Assistant Secretary knew far more about the department than his new chief could hope to learn in several months. Breckinridge realized this and referred matters to Campbell. As late as February 28, the Secretary was asking Campbell to explain to him the department's rules of procedure. Campbell, who was an independent thinker, had been convinced for some time that the Confederacy was facing inevitable defeat, and he wished to have reports from all the government bureaus listing what material or men they had on hand, and giving their opinions as to the outlook for the future. He believed that a digest of these reports would convince even the most optimistic of the futility of continuing the struggle. He believed, too, that peace could be arranged once the Confederate authorities assented to negotiations, and he hoped to stop useless bloodshed by a reconstruction of the old Union.

Breckinridge, by his own account, took over the War Department on Sunday, February 5, one day prior to the confirmation of his appointment. Two days later requests were sent out from the department to the chiefs of all government bureaus requesting from each a "clear statement of the means and resources" on hand and an estimate of the ability to continue operation.[143]

---

[142] Basil Wilson Duke, *Reminiscences of General Basil W. Duke, C.S.A.* (New York, 1911), 193.

[143] *Official Records*, Ser. IV, Vol. III, 1064.

Campbell called for these reports, a contemporary later wrote,[144] and the prevailing note of pessimism in the replies astounded Breckinridge. The bureau heads could see little hope of continuing the struggle; after digesting the reports Breckinridge decided that the key to continued operation was the Treasury Department. The failure of the Confederacy to reimburse owners for the supplies it impressed, and its inability to pay the soldiers and to meet contracts had discredited the government and spread discontent throughout the country. Breckinridge concluded that it was "plainly impracticable for this Department [War] to carry on any of its operations under such a condition of things." [145] Such a statement amounted to a confession that the Confederacy might as well sue for peace on the victor's terms.

Breckinridge considered the Confederate cause lost. After the failure of the Hampton Roads Conference he met with a few Confederate Senators to discuss the hopeless situation. The Secretary was more concerned about the plight of the Confederate soldiers from Kentucky and Missouri than with ways and means of continuing the war. He knew that, when the collapse finally came, these soldiers would be disbanded far from home with no means provided for their return. To avert hardships for others, he desired the complete surrender of the government before its forces should be captured piece by piece and the magnificent epic end in a "farce." [146] He himself was willing to surrender and take the consequences.

Meanwhile, Campbell, in an unsolicited letter, urged the necessity for an early surrender.[147] He pointed to the depleted reserves of food and materials, and explained that the commissary department found it almost impossible to obtain food, clothing, fuel, or forage for which the transportation facilities were inadequate. The government had a reserve of 25,000 arms, he wrote, but all foreign supplies were cut off and since the revoca-

144 William Edgar Hughes Gramp, *The Journal of a Grandfather* (St. Louis, 1912), 115.

145 Breckinridge to Davis, February 18, 1865, in *Official Records*, Ser. IV, Vol. III, 1094.

146 Stillwell, *John Cabell Breckinridge*, 132.

147 Campbell to Breckinridge, March 5, 1865, in John A. Campbell, *Reminiscences and Documents Relating to the Civil War During the Year 1865* (Baltimore, 1887), 26–31.

tion of army details for October, the domestic munitions industry had ceased production. Desertion increased steadily and had long since lost any stigma of cowardice. Every government bureau was paralyzed for lack of money or credit. The only sensible course, Campbell held, was to accept the old Union. Such action did not mean destruction "unless our people should forget the incidents of their heroic struggle and become debased and degraded." [148] It was the duty of a statesman and patriot, he maintained, to make peace in order to avert destruction of the Southern people.

It required no urging to convince Breckinridge that the Confederacy was doomed. During March he passed most of his time on the battlefield or in conference with men whose opinions coincided with his own. He wrote few letters in his capacity as Secretary of War. Both before and after the peace conference, Campbell, to all purposes, did the real work of the department. Breckinridge had a high opinion of Davis's courage, and the two men often conferred; but there could be no unity of purpose where one man was planning some way for the return home of his fellow Kentuckians, and the other was seeking to renew the people's will to independence and to continue the war.

The Secretary, however, was instrumental in at least one instance in effecting a major change in the departmental personnel. This was the removal of the very unpopular Colonel Lucius B. Northrop as the Commissary General of Subsistence, and the appointment in his place of Colonel Isaac Munroe St. John. Breckinridge ordered this change, he said later, because he had found the commissary department in a deplorable condition. [149] It was Jones's opinion, based on what he had heard, that the new Secretary, before accepting appointment to the War Department, had demanded the right to replace Northrop. [150] Breckinridge as Secretary made one suggestion of importance as to military strategy. He believed that the South's only hope lay in the annihilation of Sherman, and he proposed a concentration of forces by withdrawing from points of secondary im-

[148] *Ibid.,* 31.
[149] Breckinridge to St. John, May 16, [18]71, in Rowland (ed.), *Davis,* VIII, 356–57.
[150] Jones, *Diary,* II, 395.

portance. With a force equal or superior to Sherman's army and under the command of General Lee, he believed, a quick thrust might capture the audacious Yankee with all his desirable equipment. ". . . something of this sort must be done at once," the Secretary wrote Lee, "or the situation is lost." [151] Lee concurred, but stated that there were no troops. The people of the Confederacy had given their all to the fight and did not have the power to make further resistance.

When Richmond could no longer be defended and the Confederate administration was in flight southward, Secretary Breckinridge remained with the army. It was his duty to see that plans were made for the subsistence of the remnant of Lee's army. From this time on, Breckinridge ceased to regard himself as Secretary of War; he was a general in the saddle. He joined the Cabinet at Greensboro, North Carolina, but soon left to meet General Johnston and to make terms with General Sherman.

Breckinridge played a minor part in the negotiations with Sherman, which he entered as a major general, not as the Secretary of War. The meeting had its humorous side. The Secretary was in a dull and somber mood, induced by the circumstance that he had not been able to obtain his usual supply of liquor. On his arrival General Sherman suggested a round of drinks before beginning the work of the conference. John S. Wise has described what followed.

General Johnston said he watched the expression of Breckinridge at this announcement, and it was beatific. Tossing his quid into the fire, he rinsed his mouth, and when the bottle and the glass were passed to him, he poured out a tremendous drink, which he swallowed with great satisfaction. With an air of content he stroked his mustache and took a fresh chew of tobacco.

Then they settled down to business, and Breckinridge never shone more brilliantly than he did in the discussion which followed. . . .

Afterwards, when they were nearing the close of the conference, Sherman sat for some time absorbed in deep thought. Then he arose, went to the saddlebags, and fumbled for the bottle. Breckinridge saw the movement. Again he took his quid from his mouth and tossed it

[151] Breckinridge to Lee, February 21, 1865, in *Official Records*, Ser. I, Vol. XLVI, Pt. II, 1245.

into the fireplace. His eye brightened, and he gave every evidence of intense interest in what Sherman seemed about to do.

The latter, preoccupied, perhaps unconscious of his action, poured out some liquor, shoved the bottle back into the saddle-pocket, walked to the window, and stood there, looking out abstractedly, while he sipped his grog.

From pleasant hope and expectation the expression in Breckinridge's face changed successively to uncertainty, disgust, and deep depression. At last his hand sought the plug of tobacco, and, with an injured, sorrowful look, he cut off another chew.

Later the thirsty major-general remarked: "General Johnston, General Sherman is a hog. Yes, sir, a hog. Did you see him take that drink by himself?" [152]

Breckinridge's one drink, as it turned out later, was all that the Confederacy netted from the conference. He rejoined the Cabinet at Charlotte, and continued on to Washington, Georgia, with Davis. There he left the President, and added one more adventure to a career replete with them in escaping capture by the Federal forces.

There is not much to record of Breckinridge as Secretary of War. Although Jones was greatly impressed by him as compared to his predecessors, he was really less the secretary than a military commander while head of the War Department. He made no reports and wrote few letters. The idea for a survey of the Confederacy's resources, made while he was secretary, was suggested by Judge Campbell who was, in fact, Breckinridge's locum tenens in the department. Breckinridge indeed was realistic in his judgment as to the Confederacy's chances of surviving. Though he remained constant in his adherence to the President and stood by his duty to the very end, he would have favored a complete surrender of the Confederacy in February of 1865.

[152] John S. Wise, *The End of an Era* (Boston, 1900), 451–52.

V

Judah Philip Benjamin: Jack-of-All-Trades

JUDAH PHILIP BENJAMIN has been called "the brain of the Confederacy." His service to the Confederate government was rendered as head, successively, of three departments: Justice, War, and State. His work cannot be adequately treated except as a unit.

Benjamin had achieved a measure of recognition as an able lawyer and an eloquent member of the United States Senate before the Confederacy was formed. In his adopted state of Louisiana, he was the protégé of Slidell and, as such, had been accepted by its political leaders. Slidell had found Benjamin a useful and intelligent colleague in the politics of the state. Benjamin had not attained great distinction, however, as a Southern leader. When the Confederate government was organized he accepted a minor Cabinet appointment that more ambitious men had declined. He rose from the comparatively lowly post by his tact and ability to the direction, first, of the War, then of the State Department. The war had not been in progress a year when he became Davis's chief adviser.

Benjamin had had an interesting and varied life before he entered the Confederate Cabinet. He was born of Jewish parents on Saint Croix Island, August 6, 1811.[1] He was taken to Wilmington, North Carolina, and then to Charleston, South Carolina, where he lived during his early boyhood. His father was none too successful in business. His relatives and other benefactors aided young Judah to attend the Fayetteville Academy in North Carolina, a private academy in Charleston, and three

---

[1] Robert Douthat Meade, *Judah P. Benjamin: Confederate Statesman* (New York, 1943), 6. This is the best and most recent biography of Benjamin.

years at Yale University. He decided in 1828 to seek his fortune in the deep South and arrived in New Orleans with a total capital of five dollars.[2] For four years he worked at odd jobs, taught school, studied law, and was admitted to the bar. He married Marie Augustine Natalie St. Martin, a devout Roman Catholic, in 1833. When he had accumulated a fortune through his law practice, almost ruining his eyes at the same time, he invested some of his earnings in the Bellechasse sugar plantation. A disastrous flood and the failure of a friend to pay a note Benjamin had endorsed resulted in a financial loss and the sale of his new interest in Bellechasse.[3]

He began his political career in 1842 as a Whig member of the lower house of the Louisiana State Assembly. Ten years later he had been elected to the United States Senate. He drew gradually closer to the Democratic party as he realized that his own party was losing its national importance, and in May, 1856, he formally announced his switch from the Whig to the Democratic party. Three years later he was re-elected to the Senate on the Democratic ticket by a close vote. In the Senate he had never been a rabid Southern nationalist, although he had upheld what he considered the rights and honor of the South. He had favored the "Alabama Platform" at the Democratic national convention in 1860, and had approved the withdrawal of the Louisiana delegation from the convention. After the election of Lincoln, Benjamin believed that the South could no longer hope for equitable treatment from the North and the Republican party. He joined the secessionist movement at the last moment; he was not, however, elected to represent his state at the Montgomery convention. When Louisiana seceded from the Union, Benjamin resigned his seat in the Senate to return to his law practice.

Benjamin was unimpressive in appearance. Of less than average stature, his lack of inches was accentuated by his breadth of shoulders, large hands and feet, and rotund body. His features were pronouncedly Hebraic, and his full face, swarthy complexion, and short black beard were additional Jewish characteristics. An expression, half smile, half leer, hovered always upon his lips. His bright black eyes were unusually large, but

[2] Butler, *Benjamin*, 32.   [3] Meade, *Benjamin*, 89.

they did not focus perfectly. The casual observer, seeing him from a distance, would have set him down as a shopkeeper, prosperous and well-fed, but altogether undistinguished.

A realization of the strength of the Secretary's personality became apparent as one conversed with him. His manner was alert and pleasing, his voice soothing, his talent as a raconteur amusing, and his store of anecdotes seemingly inexhaustible. He could be frank and open in conversation, or reserved and diplomatic, as the exigencies of the moment might dictate. Consummate actor and student of human nature that he was, Benjamin had the gift of adapting himself to the character of every friend or acquaintance. His enemies characterized his suave manner as "oily." Although he could be deferential and complaisant, he allowed no one to treat him contemptuously. Any insinuations against his person or his race were promptly answered in kind. He was tactful, but proud and independent.

His philosophy of life was to live in and for the present, and it had a quality of Oriental fatalism. For him events of his past held little interest, and to what lay ahead of him he gave even less thought; one should live, act, and accomplish in the few fleeting moments of the present. When he had a given task before him, Benjamin would exert every effort to its accomplishment. If success attended his labor, he wasted no time in exulting over attainment; if failure came, there were no vain repinings. He did his utmost as an official of the Confederacy to achieve the goal of Southern independence. When the cause of the Confederacy was lost, he forgot it, turned his back upon the scene of his labors, and took up life anew in a distant country. Many of his contemporaries in the South believed that Benjamin had more brains and less heart than any other civic leader in the Confederacy.[4]

ATTORNEY GENERAL

The post of Attorney General was first offered to William L. Yancey. Jefferson Davis realized that nothing short of a miracle could transform Yancey into a constructive executive secretary.

[4] Wise, *The End of an Era*, 176.

In the hope of forestalling his acceptance of a Cabinet appointment, the alternative of representing the Confederacy in Europe was dangled before the eyes of the fiery Alabamian. Yancey disdained the obscurity of the attorney-generalship and accepted what he regarded as the better of two poor offices available to him.

Further political dickering ensued, and Benjamin was invited to become Attorney General. His selection was made, according to the President's account, because of his great reputation as a lawyer, his intellectual gifts, systematic habits, and capacity for labor.[5] Davis had known the rotund Senator from Louisiana, but they had not been on intimate terms of friendship. Benjamin on one occasion in the Senate had demanded from the future President of the Confederacy an apology or satisfaction for remarks that Benjamin regarded as slighting. The Senator from Mississippi, after the manner of a gracious Southern gentleman, had made a full apology before the Senate. Now his nomination of Benjamin was confirmed by the Senate on March 5, 1861, without a show of opposition.

In comparison with other departments, the office of Attorney General was a minor one, but officially it ranked as an equal in the Cabinet family. The Confederacy's scheme of government did not provide for a Department of the Interior, which savored too much of Federal paternalism, but gave the affairs which were logically domestic into the care of the first Department of Justice known in American history.[6] The department consisted of the office of the Attorney General (an assistant was later provided), the patent office, the bureau of public printing, and the legal office. Benjamin's duties as Attorney General included the organization of Confederate courts; representing the government before the Supreme Court, when and if that body should be provided for; general supervision of the court officials and the various divisions in the departments; organization of the ter-

---

[5] Davis, *Rise and Fall*, II, 242.

[6] William M. Robinson, Jr., "Legal System of the Confederate States," *Journal of Southern History*, II (1936), 464. The standard work on the Confederate Department of Justice and the Confederate legal system is *id., Justice in Grey: A History of the Judicial System of the Confederate States of America* (Cambridge, 1941). The United States Department of Justice was not established until 1867.

ritories; and advising the President and executive secretaries. The Attorney General was not overtaxed with work at a time when the country was in a state of upheaval caused by the war, and when the thoughts of the nation were concentrated on military activities.

The newly appointed Attorney General set himself immediately to the task of organizing his department and finding suitable judges, district attorneys, and marshals for the district courts. The department was in good working order, the *Charleston Mercury* reported on April 5, with all the Confederate courts established and their officers appointed. This statement was inaccurate, however, for the courts of Mississippi and Texas had not then been organized, because the judges selected in those states had declined the proffered appointments. Political expediency, as well as the factor of ability, entered into the selection of the court officers. In many cases men were appointed who had made no applications either directly or through their friends, and who did not desire the posts. Benjamin in due time completed the organization of his department and had ample time to concern himself with other matters.

Occasionally the heads of departments requested of him opinions as to the meaning of an act of Congress. Secretary Memminger, for instance, desired to know whether lemons, oranges, and walnuts should be classified as agricultural products, and, therefore exempt from tariff duties. The Attorney General in reply reasoned that walnuts were products of the earth, but as they were not the fruits of man's cultivation of the soil, they were not agricultural products. Oranges and lemons, on the other hand, were the result almost solely of cultivation, and hence were agricultural products. The conclusion naturally followed that the citrus fruits were not subject to duty, while walnuts were.[7] Benjamin, in all, rendered thirteen opinions in answer to questions submitted to him by members of the administration.[8] Seven of them were for Secretary of War Walker and related to the organization of the army, pay of soldiers, and appoint-

[7] Benjamin to Memminger, April 1, 1861, in "Records of the Confederate Attorneys-General," New York Public Library, *Bulletin*, II (1898), 196–98.

[8] Opinion Book, Opinions of the Confederate Attorneys-General, 1861–1865, New York Public Library, 2–23.

ment of officers. Of the remaining seven opinions, three were for
Secretary Memminger, and one each for President Davis, Postmaster General Reagan, and Assistant Secretary of State Browne.
Some of the questions submitted to him for opinions were of
trivial nature, but Benjamin gave all of them thoughtful consideration. In rendering an opinion he first posited the question,
then developed his argument, and in clear and definite terms
stated his conclusion.

The Department of Justice was too small for one of Benjamin's
energy and versatility. Hardly had he arrived in Montgomery
to assume the duties of his office, when he was telling an audience
that only through war could the South maintain its independence.[9] Soon it was known that Benjamin had more time to see
the crowds of importunate office seekers than any other executive in the administration. The Southern place-seeker came, not
as a supplicant for a job, but as a patriotic and public-spirited
gentleman offering his valuable services to the government. He
demanded an audience with the Executive, and to be turned
away without seeing him would have been considered an insult.
To refuse the applicant and yet retain his friendship for the
administration called for the exercise of a high degree of tact
and finesse. No one could accomplish this feat so effectively as
Benjamin. Government attachés, when in doubt, referred the
stranger to the office of the Attorney General.[10] Even the humblest caller who insisted, however, would be conducted to the
President by Benjamin.

During these early months of the Confederacy, Benjamin
became the official greeter of those who came to the capital to
observe the government at work. It fell to his lot to receive and
entertain distinguished citizens as well as inquiring foreigners.[11]
William Howard Russell found him the most open, frank, and
cordial of all Confederate officials.[12] The correspondent of the
London Times learned from him of the government's policies
and the work being done. Two Yankees would be hanged for
every Southern privateer treated as a pirate, the bellicose Secre-

[9] *Daily Richmond Enquirer,* March 9, 1861.
[10] James Morris Morgan, *Recollections of a Rebel Reefer* (Boston, 1917), 38.
[11] Butler, *Benjamin,* 230.
[12] Russell, *My Diary North and South,* 70.

tary vowed. Benjamin's contacts with the President increased as the Secretary received each day the constant flow of visitors and office seekers. The President quickly perceived the Secretary's value to him and called on him for many duties, at first of a minor nature, then more important as time passed. Benjamin's pleasing manner, no less than his methodical habits, promptness, and attention to his duties, appealed to Davis. The relations between the two men daily grew closer and their mutual regard ripened into warm friendship. Benjamin was by no means a yes man, but he had a realization of the relationship that should exist between Cabinet secretaries and the President. No task was regarded by Benjamin as too insignificant for him; his loyalty to the Confederacy was palpable and though at times he differed in opinion with the President, he never sulked or displayed temper when overruled.[13] His neatness, his conservative attire, and his calm unpretentiousness in the midst of arrogance and selfishness impressed Davis. The Attorney General really was as ambitious as other men, but he was more subtle, as well as more successful, in his efforts to achieve promotion.

Presidential errands brought Benjamin into all departments of the government. By August, he had become a frequent visitor at the War Department, and the diarist Jones noted that rumors were current that the Attorney General aspired to the office of the Secretary of War.[14] The observing war clerk was certain that Benjamin's influence with the President would be great, for the Secretary had studied the President's character most carefully and had become familiar with his likes and, more particularly, his dislikes. Already there was talk that Benjamin had too great an influence on the President in matters relating properly to the War Department.

Secretary Walker was having his troubles in that department. The rush of office seekers, the importunities of Southern patriots willing to join the army if commissioned as officers, and the tremendous task of directing an army had proved too much for him. His health failed in June, 1861, the work of the department fell behind in consequence, and stinging criticism of his conduct of the office added to his worries. In September he resigned. The

13 Butler, *Benjamin*, 239.   14 Jones, *Diary*, I, 71.

President on September 17 appointed Benjamin as acting Secretary of War.[15]

The former Louisiana statesman had come a long way in a short time. Within a period of less than seven months he had progressed from the office lowest in the scale of government departments to the most important of all. The Department of Justice had served him well as an apprenticeship. He had shown his willingness to work hard for the cause and had seized every opportunity to serve. It was plain that he had great potential ability; his tact and knowledge of men did the rest. In his immediate need for an executive to succeed Walker, the President naturally turned to Benjamin.

Not much can be said either in praise or adverse criticism for Benjamin as Attorney General. He organized the department, set the various bureaus in motion, and established the system of Confederate justice by the appointment of judges, attorneys, marshals, and other officers. He rendered a few legal opinions for other secretaries, but any able lawyer could have performed the same service. His administration of the Attorney General's office was capable but not brilliant. He left the office virtually unnoticed by the Southern newspaper press. It was as an individual that Benjamin stood out, and he was to have in the War Department the opportunity to demonstrate his true worth.

SECRETARY OF WAR

As Congress was not in session, Benjamin was appointed Secretary of War *ad interim*. It is evident that the President considered the appointment a stopgap until a permanent secretary could be found, for Benjamin continued to act as Attorney General. The *ad interim* Secretary's habitual smile seemed, to Jones at least, to fade as he realized the importance of his post and its arduous duties, but he was robust in health and equal to any demands the office should make upon him. Perhaps, the diarist added, Benjamin's smile had vanished because he realized his appointment was temporary; but again, perhaps, the President

15 For the story of Walker, see pp. 104–120.

would make the appointment permanent, because Benjamin knew how to please the Chief Executive.[16]

In the meantime there were speculations upon the probable choice for the permanent appointment. Major General Leonidas Polk, formerly a Bishop of the Episcopal Church, was suggested by the *Richmond Examiner* as a selection the public would approve. Major General Felix K. Zollicoffer, John Branch of North Carolina, John C. Breckinridge, and Robert E. Lee were other names suggested for the appointment. There was no need for haste, the *Examiner* concluded, for the position "is now filled by a man of most varied ability, who has never failed to master any business he undertook, and whose wonderful capacity for work will qualify him for grappling with the herculean labours of the office." [17] The *New Orleans Picayune* believed that Benjamin's adaptability would enable him to be more than satisfactory and hoped that Yancey could be recalled to fill the Attorney General's office.[18]

Benjamin immediately became a popular Secretary of War, if contemporary newspaper comment accurately reflected public sentiment. The *Picayune*'s correspondent considered Benjamin well fitted for the war office, despite a lack of military knowledge.[19] The *Richmond Dispatch* believed that Benjamin proved his eminent qualifications for the post while Acting Secretary of War, and in the opinion of the *Petersburg Express* Benjamin was better qualified for the position than any other man.[20] A correspondent of the *Charleston Courier* wrote:

Renewed vigor and industry characterize the War Department. The new Secretary, Mr. Benjamin, (let us hope he will be the permanent appointee) is just the man for the position. No one comes for an interview with him who does not speak in terms of wonder and admiration at his quickness of perception and promptness of decision. He dispatches more business in one hour than most men could accomplish in a day. Though he entered the Department comparatively

16 Jones, *Diary*, I, 79.
17 *Daily Richmond Examiner*, September 19, 1861.
18 *New Orleans Daily Picayune*, October 12, 1861.
19 *Ibid.*, October 19, 1861.
20 *Richmond Daily Dispatch*, November 22, 1861; *Petersburg Daily Express*, October 21, 1861.

unacquainted with its details, in a few days he had made himself thoroughly conversant with the whole scope and range of his duties as a War Minister. Mr. Benjamin is one of the most extraordinary men in America, and is almost indispensable to the Confederacy. No public man has a larger share of the confidence of the President.[21]

A sour note in all this paean of newspaper praise was struck by the *Charleston Mercury*, which, although not doubting Benjamin's ability, feared he was an ardent supporter of defensive warfare.[22] The newspapers, as was so often the case, had no factual basis for their praise of the acting Secretary. They were merely quoting rumors that the former Attorney General had brought new life into the War Department and was acting promptly on all questions, which they regarded as a pleasing contrast to the unsystematic methods of the former head of the department. It was no surprise, therefore, when the President nominated Benjamin for the permanent secretaryship and the provisional Congress confirmed the appointment on November 21, 1861, without referring it to a committee.

The new Secretary had already found the duties of the War Department extremely arduous. Jones reports that on one occasion he saw Benjamin surrounded by a large circle of visitors, without the slightest idea as to whom he should see next. His predecessor, Walker, had made the mistake of personally attending to the details of the department, with the result that important business was delayed. Benjamin introduced a more systematic policy by which the office was enabled to keep up with its duties. He carefully allotted tasks, delegated authority, and disposed of accumulated correspondence. He was a hard worker, but he was not by any means a slave to his office. He so planned it that the routine work of the department was carried on by subordinates, thus affording the Secretary more time for official conferences or for personal affairs.

Benjamin came to the War Department at a critical time. Walker had organized the department and directed the work of creating an army. War materials, such as gunpowder, shot and shell, guns and heavy artillery, were scarce. The first available

[21] *Charleston Daily Courier*, October 6, 1861.
[22] *Charleston Mercury*, October 30, 1861.

supplies of these necessities of war had been sadly depleted, and as yet the hoped-for importations from Europe had not arrived. Domestic facilities for production of war materials were in course of being completed, but at the moment, and for some months to come, the scarcity was acute and the outlook dark. The country was in a glow of enthusiasm over one victory and felt that the danger from "Bull Running Yankees" could not be great. There was danger that national overconfidence might easily bring disaster. Benjamin faced an almost impossible task in the fall of 1861.

In his first report to the President, Secretary of War Benjamin emphasized the need for soldiers, stating that he viewed with fear the time when the twelve-month enlistments should expire. Experience had definitely proved the bad features of short-term enlistments, he said. A recruit's first months were passed in instruction camps and by the time he was fit for active service winter had set in, with consequent inactivity. Benjamin placed the average time of usefulness of a twelve-month volunteer at only three months. The system not only was extremely costly, but, more important, it also prevented the army from being welded into an efficient unit. The Secretary urged a policy of granting moderate furloughs and liberal bounties for re-enlistment.[23] Congress acted on this recommendation by voting a grant of fifty dollars to soldiers whose term of enlistment was extended for three years, and furloughs of not more than sixty days to men who had enlisted for twelve months.

Benjamin in December, 1861, continued to urge the necessity for long-term enlistments. In a brief review of the situation, he stated that when he first took office the department in a single day refused as many as five thousand volunteers for the twelve-month term of enlistment. When it was realized that the government would not accept troops for less than three years unless they furnished their own arms, there was a great increase in long-term enlistments. The state governments, however, began to raise independent armies, to keep their arms and ammunition within their states, and to call for short-term volunteers for their state forces. This had the effect of inducing companies that were

[23] Benjamin to Davis, November 30, 1861, in *Official Records*, Ser. IV, Vol. I, 763.

ready to be mustered into the service of the Confederacy to march out for service with the state forces, lured by the attraction of enlistment for a term of three to six months. Against this ruinous state policy the Confederacy could only interpose the weight of reasoning. The Secretary, in closing his review, declared that the cost of war conducted under the six-month enlistment term would be three times as much as one fought under a three-year term.

In his third report to the President the Secretary summed up the work done by his department during the four months just ended. Although only 15,000 stands of arms had been imported, 9,000 more were expected to be received within the next few months. Between the government and private sources, 110 tons of gunpowder and more than $2,500,000 worth of blankets, medicines, and other supplies had been added to its store of war materials. The attention of the department had been mainly directed toward the development of the Confederacy's domestic resources, and the manufacture of powder had reached a production of three tons per day. The foundries had delivered an average of three field guns daily since August. Contracts had been let for thousands of tons of iron, shot and shell, and saltpeter; and departmental lead mines were producing about ten tons of that metal each day. The department also had in operation woolen mills, a large wagon factory, and miscellaneous plants making harness, tents, and camp equipment. In February, 1862, the army strength was 435 regiments, about two thirds of the troops being twelve-month men. Four fifths of these short-term volunteers, Benjamin was sure, would re-enlist for the duration of the war under the inducements of bounties and furloughs.

At the request of Congress for information on the military needs of the Confederacy, the Secretary stated that 350,000 men, 500,000 small arms, 1,000 pieces of artillery, 2,000 tons of powder, and appropriations of $200,000,000 were additional requirements.[24] The Secretary, realizing that this was impossible of fulfilment at the time, stated the minimum requirements as 200,000 rifles, 20,000 pistols, 500 Blakely guns, and 1,000 tons of powder. The President in his communication to the House

[24] *Id.* to *id.,* March 4, 1862, *ibid.,* 970.

of Representatives tripled Benjamin's estimate of the number of rifles needed, and asked for five times the quantity of powder and guns the Secretary had named.[25] By March 15, Benjamin was able to report that the Confederate powder factories had a capacity equal to the army's needs but that the supply of saltpeter was insufficient for making all the powder required. Not one tenth of the required quantities of small arms could be supplied by Southern factories. Nor could this latter situation be remedied, since farmers could not be converted by legislation into capable gunsmiths.

The army's needs were never supplied during Benjamin's incumbency of the War Department. Efforts to obtain materials in Europe were continued, but the results were disappointing. A brighter side was presented at home where a policy of encouraging private industry, through placing large contracts, and of establishing government-operated plants was proving satisfactory. Efforts to obtain war materials from the states, however, met with little success. The component parts of the Confederacy were never quite willing to entrust the entire defense of the country to the central government. Inability to obtain military equipment in sufficient quantity necessitated the refusal of many short-term volunteers,[26] for to have enlisted men for whom there were no guns would have increased the cost of the service. The department was never so fatuous as to heed the advice of the optimists who urged that it send unarmed men to fight the Yankees and obtain guns from the routed foe.

Benjamin in the course of his direction of the War Department soon incurred the hatred of General Joseph E. Johnston. The Secretary had been in office only a few days when he complained that the department had not had a single return from General Johnston's army as to the quantity of its ammunition, artillery, means of transportation, or the number of men rendered ineffective because of illness.[27] Benjamin never did receive satisfactory returns from Johnston; the latter, however, was soon

---

[25] Davis to the Speaker of the House of Representatives, March 4, 1862, *ibid.*, 969–70.

[26] Owsley, *State Rights in the Confederacy*, 22.

[27] Benjamin to Johnston, September 29, 1861, in *Official Records*, Ser. I, Vol. V, 883.

accusing the Secretary of interfering with the army. Most of the controversy arose over furloughs, the granting of which the department had hoped would stimulate enlistments for the duration of the war. Efforts to get the generals to furlough men were as a rule unsuccessful. Frequently, direct orders were sent to General Johnston to issue furloughs to soldiers whose names were given. The General complained that the Secretary granted furloughs, ordered troops into the military department, moved companies from point to point, and gave officers authority to raise companies among the twelve-month men, all without having notified him. Johnston appealed to the President, stating that Benjamin "has not only impaired discipline, but deprived me of the influence in the army, without which there can be little hope of success." [28] General Johnston found little satisfaction in the President's attitude.

Benjamin in turn complained that his orders, which did not invade the rights of a commander, were not executed, and asserted he could cite many instances to justify his charge of noncompliance.[29] Furloughs, to which Johnston objected, had been granted to avert possible legislation which threatened a wholesale system of leaves for the troops. It was suggested to General Johnston that spurious orders had been passed off on him, for the Secretary had not granted any furloughs within the past month. The President's support of Benjamin served to increase the bitterness of Johnston, who, according to Jones, declared "that there could be no hope of success as long as Mr. Benjamin was Secretary of War." [30]

General Thomas J. (Stonewall) Jackson soon objected to an order by Benjamin. Eleven officers protested on January 25, 1862, against being stationed in winter quarters at Romney, Virginia, and their action was approved by their commander, Brigadier General William Wing Loring. General Jackson forwarded the officers' petition with his disapproval to the War Department.[31] There were valid objections to the retention of Romney and on the receipt of intelligence of a move by the enemy to cut

---

28 Johnston to Davis, March 1, 1862, *ibid.*, 1086–87.
29 Davis to Johnston, March 4, 1862, in Rowland (ed.), *Davis*, V, 210.
30 Jones, *Diary*, I, 116.   31 *Official Records*, Ser. I, Vol. V, 1046–48.

off Loring's command, Benjamin instructed General Jackson to withdraw the forces and station them at Winchester. The order stirred up a hornet's nest. Jackson, on January 31, asked that either he be transferred from his command to his former professorship at the Virginia Military Institute, or that his resignation be accepted.[32] General Johnston immediately protested to the President, meanwhile holding up Jackson's resignation. Pressure was brought to bear on General Jackson to reconsider his request, which he did after obtaining assurance that his discipline would never again be interfered with. Brigadier General Loring was ordered to Georgia and his troops were given to other commands.[33]

Benjamin's popularity was greatly, and unjustly, hurt by the incident. Jackson's ability as a Confederate commander was everywhere recognized and, when it became known that the interference of the Secretary of War had nearly resulted in Jackson's resignation, Benjamin was the object of general anger. Benjamin's contemporaries were quick to condemn him. Even the able military historian Colonel G. F. R. Henderson wrote: "The omniscient lawyer asked no advice; . . . he had acted entirely on his own initiative." [34] The truth was that Benjamin sent the order at President Davis's direction.[35] Moreover, the petition of discontented officers at Romney had had little to do with the order of withdrawal. The military danger attending the occupation of Romney, not the discomfort of a few disgruntled officers, had influenced the President. General Johnston had been

[32] Jackson to Benjamin, January 30, 1862, *ibid.*, 1053.

[33] For an account of the Jackson-Benjamin controversy, see Douglas Southall Freeman, *Lee's Lieutenants: A Study in Command* (New York, 1943), I, 122–30.

[34] G. F. R. Henderson, *Stonewall Jackson and the American Civil War* (New York, 1934), 156. Henderson's statement is: "Mr. Benjamin's action was without excuse. In listening to the malcontents he ignored the claims of discipline. In canceling Jackson's orders he struck a blow at the confidence of the men in their commander. . . . Nor was his interference the crown of Mr. Benjamin's offense. The omniscient lawyer asked no advice; . . . he had acted entirely on his own initiative. It was indeed time that he received a lesson.

"Yet the Southern soldiers had never to complain of such constant interference on the part of the Cabinet as had the Northern; and to Jackson it was due that each Confederate general, with few exceptions, was henceforward left unhampered in his own theatre of operations." *Ibid.*, 156–57.

[35] Benjamin to Johnston, February 3, 1862, in *Official Records*, Ser. I, Vol. V, 1059.

instructed to visit Romney and, after an examination, to give the proper orders. Johnston, however, sent an inspector only as far as Winchester. "Had you given your personal attention to the case," the President wrote Johnston, "you must be assured that the confidence reposed in you would have prevented the Secretary from taking any action before your report had been received." [36] The President had acted in the absence of the required information because he feared Loring's command might be cut off. But these hidden factors did not become known for many years and the public condemned Benjamin because it credited the rumor that he had personally interfered with a general's command on behalf of a few malcontents.

Other commanders and state officials clashed with the Secretary of War. Benjamin refused to allow the execution of General Beauregard's orders to recruit a company to serve as a rocket battery. A wordy correspondence ensued, and the General threatened to resign because he was in a false position without a real command. The Secretary replied sharply, "It is not your position which is false, but your idea of the organization of the Army. . . . You are second in command of the whole Army of the Potomac, and not first in command of half the Army. . . ." [37] Beauregard therefore appealed to the President, but got no consolation from him. Davis, indeed, half apologized for the tone of Benjamin's letter, but assured the General that the Secretary had the highest regard for him. ". . . let me entreat you to dismiss this small matter from your mind," the President wrote, for "in the hostile masses before you, you have a subject more worthy of your contemplation." [38] Other controversies were those with Brigadier General Alexander Robert Lawton over the seizure of the army supplies at Savannah, and with Brigadier General Henry A. Wise about the defenses of Roanoke Island. Governor Brown of Georgia threatened to resist with force the Confederacy's impressment of railroad engines unless Benjamin acted to restrain his military subordinates.[39] The Secretary wrote to Governor Henry Toole Clark of North Carolina letters that

---

[36] Davis to *id.*, February 14, 1862, *ibid.*, 1071.
[37] Benjamin to Beauregard, October 17, 1861, *ibid.*, 904.
[38] Davis to *id.*, October 25, 1861, *ibid.*, 920.
[39] Joseph E. Brown to Benjamin, October 1, 1861, *ibid.*, Ser. IV, Vol. I, 666.

contained both plaintive appeals for cooperation and sharp rebukes. Departmental correspondence reflected no credit on either Benjamin or his critics.

Abundant evidence exists to support Benjamin's reputation as the most tactful man in the administration so far as his personal relationships were concerned. He was far from being tactful, however, in his correspondence. His letters showed little consideration for the touchy dignity of state executives and army officers. The fact that letters written to him were far more offensive than his own does not absolve Benjamin from blame. It was his job as Secretary of War to harmonize conflicting interests and obtain cooperative effort, and he failed to accomplish this. He was a man of action who pushed steadily forward to attain the broader objectives he had in view. In carrying out his program he made enemies of those whose friendship was needed by the administration. His controversies with generals engendered the enmities of important and popular army officials, from whom the common soldier took his cue. More and more the men in the ranks came to regard Benjamin as the embodiment of all they viewed as evil in the administration. In part, the cause of Benjamin's unpopularity can be traced to his correspondence with subordinate officials.

The military reverses of the Confederacy during his term of office, however, constituted the most important cause for the Secretary's unpopularity. While Walker was Secretary of War the people had been able to forget minor reverses because of smashing victories. A period of quiet had come after the battle of Manassas while both sides gathered their forces, and many a Southerner was puzzled and perturbed because the South's victorious army did not march upon Washington. As the period of inactivity lengthened some impatient ones expressed the belief that Benjamin's influence had been cast on the side of a defensive policy. By late winter the Union forces had taken the offensive, capturing the important Forts Henry and Donelson in the West and Roanoke Island on the east coast.

Only a minor share of the blame for the loss of the forts was laid upon Benjamin, but it was different in the case of the Roanoke Island disaster. The defense of the island had been entrusted in January, 1862, to Brigadier General Wise, a popular Virginia politician. Hardly had he reached his post when he asked for reinforcements of men and supplies. When he failed to obtain favorable action by correspondence, the General left his command and went to Richmond. Benjamin frankly told him that the department had little to give but would make every effort to obtain powder and guns. The Secretary endured Wise's constant demands until his patience gave out, then he ordered him back to his post. Wise not only failed, in a military sense, in not accomplishing as much as possible with the means he had, but he had also been insubordinate in going to the War Department over the head of his superior, General Benjamin Huger. On January 31, the Secretary wrote General Huger instructing him to take immediate and energetic steps to strengthen the island's defenses.[40] Far too little attention had been paid to General Wise's needs, however, and in a little more than a week a large Federal force captured the island, killing or taking prisoner most of its defenders.

News of this reverse shocked and dismayed the South more than any setback it had suffered thus far. Mixed with the popular anger was the fear that the island now in the enemy's possession would be used as a base for an attack on Richmond. The public's indignation centered on Benjamin. General Wise could show that he had repeatedly warned the War Department of the danger. Besides, his own son, Captain O. Jennings Wise, had been killed in the island's defense, and general sympathy, not disapproval, was expressed for the gallant Virginia leader.

Blame for the capture of Roanoke Island, in a final analysis, must be placed upon General Huger. His was the direct responsibility for the general defense of the sector in which the island was included. The War Department left the conduct of military operations to the commander, but urged him to pay particular attention to the island's defenses. There was not much Benjamin

---

40 Benjamin to Huger, January 31, 1862, *ibid.*, Ser. I, Vol. IX, 147. Benjamin had been impressed more by the facts presented in a report of Captain William Francis Lynch on the deficiences of the naval defenses of Roanoke Island than by the demands of General Wise. General Huger was instructed to give Captain Lynch men for his gunboats, although it meant weakening the force under Huger at Norfolk.

could have done without being accused of interference with commanders in the field. It was true that the War Department had not the men and munitions to reinforce General Wise, but the Norfolk sector had men and supplies in numbers and quantity equal, if not superior, to those possessed by other military departments. Had General Huger aided General Wise, or had the latter been an abler officer, Roanoke Island might have been saved. Any blame that may be laid to Benjamin is on the score that he erred in believing that the Federal attack would come at another place. It is true General Wise had made urgent appeals for aid, but nervous commanders were always sending the War Department reports of impending enemy attacks. Benjamin lacked the resources to strengthen the Roanoke Island defenses, and saw no reason to interfere with General Huger's military plans.

The loss of Roanoke Island revived the smoldering opposition to the administration. Benjamin was denounced as the sole cause of all Confederate disasters by Representative Henry S. Foote and other critics in Congress.[41] A Congressional investigating committee was appointed. The Secretary of War agreed that a strict inquiry should be conducted and invited Congress to make a thorough investigation.

In the meantime the newspapers began to criticize Benjamin. The *Southern Literary Messenger* in December, 1861, called him the "chief thief in a cabinet of liars." [42] The *Richmond Examiner* was dissatisfied with the War Department because of the paucity of news it gave out. Public opinion held, the newspaper reported, that this dearth of intelligence was a fixed policy of a busy War Department. Actually, however, its whole work, said this journal, was taken up with applications for office and the communications of a mutual admiration society in the army.[43] Benjamin was a very worthy and estimable gentleman, in the opinion of the *Petersburg Express,* but he did not possess the practical knowledge and military experience needed to head the War Department.[44] The Secretary had a defender in the *Savan-*

---

41 Jones, *Diary,* I, 118.
42 "Editorial," *Southern Literary Messenger,* XXXIII (1861), 466.
43 *Daily Richmond Examiner,* February 28, 1862.
44 *Petersburg Daily Express,* February 24, 1862.

nah Republican, whose editor suggested that Benjamin was under the direct control of the President.[45] The *Charleston Mercury* enlarged upon this idea at a later date, declaring that Benjamin was only the agent and instrument of a despotic Executive; responsibility for all the blunders and inefficiencies, the *Mercury* asserted, was practically and constitutionally on the commander in chief, Jefferson Davis.[46] The purpose of the press was to discredit the President, yet major censure fell on Benjamin.

The Secretary, however, had his defenders. A most elaborate vindication was that written by "Justice." [47] The position of Secretary of War under the old government had been considered arduous, said "Justice" in the *Petersburg Express,* but Benjamin had an army thirty times as large and a task fully sixty times as hard as any War Secretary of the United States had had before 1861. Less than a year ago the Confederacy had nothing; now it had nearly half a million men in the field and factories of all types in operation. The speed and efficiency with which this modern miracle had been accomplished was the wonder of the world, and virtually all of this had been done under the direction of Benjamin, who had toiled from early morning until after midnight. He did not work at useless tasks but with a purpose in mind, wrote "Justice," recalling that he had often visited the Secretary on business when from eighteen to twenty callers waited ahead of him. Yet Benjamin invariably would see all in less than an hour. "His keen perception enables him to seize at once upon the tangible points of each proposition, to form his conclusions upon it with the promptness of electricity, and announce them clearly and satisfactorily to his applicant."

Where could the President find another man of Benjamin's capabilities, "Justice" asked, should he heed the critics' advice and remove him?

Who has his shrewd common sense, his keen perception, his wonderful power of analysis, his perfect acquaintance with the law and usage of his department, his patience to listen, his industry to ascertain, and his quickness to decide, joined with his habits of labor, and

[45] *Charleston Mercury,* February 28, 1862, quoting the *Savannah Republican.*
[46] *Ibid.,* May 13, 1862.
[47] *Petersburg Daily Express,* February 26, 1862.

a power of physical endurance that enables him to bear ten or twelve hours of the severest mental labor with unflagging energy—for all these requisites are indispensable to the position? [48]

This praise was no more biased than Representative Foote's criticism. In the same breath, that legislator could trace all the disasters of early 1862 to Benjamin, and accuse him of being a "mere clerk" doing the will of the Executive.[49] Foote was not content to denounce the Secretary as inefficient; he also impugned his honesty in the Houmas land speculations. Benjamin, as his Congressional foe portrayed him, was incapable of directing any legitimate enterprise.

Disaster and criticism seemed only to strengthen the relations between the President and Secretary. The mutual respect that had existed from the first developed into a solid friendship. The President knew the handicap under which the Secretary labored. He understood that the public had unreasoningly visited upon Benjamin its rage and disappointment at Confederate defeats, reverses that rightly should be attributed, not to the War Department's remissness, but to the superiority in resources of an industrialized nation at war with an agrarian country. The President believed, too, that in the epistolary warfare between the Secretary and army officers, the latter had been more at fault than Benjamin. Davis had seen all the correspondence and, while conceding that Benjamin's letters were phrased like those of a lawyer, he considered them models of virtue compared to those written by glory-seeking generals like Johnston and Beauregard. Davis contrasted the touchy dignity and self-seeking of the generals with the Secretary's unassuming attitude. The President's admiration for Benjamin grew. The generals too often seemed to be upholding their positions by attempting to throw the blame for failures upon others, rather than striving to achieve the fundamental aim of national independence. Their vision did not extend beyond their own armies, the success of which would reflect honor upon the commanding officer. Benjamin, on the other hand, seemed to care little for the fleeting honor of the moment.

[48] *Ibid.*
[49] Henry S. Foote, *War of the Rebellion; or Scylla and Charybdis*, . . . (New York, 1866), 352.

He presented an indifferent front to praise and abuse alike. He was content to let false accusations go unchallenged, and he sought no personal acclaim. Davis believed in the Secretary's integrity of purpose, had faith in his ability, and increasingly sought his advice.

Benjamin's attitude toward the President was marked by respect and understanding. Never did he forget that he was an appointed subordinate to an elected chief. The ultimate responsibility for the loss or winning of the war would be the Executive's, and Benjamin considered that the President's should be the final voice in determining the policies of the nation. His tact enabled him to aid in directing the course of a President who wanted assistance. Davis followed Benjamin's advice more often than not. The President controlled where military planning was concerned, although he and Benjamin worked out the plans together. The Secretary had virtually a free hand in the business management of the department. The charge that he was no more than a clerk in his department had no basis in fact. He was the strong active head of the most important department of the government, just such a man as the President wanted in that post. Davis believed he had found in Benjamin the qualities he required for successful conduct of the War Department, and gave the Secretary his full confidence and support. Benjamin never abused either.

The two men had distinct and contrasting physical and mental characteristics. Benjamin, short in stature, and of well-fed appearance; the President, tall and gaunt, presented a study in opposites. Physically, Benjamin had a resiliency that the President did not possess; after a long, hard day's work the Secretary would still be fresh and full of energy, while the President would be a mass of jangled, throbbing nerves.[50] Davis, usually half-ill, must have envied Benjamin his powers of endurance and recuperation. Benjamin also enjoyed the advantage of a mental detachment that Davis lacked. The President's hypersensitiveness to criticism was matched by the Secretary's imperviousness to attacks. Benjamin's indifference to criticism went so far, in fact, that because of his failure to defend himself from accusations he

[50] Butler, *Benjamin*, 333.

shouldered much criticism that by right should have been directed at the President. Benjamin regarded it a Cabinet member's duty to ease the President's burden.

It was not strange that, under the circumstances, Davis resented the attacks upon his Secretary of War. The criticisms of Benjamin for the most part were vague and general. Only when they charged that he was responsible for the losses of Forts Henry and Donelson and of Roanoke Island were his critics specific. These reverses, in the President's opinion, could not justly be attributed to any ineptness or dereliction on the part of the Secretary. Davis desired to continue Benjamin at the War Department for considerations of the Confederacy's good, not less than for personal reasons of friendship. He made every possible effort to retain the Secretary when the permanent government was established in February, 1862, if the biased Foote can be credited. For a period of four weeks the President withheld the Cabinet nominations while pressure was exerted on Senators to accept Benjamin.[51]

Davis's opponents in the House of Representatives in the meantime sniped at the Secretary of War. On March 5, 1862, Representative Foote moved that the office of Secretary of War be abolished for the duration of the war, as the House had under consideration a bill to authorize the appointment of a commander in chief.[52] Later, Representative James W. Moore of Kentucky offered a resolution declaring a lack of confidence in the Secretary:

. . . J. P. Benjamin, as Secretary of War, has not the confidence of the people . . . nor of the Army, to such an extent as to meet the exigencies of the present crisis, and that we most respectfully suggest that his retirement from said office . . . is a high military necessity.[53]

Neither the move to abolish the War Department nor to pass a resolution of censure succeeded. The introduction of the resolution was farcical technically, because the new government had come into being in February. Neither Benjamin nor any other secretary would officially hold office until nominated by the President and confirmed by the Senate.

[51] Foote, *War of the Rebellion*, 356–57.   [52] *Journal of Congress*, V, 45–46.
[53] *Ibid.*, 57.

It would have been the part of wisdom for the President to have yielded in the matter of Benjamin's appointment. The continuance in office of one so cordially disliked by the army must have been detrimental to the Confederacy. The President, however, would not calmly accept defeat, but exerted every effort to obtain continued tenure for Benjamin. Only when Davis became certain that the Senate would not confirm Benjamin did he arrange a compromise by which Benjamin was promoted to be Secretary of State. Thus he salved his own conscience and made amends for the injustice done his friend and trusted adviser.

As acting and appointed secretary, Benjamin had conducted the War Department for a little more than six months.[54] It had been a period of stress for both the Confederate and Union armies, but especially for the former. Hope of an early recognition of the Confederacy as a result of the victory at Manassas had given way to fear of a long war. The Confederacy needed trained men and war supplies in order to defend a long frontier. It needed wise direction to unify and coordinate its potential power for defense. What, if anything, had Benjamin's efforts contributed to the strength of the South during his term of office in the War Department?

He had continued the policies adopted under his predecessor, Walker, the first Secretary of War, a cardinal policy which had been to promote the development of manufacturing in the South. Benjamin made little change in the plans for the domestic production of guns, powder, and camp equipment. By the end of his term, Southern factories were supplying the greater part of the Confederacy's requirements in the way of war materials; Southern powder mills could have produced all that the army needed had the raw materials been available. Another important policy of the department had been the supplementing of home production of munitions by purchases abroad. The government had sent its agents to Europe for this purpose; naturally, Benjamin continued this plan. But it had required

[54] Officially, Benjamin's term of office was from November 21, 1861, to March 17, 1862, but actually he directed the War Department from September 17, 1861, to March 24, 1862.

time to get the agents abroad. Often they had arrived only to find that agents of the United States, on a similar mission and better supplied with funds, had purchased the entire stock of available munitions. In such cases it had been necessary to make contracts, and the guns when manufactured had to be shipped to the Confederacy through a blockade which was fast tightening. To the layman, who knew little or nothing about the difficulties and unavoidable delays attending these foreign purchases, it seemed that too much time was lost. It was not until the very end of his term that any considerable amount of supplies reached the Confederacy from sources abroad. Little credit for the increase in war material can be given to Benjamin, for he merely carried out a policy of the department already in effect when he took office. Perhaps, however, he was more aggressive in his attack on the problem than Secretary Walker had been.

Next in importance to the task of obtaining war supplies was the problem of recruiting men for the armies. The Confederacy at first had enlisted for a short term of twelve months, but soon adopted the policy of accepting volunteers for the duration of the war only. An exception was made, however, in cases where a fully equipped company volunteered for a short term. Under Benjamin's administration of the department, this policy was continued, but with even greater emphasis upon the long-term enlistment. The problem of keeping short-term volunteers in the service was not solved by Benjamin. By the end of 1861, more than two thirds of the Confederate forces consisted of twelve-month volunteers; [55] at the end of Benjamin's term the situation had not appreciably improved. Benjamin was no more successful than Walker in satisfying the army's pressing need for long-term volunteers.

Subordinate to the War Department's two main problems— munitions and men—was the delicate matter of establishing and maintaining harmonious relations between the administration and commanders in the field. Sensitive generals had to be handled with tact. The records indicate Benjamin either failed to recognize this fact or chose to disregard it. He did not bring conciliation and a spirit of cooperation to the department; he left it

---

[55] Benjamin to Davis, December 31, 1861, in *Official Records,* Ser. IV, Vol. I, 796.

with military men and civil administrators at swords' points. Benjamin, supposedly a master of tactful dealing, had written letters whose repercussions had required the offices of the supposedly tactless President to smooth the ruffled feelings of recipients. Benjamin's conciliatory letters failed of their purpose because his phrases were too honeyed, or he too greatly emphasized his own hard work. The Secretary failed completely to bring into harmony the civil administration, the military commanders, and the state executives.

The great task before the War Department, one which was indeed the reason for its being, was to achieve military success against the enemy. Above all, the people demanded victory, and when it was not forthcoming they looked about for someone upon whom to fix the responsibility. Benjamin's conduct of the War Department was a failure from a military point of view, and he was blamed for reversals in the field. By the end of March, 1862, he was the most unpopular and most hated man in the Confederacy. Neither the army nor the people wanted him reappointed Secretary of War.

Benjamin had qualities as an executive that in a measure offset his faults. He was aggressive in conducting his work; he saw clearly what was needed; and he issued his orders promptly for the accomplishment of desired ends. He made mistakes, but at least he did not fear to try. Had the public been more patient in the face of the army's temporary reverses, Benjamin perhaps would have made a capable permanent Secretary of War. This was the opinion, at least, of the President, who was a good judge of men. In the performance of the purely administrative work of the department, Benjamin was businesslike and brought system and order to a disorganized department; correspondence was quickly answered and personal interviews were taken care of methodically and efficiently. Benjamin could soothe a complainant, turn down a job-hunter in such a manner as to make the rejection painless, and quickly detect whatever value a suggestion possessed. He was a force in promoting good feeling among the members of the Cabinet. In social intercourse, as well as in his official capacity, he could bring out a community of interests between differing personalities. His optimism and philo-

sophic temperament contributed to the development of an *esprit
de corps* that was of value to the administration. As an adviser
to the President he was in the Chief Executive's confidence, and
his counsel was excellent. The President respected him as a
secretary, and cherished him as a friend in whom he could confide
and upon whom he could place responsibility.

It is very doubtful whether any other Southerner, in identical
circumstances, could have accomplished more than Benjamin
did. He did not exhibit any great talent as a war administrator;
his administration, in fact, was not as productive in tangible
results as that of his predecessor. But Benjamin was an abler
executive than Walker, and a far more valuable assistant to the
President.

SECRETARY OF STATE

There was much speculation as to Hunter's probable successor in the State Department when it was definitely known that
he would not retain his Cabinet post. Benjamin's appointment,
however, had not been advocated or suspected by the newspapers.
The general desire was for the selection of William Cabell Rives,
said the *Savannah Republican*,[56] but "Hermes," the *Charleston
Mercury* correspondent, believed it was hardly likely that there
could be any accord between Rives and Davis.[57] The editor of the
Mercury suggested either James A. Seddon or William L. Yancey
for the post.[58] Seddon was a close personal friend of the President,
and was a distinct possibility for nomination as Secretary of
State. The *Mercury* on March 3, 1862, however, reported that
the *Richmond Examiner* had a new Cabinet in which Benjamin
held the portfolio of Secretary of State.

The members of the Louisiana delegation in Congress were
active in support of Benjamin for a Cabinet post. Several of them
lived with him and were his intimate friends. The President
nominated him for the post of Secretary of State and the Senate
confirmed the nomination. Edward Sparrow, one of the two
Louisiana Senators, voted against a reconsideration of Benjamin's

[56] *Savannah Republican* item, January 31, 1862, in Marcellus Stovall Scrapbook,
Southern Collection, University of North Carolina.

[57] *Charleston Mercury*, February 3, 1862.   [58] *Ibid.*, March 3, 1862.

confirmation, and Thomas Jenkins Semmes, Sparrow's colleague, voted for it.[59] Semmes favored Benjamin for the office; he voted with the opposition in order to be in a tactical position to move a reconsideration of the vote had it been against his fellow Louisianian. Both Senators on February 13, 1865, voted against the resolution declaring the nation lacked confidence in Benjamin.[60] Only one Louisiana representative voted in 1865 for printing the resolutions condemning Benjamin after his speech in the African Church.[61] The evidence is conclusive that Benjamin had the support of his fellow Louisianians.

Unquestionably, Benjamin's appointment to the State Department was unwise on the President's part. It would have been more astute of him to have retained Benjamin as an unofficial adviser or even as a Presidential aide "without portfolio." Benjamin had incurred too much enmity and unpopularity as Secretary of War for his retention in the Cabinet to be received with general favor. Strangely enough, his nomination did not cause any pronounced outcry from the press. Most of the newspapers quietly accepted the change, without reflecting in any great measure the resentment felt by the people. Benjamin had not been forgiven for the Roanoke Island disaster, however, and his appointment to another Cabinet position ostensibly higher in rank was regarded as a defiant gesture by the President. Benjamin's enemies had prevented his reappointment to the War Department, but they could not block his confirmation as Secretary of State. Their enmity persisted. They spread the idea that the "little Jew" was not only incompetent, but in his new post would have time to meddle in every department of the government. Nor did they omit to harp on the theme that Davis, in arbitrarily appointing an unpopular man to a Cabinet post, had flouted the will of the people. Criticism of the new Secretary of State became a handy vehicle for carrying the opposition's concentrated attacks on the President.

The Confederacy's foreign policy had been fairly well determined when its third Secretary of State took office on March 18,

---

[59] *Journal of Congress*, II, 73–74.   [60] *Ibid.*, IV, 552–53.
[61] *Ibid.*, VII, 582. Benjamin's confirmation by the Senate was accomplished with ease. There was a move to reconsider the confirmation but it failed.

1862. At the heart of this policy was the South's unshaken faith in the omnipotence of King Cotton and the inducements the Confederacy had to offer in the way of trade advantages. The South had counted on these trump cards to win foreign recognition of its statehood, but the State Department had succeeded in obtaining no more than an acknowledgment of the belligerent rights of the Confederacy. Nothing else of note had been accomplished. Benjamin's purpose, as it had been his predecessors', was to obtain foreign recognition of the Confederacy's independence.

The methods the new Secretary of State employed in his efforts to realize his goal are worth reviewing. For a time there was relatively little change in the department's policy. As before, the efforts to obtain foreign recognition were concentered on England and France. Benjamin had received no reports from the recently appointed commissioners to Europe and, in the absence of intelligence from them, the instructions of September 23 and February 8 remained unaltered.[62] The Secretary, however, charged the commissioners to stress the fact that, under the terms of the Declaration of Paris, a blockade to be binding must be effective. From first to last, Benjamin sent many reports to Mason and Slidell listing ships entering Southern ports, as evidence of the ineffectiveness of the blockade. The Secretary urged the commissioners to make it clear to the foreign governments that recognition alone would bring an end to the war; that the very fact of nonrecognition rendered Lincoln powerless to accept Confederate independence; and that, as long as neutral powers remained silent, the North would persist in believing the conquest of the South possible. On the other hand, recognition of the Confederacy by neutrals would be considered the verdict of an impartial jury, and a large part of the United States would then refuse to continue its support of the war. Recognition, the Secretary wrote, meant peace and the restoration of a prosperous intercourse with the South.[63] The twin arguments—the blockade's ineffectiveness and the idea that recognition meant peace,

---

[62] Benjamin to John Slidell, April 8, 1862, in Richardson (ed.), *Messages and Papers*, II, 216.

[63] *Id.* to James M. Mason, April 12, 1862, *ibid.*, 227.

not war, for England and France—became Benjamin's stock in trade, but he never made a sale.

In time, the Confederacy ceased to explain the reasons for secession or to attempt to show the legality of the act; instead it demanded recognition as a right. Particularly was this the case in dealing with minor nations that were regarded as of little value to the Confederacy. Lucius Q. C. Lamar, commissioner to Russia, was told that it was not necessary for him to maintain the right of secession, although he should explain the South's position if the Tsar's government should ask about it. Rather, Lamar was instructed to direct special attention to the fact that the Confederacy had already won its place among nations, and that lack of recognition encouraged the North to persist in waging a needless and hopeless war.[64] Similar instructions were given the commissioner to the Dutch government.[65] No longer would the Confederacy explain its course and beg for recognition. It would demand it as a right, and the demand should carry the implied threat of future commercial restrictions against a nation that withheld the right. This drastic change in policy was induced by the failure of the former method.

This demanding, half-threatening tone was not used at first

[64] *Id.* to L. Q. C. Lamar, November 19, 1862, *ibid.*, 365–67.

[65] *Id.* to Ambrose D. Mann, August 14, 1862, *ibid.*, 313–14. Benjamin wrote that at first it was proper for representatives of the Confederacy to explain the true nature of the former Union. "But, now, when appeal to the common sense of justice of the nations has failed to elicit any further response than a timid neutrality scarcely covering an evident dread of the power of our arrogant foe, we prefer speaking in other tones and insisting that an admission into the family of nations is a right which we have conquered by the sword. . . . The very nations that now halt and hesitate as to our power to maintain our independence are plainly withheld from its acknowledgment by their reluctance to provoking the hostility of a foe whom they fear, but whom we resolutely resist and overcome. . . . In the code of modern international law, the nation which presents itself with an organized government and an obedient people, with the institutions created by the free will of the citizens, and with numerous armies that crush all the attempts of the most powerful foe to subjugate it, which is aiming at no conquest, seeking no advantage and steadily bent on securing nothing but the inherent rights of self-government—such a nation may insist upon, and with some degree of stern self-assertion demand, its right of recognition from those who may expect hereafter to maintain with it relations of mutual advantage in the exchange of good offices and the freedom of commercial intercourse. It is preferred, therefore, that in any communication you may now initiate with the Dutch Court, while the utmost deference and courtesy are observed, the tone of official correspondence be placed on the high ground above indicated rather than on any argument in support of the justice of our cause."

toward England. As Benjamin became convinced that Queen Victoria's government would not respond to the milder representations, he was ready to adopt the bolder attitude. Mason advised that he be authorized to present a demand for recognition and to withdraw immediately if the English government should refuse it.[66] The President and Secretary of State discussed the advisability of adopting the suggestion. They agreed that Mason's attitude should not be one of supplication, but Benjamin was careful to point out that it would not serve any useful purpose for the commissioner to quit England.[67] Even though the British government refused recognition, a Confederate representative at the Court of St. James would be in a position to correct false opinions, and would be the center around which interests friendly to the Confederate cause would rally.

Almost a year later, Benjamin wrote Mason that the President, after studying the debates in Parliament, believed that England intended to take no action in the Confederacy's case. Mason was instructed, therefore, to leave London unless he judged that there was evidence of a possible change in the British Cabinet's attitude.[68] Mason saw no such evidence and after consulting with Slidell, he left England for Paris about October 1, 1863.[69] As far as England was concerned, the recourse to strong demands was no more effective than supplications had been.

Benjamin never quite understood why England stood out against recognition. He did his utmost to show the British that the blockade was ineffective, that recognition would not involve England with the United States but would stop a needless war, that the South could not be conquered, and that England would gain from a Confederacy dedicated to free trade. England politely rejected all these reassurances, as well as the appeal to its self-interest. Lamar, when visiting in Parliament, was elated to hear the cheers for the heroism of Confederate armies and the praise of the statesmanship of the Confederate leaders; but he was convinced that England had nothing but sympathy to offer the Confederacy. "They [England] will recognize us," he wrote,

---

[66] Mason to Benjamin, June 23, 1862, *ibid.*, 258.
[67] Benjamin to Mason, September 18, 1862, *ibid.*, 323.
[68] *Id.* to *id.*, August 4, 1863, *ibid.*, 540.
[69] Mason to Benjamin, September 25, October 2, 1863, *ibid.*, 572–74.

"when we conquer a recognition from the North—never before, unless forced to it by Louis Napoleon who is the only statesman in Europe." [70]

The attitude of British legislators toward the Confederacy was summarized by a friendly member of Parliament, William Henry Gregory, in a letter to William Porcher Miles.[71] He believed that nine tenths of the members of both houses favored the South, but that there was an almost universal disinclination to interfere in the war. In the first place, they believed the South could not be conquered. Recognition unless accompanied by intervention would be no more than an empty compliment. Recognition without intervention, Gregory's colleagues believed, instead of aiding the South would bring together Democrats and Republicans in the Union and stiffen the determination of the United States to continue the war until the South should be brought to its knees. Left alone, the South would win its independence. Gregory, in fact, spoke for a large number of British legislators who wanted a hands-off policy continued. Davis and Benjamin became convinced that the Confederacy could not hope for any help from England.

Benjamin attempted, almost from the time he took office as Secretary of State, to develop a cleavage in the common attitude of England and France toward the Confederacy. In expressing the belief that England would recognize the Confederacy only if forced to do so by Napoleon III, Lamar had echoed Benjamin's opinion. The Secretary of State, as early as April 12, 1862, sought some method of breaking the two nations' apparent concert of action in foreign affairs. He was convinced that their interests really conflicted.[72] He adopted the plan of giving the French Emperor an incentive to act independently of England. Slidell was instructed to suggest a commercial convention whereby, in return for the breaking of the blockade by Napoleon, French products would be admitted into the Confederacy free of duty. Furthermore, as a subsidy for the Emperor's depleted exchequer,

---

[70] Lamar to Virginia C. Clay, August 8, 1863, in Clay Papers.

[71] Gregory to Miles, April 9, 1863, in Miles Papers.

[72] Benjamin to Slidell, April 12, 1862, in Richardson (ed.), *Messages and Papers*, II, 228.

the Confederacy would deliver 100,000 bales of cotton at certain Confederate ports.

Slidell laid the proposal before the French government, offering cotton valued at 100,000,000 francs, free importation of French products during the war and for a short time thereafter, and a defensive and offensive alliance of the two nations for Mexican affairs. The plan was excellent in theory, but it failed to reckon with the troubled situation in Europe. Napoleon feared the rising tide of nationalism in Germany; he had made enemies by his sympathy for the rebellious Poles; and he dared not do anything that would offend England. The canny Emperor did not summarily reject the Confederacy's proposal. Slidell's reports, indeed, encouraged Davis and Benjamin to believe that there was hope of favorable action by France. But Napoleon would not act alone. He feared that his intervention would cause the United States to declare war against France, and he could not afford a war. He had too many enemies in Europe, and was none too popular with his own people in France.[73] In the end, Napoleon followed England's lead, and Davis and Benjamin concluded that the Emperor had double-crossed the Confederacy.

While negotiations with Napoleon were in progress Benjamin was trying another device to bring about recognition. He planned to create a material interest in the Confederacy for England and France by inducing their merchants to buy and store cotton, tobacco, rice, and naval stores in Southern ports. This was not an innovation, but Benjamin put new energy into it. He hoped that the British and French merchants would in the end force their governments to aid the South in order to prevent the confiscation of their goods in the event of the defeat of the Confederacy.[74] Benjamin also urged European merchants to store large depots of goods in West Indian islands until peace should actually be restored. With so much wealth at stake, he thought it possible that England and France would demand a six-month armistice between the North and South. Once the United States

---

[73] Owsley, *King of Cotton Diplomacy*, 564.

[74] Benjamin to Mason and Slidell, December 11, 1862, in Richardson (ed.), *Messages and Papers*, 369–77.

agreed to a pause in hostilities, he believed it most unlikely that
the war would be resumed. Should no armistice be declared,
however, a true enforcement of the Declaration of Paris would
open many Southern ports and the needs of the Confederacy
would be supplied. Benjamin's plan was partly successful. Foreign merchants bought goods of the South and brought pressure
to bear upon their governments, but the governments failed to
act as Benjamin desired.

When all these efforts had failed, Benjamin prepared to play
what he believed was an ace in the hole. England and France, he
concluded, would never recognize the Confederacy as long as
the slave system was retained. Early in the war a few Southern
men were convinced that slavery would be abolished no matter
what the outcome of the conflict. Benjamin gradually accepted
this idea and sought to convince the President. By 1865, Davis had
come to believe that the only hope for the South's independence
lay in recognition and that this, in turn, was contingent on the
abolition of slavery. Because of the need for secrecy, it was decided to send a special representative to Europe to lay the offer
before the governments. Duncan F. Kenner, a member of the
Confederate House of Representatives from Louisiana and at
one time one of the largest slaveholders in the South, was
selected for the mission. He was instructed to promise abolition
of slavery in return for recognition of the Confederacy by England and France. Reports of a new policy of the Confederacy
reached Europe before Kenner arrived.[75] Mason was astonished
at the news brought by grapevine report and protested to Kenner
against the policy. The Virginian stifled his scruples against
abolition, however, when he learned that he would be suspended
unless the order was obeyed.[76] The friendly *London Times,* in
an editorial on February 13, 1865, warned the South that abolition of slavery would not change British policy.[77] England had
remained neutral from abstract principles of policy, this newspaper said, and while the abolition of slavery would make it
clear that the United States was fighting for imperial domination,

[75] Callahan, *The Southern Confederacy,* 262.

[76] C. S. Henry, "Kenner's Mission to Europe," *William and Mary Quarterly,*
XXV (1917), 12.

[77] *Richmond Daily Dispatch,* March 4, 1865, quoting the *London Times.*

the question of recognition would remain exactly where it had stood. The French Emperor continued to promise recognition in the event England granted it, but the English Prime Minister would have none of it.[78] The Secretary's last recourse had failed.

Benjamin was both perplexed and infuriated by the attitude of Europe. He had tried everything in his power, but nothing had budged England from her position. Benjamin's last letter to Slidell sadly recounted his three years of fruitless effort and his disillusionment. The Confederacy, he maintained, would have defeated the North but for the aid the Union had received from Europe. Yet the Confederacy was fighting the battle of England and France, for a victorious United States would be all-powerful. The South had maintained its independence for four years and had no purpose other than that of achieving self-government. England and France had not only remained aloof, but had never explained their intentions or their reasons for nonrecognition. The South would have been willing to grant them concessions, but they had never made any proposals. The Confederacy, uninformed of any basis for an agreement, had been obliged to grope in the dark for some way to appeal to the European nations, whose failure to recognize the Confederacy had made the war the bloodiest in history. Benjamin could not understand the situation. The only logical conclusion he could arrive at seemed to be that England feared the United States.[79]

The Confederate State Department also sent representatives to Russia, Holland, Denmark, and Spain. A special representative was sent to the Pope in an attempt to check the enlistment of foreign soldiers, especially Irish, in the United States armies. The commissioner to the Holy See was courteously received, but he accomplished nothing more than a letter from the Pope addressed to Jefferson Davis as "President of the Confederate States." This salutation was the nearest approach to a recognition

[78] Henry, "Kenner's Mission to Europe," *loc. cit.*, 12.

[79] Benjamin had found the fundamental reason for the failure of England to intervene. Frank Lawrence Owsley, the authority on Confederate diplomacy, states that England did not recognize the Confederacy because England feared a war with the United States would follow such action. In event of war with the United States, England would probably lose Canada, the English carrying trade, and the profits the American war was bringing to English merchants and industrialists. Owsley, *King Cotton Diplomacy*, 578.

of the Confederacy that Benjamin obtained. The missions to the smaller countries were relatively unimportant and Confederate diplomacy concentrated on the two major European powers. Benjamin reasoned that once England and France recognized the Confederacy, the lesser nations would fall into line.

The activities of foreign consuls resident in the Confederacy constituted a problem for Benjamin throughout his term of office. When the war began they were allowed to remain in the South without presenting credentials to the newly formed government. This policy had been followed on the theory that the Southern states were under an obligation to continue the recognition given the consuls by the state's former agent, the United States. As the war progressed it was found that the consuls were being used by aliens in their efforts to avoid being drafted into the army. Confederate laws gave foreigners residing in the South ample time in which to leave the country, but upon the expiration of the time limit the government began to draft them. No doubt a few subjects of foreign governments were drafted, but Benjamin was convinced that the British consuls, in accepting without question the statement of any man claiming to be a British subject, protected many who had no valid claim to exemption from military service.[80] The Secretary of State, in the absence of the President, called a meeting of the Cabinet on October 7, 1864, and the secretaries voted unanimously to expel the British consuls.[81] Benjamin's act of expulsion met with public approval, for the newspapers had long been criticizing the policy of allowing the consuls to reside in the Confederacy. For the moment, the Secretary of State was restored to public favor. The consuls continued to live in the Confederacy, however, although they were not permitted to exercise any official functions.

Benjamin also had a part in the various efforts for the establishment of peace with the Union, the most important of which was the final effort in 1865 at the Hampton Roads Conference. President Davis, against his better judgment, agreed to send

[80] Benjamin to Slidell, October 8, 1863, in Richardson (ed.), *Messages and Papers*, II, 582.

[81] Milledge Louis Bonham, *Studies in History, Economics and Public Law*, Vol. XLIII, No. 3, *The British Consuls in the Confederacy* (New York, 1911), 232.

commissioners to this meeting to discuss terms of peace. President Lincoln had shown his willingness to bring "peace to the people of our one common country." Alexander H. Stephens, Robert M. T. Hunter, and John A. Campbell were selected to represent the Confederacy at the conference, and Benjamin drew up simple instructions for their guidance. They were instructed that, in compliance with Lincoln's letter, "you are hereby requested to proceed to Washington City for conference with him upon the subject to which it relates." [82] President Davis feared this phrasing would be construed as an admission that peace would be made on the basis of "one common country," in other words, a restoration of the Union. Benjamin had purposely made his reply vague, as he was eager for the conference and had no objection to one conducted on the "one country" basis.[83] The instructions were finally changed, however, to read: "In conformity with the letter of Mr. Lincoln, . . . you are requested to proceed to Washington City for informal conference with him upon the issues involved in the existing war, and for the purpose of securing peace to the two countries." [84] This rephrasing, of course, changed the possible nature of the conference. It had the approval of Davis, and meant that Southern independence was to be a *sine qua non* of peace. The conference was a failure, but it is conceivable that under Benjamin's original draft a reconstruction of the Union might have taken place.

This is not necessarily to say that Benjamin favored reunion with the Northern states. The evidence indicates that he was extremely eager that the conference be held and desired that nothing be done that might prevent a meeting. He believed a conference would have the effect of stiffening Southern resolution, for he was convinced that Lincoln would demand the Confederacy's unconditional surrender. Faced with this uncompromising attitude, he thought, the South might rally. The Northern people, on the other hand, would have yet another example of the readiness of the Confederacy to make peace, and this, Benjamin reasoned, might weaken Northern support of the

82 Benjamin to Davis, May, 1877, Southern Historical Society, *Papers,* IV (1877), 214.

83 *Ibid.,* 213.   84 *Ibid.,* 214.

Lincoln administration. What appears on the surface to be a wide difference between the ideas of the President and the Secretary is deceiving. They were, in reality, in accord on the fundamental principle of Confederate independence.

The change in Benjamin's original instructions so as to read "peace to the two countries," delayed the meeting, the commissioners reported. Davis was accused of preventing an end to the war by his demand for independence, but the accusation can hardly be substantiated. The commissioners were acquainted with the wording of their instructions and had they been contrary to their principles, could have declined to accept the mission. Despite the final phrasing of the instructions, the discussion at the meeting with Lincoln satisfied the Southern representatives that complete surrender or continued war were the only terms the United States had to offer. After surrender, penalties or conditions to be imposed upon the South would be decided upon. President Lincoln unquestionably would have made every effort to readmit the Southern states into the Union without reprisals upon the men of the South. The Southern leaders, however, who had been fighting a ruthless foe for years, did not, and could not trust themselves to the mercy of their enemy's leader. Rather than surrender unconditionally, they endeavored to arouse Southern patriots to renewed efforts.

Benjamin failed in his foreign policy, yet he was an extremely valuable man to the President of the Confederacy. The close relation between Davis and Benjamin as Secretary of War became even more intimate while Benjamin was Secretary of State. True, he was no longer the President's chief adviser on military plans. Lee, Seddon, and Bragg had replaced him there, but Benjamin continued to be the President's intimate in the Cabinet. He became again, as he had been during his service as Attorney General, the administration's handy-man, a jack-of-all-trades. There were few matters of importance in the Confederacy with which he was not conversant. Davis often called in his friend and trusted Secretary for long conferences, and visitors at the custom house frequently saw the President in Benjamin's office.

Benjamin's activities included more than those relating to his office as Secretary of State. An early biographer believed that he

had a hand in other departments of the government.[85] Benjamin
is generally believed to have been the author of many able letters written in defense of the administration, and he said in
1871 that Davis had called on him to write various Presidential
messages to Congress.[86] He also drew up bills for introduction in
Congress or polished the rough draft of bills drawn up by others.
The conscription bill, for instance, was turned over to him to
be put into final shape.[87] He was directed at times to inquire
as to the treatment of prisoners of war and to make reports
personally to the President.[88] Additional tasks were assigned to
Benjamin because of his expeditious handling of work. L. Q.
Washington, Assistant Secretary of State, had seen his superior
draft at one sitting a twenty-page state paper, so accurately
drawn that few changes were required for the final draft.[89]

Benjamin did not lack for time to devote to problems, both
major and minor. Jones, the war clerk, was amused by Benjamin's
efforts to keep himself occupied. On one occasion he personally
called on Seddon in his office to obtain his promise to sit for
an oil portrait to complete a set of paintings of Cabinet members.
Another time Benjamin bestirred himself in the project of
better arrangements for obtaining the delivery of Northern newspapers for the State Department. The *Richmond Examiner* described the department as a file room for current periodicals and
dubbed it the "Confederate Reading Room." The *Richmond
Enquirer,* which had pretty consistently supported the administration, thought Benjamin should resign on the plea of lack of
work. The *Charleston Mercury*'s correspondent, "Hermes," reported that the country was indebted to the Secretary of State

---

[85] Butler, *Benjamin*, 328.

[86] Benjamin to Mason, February 8, 1871, *ibid.*, 396. "I have hardly anything to
which I can refer to refresh my memory, but I have the *original* report made by
the commissioners who went to Hampton Roads, and a bound copy of the President's messages to Congress which you (who were in our secrets) know to have
been written by me, as the President was too pressed with other duties to command
sufficient time for preparing them himself."

[87] Freeman, *R. E. Lee*, II, 29.

[88] Benjamin to Randolph, October 10, November 10, 1862, in *Official Records
of the Union and Confederate Navies in the War of the Rebellion* (Washington,
1894–1927), Ser. I, Vol. XXIII, 705–706, 708. Cited hereafter as *Naval Records*.

[89] L. Q. Washington, "Confederate States State Department," Southern Historical Society, *Papers*, XXIX (1901), 348.

for a translation of an article in *La Patrie,* a semiofficial French newspaper, in which the United States and Russia were excoriated and held up as despotisms to be feared by the world.[90] Benjamin was also the author of a circular that proved "conclusively that the Yankees would never pay their debt," a fact, the *Mercury* commented, that was known to all except stupid Dutchmen, and even they were coming to their senses. The State Department's correspondence was voluminous; frequently the Secretary decoded cipher messages so confidential in nature that they could not be entrusted to clerks.

Once again Benjamin became the President's intermediary and the welcomer of important strangers. When Count Henri Mercier came to Richmond to obtain firsthand knowledge of the spirit of the Confederacy, it was Benjamin who convinced him that the South would fight to the last man before submitting to the North.[91] It was Benjamin, too, who explained to an English visitor, Lieutenant Colonel Arthur James Lyons Fremantle, the reasons justifying secession and why recognition by England would forthwith end the needless war. James Roberts Gilmore, a visitor from the North, found the State Department room unattractive. Maps and battle plans were on the walls; a tier of shelves loaded with books was in one corner; and a green-baize covered black walnut desk, littered with state papers, occupied the center of the room. At the desk was seated a "short, plump, oily little man."[92] His manner was cordial, but mingled with his pleasantness was diffidence amounting almost to timidity. The Northern author concluded that Benjamin had no moral force, but had a "Keen, shrewd, ready intellect, but not the stamina to originate, or even to execute, any great good, or great wickedness."[93]

Davis left the direction of the State Department almost wholly to Benjamin. The President had far too many duties to attempt to conduct the affairs of the State Department. The Secretary kept him informed of the important operations of the depart-

[90] *Charleston Mercury,* March 4, 1864.
[91] Owsley, *King Cotton Diplomacy,* 311.
[92] Edmund Kirke (James Roberts Gilmore), *Down in Tennessee and Back by Way of Richmond* (New York, 1864), 267.
[93] *Ibid.,* 268.

ment, "but its management, its instructions, correspondence, and policies were those of its accomplished head." [94] Hardly a day passed without a conference or visit between the two men, yet the President sought his Secretary not so much to give advice as to listen. The tired and often discouraged Chief of the Confederacy found conversation with the reassuring, ever-hopeful Benjamin pleasing and encouraging. This intimate relationship gave rise to the rumor that Benjamin was responsible for administrative policy and brought down upon him bitter denunciation. Representative Foote reported that

On the occasion of the recent visit of M. Erlander, Minister Plenipotentiary and Envoy Extraordinary from His Highness, the Emperor of France, to his Highness, the-would-be Emperor of the Confederate States, Judah Iscariot Benjamin had spoken French for two hours.[95]

Slurring references to Benjamin's racial origin were made by critics and unfriendly newspapers. If the policy of the government displeased someone, or he had a personal grievance against the administration, it was most convenient to blame everything on the representative of the "Jewish Synagogue" in the Cabinet. In the absence of direct evidence of his incapacity, it was enough in the 1860's that the object of attack was of the Jewish faith. Benjamin was not ashamed of his faith, nor did he allow a derogatory reference to it to go unanswered, but he was not greatly concerned about religion. Not only was Benjamin a Jew, he was also stout and sleek at a time when many found it difficult to obtain sufficient food. The diarist Jones, along with others, resented the Secretary's well-fed appearance.

Newspapers printed bitter attacks upon the Secretary of State, declaring that neither the people nor the soldiers had forgiven him for the defeats the Confederacy had suffered during his service as Secretary of War. The newspapers, seeing in him the evil genius of the Confederacy, seemed to take delight in printing accounts of his inefficiency. The *Richmond Sentinel* alone of the five Richmond papers supported him. The *Rich-*

[94] Butler, *Benjamin*, 331, quoting L. Q. Washington.
[95] Max J. Kohler, "J. P. Benjamin, Statesman and Jurist," American Jewish Historical Society, *Publications*, XII (1904), 79.

mond Enquirer stated that 90 per cent of all Virginians opposed him.[96] Challenged to adduce evidence of Benjamin's derelictions, the *Enquirer* referred to his failure as a Secretary of War and its desire to get rid of him after the fall of the forts and Roanoke Island.[97] The enterprising *Sentinel* in reply published extracts from the *Enquirer* of 1862, in which Benjamin was supported and General Huger was held responsible for the loss of Roanoke Island. The *Sentinel* furthermore searched the files of the *Enquirer* and found no criticisms by that newspaper when Fort Donelson fell, nor any objection by it to Benjamin's transfer to the State Department.[98] Confounded by the words of his own mouth, the *Enquirer's* editor could answer only with vague accusations.

In its zeal to destroy Benjamin the *Enquirer* was subjected to further embarrassment. The paper had criticized the appointment of James Spence as Confederate agent in Europe, because on page eighty-three of Spence's book, *The American Union,* the *Enquirer* had found a criticism of slavery. This discovery led the newspaper to expose Benjamin for appointing an abolitionist to represent the South. The *Sentinel* defended Spence, at the same time informing its contemporary that Memminger, not Benjamin, had appointed the author as financial agent.[99] The *Enquirer,* a supporter of Memminger, was caught off guard, and lamely advised the *Sentinel* not to attempt to saddle Spence on the Secretary of the Treasury, but to put him on shoulders other than the burdened ones of Memminger. ". . . for humanity's sake, leave him on Mr. Benjamin, who has so little on his mind and shoulders." [100]

Newspapers complained that Benjamin's rosy hopes never materialized. The Secretary's press releases often held forth the prospect that recognition and the end of the war were just around the corner. In 1863 Benjamin wrote that good crops had assured an ample supply of corn for two years, and that there was no danger of the Confederacy's being starved.[101] In the same letter

[96] *Daily Richmond Enquirer,* September 14, 1863.   [97] *Ibid.*
[98] *Richmond Sentinel,* September 18, 1863.   [99] *Ibid.*
[100] *Daily Richmond Enquirer,* September 17, 1863.
[101] Benjamin to Mason, May 20, 1863, in Richardson (ed.), *Messages and Papers,* II, 488.

he stated his conviction that the Confederacy's tax system was devised to enable the South to resist the United States for an indefinite period. "Every hour produces fresh evidence of the early and disastrous break-down in Northern resources both of men and money," he wrote Slidell in 1864.[102] No doubt Benjamin was following a deliberate policy in painting these bright pictures.

Many of Benjamin's critics held that the Confederacy had been dishonored by the treatment to which its commissioners had been subjected in Europe. They wished to have these envoys recalled and foreign consuls expelled in retaliation. Some of those who advocated this action were animated by a spirit of revenge; others regarded the entire State Department and its representatives as a waste of money, since they were convinced that European recognition would come only in case of the Confederacy's victory.

Congress occasionally meddled in the State Department's affairs. Benjamin promptly complied with requests from Congress for information, unless he judged that the information desired might be used to the disadvantage of the administration. In such cases he evaded the issue on the plea that secrecy was vital to the success of governmental policies. In March, 1863, the Secretary desired to send a commissioner to the Spanish government. His friends in the Senate, however, told Benjamin that the appointment of another commissioner would not be confirmed.[103] Determined attempts were made in Congress to pass a resolution demanding the recall of all Confederate commissioners abroad. Lucius Q. C. Lamar, commissioner to Russia, was recalled because the Senate had adjourned in May, 1863, without having confirmed his nomination.[104] Benjamin resented the

---

102 *Id.* to Slidell, April 23, 1864, *ibid.*, 643.

103 *Id.* to *id.*, March 26, 1863, *ibid.*

104 *Id.* to Lamar, June 11, 1863, *ibid.*, 505–506. Complaints were made against the men selected to represent the South in Europe. Paul du Bellét gives an amusing and highly colored account of a meeting between a Confederate agent in France, Thomas Cooper DeLeon, and the French Minister of Agriculture and Commerce.

"On the appointed day our young diplomatist was ushered into the presence of the *Ministre;* and when the sacramental question was asked 'What can I do for you, Sir?' he coolly unfolded an engraving and presented it to His Excellency saying, 'I have been sent to Paris by His Excellency Jefferson Davis to fill a very important mission, *a mission upon which depend the lives of eight millions of people!'*

Senate's action. He charged the Senate with meddling in administrative departments at a time when the Senators should have been devoting themselves to the enactment of needed legislation. This Congressional meddling did add to the difficulties of the State Department and forced the Secretary to compromise on the question of foreign commissioners; but it made little difference in a situation where, as his critics were fond of reminding him, recognition was dependent, not on the activities of the State Department, but upon the success of the Confederate armies.

Benjamin's official letters and public utterances were sometimes couched in undiplomatic language. There was some excuse perhaps for the vehemence of his criticism of the North when uttered for public consumption, but there was no necessity for some of his characterizations of the Northern people contained in letters to men like Mason and Slidell. "No crime is too revolting for this vile race," the Secretary wrote to Slidell, "which disgraces civilization and causes one to blush for our common humanity." [105] To Mason he wrote that the Northern people were "execrable savages who are now murdering and plundering our people." [106] Benjamin had no doubt that hundreds of thousands of people in the North would be "frantic with delight" if they should hear of the universal massacre of the Southern people. In his opinion, one could never say too much in condemnation of a people who cheated in the exchange of prisoners, violated the honor of women, and murdered prisoners in cold blood. Enraged at what he considered double dealing by Napoleon III, Benjamin excoriated the French Emperor as one "who had not *hesitated* to *break* his *promises* to us in order to *escape* the *consequences resulting* from *his un-*

"'I beg permission to offer to your Excellency the likeness of our beloved President!'

"The *Ministre*, taking the portrait, said 'You are extremely kind, Sir; I am much obliged to you for the trouble you have *taken in bringing it yourself*.'

"A deadly silence then prevailed, which not being interrupted, His Excellency walked towards the door and made a low and respectful bow to his visitor who understood then *that the time had come for him to make his exit*." Paul du Bellét, "The Diplomacy of the Confederate Cabinet," 58–59, in Col. John T. Pickett Papers, Manuscripts Division, Library of Congress.

[105] Benjamin to Slidell, January 8, 1864, in Richardson (ed.), *Messages and Papers*, II, 619.

[106] *Id.* to Mason, May 20, 1863, *ibid.*, 489.

popular Mexican policy." [107] He concluded that the Confederacy would receive with extreme distrust "any *assurances* whatever that may *emanate* from a *party capable* of the *double dealing* displayed *toward us* by the *Imperial Government*." [108] Letters as extravagant and unrestrained as these could not serve any good purpose. They were, in fact, highly dangerous, as the State Department's correspondence was always subject to the risk of interception.

The opposition to Benjamin reached its climax shortly before the collapse of the Confederacy. The Secretary for some time had been converted to the plan of using slaves as soldiers, and he favored rewarding those slaves who enlisted with freedom. He worked quietly and, to some extent, under cover, for the plan. He wrote letters to congressmen, generals, and newspapers requesting an expression of their opinions and asking them to use their influence to bring about the use of Negroes as soldiers. Benjamin came out openly for the enlistment of Negro troops at a demonstration held in Richmond at the African Church, on February 9, 1865. At this meeting, held to renew the people's will to resistance, Benjamin said: "Let us say to every negro who wishes to go into the ranks on condition of being made free—Go and fight; you are free." [109] Benjamin declared slavery to be the best system ever devised for the improvement of the Negro and the freedom of white people, but since the Confederacy was no longer able to protect slaves, the best system of control should yield to the next best.

This was revolutionary doctrine, enunciated, moreover, by an unpopular member of the Cabinet, and it immediately evoked criticism. Senator Wigfall on February 11 introduced a resolution in the Senate declaring that Benjamin had lost the confidence of the nation.[110] On February 13, the Wigfall resolution was amended to read:

Whereas the Honorable J. P. Benjamin was appointed to the office of Secretary of State, by and with the advice and consent of the Senate; and

[107] *Id.* to Slidell, April 23, 1864, *ibid.*, 654.
[108] *Id.* to *id.*, April 23, 1864, *ibid.*, 655.
[109] *Richmond Daily Dispatch*, February 10, 1865.
[110] *Journal of Congress*, IV, 550.

Whereas that body is now satisfied that the appointment has proved unfortunate, and is one which would not now be advised or consented to, and that the said J. P. Benjamin is not a wise and prudent Secretary of State, and has not the confidence of the country: Therefore, *Resolved*, That the President be advised of this opinion of the Senate, and most respectfully requested to take such action in the premises as he may deem proper.[111]

The amended resolution was considerably milder than the original. Senator Sparrow of Louisiana moved further to amend it by inserting after the word "country" the phrase "except the State of Louisiana." The amendment was lost. A vote on the resolution was demanded, and a tie resulted, eleven voting for and eleven against its adoption. Two days later James T. Leach in the House of Representatives offered a resolution declaring that the ideas expressed by Benjamin on February 9 were derogatory to his position and an insult to public opinion. The resolution was laid on the table, however, and an effort to have it printed was defeated by a vote of 46 to 24.[112]

It made little difference whether the resolution passed or failed. The President ignored what he regarded as Congressional meddling in a purely Executive field. Opposition to Benjamin had the effect of drawing the President closer to the Secretary. Nor was there any likelihood that Benjamin would resign, as Secretary of War Seddon had done, because of criticism in Congress.[113] General Lee's public advocacy of slave enlistment relieved Benjamin of further attacks on this score.

Judged on his actual accomplishments, Judah P. Benjamin was a failure as Secretary of State. He did not achieve a single purpose or objective of the Confederacy. He had failed to obtain recognition of the Confederacy, foreign intervention, the breaking of the blockade, or trade treaties, all vital items in the nation's program of foreign policy. He had used every means in his power to attain his ends. His attitude had varied from that of a suppliant to that of one demanding a right. No man in the South could have obtained recognition for the Confederacy.

---

[111] *Ibid.*, 552.　　　　　　　　　　　　[112] *Ibid.*, VII, 582.

[113] On February 21, 1865, Benjamin wrote Davis of his willingness to resign, if such action would be of service to the administration, but expressed his indifference to Congressional and press opposition. Meade, *Benjamin*, 308–309.

Benjamin was a victim of the same peculiar world conditions that so adversely affected his country. Surplus cotton, failure of the European wheat crop, the diplomatic situation in Europe and Confederate military defeats at critical moments, the Federal blockade, all checkmated the Secretary's every move.

Benjamin was unquestionably a man of ability. His state papers and his letters, in spite of their occasional invective, give evidence of his mental powers. His instructions were clear, unequivocal statements, phrased in good English. He was a shrewd little man who had an instant grasp of questions and could make his decisions quickly. A man of action, he often made mistakes that antagonized men slower in their movements and mental processes. The affairs of his office were kept in order; rarely was the machinery of his department slowed up by unfinished business. He assigned to his assistants duties for the performance of which he allowed them considerable freedom and responsibility. He kept his own duties down to a minimum, which partly explains his availability for other services to the President. His versatility, originality, and retentive memory enabled him to meet almost any situation.

The Secretary possessed characteristics that were frequently overlooked or were unsuspected because they were hidden beneath his masklike exterior. Few among the members of the Cabinet could hate as bitterly as Benjamin, and he rarely made any effort to compromise with an avowed enemy. Nor did he love any man or cause with an intense devotion. For him life was a transition from one job, or case, to another. He gave his all in thought and service to the accomplishment of the purpose of the moment. When the battle ended, win or lose, he shrugged away the past. Friendship and companionship were for him the means to an end. During the four years of the war he was on terms of close friendship with President Davis and Secretary of the Navy Mallory. Yet after the fall of the Confederacy he dropped them as a tree sheds its leaves in autumn. The distance that separated him from these friends may account for what seems indifference, but it hardly explains his failure to write them for the sake of old acquaintance. The more one studies his unique personality, the more one has a sense of something lacking in his character. It may have been a want of moral stability and devotion to principles.

Benjamin's value in his work for the Confederacy was as an adviser and aide to the President; he was superior in this respect to any member of the Cabinet. Endowed with cheerful courage and an optimistic nature, he was willing to take censure for mistakes, or to accept reversals, without a murmur; thus, he shared the burdens of the presidency without demanding its attendant prestige. During periods when Davis was ill Benjamin did much to keep the departments working in harmony. It was generally recognized that he was the President's alter ego; otherwise it is hardly likely that he would have called a Cabinet meeting and asked for an important decision in the absence of the head of the government.

Attorney General, Secretary of War, Secretary of State—Benjamin in truth was the Confederacy's jack-of-all-trades. And far from being good at none, he was capable at all. Pre-eminently an able lawyer, he was also a good administrative officer and a perfect adviser to the man who presided over the Confederacy.

VI

Dealers in Paper

FINANCIALLY, the Confederacy's plight was far worse than its situation in respect to the possession of war materials or its ability to produce them. The South was the home of the agrarian; it was a debtor section. There was wealth in the South, but it was largely in land and in slaves. Its assets could not be liquidated readily to pay the cost of the war. The planter was a speculator who put his profits, when he made profits, into land and slaves. In most instances he could not give credit; he stood in need of credit. The agrarian South held the North responsible for this situation. The South was convinced that the Federal system of economy had favored the commercial class and the Northern financial institutions at the expense of the farmer and the Southern banks.

The South, however, possessed creditable financial institutions. No stronger or better managed banks than those in Louisiana could be found in the country. From 1850 to 1860 there had been a remarkable expansion of bank deposits and credit facilities. In fact, the slave states possessed, on a comparative basis of population and business turnover, almost as much specie as did the free states. The newborn Confederacy numbered among its citizens many who had training and ability in political economy. A foreign-born commercial lawyer, Christopher G. Memminger of South Carolina, had worked long, and with some success, to establish sound banking principles in his state.

The problem of finance did not greatly engage the thought of the fathers of the Confederacy, notwithstanding the lack of liquid capital in the South. Their government would be a simple one with few financial requirements. A low tax on imports, added to an export duty on cotton, would supply the government's needs. The export tax was especially favored. Cotton, being king, would command his market, and the Southerner convinced himself that the buyer, not the producer, would pay the tax. Should an unexpected need for revenue arise, a small direct tax might be levied. The problem of national economy was easily solved. Once separated from the "leech-like" North, the individual lot of the Southerner would be improved, for a credit system adapted to an agricultural economy would result. Southerners were vague as to how this could be arranged, but were confident that secession would abolish the old system of control by the North. With a financial system planned for an agrarian economy and with Southerners in control, the planter, farmer, and business man would prosper in an independent South.

Money was the most immediate need of the Confederacy. The government could not function until a well-regulated Treasury Department should be established to provide funds. President Davis considered Robert Toombs, of all the politicians known to him, the most suitable to head the Treasury Department.[1] Davis had been impressed by Toombs's financial acumen as a Senator, and his opinion as to his ability had been further strengthened by Toombs's selection as chairman of the Committee on Finance in the provisional Congress. Howell Cobb believed that a choice of appointment to the State or Treasury Department had been offered Toombs.[2] The State Department appointment, however, was offered to Robert Barnwell, who declined it,[3] and the South Carolina delegation urged Christopher G. Memminger for the Treasury Department.[4] The South Carolinian was nominated by the President and his appointment was confirmed without opposition by the provisional Congress on February 21.[5]

---

[1] Davis, *Rise and Fall*, I, 242.

[2] Howell Cobb to his wife, February 20, 1861, in Phillips (ed.), *Correspondence of Toombs, Stephens, and Cobb*, 544.

[3] Laura Amanda White, *Robert Barnwell Rhett: Father of Secession* (New York, 1931), 195; Davis, *Rise and Fall*, I, 241-42.

[4] Davis, *Rise and Fall*, 242.

[5] Robert Barnwell Rhett longed for office. After the war R. B. Rhett, Jr., denied that the South Carolina delegation recommended Memminger. "The Confederate

Two days later the *Charleston Mercury* congratulated Memminger on his appointment, and the Confederacy on having one so well fitted to perform the duties of the Treasury Department on sound economic principles. There were few men in the South, Rhett's paper asserted, possessed of greater business capacity than the studious Memminger, who had great intellect, initiative, and experience. Thomas R. R. Cobb, while not rating the appointee's talent highly, thought he was "shrewd as a Yankee." [6] Memminger's appointment, a friend wrote William Porcher Miles, gave very general satisfaction because of his eminent ability and fitness for the position. At the same time, Miles's correspondent feared the South Carolinian's lack of experience in Washington might lead him to "think all men honest, but I know he will not be very long in his present position, before he becomes satisfied that there is yet a plenty of Puritan blood in the land, South as well as North." [7] The Confederacy was well pleased with its Secretary of the Treasury.

CHRISTOPHER GUSTAVUS MEMMINGER

Alien-born as he was, Christopher Gustavus Memminger had won for himself an enviable place in his adopted state when he became the Confederacy's first Secretary of the Treasury.[8] He was born in Nayhingen, in the Duchy of Württemberg, on January 9, 1803, and brought to Charleston as an infant in arms by his mother and grandfather. Orphaned at an early age, he became a charge of Charleston's famed Orphans' Home, where he remained until Thomas Bennett, who later became governor of

---

Government at Montgomery," in Johnson and Buel (eds.), *Battles and Leaders of the Civil War*, I, 104.

Rhett's *Charleston Mercury* of February 26, 1861, however, printed a letter that stated: "The individual members of the delegation, including Mr. Barnwell, recommended . . . [Memminger]." On March 9, the *Mercury* denied that Memminger had been recommended by the individual members of the delegation, but admitted that Robert Barnwell, representing them, had recommended Memminger.

6 Hull (ed.), "Correspondence of Thomas Reade Rootes Cobb, 1860–1862," *loc. cit.*, 174.

7 G. N. Reynolds to Miles, February 23, 1861, in Miles Papers.

8 The summary of Memminger's life is based on Henry D. Capers, *The Life and Times of C. G. Memminger* (Richmond, 1893); *Dictionary of American Biography*, XII, 527–28.

South Carolina, adopted him. His foster father sent him through South Carolina College and gave him an opportunity to study law. Memminger became a naturalized citizen in 1824, and it was not long before he was regarded as a leading practitioner in Charleston, notably in commercial and constitutional law.

He had identified himself with the Union States Rights party, and in 1832 he wrote *The Book of Nullification*. Despite this attack on influential leaders, Memminger was elected to the South Carolina House of Representatives in 1836. Two years later he became chairman of the House Ways and Means Committee, and for twenty years retained the chairmanship. Memminger steadfastly upheld the principles of sound banking; in 1839 he opposed a law allowing the suspension of specie payments, and later conducted the prosecution of the state banks for suspending specie payments. His sound and practical views on finance are evidenced in the arguments he made when bank legislation was under consideration.

Memminger was a man of independent thought and liberal sympathies. When Samuel Hoar came to South Carolina as the agent of Massachusetts to test the constitutionality of the act of 1835 that prohibited the landing of Negro seamen, Memminger alone of 118 House members opposed a resolution requesting the governor to expel the Northern agent. He displayed a truly liberal spirit in his investigations of comparative educational systems, and was responsible for a reorganization of education in his state. It was owing primarily to him that the Charleston schools were among the best in the nation in 1860.

With the passage of the years his early Unionist sentiment changed. He belonged to the cooperative division of the Democratic party in the 1850's, and desired a Southern convention to obtain either redress of grievances or cooperative secession. After introducing a resolution in the South Carolina legislature for such a convention he was appointed a commissioner to Virginia to obtain the cooperation of that state. In Richmond, however, he soon became disgusted with the lack of favorable response, and reported to Miles: "It seems to me that we shall finally be brought to the point of making the issue alone and taking our chances for the other states to join us, whenever a

Black Republican has the rule over us."[9] When the "Black Republican" was elected to the presidency, Memminger voted for secession and was elected a delegate to Montgomery. There he became one of the most active members of the provisional Congress.

His work in the Congress was curtailed by the pressure of his official duties as Secretary of the Treasury. Even before his nomination had been confirmed, Henry D. Capers, who became chief clerk of the department, had been busy furnishing and setting to rights an office in the bank building for the Secretary's occupancy. In the meantime, Memminger obtained temporary credit for the government from the Central Bank of Alabama. Congress on February 8 accepted the offer of a $500,000 loan from Alabama, but it appears that the first actual money came to the Treasury from Louisiana on March 14. This was the sum of $536,787.12, of which $389,267.46 was from the Bullion Fund, coin kept at the New Orleans mint for the purchase of bullion, and $147,-519.66 from the New Orleans customs receipts.[10]

With the aid of temporary bank loans, the Treasury Department was organized and ready to function within a week. The major offices were filled by former officials of the United States Treasury, and they were free to choose their own assistants. Every clerk in the department was appointed for a six-month period with the guaranty of permanent employment should his work prove satisfactory. Memminger set strict rules as to the hours of work, and imposed regulations designed to prevent the department from being turned into a politicians' social club. The department personnel murmured at his strictness, but the close supervision enabled the department to function in a business-like manner.

Memminger himself observed the rules he laid down for his subordinates. He was in his office daily from nine o'clock in the morning to three in the afternoon, unless prevented by attendance at Cabinet meetings or sessions of Congress. Frequently he came earlier and remained at his desk until late at night. Pollard

[9] Memminger to Miles, January 30, 1860, in Miles Papers.

[10] *Journal of Congress*, I, 32; Earnest Ashton Smith, *The History of the Confederate Treasury* (Richmond, 1901), 5.

has left an inaccurate impression of him as a religionist who wasted his time in ransacking bookstores for works on theological controversies. The Carolinian's training had instilled in him habits of hard work, and he held steadfastly to his task in success or failure.[11]

He was sometimes criticized for his methods in dealing with visitors. As the duties of office grew more pressing he found himself unable to receive any and every caller at the department, and to conserve his time he made rules to eliminate all except important visitors. Even they had to state their business to a clerk before they were admitted to the Secretary's office. This necessary preliminary caused some visitors to leave the department in high dudgeon, enraged at what they regarded as "red-tape-ism" and manifestations of "royal customs" in the Confederacy.[12] Their complaints had little basis in fact, for it was comparatively easy to obtain access to the Secretary if one were willing to state his business and await his turn. Too often, however, the caller who was admitted to the Secretary's office left it resentful of Memminger's attitude. Memminger was of morose temperament and did not give or inspire confidence in his relations with other men. It was not that he was unfriendly, but he lacked the faculty of making friends or of placating enemies. Even his colleagues in the Cabinet were on none too friendly terms with him. Reagan, Mallory, and Seddon at times were at odds with him on financial questions. Memminger was a stickler for a close adherence to the letter of the law in honoring requisitions, and promptly demanded the correction of any irregularity in applications for money.

The Secretary of the Treasury, on his part, took umbrage at irregular demands by the other secretaries, and fell back on President Davis for support. He hoped that his colleagues would realize the difficulties attending the obtaining of funds for the government, and that they would cooperate with him for the well-being of the Confederacy. The secretaries, of course, comprehended the magnitude of the task before the Treasury, but each nevertheless demanded of it what he considered the due of his department. When debatable financial controversies were

[11] Capers, *Memminger*, 309–14.
[12] Hamilton (ed.), *The Shotwell Papers*, I, 382.

submitted to him, the President acted upon the opinion rendered by the Attorney General. In cases where the Treasury was plainly in the right, as in the instance of General Beauregard's seizure of the specie of the Columbus banks and his refusal to deliver it to the Treasury agents, the President upheld the Secretary. In the controversy mentioned, Davis rebuked General Beauregard.[13]

Prior to the organization of the Confederacy, Davis had not been acquainted with Memminger, but the two men quickly developed a mutual respect. Their official association never went beyond that stage, however, as both were of the type who, while readily responding to friendly advances, were diffident about making the overtures. Davis's contacts with the Treasury head, even though their relationship was not that of warm friendship, made him confident of Memminger's competence, and he gave the Secretary a free hand. This was especially easy to do, for the President also knew that the fiscal plans of the Confederacy had been made after consultation with able financial authorities. Memminger had turned for advice to Robert M. T. Hunter and Howell Cobb, both experienced in public finance, and to the South's leading bankers and merchants, particularly George A. Trenholm of South Carolina and James Denègre of Louisiana. Important plans of the Treasury Department were fully discussed at Cabinet meetings, and the President generally supported suggestions made by the Secretary.

Aside from the respect that each had for the other's ability, the President and the Secretary held interests in common. Both were students of religion and certainly enjoyed discussions in private on this subject. They had in Colonel Lucius B. Northrop a common friend through whom they were brought into closer personal association. Memminger, like the President, was a man of cultured thought and tastes: each enjoyed a well-turned jest or a witticism with a literary flavor.[14] The Secretary's industry, his attachment to the ideal of the South's independence, and his optimism, impressed the President. The Congressional criticism of Memminger in 1863, that Davis thought unfair and unneces-

[13] Davis to Randolph, May 27, 1862, in *Official Records,* Ser. IV, Vol. I, 1130–31.
[14] Capers, *Memminger,* 31.

sary, brought the two men closer together. Memminger, after all, was accomplishing much with little resources, and could have done even better, Davis believed, had Congress given more heed to administrative plans. In 1864, when the Secretary's foes in Congress were attempting to force his resignation, the President was begging the Secretary to disregard the carpings of "little men" and to remain in the Cabinet. The unorganized opposition to the Confederate administration had brought Davis and Memminger more closely together than ever.

At first there was little criticism, but considerable praise, for Memminger's conduct of the Treasury Department. A correspondent of the *Richmond Examiner* in May, 1861, regarded the Secretary as a very successful administrator.[15] A few months later this newspaper declared: "Our Government has established a financial policy that more than anything else has contributed to the economy, simplicity and positive elevation of our political system." [16] The *Charleston Courier,* in 1861, considered Memminger the most able and faithful of all the Cabinet members, most of whom, the newspaper asserted, had been selected as graduates of Washington or as a means of satisfying regional claims. The Secretary of the Treasury, on the other hand, had been chosen because of his experience, ability, and skill in financial matters. Viewing Memminger's excellent management of his department, despite the burdens added to it by "sleepy" secretaries of War, Navy, and Post Office, the *Courier* expressed the wish that in the future all Cabinet members be selected on the basis of ability.[17] The newspaper expected that Memminger, among the best, if not the best, Cabinet appointments of the provisional government, would be nominated and confirmed as Secretary of the Treasury of the permanent government.[18] He was appointed, and the Senate on March 18, 1862, confirmed the nomination without objection.

The criticism of Memminger in the first year of his term related to minor matters and was made in a spirit of friendliness. Intelligent men realized that many delays in the work of the

15 "Ariel," *Daily Richmond Examiner,* May 13, 1861.
16 *Ibid.,* August 5, 1861.   17 *Charleston Daily Courier,* November 27, 1861.
18 *Ibid.,* March 2, 1862.

Treasury Department were unavoidable. The South could not
supply notepaper for currency and bonds, and it was necessary to
bring lithographers from Scotland under contract to work for the
government.[19] Poorly made treasury notes soon became abundant
throughout the Confederacy, but there were only a few cases of
fraud by government employees.

The primary concern of the Confederate Treasury Department
was to obtain money. The complete story cannot be told here; a
consideration of Memminger's ideas in relation to the fiscal policy of the Confederacy is more germane to the present study. It
was realized clearly at the outset that the young government
would have to depend upon taxes and loans as its main sources
of revenue. Congress on February 28 provided for an issue of
$15,000,000 of 8 per cent bonds, the interest and principal of
which were assured by an export levy of one eighth of one cent per
pound on cotton. Memminger arranged to float one third of this
bond issue at par to obtain specie. He hoped that the allotment
would be oversubscribed by double the amount. The Treasury
received bids for more than $8,000,000 worth of bonds. Subscrib-
ers found it difficult, however, to obtain specie to meet the required deposit of 5 per cent, and impossible to obtain cash to
make the final payment on May 1. Most of the Southern banks
had suspended specie payments and holders of bank notes could
not convert their paper currency into cash. The bankers, however, agreed to redeem in specie all notes used in the purchase of
the first Confederate bonds. It was clear, from the response to the
first loan, that the Treasury could not depend on the sale of bonds
to provide cash for the needs of the government.[20]

Congress, in the meantime, authorized an issue of $1,000,000
in twelve-month notes bearing interest of 3.65 per cent. This was
the forerunner of subsequent legislation that taxed the capacity
of the South's printing presses to produce a quantity of treasury
notes sufficient to meet the demands of inflation.

Increased demands, arising in every department after the opening of hostilities, accentuated the inadequacy of the government's

[19] Trenholm to Seddon, February 4, 1865, in Treasury Department, Confederate
States of America, Miscellaneous Letter Book, January 22 to April 2, 1865, Confederate Museum, Richmond.
[20] Report of July 29, 1861, in Memminger Papers.

income, and caused the Secretary to turn for advice to the leading bankers in the Confederacy. His own thought was to call for the remainder of the $15,000,000 loan, but Denègre, president of the Citizens' Bank of New Orleans, opposed this recourse on the ground that the people had no money and would not have any until they should sell their crops. His suggestion was that treasury notes in the amount of $20,000,000 be issued and a direct tax, payable on March 1, 1862, be levied.[21] Memminger reopened the loan on May 7, however, but the response was disappointing, and it was not until November following that the full $15,000,000 was finally subscribed.[22] Denegree's suggestions were embodied in Memminger's outline of fiscal policy contained in his report of May 10. He called for a tariff of 12½ per cent, a direct war tax up to $15,000,000, an issue of not more than $20,000,000 in treasury notes, and a $50,000,000 foreign and domestic loan for which produce would be accepted.[23]

Memminger first issued treasury notes as an experiment to discover public reaction to this type of currency. When he found that it was favorable, he sought to establish a system of national currency based on the government-backed notes. If this was successful, he believed that the administration would not only be enabled to obtain supplies, but that a uniform currency would also help trade by offering a medium of exchange to take the place of vanishing specie. At the Secretary's suggestion, a conference of bankers was called in June, 1861, and the bankers agreed to accept treasury notes when issued. Memminger, in a circular to the banks in the Confederacy, pointed out the advantage of a common medium of exchange sustained by the credit of the Confederacy. Only the banks of New Orleans refused to follow his suggestions. Pressure, both direct and indirect, was applied to them, however, and in the fall they suspended specie payment to accept the new Confederate currency.

It was never Memminger's intention that there should be wild inflation through treasury notes. He assumed that accumulated notes would be used to purchase interest-bearing bonds, and that

21 Smith, *The Confederate Treasury*, 6–7.
22 Report of November 20, 1861; Circular of the Treasury Department, November, 25, 1861, in Memminger Papers.
23 Report of May 10, 1861, *ibid.*

the treasury notes in circulation would remain almost constant. He estimated that a circulation of $100,000,000, or possibly $150,000,000, could be absorbed. This calculation was based on the average circulation and deposits for a six-year period, 1852–1858, in the eight states of the Confederacy in which banks existed.[24] Later, upon the advice of bankers, Memminger raised the estimate to $200,000,000. He qualified his estimate by pointing out that an essential part of the Confederacy's fiscal policy was the levying of a direct tax. The system provided for a fairly constant national currency, sufficient to meet the needs of exchange without serious inflation.

His plans were carefully studied and represented a synthesis of the advice given by Southern men versed in finance. The plan depended for its successful operation upon the cooperation of the states, the Congress, and the people. Memminger was to be disappointed in his hopes for this cooperation. Local governments swelled the total circulation by lavish issuances of notes of many types. Congress failed to respond fully to the Secretary's program, and the people never rushed to buy government bonds. Added to these difficulties was the loss of confidence in the government brought on by military reverses.

Fundamentally, Confederate fiscal policy was to meet the current expenses of government by the sale of bonds. Only if the public bought liberally could inflation be averted. From the first, public support of the Treasury policy was decidedly lacking. The response to the first loan, Memminger reported on July 29, 1861, had been so discouraging as to prove that bonds could not be depended upon as an immediate source of revenue.[25] The issuance of treasury notes had been resorted to as the only immediate means of continuing the government's financial policy. To further the sale of bonds, produce was accepted as payment in lieu of cash. Treasury agents, in effect, took for security promises of a percentage of the 1861 harvest, the agricultural products to be sold through regular channels and the proceeds to be turned over to the government. Although many of the bonds were sold on these terms, the Treasury received no immediate aid. A principle similar to the produce loans was applied in obtaining industrial

[24] Report of July 20, 1861, *ibid.*   [25] Report of July 29, 1861, *ibid.*

products, raw materials, and services. First, the manufacturers
and the railroads were induced to take bonds in payment for
goods and services. Later, the Treasury required other departments of the government to take a part of the amount of their
requisitions in bonds. In this way the government paid for its
purchases partly with treasury notes, at the same time sparing no
efforts to have these certificates funded in bonds.

Efforts to sell securities outright were supplemented by inducements to fund treasury notes. In the beginning, appeals were
made to the public to assist voluntarily in the funding arrangements. Notes could be exchanged for 8 per cent bonds or for
interest-bearing certificates, at the owner's option. Another
scheme to reduce the circulation was the establishment of depositories, in which notes were accepted as deposits on call at 6
per cent interest. The Southern man thought more of his money,
however, than he did of securities redeemable at a future date,
and there was only apathetic response to the appeals. The suggestion was then made that those who failed to fund their notes
be penalized. The Secretary proposed that all notes issued prior
to December 1, 1862, should cease to be recognized as currency
and after July 1, 1863, the notes could no longer be exchanged
for bonds.[26] Although withdrawn from circulation, the notes were
then to become fixed noninterest-bearing obligations of the
Treasury. Memminger believed that holders naturally would
fund their notes before the expiration of the deadline. But even
this measure, closely approaching repudiation, failed of the desired effect; inflation grew beyond control. Memminger in his
report of December 7, 1863, recommended the adoption of a
comprehensive scheme for funding. Congress was asked to provide a billion-dollar 6 per cent bond issue for the purpose of
taking up the surplus currency and providing for current appropriations. Certificates entitling the holders to bonds would be
given in exchange for deposits of treasury notes. In order to entice
exchange, any bonds issued prior to February, 1864, would be
forever tax-exempt. A new issue of currency, rigidly limited to
$200,000,000 or less, was favored by the Secretary. Old notes, not
funded, after April 1, 1864, would cease to be currency, although

26 Report of January 10, 1863, *ibid.*

they would continue to be obligations of the government. The plan recommended by the Secretary was substantially that recommended by the bankers' convention held at Augusta, Georgia. Memminger made changes in detail only and these strengthened the original plan.

Congress questioned the proposal. Its attitude toward the Secretary was never cordial. Memminger repeatedly urged the necessity of adopting means other than the issuance of treasury notes to meet current expenses. Congress accepted the suggestion for funding notes, but in reality defeated the purpose by adding a provision allowing bonds to be re-exchanged for notes. The Confederate Congress, however, in 1864 altered the whole conception of Memminger's plan. An act of February 17, 1864, proposed to reduce the currency by compelling holders to fund notes. All noninterest-bearing notes of denominations above five dollars could be funded at par in 4 per cent twenty-year bonds up to April 1, 1864 (July 1 in the Trans-Mississippi), and at two thirds their face value until January 1, 1865, after which latter date they would be taxed out of existence. A new issue of treasury notes was authorized, for which the old notes could be exchanged on a three-for-two basis. The act was as complicated as it was unwise. Congress, in effect, repudiated obligations of the Confederacy and failed to provide the Treasury with ways to obtain funds.

Memminger was no more successful with Congress in the field of taxation. That body neither took the initiative in devising legislation for taxes nor acted upon Memminger's repeated suggestions. From first to last the Secretary recommended the adoption of a fiscal policy to be erected on a solid basis of taxation. Experience had fully established, he reported, "that the expenses of modern war cannot be maintained by taxes, to be levied during a state of war. The utmost that can be obtained by taxes, at such a time, is the establishment of a solid basis for loans, and the pledging of sufficient amount of annual income to discharge the principal and interest of such loans, as they become payable." [27] This mild statement does not give a true insight into Memminger's views on taxation for he was a confirmed believer in hard

[27] Report of March 14, 1862, *ibid.*

money and the necessity of taxing to the limit. His recommendations to Congress on taxation are in curious contrast to the emphasis he placed on it in personal letters and messages to Congressional leaders.[28] The inconsistency perhaps is best accounted for by the attitude of Congress. Memminger no doubt was informed that pressure by him for taxation would create immediate opposition to the administration in the economy-minded Congress. The public was opposed to taxation. Some Southern leaders realized that unity in the South was not a certainty. Under the circumstances it appeared to the legislators to be the wise course to be chary of placing direct burdens upon the people. Not only Congress, but also the state governments winced at the thought of taxation. The state governments avoided it by borrowing or issuing notes. The Southerner, living in a region of staple agricultural products, saw no good reason why he should be burdened when import and export duties imposed after the war would very soon liquidate all the debts that had been contracted by the government.

As the policy of credit failed, taxation developed as an alternative. Memminger, in his first report, advocated a direct tax of $15,000,000.[29] This tax was to be levied upon the states on a population basis, with a liberal discount granted to any state electing to pay in advance. Even this small tax was not to be collected until June, 1862. The *Petersburg Daily Express* approved of the levy and thought that the Confederacy would thereby be more than able to meet all financial difficulties. Men of wealth, the newspaper believed, would gladly pay, for "the South saves by non-intercourse with the North at least *two hundred millions of dollars per annum. . . ."* [30] The states assumed the burden of

[28] Smith, *The Confederate Treasury*, 9. Memminger repeatedly requested taxes of Congress, as illustrated by his reports of May 1, May 10, July 20, July 24, July 29, 1861. Memminger Papers. On July 24 he suggested an ad valorem tax on slaves, real estate, merchandise, and stocks to raise $25,000,000. Five days later he reduced this to $20,000,000. His fault was, not in failure to recommend, but in failure to demand taxes. The Southerner did not want taxes and did not believe them necessary even in the amounts recommended by the Secretary.

[29] Report of May 1, 1861, in Memminger Papers. The actual figure was $15,438,581. Memminger believed $23,700,000 could be collected in customs and duties.

[30] *Petersburg Daily Express*, August 17, 1861.

the tax, thereby pleasing the people, never at any time eager to take on financial burdens.

The Southern press by late 1862 began to call for a fixed system of taxation. Currency was rapidly depreciating, and everyone felt called upon to advise the Treasury Department. By 1863 the demand for increased taxation could not be ignored. The clamor was pleasing to Memminger, and in his report of January 10, 1863, he called for taxation amounting to $63,000,000 a year. Congress responded with the act of April 24, 1863, levying a comprehensive tax on agricultural products, money, salaries, professions, property of all kinds, and business enterprises. Confederate taxation had been slow in coming, but when Congress finally acted, it was no halfway measure. Citizens were confused at the returns called for, and they resented the demands made upon their incomes. Taxation never brought in the revenue it should have. By 1863 much of the Confederacy's territory was under control of the invaders, and a strong opposition to the taxes had developed, defeating to a great extent tax collections within the country. Memminger's compromising spirit had prevented him from forcing the issue of taxation upon a reluctant nation in 1861, but had he stubbornly insisted upon a policy of demanding burdensome levies early in the war, he would have met with an equally stubborn resistance.

Unable to obtain sufficient revenue from the sale of bonds or from taxation, the Treasury was faced with the necessity of depending on paper currency unless some other source of income could be discovered. Certificates of indebtedness and impressment of goods were resorted to, but these methods were extremely unpopular. There remained the hope that foreign investors would buy Confederate securities. This would not only bring in money, but would also tie foreign men of wealth to the Confederacy. It was reasoned that, as the safety of their investment depended on an independent South, they would work to force recognition of the Confederacy. In March, 1861, Memminger planned to sell Confederate bonds in New York, but the outbreak of the war destroyed his hopes of disposing of the securities in Wall Street. The efforts to develop a market for the bonds in

Europe were inaugurated when the first agents had orders to pay
for supplies in Confederate bonds whenever possible, but European industrialists were unwilling to accept 8 per cent bonds
which were backed only by the credit of the Confederacy. In 1862
Memminger began to use cotton as a basis for foreign credit by
issuing certificates of deposit on the cotton stored in the Confederacy. Treasury Department agents were willing to sell these
certificates at a discount of 50 per cent if necessary.[31]

The French banking firm of Erlanger et Compagnie saw an
opportunity to float a loan in Europe on this basis, and Baron
Émile Erlanger came to Richmond to discuss terms. The outcome of his visit was a contract signed for the floating of the first
and last Confederate foreign loan. The contract called for an
issue of 7 per cent bonds to the amount of $15,000,000, one for-
tieth of the principal to be repaid semiannually from March 1,
1864, each bond to be exchangeable for cotton at a price of six
pence per pound not later than six months after peace was established. The French banking firm guaranteed to underwrite
the bonds at 77 per cent of their face value, but its 5 per cent
commissions and allowance for service charges reduced this figure to 70 per cent.[32] The securities were placed on sale at 90 on
March 19, 1863, and rose to 95½ in the open market.[33] Before
the date for payment of the second installment on the bonds, the
price had dropped well under the original flotation price. Mason
in Paris, fearing that subscribers would not take the bonds, was
persuaded to use over 1,500,000 pounds in bulling the market.[34]

[31] Mallory to James Dunwoody Bulloch, September 20, 1862, in *Naval Records,*
Ser. II, Vol. II, 269–71.

[32] Benjamin to John Slidell, January 15, 1863, in Richardson (ed.), *Messages and
Papers,* II, 406.

[33] John Christopher Schwab, "The Confederate Foreign Loan: An Episode in
the Financial History of the Civil War," *Yale Review,* I (1892), 180.

[34] Mason to Slidell, May 14, 1863, in *Naval Records,* Ser. II, Vol. II, 422–23.

Most of the bonds bought by Mason were later used to pay Confederate debts
or buy material. The Erlanger Bonds sold for 37 in the London market in
December, 1863. In 1864 they recovered and reached a high of 84, but the market
broke in September when the bonds fell to 57. The price trend continued down-
ward until the news of the peace conference at Fortress Monroe when the bonds
ran up to 59. John Christopher Schwab, *The Confederate States of America, 1861–
1865; A Financial and Industrial History of the South During the Civil War* (New
York, 1901), 36–37.

There were a number of reasons for the recovery in the price of the bonds in
1864. Lee was holding Grant's powerful army. The appointment of McRae and

In the end, the Confederate government realized about 40 per cent of the face value of the loan.

Memminger was criticized for not attempting to float a larger loan. Erlanger had offered to take a $25,000,000 bond issue, but Confederate officials were not willing that the issue should exceed $15,000,000, and only agreed to that figure because of Slidell's argument that a foreign loan would have resulting political benefits for the Confederacy.[35] Memminger did not believe that he had been authorized by Congress to float a loan of more than fifteen to twenty million dollars in the foreign market.[36] The Confederacy's venture in foreign financing was a failure, partly due to Mason's gullibility and partly to Baron Erlanger's shrewdness. In September, 1863, both Mason and Slidell reported that it would be impossible to float another loan in Europe.[37] By 1864 Memminger was glad to sell regular Confederate bonds at twenty-five cents on the dollar.[38]

Military defeats and the South's inability to get cotton through the blockade were the main causes of the Confederacy's failure to float bond issues abroad. The staple, which the South considered all-powerful, was shorn of its might by the blockade; cotton, which was believed to be the Confederacy's strength, proved to be one of its greatest weaknesses. There were those who retained their faith in King Cotton and who maintained that its potentialities had been nullified by inept management. Stephens had a plan for utilizing the power of the staple. His theory was that by taking two million bales of the 1861 crop, paying $100,000,000 for them in 8 per cent bonds, and adding to them two million bales of the old crop at the same price, the Confederacy would be enabled to acquire fifty ironclad steamers to protect the cotton in transit to Europe. Once there, the staple would be stored until its

---

Bayne resulted in more cotton reaching Europe. (See pages 223, 224.) One twentieth of the bonds were paid off each year and there was hope on the part of speculators that the Confederacy would allow the immediate conversion of bonds into cotton.

[35] Benjamin to Mason, January 15, 1863; *id.* to Slidell, January 15, 1863, in Richardson (ed.), *Messages and Papers*, II, 399–400, 406.

[36] Memminger to Slidell, November 7, 1862, in Capers, *Memminger*, 359–60.

[37] Mason to Benjamin, September 5, 1863, Slidell to *id.*, September 22, 1863, in Richardson (ed.), *Messages and Papers*, II, 561, 565.

[38] Mallory to James Dunwoody Bulloch, January 25, 1864, in *Naval Records*, Ser. II, Vol. II, 578–79.

price reached fifty cents a pound, when it would be sold for $1,000,000,000, giving the Confederacy a clear profit of $800,-000,000 in sterling.[39] The *Richmond Dispatch* in reviewing the plan expressed regret that Stephens was not Secretary of the Treasury.[40] Later, General Joseph E. Johnston blamed the defeat of the Confederacy on the administration's failure to inaugurate a cotton scheme similar to that suggested by "Little Alec." [41]

Stephens's plan, however, evidenced both his visionary nature and his lack of business judgment. Upon any consideration, the scheme was as full of holes as a sieve. In the first place, there were only a few hundred thousand bales, not two million, of the 1860 crop left in the South in 1861, and the planters would not have sold their cotton in exchange for bonds. Instead of being ready to aid the government, they were calling loudly for financial help from the Confederacy's Treasury. Nor was there any assurance that money would have bought the ironclads; in fact, the Confederacy found that it would not. Finally, the idea that the Confederacy could have held four million bales in storage in England for any length of time, or that with four million bales in storage the price of cotton would have risen to fifty cents a pound, was fanciful.

Stephens's scheme was based on two fallacious beliefs. The first, which was held by many, was that the Secretary of the Treasury personally desired to prevent the export of cotton in order to produce a famine of the staple that would force foreign recognition of the Confederacy. The fact was that Memminger, at the outset, made plans for shipping the staple out of the country, and in the first meetings of the Cabinet he urged early shipments of cotton and proposed that two steamship lines, one to Bermuda and another to Havana, be established for this purpose.[42] Memminger made inquiries of a leading New York merchant about vessels in which to transport cotton, which was not being exported in quantity because the South lacked ships. Furthermore, the Confederacy never officially restricted the export of cotton for

---

39 Stephens, *Constitutional View*, II, 783.
40 *Richmond Daily Dispatch*, September 21, 1863.
41 Joseph E. Johnston, *Narrative of Military Operations, Directed, During the Late War Between the States* (New York, 1874), 421–24.
42 Memminger to Davis, September 25, 1877, in Rowland (ed.), *Davis*, VIII, 25–27.

any reason other than to prevent it from falling into the hands of the enemy. An act of May 21, 1861, forbade the export of cotton except through the seaports of the Confederacy. From that date until the end of the war, the purpose of governmental legislation was to prevent the products of the South from reaching the North and to facilitate shipments to aid the Confederacy.

The official acts of the Confederate government fail to paint an accurate picture of the situation. Members of the Congress, governors, cotton factors, merchants, planters, and newspaper editors were firm believers in the embargo as an effective weapon to force recognition from England.[43] The state authorities and local committees of public safety sought by every possible means to prevent the export of cotton. These "extra-legal and voluntary" embargoes were effective.[44]

Memminger did not lend his support to this movement. In a telegram protesting an embargo placed by the authorities of Galveston, Texas, he stated that the general government alone had power over foreign trade and "it totally disapproves of any obstruction to commerce in our ports." [45] In the spring of 1862 the governor and council of South Carolina by resolution forbade the export of cotton, but suspended the order when Memminger objected.[46] The *Charleston Courier,* a supporter of the Secretary, opposed from time to time the embargo on exports.[47] The responsibility for the mistaken embargo of 1861 does not rest on the shoulders of Memminger.

The second erroneous belief on which the Stephens scheme was based was that the primary purpose of the cotton purchase plan was to aid the Confederate Treasury. Southern farmers in the fall of 1861 found it difficult to obtain credit. The suggestion

[43] Owsley, *King Cotton Diplomacy,* 31.

[44] See chapters I and II, *ibid.*

[45] Memminger to T. H. Hatch (Collector at the Port of New Orleans), April 23, 1861, in Treasury Department, Confederate States of America, Telegrams, February 27, 1861, to July 30, 1864, p. 89, National Archives.

[46] Memminger to F. W. Pickens, April 15, 1862, in Memminger Papers; *Charleston Daily Courier,* April 23, 1862.

[47] The *Courier* printed many letters from subscribers who favored the embargo. The reader should not confuse the editorial policy of the *Courier* with the letters printed in the paper. The *Courier* was not consistent, but generally opposed the embargo. See letters and editorials of September 4, 23, 24, 25, 26, 27, and October 14, 16, 24, 1861, as well as of April 23, 1862, *supra.*

was then made, primarily to aid the planters, that the government buy their cotton. Such purchases, it was argued, would relieve the owners and furnish a basis for government credit. The scheme, according to the *Richmond Examiner,* would cost $200,000,000. ". . . it would be a vast Federal stretch of power for our new Government, and a frightful example of soup-house legislation. It would steep the country in debt upon a commercial speculation. It would be a financial blunder, a social canker, a political monster." [48] The *Examiner's* editor, Edward A. Pollard, when writing the second volume of his *History of the War,* berated Memminger for not buying cotton, and accused him of dismissing the Stephens scheme as "soup-house legislation." [49] It is true that Memminger in the fall of 1861 opposed government buying of cotton on constitutional grounds and because the Treasury lacked funds. Pollard's *Examiner* at that time published Memminger's letter opposing the plan and praised the Secretary for his forceful stand. [50] A year later the *Examiner* said the great fault of the administration was its lack of originality and its failure to accept the cotton purchase idea, which the *Examiner* declared it had favored from the first. The *Richmond Enquirer* pointed out the fallacy in the *Examiner's* argument, quoting directly from a series of the *Examiner's* editorials. [51] In its defense, the *Examiner* lamely explained that those early editorials did not represent its policy which, although not expressed, favored the purchase of cotton. Contemporary evidence supports the conclusion that the suggested plan in 1861 to buy cotton originated as a scheme to benefit the South's agricultural interests. Later, the idea of transporting and storing the cotton in Europe was tacked on, and this added feature was adduced in criticism of the administration's fiscal policy.

The Confederate government did buy cotton from the planters. By January 10, 1863, Memminger reported the purchase of 69,507 bales and the probable purchase of 250,000 additional bales. [52] The Secretary's report of December, 1863, stated that

[48] *Daily Richmond Examiner,* October 12, 1861.
[49] Pollard, *Southern History of the War,* II, 184.
[50] *Daily Richmond Examiner,* October 19, 1861.
[51] *Daily Richmond Enquirer,* October 21, 1862.
[52] Report of January 10, 1863, in Memminger Papers.

399,753 bales had been obtained since April 30, 1863.[53] This cotton was secured from the produce loans,[54] the objectives of which were to obtain needed military supplies for domestic use and other commodities, especially cotton, that could be used as a basis for foreign credit. Certificates and bonds backed by government-owned cotton to the extent of $9,000,000 had been forwarded to Confederate agents in Europe by February 4, 1863.[55] In this way the cotton owned by the government was utilized although still in the Confederacy.

The Confederate Cabinet and the agents of the government were not satisfied with these instruments of credit, but desired to ship cotton directly to Europe. Unfortunately, there were too many agents of the various administrative departments both in the Confederacy and in Europe whose work often resulted in confusion and prevented the full exploitation of cotton.[56] In September, 1863, Memminger, Seddon, and Mallory with the approval of Davis and Benjamin agreed to center control of all finances and supervision of all foreign agents in Collin J. McRae.[57] It was also necessary to bring under one head the tasks of buying and shipping cotton from the Confederacy. Thomas L. Bayne, who had charge of the War Department's blockade-runners, was selected for the job.[58] The newly appointed director used the authority given by Congress on February 6, 1864, which vested control of the exportation of cotton, tobacco, sugar, rice, and naval stores in the President, to establish centralized control over the purchase and export of cotton. Colonel Bayne's accomplishments in his difficult task brought him additional grants of power. By the summer of 1864 he was the war "Tsar" of all shipping and his activities, together with the able work of McRae in England, brought order where chaos once ruled supreme. The

[53] *Ibid.*, December 7, 1863.

[54] Provisions were made for these produce loans on May 16, August 19, and December 24, 1861, April 21, 1862, February 20 and April 30, 1863.

[55] Mason to Slidell, January 28, 1863, in James M. Mason Papers, Manuscripts Division, Library of Congress; Owsley, *King Cotton Diplomacy*, 396.

[56] In the first nine months of 1863 the central government, state governments, and private individuals or companies succeeded in getting 100,000 bales of cotton to Liverpool. Samuel Bernard Thompson, *Confederate Purchasing Operations Abroad* (Chapel Hill, 1935), 72.

[57] *Naval Records*, Ser. II, Vol. III, 617–18.

[58] *Official Records*, Ser. IV, Vol. III, 370.

cotton from the produce loans was utilized to better the credit of the Confederacy in Europe and to obtain military supplies from that continent.[59]

The purchase and sale of cotton had no salutary effect on Confederate finances at home. As the currency continued to depreciate, reform of the monetary system became an important consideration. Open letters printed in newspapers suggested legislation to make Confederate notes legal tender. Such a measure was favored by Duff Green, who thought that the treasury notes with their promise to pay in gold six months after peace were a palpable fraud and caused people to distrust the currency.[60] Memminger in 1862 had considered the idea of making the notes legal tender, but had rejected it. Since the notes were accepted as currency, he believed they did not need any assistance to enable them to perform the functions of legal tender, but that a law to compel their acceptance as such would create suspicion and distrust of the currency.[61] The Secretary approved of another suggestion that each state guarantee its pro rata share of the Confederate debt.[62] He believed that such a guaranty would enable the Treasury to sell more bonds at a lower interest rate. Stephens protested against this plan and was pleased that the *Augusta Constitutionalist,* in fighting the guaranty proposal, made use of his arguments.[63] The Vice-President held that the agency that created a debt should be responsible for its payment. He expressed fear that the State of Georgia eventually would have to assume a debt of $100,000,000, and he warned that the proposal to guarantee bonds was a scheme of the President to obtain power.[64] The plan was never tried, although a few states declared their willingness to guarantee Confederate bonds.

Toombs was among those concerned about the currency situation. His views, set forth in a letter to the editor of the *Augusta Constitutionalist,* sent from his Washington, Georgia, retreat, are

---

[59] For an excellent account of the Confederate efforts to better the import and export program, see Thompson, *Confederate Purchasing Operations Abroad,* chapter IV.

[60] *Sumter Republican,* February 13, 1863.

[61] Memminger to Lucius Jeremiah Gartrell, March 13, 1862, in Capers, *Memminger,* 488–89.

[62] Report of December 7, 1863, in Memminger Papers.

[63] Johnson and Browne, *Life of Stephens,* 430.   [64] *Ibid.,* 441.

of interest because he had been prominently mentioned in 1861 as the most suitable choice for the Treasury post. Toombs wrote that the Confederacy started with immense resources, but with two errors: the attempt to carry on a war without taxation, and a dependence on treasury notes. These mistakes, he said, had wasted the country's resources. He believed that the Treasury should depend on taxation and loans, issuing "new bonds with principal and interest payable in gold and silver." [65]

This letter was praised by the administration's opponents, who regretted that Toombs was not Secretary of the Treasury. The Georgian's letter, however, did no more than express the commonplace thought of the day. The "wisdom" displayed by the former Secretary of State amused Memminger, who had himself always been a consistent believer in taxation and the sale of bonds. Few Southern men were more devoted to sound money finance than Memminger, who had started out by paying interest on bonds in specie. Indeed, he had been induced to abandon his scheme to increase bond sales by paying interest in gold under the persuasion of Trenholm and Denègre. [66]

Toombs had told the country nothing that the humblest citizen did not know, the *Richmond Enquirer* thought, and the newspaper reproached him for not having presented his financial plans when he was a power in Congress and in the Cabinet. This criticism struck home, for Toombs in 1861 had held that a small tariff duty would amply supply governmental needs. [67] His letter informed the country of the Treasury's shortcomings, but gave no practical method of relief. Bonds bearing interest payable in gold or silver, as Toombs suggested, could have been sold, but the problem was to find the gold and silver. In commenting on Toombs's advice to stop issuing paper money, the *Richmond*

---

[65] Toombs to the Editor of the *Augusta Constitutionalist*, August 12, 1863, in Phillips (ed.), *Correspondence of Toombs, Stephens, and Cobb*, 622–27.

[66] Trenholm to Memminger, June 9, 1862, in Memminger Papers; Smith, *The Confederate Treasury*, 17.

[67] *Charleston Daily Courier*, March 5, 1861. Many Confederate leaders looked to customs duties for the Confederacy's chief source of revenue. "Mr. Toombs, especially, seemed incapable of imagining the expediency of any other mode of raising a revenue, even under the present peculiar condition of affairs. . . ." Gamaliel Bradford, "Blunders of the Confederate Government," *De Bow's Review*, After War Series, V (1868), 485.

Enquirer said such action would "stop the war and wind up the government itself." [68] It was easy enough to indicate the fiscal needs of the Confederacy, but far from easy to offer a plan to meet them.

The plan adopted by Congress embodied a combination of ideas. It was contained in the Funding Act of February 17, 1864, which leaders in Congress and newspaper editors believed would soon restore Confederate notes to face value. In enacting it, the *Sumter Republican* declared, Congress did the very thing needed to restore the credit of the nation.[69] Publication of the act, however, caused prices to soar. Whiskey that had been selling for ninety dollars a gallon leaped in price to more than one hundred and twenty dollars, and many dealers closed their shops entirely. The *Richmond Enquirer* believed, however, that prices would fall after the volume of currency was reduced.[70] When prices continued their upward flight, critics looked about for someone to censure. The *Charleston Mercury* recalled that Memminger had opposed many parts of the Funding Act while it was pending, and suggested that he would not administer it in the way Congress intended or in such manner as to effect a reduction in prices.[71] It was true that the Secretary had opposed the act and had considered resigning in protest against it. He had consented to remain in office after a conference with the President, who feared that a new secretary would be unable to put into effect the complex and extensive terms of the Funding Act within the forty-day limit set by Congress.[72]

Blame for inflation fell upon Memminger as it became increasingly evident that the plan of Congress to deflate the

[68] *Daily Richmond Enquirer,* September 4, 1863.

[69] *Sumter Republican,* February 19, 1864.

[70] *Daily Richmond Enquirer,* February 24, 1864.

[71] *Charleston Mercury,* March 21, April 11, 1864. The *Mercury* accused Memminger of planning to do everything possible to nullify the act by issuing up to $400,000,000 in new currency which would be "quite enough to begin with, to bring us speedily back to the normal condition of our finances under the Administration, of inflation, complication, derangement and distress, unless Congress can find some words which can be potent enough to arrest his construction." Memminger had no intention of trying to inflate the currency. By June 17, the *Mercury* was criticizing him for issuing only $57,000,000 of new currency when he should have printed $225,000,000.

[72] Memminger to Davis, June 15, 1864, in Memminger Papers.

currency would not bring relief. Dissatisfaction with the Secretary had been growing. Senator Wigfall in the summer of 1863 despaired of improving the currency as long as Memminger remained in office, and suggested the abolition of the Treasury Department and the employment of a public printer. This at least would save the Secretary's salary, he said.[73] Memminger reminded the *Richmond Dispatch* of a boy holding a cow's tail while she ran full speed downhill. The Secretary could stop printing treasury notes but, like the boy, he could not let go without falling.[74] The *Richmond Examiner* taxed the President, who had had a host of excellent men to choose from, with selecting a poor man, to whom he had given complete control of the Treasury Department, and whom he had failed to replace when, during the first months of the war, it became plain that he was incapable. The result was, the newspaper concluded, a currency past redemption and a national debt double what it should have been under able management of the Treasury.[75] The Confederacy needed for Secretary of the Treasury, the *Examiner* declared at a later date, "a man possessing brains and practical capacity; and not an aged spider, stuck in a dusty corner of the Treasury, ever busy, to excess, at weaving tangled, incomprehensible, but flimsy webs." [76] The Secretary was accused of intentionally interpreting the act of February 17, 1864, in such way as to defeat its purpose; of planning to inflate further the currency by the lavish issuance of notes; and of failure to print the new notes to spite Congress. The act, in the *Examiner*'s opinion, was good, but ineffective when administered by a Secretary who left undone all that should have been done and did all that should not have been done.[77]

When Congress convened in May, 1864, the Senators and Representatives opposed to the Davis administration began to turn their fire on Memminger. Attention could be diverted from their own shortcomings by heaping upon the Secretary all the responsi-

---

[73] Wigfall to Clement C. Clay, August 13, 1863, in Clay Papers.
[74] *Richmond Daily Dispatch*, September 21, 1863.
[75] *Daily Richmond Examiner*, December 30, 1863. The *Examiner* had failed to realize Memminger's early incompetence; rather the newspaper had praised him for his good management. See p. 210.
[76] *Ibid.*, January 18, 1864.　　　　[77] *Ibid.*, June 16, 1864.

bility for the failure of the Funding Act. A resolution asking for the Secretary's removal was offered by Representative Henry S. Foote on May 27. A motion to lay the resolution on the table was defeated by a vote of 45 to 37, and the resolution was ordered printed.[78] Three days later Foote was defeated when the House by a 43 to 37 vote buried the resolution in the Judiciary Committee. Foote's resolution was carefully worded so as to catch as many votes as possible, but it failed nevertheless. Foote afterwards said that he had refrained from demanding a final vote on the resolution because he was assured by friends of Memminger that the Secretary would resign when Congress adjourned.[79] The caustic Representative overestimated his power, however, in attributing Memminger's resignation to his censure. Memminger could have remained in the Cabinet, with the President's strong support, even if the resolution had not failed, but he had already decided to resign. After Congress passed the Funding Act of February 17, 1864, he had retained office only at the President's request. He had agreed, upon the advice of Trenholm, to give Congress another chance to cooperate with his department, but when in its session of May, 1864, the legislative body hardly noticed his recommendations, Memminger definitely resolved to leave the Cabinet. His decision was not so much influenced by the possibility that a resolution of censure might be passed as it was by the refusal of Congress to consider his financial recommendations.

Memminger informed the President in June of his decision to retire from office. In a personal letter to Davis he expressed his gratitude for Davis's kindness and his admiration of his talent as an executive.[80] In an official letter the Secretary referred to his prior intention to resign, from which he had been dissuaded by the President, who insisted that he needed an experienced man to put the Funding Act into operation. As funding of the currency was nearly complete, Memminger felt that the public interest would not suffer during the time when a successor was becoming familiar with the duties of office. The President still

---

[78] Journal of Congress, VII, 110.   [79] Foote, War of the Rebellion, 357–58.
[80] Memminger to Davis, June 2, 1864, in Memminger Papers.

opposed his retirement, but Memminger insisted that his resignation be accepted and that a successor be appointed whose views were in harmony with those of Congress. The Secretary said that he parted with the President and the Cabinet with deep emotion and assured Davis that he had never, even in confidential intercourse, heard a word or suggestion indicating anything other than a conscientious and disinterested desire to do what was best for the Confederacy.[81] The President agreed to accept Memminger's resignation, but asked him to remain in office until a successor could be found. In his letter to Memminger, Davis thanked the Secretary for having subordinated his personal inclinations to public duty by retaining the office so long, and complimented Memminger on his cheerful and unremitting devotion to public service.[82]

Memminger did not give up the office until the middle of July; meanwhile, newspaper criticism of him continued. An Alabama newspaper, overjoyed to hear rumors of Memminger's resignation, said that some called him "a great old rascal." Others thought that he was, in truth, utterly unfit for his place, and that to spite Congress he had been adding to the hardships of the people in funding the old currency at three to two.[83] The *Richmond Whig* asserted that ability had never been considered in selecting Memminger, "the favorite of a favorite of the Executive." [84] An Augusta newspaper demanded that the Secretary be ousted for lack of energy, foresight, and intuitive genius in handling the Treasury Department.[85]

Memminger, however, had his defenders among the press. The *Savannah Republican* hoped he would pay no attention to the senseless clamor against him, for "we have seen no evidence of public sentiment being against him as Chief of the Treasury Department, and believe that four-fifths of the people would be gratified to have him retain his present position." [86] The *Charles-*

---

81 *Id.* to *id.*, June 15, 1864, *ibid.*
82 Davis to Memminger, June 21, 1864, *ibid.*
83 *Mobile Advertiser and Register*, June 24, 1864.
84 *Charleston Daily Courier*, July 12, 1864, quoting the *Richmond Daily Whig*.
85 *Augusta Daily Chronicle and Sentinel*, June 22, 1864.
86 *Charleston Daily Courier*, July 8, 1864, quoting the *Savannah Republican*.

ton Courier agreed with the *Republican,* but believed that four fifths of the people desired that the Secretary no longer subject himself to a "foolish" Congress.[87] Another South Carolina newspaper attributed the criticism of Memminger to faultfinders who, like mad dogs, care little whom they bite as long as they bite some one.[88]

The Secretary was vigorously defended by the *Richmond Sentinel,* the *Richmond Enquirer,* and the *Charleston Courier.* Three types of people were opposed to Memminger, the *Sentinel* said: the Ishmaelites who oppose everything and everybody, the President's enemies, and the speculators whose occupations were taken from them. Admitting that the Secretary made mistakes, the newspaper remarked that the greatest minds in the country also erred, for they had been the advisers of the Treasury Department. Memminger, his newspaper defender continued, had brought to a difficult task a mind well-stored with the principles of political economy, experience in financial management, and patient industry, and had been aided by the wisest counselors in the country. It was a well-recognized fact that the Confederacy's financial troubles arose from the war, the *Sentinel* declared, and Memminger should not be blamed for a condition over which he had no control.[89] In defense of the Secretary the *Courier* said that, although his critics held that it should have been easy for the Secretary to foresee and plan for a long war, these prophets, in the management of their personal affairs, had never considered in 1861 the possibilities of an extended war.[90] Memminger was not responsible for inflation, in the opinion of the *Enquirer,* and neither his resignation nor the appointment of a successor would improve the financial condition of the country. This newspaper blamed Congress for providing the treasury notes while neglecting to arrange for their reduction or redemption. In such circumstances, said the *Enquirer,* it was impossible to prevent depreciation or the consequent rise of prices. A people disappointed in expectations were not likely to give justice to an official, the *Enquirer* concluded, but it believed that in years to

[87] *Charleston Daily Courier,* July 8, 1864.
[88] *Daily South Carolinian,* July 14, 1864.
[89] *Charleston Mercury,* July 27, 1864, quoting the *Richmond Sentinel.*
[90] *Charleston Daily Courier,* July 7, 1864.

come the historian would give Memminger his rightful place among the best servants of the country.[91]

It was generally rumored during June and early July that Memminger had resigned, and the rumor was confirmed on July 19, 1864, when the correspondence between the Secretary and the President was released and the appointment of Memminger's successor was announced. Memminger retired to his country home at Flat Rock in western North Carolina. Except for raids of marauding soldiers and the temporary seizure of his property in Charleston, the former Confederate official was not molested at the close of the war.

It was difficult for his contemporaries (and it remains so today) to evaluate Memminger's contribution to the Confederacy as Secretary of the Treasury. A great many Southerners in the 1860's were under the delusion that their section was rich enough in resources to provide a sound basis for financial stability under any circumstances. In retrospect, one can see how really meager these resources were and one can realize the magnitude of the task of creating a stable fiscal system for a newly organized nation in the time of war. The Secretary of the Treasury of the United States had a gigantic task in financing the war, but Salmon P. Chase's difficulties were minor in comparison with those of Memminger. It is easy to discover mistakes in Confederate fiscal policy, but it is debatable whether any secretary could have avoided the pitfalls that beset Memminger.

It is less difficult to appraise Memminger's character and certain phases of his public service. He came to the Treasury with a record of achievement and a training that embraced experience in the theory and practice of public economy. His industrious application to duty while in office, his honesty, and his unselfish loyalty to the Confederacy are beyond question. He kept the business of the Treasury in order and up to date, and in the technical phases of his administration he was a capable executive, although somewhat of a martinet toward his subordinates.

He was not a colorful personality, but he was not by any means

---

[91] *Wilmington Daily Journal*, June 24, 1864, quoting the *Daily Richmond Enquirer*.

a humdrum plodder devoid of ideas. His problem was to obtain revenue for the government. Seeking to accomplish this purpose he not only used his own resourceful mind but also called for assistance from the South's financial leaders. The financial plans he evolved were syntheses of his own ideas and those of bankers, merchants, and politicians. The Confederacy's fiscal system was not a commonplace, unimaginative creation. Memminger planned to provide a national currency backed by taxation. He depended upon the sale of bonds to supply funds. When he found it difficult to sell bonds, he accepted produce in lieu of money, forced governmental departments to pay for materials and services in securities, issued certificates of indebtedness convertible into bonds, provided for the exchange of treasury notes into securities, endeavored to sell Confederate bonds in foreign markets, and floated a loan abroad. From the first he desired taxation, but he failed in his official reports to advocate heavy levies as vigorously as he should have done. It must be recognized, however, that even with a people willing to pay, and living under a well-organized government, it requires time for a scheme of taxation to bring in revenue. Memminger had to contend with a people set against taxation.

The inherent weakness of Confederate fiscal policy was the issuance of and dependence upon treasury notes for revenue. Memminger never desired this; it was forced upon him. Congress, on one hand, was unwilling to tax; on the other, the people were unwilling, or unable, to buy bonds in sufficient quantity. Thus blocked by two immovable obstacles, Memminger could obtain loans only by issuing more and more treasury notes. When inflation set in, the Secretary, along with others, attributed the monetary ills solely to the redundancy of the currency, and believed the situation would be corrected by a reduction of the circulating medium. To effect this, he provided for voluntary funding and later utilized a modified form of repudiation to force the exchange of notes for bonds. Congress went further, virtually repudiating the currency, thereby shaking the people's faith in all government securities. What Southern politicians failed to realize was that the country's monetary ills were caused as much, if not more, by the people's lack of faith in the Confederacy's ability to win the war as by the excessive issues of treasury notes.

Memminger's administration of the Treasury was handicapped by a non-cooperative Congress. Early in the war Congress and the Secretary were in virtual agreement, except upon the question of taxation. Later, as confidence in the South's ultimate victory waned, Congress tended to lay responsibility for the fiscal muddle on the shoulders of the Secretary of the Treasury. Congress, throughout Memminger's term, had altered important parts of the Secretary's plans, and in 1864 it assumed complete control of financial policies. The Secretary's fiscal ideas were superior to those of Congress, but his failure to retain the good will of the legislative branch of the government was a major mistake. Perhaps no man could have appeased the opposition in Congress, but Memminger especially did not possess the faculty of inspiring confidence and obtaining harmony.

An outstanding defect in the Secretary was a personality unsuited to the give and take of politics. He was headstrong, haughty, and a bit overbearing in his relations with others.[92] Although he was not given to temperamental outbursts, he was uncompromising in his demands and morose in his demeanor. In his zeal to defend what he considered the interests of the government, he would not allow any deviation from the rules. Those who had dealings with the Treasury were treated justly, but it was an exact justice, strictly and severely interpreted. Any Confederate Secretary of the Treasury was bound to be unpopular, but Memminger added to his own difficulties by an irritating manner, a disagreeable demeanor, and a stony presence.

Because he failed to foresee a long war, Memminger did not plan a fiscal program adequate to the extended conflict. In this lack of foresight he was not unique among Southerners. It is true that optimistic political leaders in the South in 1861 never hoped to conquer a vastly more powerful North without aid from sources outside itself. But the South was convinced that, if the United States did not itself break into warring factions, cotton would win for the Confederacy the intervention of Euro-

---

[92] Jones explained this deficiency in the Secretary's character by saying, "he is no Carolinian by birth or descent." Jones, *Diary*, I, 242.

pean nations. Without support from an outside source, the South had no chance of maintaining its independence; few Southern leaders would have favored secession had they not expected foreign aid.

Memminger underestimated the financial requirements of his government, and overestimated the revenue to be obtained from import duties. His estimates of government needs, however, were based on the budgets of other departmental secretaries that were considerably less than the actual sums necessary to operate their offices. Criticisms of Memminger for not employing the power of cotton to the full were shallow. Memminger, perhaps, could have obtained a small additional revenue by government buying of cotton and its shipment abroad in 1861. But it was unreasonable to believe that any man could establish a form of state socialism within the Confederacy at the beginning of the war, with the Southerners' belief in the principle of government being what it was. Memminger, moreover, protested against attempts to put embargoes upon cotton exports, and he encouraged private initiative to ship cotton abroad. It was through such shipments that Southern owners acquired foreign exchange which the Secretary bought for the use of the government. Lacking in foresight he may have been, yet the much-abused Secretary was more forehanded than many of his contemporary critics.

GEORGE ALFRED TRENHOLM

Memminger's resignation was accepted by the President on June 21, 1864, but it was not until July 18 that his successor was appointed. The newspapers in June were confident that John A. Campbell, Assistant Secretary of War, would be nominated to the Treasury office. The President, however, passed over the former Justice of the United States Supreme Court, and determined to appoint George A. Trenholm, probably the wealthiest man in the Confederacy and a friend of the retiring Secretary.

The Charlestonian at first rebuked those who suggested that he be appointed Memminger's successor. The *Charleston Courier* on July 7 suggested Trenholm for the office, but four days later published a letter which stated that Trenholm did not approve of the suggestion. Trenholm, himself, on June 28 asked that his name be not considered for the Treasury Department, for his views "were in direct opposition to the whole policy of Congress as exhibited in the important acts passed by that body, upon the two great and kindred subjects of taxation and currency." [93] He believed that the President would not desire to appoint anyone as secretary whose views did not coincide with those of Congress. Furthermore, he had advised Memminger to resign if Congress failed to bring its acts into harmony with the views of the Secretary, and it seemed inconsistent to Trenholm to allow himself to be placed in exactly the position from which he had advised another man to retire.[94]

Despite his objections, Trenholm was recommended to the President for the appointment. Davis wanted for Secretary of the Treasury a man whose fiscal ideas were similar to those of Memminger, and he requested Trenholm to come to Richmond for a conference. After his visit to the President, Trenholm wrote to his son that he had repeated to Davis his reasons for his unwillingness to accept the appointment, but that the President declared he would never appoint to the Treasury anyone who entertained the same views on finance as Congress. Both the President and his Cabinet were at variance with the Confederate legislature as to financial policy. Davis wished, he told Trenholm, to select a secretary who held opinions that would tend to ease the "mess" to which legislation by Congress would eventually lead.[95] Trenholm found the President kind, courteous, and sensible of the personal sacrifice Trenholm would have to make in accepting the appointment. Davis assured him that the country was most receptive to his selection for the Treasury post, and that his popularity would compel respectful consideration from Congress. The members of the Cabinet joined the President in urging Trenholm to accept and promised to cooperate with him and aid him to the full extent of their ability.[96] Trenholm

[93] Trenholm to Henry Gaidin, June 28, 1864, in George A. Trenholm Papers, Manuscripts Division, Library of Congress.
[94] *Ibid.*
[95] George A. Trenholm to William Lee Trenholm, July [no day], 1864, *ibid.*
[96] *Ibid.*

was pleased with the warmth of the welcome given him, and, as he was convinced that Memminger would not resent his taking the place he had vacated, accepted the appointment.

Trenholm's appointment was beneficial to Confederate morale. Trenholm would succeed, the *Charleston Mercury* believed, if it were possible for any man to do so.[97] The *Richmond Dispatch* was pleased that Trenholm was not a politician with a party affiliation, but a man conversant with world trade and on a par with the class of men from whom England derived its knowledge of finance.[98] Many newspapers welcomed the newly appointed Secretary as the man best able to reconstruct a demoralized financial system.[99]

George Alfred Trenholm was born in Charleston, South Carolina, on February 25, 1807. The death of his father, William Trenholm, necessitated the son's leaving school at an early age. When he was sixteen years old he was employed by John Frazer and Company, a shipping and commission firm of Charleston. His advancement in this company was rapid; he became its head, and before 1860 was one of the wealthiest men in the United States. Besides his vast interests in steamships, wharves, hotels, cotton presses, plantations and slaves, he was director of the Bank of Charleston and of the South Carolina Railroad and the Blue Ridge Railroad.[100]

Trenholm first manifested an interest in the politics of his state in 1830, when he ardently supported the cause of nullification. Until 1852, however, when he was elected a representative in the South Carolina legislature, he had not held any public office. He was suggested for the Confederate Congress in 1861, but refused the nomination and instead devoted his time and energies to blockade-running. His firm, John Frazer and Company of Charleston, and its foreign affiliate, Frazer, Trenholm

97 *Charleston Mercury*, July 20, 1864.

98 *Richmond Daily Dispatch*, July 20, 1864.

99 Three Richmond papers—the *Sentinel*, the *Enquirer*, and the *Courier*—and the *Augusta Daily Chronicle and Sentinel, Columbia Triweekly Guardian, Daily South Carolinian*, and *Savannah Republican* carried editorials that lauded the appointment of Trenholm.

100 The author is greatly indebted to Mr. Alfred Jackson Hanna for the privilege of using his notes and his article on George Alfred Trenholm, written for the 1944 supplement to the *Dictionary of American Biography*.

and Company of Liverpool, brought in the first forty thousand rifles for the Confederacy.[101] Trenholm, as head of John Frazer and Company, controlled a fleet of more than fifty blockade-runners, and in the first part of the year 1863 he was able to ship 18,022 bales of cotton to England. Besides this staple, his ships regularly sent tobacco and turpentine to England, and brought back to the Confederacy through the Federal naval cordon, supplies of salt, coal, iron, arms, ammunition, and other commodities.[102] The companies controlled by Trenholm adhered to a policy of cooperation with the government; while their blockade-running activities were immensely profitable, they would undoubtedly have been far greater through the importation of articles of luxury instead of those vital to the Confederacy.

Secretary Memminger, in May, 1861, sent Trenholm to the Bankers' convention in Atlanta, Georgia, to present the views of the Treasury Department to that body,[103] and from that time until July, 1864, Trenholm continued to be Memminger's unofficial adviser, aiding him in shaping the fiscal policy of the Confederacy.

As Secretary of the Treasury, Trenholm naturally continued the financial measures of his predecessor. The Treasury under his direction continued to issue certificates of indebtedness, to sell bonds, and to print treasury notes. The Secretary, in letters usually printed in the newspapers, opposed increases in prices, advocated the establishment of depositories, stated his determination not to inflate further the currency, and asked for cooperation by the banks and the public.[104] Trying to explain the failure of funding to effect a material reduction in the price level, he wrote that a lack of confidence, not a redundancy of the currency, was mainly responsible for the depreciation of treasury notes; and he held out the hope that the enactment of legislation by Congress would restore morale. In the same letter the Secretary bespoke popular support of the government and

---

101 *Richmond Sentinel,* July 22, 1864, quoting the *Columbia Triweekly Guardian.*
102 See note 100, *supra.*   103 *Charleston Mercury,* June 6, 1861.
104 *Ibid.,* July 23, August 26, October 18; *Charleston Daily Courier,* August 9; *Richmond Sentinel,* August 27; *Richmond Daily Dispatch,* August 23, 1864; Trenholm to T. S. Metcalf, July 19, 1864, in Treasury Department, Confederate States of America, Telegrams, 473.

sought to discourage speculation by recommending bonds of the Confederacy as a safe investment.[105] The Confederacy, in his opinion, was making a new start in finances under circumstances that were by no means discouraging or unfavorable to the South.

Although the Treasury was using the same means to obtain revenue as had been employed before, Trenholm informed the public of the work being done by his department. The *Richmond Dispatch* applauded the Secretary's efforts to get over the idea of a "Treasury of the People," in contrast to the former policy which seemed to set the department over, and independent of, the Confederate citizen.[106] The Secretary had encouraged the people, the *Charleston Mercury* said, and had restored confidence by communicating with them and laying before them financial measures that should be adopted.[107]

Trenholm, unlike his predecessor, was a man of distinguished appearance with the faculty of making friends easily, and he won the confidence of the people through his relations with them. His effort to advertise the Treasury Department was distinctly wiser than the course pursued by Memminger. It not only stilled newspaper criticism, but also won over elements in Congress that had opposed Memminger. In a Congressional resolution Representative Foote referred to the Secretary's "admirably digested financial views," and asked Congress to draw up a fiscal plan in consonance with the Secretary's ideas.[108] There was little criticism of Trenholm in Congress, even though Trenholm often placed the blame for the Confederacy's financial muddle on that body. Some suggested, however, that by his direction of the Treasury Department, Trenholm had made it possible for his trading companies to obtain large profits; and the *Richmond Enquirer* complained that his policy appeared to be limited "to persuasive advertisements and urgent appeals to the people"

[105] Trenholm to Milleadge Luke Bonham, August 5, 1864, in *Richmond Daily Dispatch*, August 23, 1864.

[106] *Richmond Daily Dispatch*, August 23, 1864.

[107] *Charleston Mercury*, July 23, 1864.

[108] *Journal of Congress*, VII, 274. Foote later characterized Trenholm as "a most competent and efficient officer, and a most meritorious and worthy gentleman." Foote, *War of the Rebellion*, 358.

for their favor.[109] Later this newspaper, as if in apology, published an editorial praising the financial acumen of the Secretary.

While both the people and Congress gave evidence of warm approval of the Secretary, neither supported his proposals. The sale of Confederate bonds dwindled to almost nothing, and many contractors refused to accept in payment either bonds or certificates of indebtedness. By the last quarter of 1864 bureau heads of the War Department were complaining that it required two months for the Treasury Department to honor requisitions. Secretary Seddon wrote that the failure to meet obligations had resulted in desertions, marauding, and the sale of personal equipment by the soldiers; that it had prevented the accumulation of supplies; and that it would necessitate closing the work of the War Department if relief were not forthcoming.[110] Soldiers' pay was months in arrears, and the men placed little value on treasury notes when an entire month's pay would buy only one night's lodging away from camp.[111] Confederate money was "utterly valueless in Western Texas," Kirby Smith wrote; [112] and the *Charlottesville Chronicle* suggested that all the notes be burned and barter be used in business transactions.[113]

The Treasury Department's supply of the almost valueless currency was running short. The Secretary estimated that the Treasury would have no notes by January 1, 1865, and he was determined not to print any money in excess of the limit set by Congress. Jones, late in January, noted that the Secretary was selling cotton and tobacco to foreign agents and using their sterling bills of exchange to buy treasury notes at the market

[109] *Daily Richmond Enquirer,* October 4, 1864. There was no truth in the accusation that Trenholm used his official position for personal gain. On the contrary, Trenholm's tenure of office was costly to him.

[110] Seddon to Trenholm, December 29, 1864, in *Official Records,* Ser. IV, Vol. III, 975.

[111] *Charleston Daily Courier,* November 26, 1864, quoting the *Daily South Carolinian.*

[112] Smith to Davis, December 13, 1864, in *Official Records,* Ser. I, Vol. XLI, Pt. IV, 1109.

[113] *Mobile Advertiser and Register,* September 25, 1864, quoting the *Charlottesville Daily Chronicle.*

price.[114] As a result, gold quotations in terms of the notes dropped from eighty to fifty to one. Evidently, Trenholm had hoped that the purchase of currency would tide the government over until Congress should provide a revenue measure. All that Congress did, however, was to authorize a loan to obtain $3,000,000 in gold and, in case that sum was not obtained by April 17, 1865, to impose a tax of 20 per cent on all hard money, bullion, or foreign exchange in the Confederacy. Trenholm was able to borrow about one tenth of the loan from Virginia banks. In the meantime, the Treasury asked for gifts of money, jewelry, and food. Trenholm himself gave $100,000 in bonds and a like amount in currency; Benjamin donated $7,500 in bonds to the Treasury.[115] The work of the Confederacy's Treasury Department, along with other agencies of the government, was drawing to a close.

Responsibility for the collapse of Confederate finance, Trenholm believed, rested on Congress. In his report of November 7, 1864, he called for a return to a fiscal system that would assure the eventual resumption of specie payments. In order to accomplish this, he recommended that there be no further increase in the amount of treasury notes and that one fifth of all tax collections be applied to a reduction in volume of currency. To effect an immediate reduction of outstanding treasury notes, the Secretary proposed a continuation of the tax in kind after the war, the tax to be payable in currency at the existing prices of cotton and other agricultural products. Under this plan, a producer who surrendered treasury notes would receive tax-exempt certificates from the Treasury which would be accepted in lieu of a tax in kind when the war should end. An immediate reduction of the currency, with its consequent appreciation in value, would thus be effected. Trenholm also proposed that Congress sell bonds and levy a tax to raise $360,000,000 for the expenses of the government.[116] Trenholm asked Congress either to accept his plan or to formulate one which would restore the currency gradually and by voluntary action.

---

[114] Jones, *Diary*, II, 393. On March 5, 1865, the Treasury was buying notes at 60 to 1 in gold. *Ibid.*, 440.   [115] *Richmond Sentinel*, March 30, 1865.

[116] *Daily Richmond Examiner*, November 12, 1864; Schwab, *The Confederate States of America*, 78–80.

The Secretary's report was warmly acclaimed by the Richmond press,[117] but Congress failed to act favorably upon it. The program was endorsed by the President; and the House of Representatives passed a bill which embodied most of Trenholm's recommendations, but the Senate threw it out. Trenholm, in mid-January, 1865, suggested that Congress raise $720,000,000 by taxation. Congress not only failed to heed the Secretary's recommendations, but attempted to pass, over the President's veto, a bill increasing the amount of treasury notes by $80,000,000.[118]

Trenholm's tax recommendations were impracticable, but the inactivity of Congress disgusted him. The only recourse, he believed, was an appeal to the patriotism and generosity of the people. Discouraged and tired, he saw the end, for he realized that neither through taxation nor the sale of securities could the Treasury raise the billion dollars needed to carry the Confederacy through another year.

Trenholm believed that only by obtaining a foreign loan of substantial proportions could there be any hope of averting the disaster, and he saw no chance of obtaining such a loan. Trenholm had responded enthusiastically to the suggestion of a bond issue of $75,000,000 to be sold by French bankers. In December, 1864, B. S. Baruc, representing French interests, had come to Richmond to continue negotiations initiated by Collin J. McRae. A preliminary contract had been drawn up which provided that half the sum of the loan was to be delivered in gold; the balance was to be paid in bills of a specially created bank and used solely to purchase and retire Confederate currency and

---

117 *Richmond Sentinel,* November 9, 1864; *Daily Richmond Enquirer,* November 10, 1864. The Editor of the *Dispatch* thought the Secretary's report gave such evidence of business and financial knowledge that Confederate finance should be turned over to Trenholm, whose views and suggestions should be given the force of law. The *Examiner's* Editor declared the report the most encouraging document that had ever come from the administration.

118 *Official Records,* Ser. IV, Vol. III, 1154; *Journal of Congress,* IV, 742. Schwab, *The Confederate States of America,* 80, states that Congress passed the act over the veto of the President. This was not the case. On March 18, 1865, the veto message of the President was considered in the Senate. Thomas Jenkins Semmes was the only Senator to favor the President's stand. There was not a quorum in the Senate, however, and no official action could be taken. The Senate adjourned on March 18 and never met again. *Journal of Congress,* IV, 742.

bonds. The French underwriters, in addition to the commissions to be paid them, were to be aided in obtaining from the South Carolina legislature a charter for a French-American bank.[119] Through Trenholm's influence in his home state, South Carolina had granted a bank charter giving to the French promoters virtually unlimited powers in agricultural, commercial, and industrial trading, as well as in banking operations.[120]

The President had supported Trenholm in his efforts to float the loan. Secrecy of the negotiations was necessary, and Duncan F. Kenner, an agent of the State Department in the proposal to free the slaves in return for recognition by England, had been appointed the Confederacy's financial agent. He had full power to contract for a loan at a price not lower than 50 per cent of par value in return for the liberal bank charter granted by South Carolina.[121] Kenner had found that the sale of Confederate securities in Europe would depend upon recognition of Southern independence, and the negotiations had been abandoned.

Had Trenholm succeeded in floating a $75,000,000 loan at a discount of 50 per cent, it would not have saved the crumbling Confederacy. Soon after Kenner reached England, General Grant captured Richmond and the Confederate administration was in flight. Ill though he was, Trenholm accompanied the President and the Cabinet as far as Fort Mill, South Carolina. His physical condition prevented him from going farther with the party and, on April 27, 1865, he regretfully asked the President to accept his resignation.[122] Davis acceded to the Secretary's request, and thanked him for the zeal, ability, and patriotism he had exhibited in his conduct of the Treasury Department.[123]

Davis had given Trenholm his full confidence and support in the administration of the Confederacy's fiscal affairs. When Congress failed to act on his recommendations in 1864 and 1865, Trenholm asked the President to relieve him of his office, but Davis persuaded him that it was his duty to remain in the Cabi-

---

[119] Baruc to Trenholm, December 9, 1864; Trenholm to Duncan F. Kenner, January [no day], 1865, in Trenholm Papers.

[120] William Lee Trenholm to George A. Trenholm, December 23, 1864; Act of South Carolina to establish a Franco-Carolina Bank, *ibid.*

[121] George A. Trenholm to Kenner, January [no day], 1865, *ibid.*

[122] *Id.* to Davis, April 27, 1865, *ibid.*

[123] Davis to Trenholm, April 28, 1865, *ibid.*

net. The President doubted that anyone could improve the currency situation, as Congress was in open warfare against the administration; Davis also felt the need of Trenholm's able counsel and moral support.[124]

Trenholm had enjoyed the confidence of the President, had been lauded by the press, and had been on terms of friendliness with members of Congress; yet despite all these favoring circumstances he had been unable to reorganize the financial system of the Confederacy. His failure was due to the increasing loss of confidence in the South's ability to win the war. There were but few leaders in 1864 and 1865 who openly advocated surrender, yet not many in the South believed that victory for the Confederacy was possible. Under such circumstances no Secretary of the Treasury could have restored the people's confidence in a discredited currency. George A. Trenholm undertook an impossible task in July, 1864, and as was inevitable, he failed.

[124] Morgan, *Recollections of a Rebel Reefer*, 225.

VII

True to the Navy

LITTLE preliminary thought had been given to a navy by the men who led the South into secession. These fervid nationalists considered navies necessary only to imperial and industrialized nations. The South let it be known to the world that its ports would be open to all countries. Southern leaders believed that commercial nations would ensure the freedom of Southern trade in order to obtain Southern cotton, tobacco, and rice. The South would have little need of men-of-war, having no carriers to protect, no traders to cause disputes in lands overseas, and no colonial territories. Navies were essential for the protection of private enterprise and, in the minds of the South's leaders, were associated with raids on the Treasury.

The provisional Congress of the Confederacy on February 12, 1861, appointed a naval committee, which was instructed to call to Montgomery naval officers to advise what steps should be taken in respect to a Confederate navy. Ten days later the committee reported to Congress. It appeared impracticable to the committee to contemplate any extensive naval preparation in time to meet threatened dangers, since the South had only one navy yard and that under the hostile guns of Fort Pickens. The committee, therefore, had limited its consideration to craft that would serve as auxiliaries at forts and arsenals and cooperate with land forces in the defense of rivers and harbors.[1] Although Congress was considering only a small naval auxiliary to cooperate with the army, it nevertheless provided for a regular Navy Department.

John Perkins, Jr., of Louisiana was reported to be the President's choice to head the department. The *Charleston Mercury*

[1] *Journal of Congress*, I, 75.

was not enthusiastic at the prospect of his appointment, recalling that his educational training had been obtained at Yale and Harvard, and that his experience was limited to the circuit court and the operation of a large plantation. The newspaper did not question Perkins's high character, but could only hope he would prove equal to the task.[2] Perkins was not to be put to the test, however, for as so often happened in the Confederacy, the rumor of his appointment proved false.

STEPHEN RUSSELL MALLORY

President Davis on February 25 sent to Congress as his selection for Secretary of the Navy the name of Stephen Russell Mallory of Florida. He had nominated Mallory without consulting him, nor had any mention of the choice been made to the Florida Congressional delegation, most of whom later opposed confirmation of their fellow Floridian.[3] Davis had known Mallory when the Floridian was chairman of the United States Senate Committee on Naval Affairs, and believed him to be well acquainted with navy personnel and to have a practical knowledge of naval affairs and maritime law. Mallory accepted the secretaryship reluctantly, and only after the President had repeatedly and urgently requested him to do so.

Mallory's nomination was the only Cabinet appointment of the provisional government held up by Congress. When his name was submitted, Jackson Morton of Florida moved that the nomination be referred to the Committee on Naval Affairs. Three days later a majority of the committee reported favorably on the nomination, a minority reporting unfavorably. At the request of two Florida delegates, Morton and James B. Owens, consideration of the reports was postponed until March 4, when Mallory's nomination was confirmed by a five to two vote, with two of the three Florida delegates voting against it.[4] Morton and Owens openly fought Mallory's confirmation on the ground that he had opposed secession and had been in concert with the

[2] *Charleston Mercury,* February 23, 1861.

[3] Clubbs, "Stephen Russell Mallory," 199.

[4] *Journal of Congress,* I, 95–96, 105–106. Florida and Texas voted against confirmation; the individual vote for confirmation was 30 to 7.

United States government in acting to prevent the seizure of Fort Pickens.[5] Mallory was accused of seeking to gain political preferment as a conciliator and also of bad faith toward Florida.[6] The absence of substantiation of these charges and the sense of deference Congress owed the President prevented the rejection of the nominee.

Mallory, in truth, was not an ardent secessionist. In his petition for amnesty in 1865 he avowed his attachment to the Union and stated it as his belief that secession was only another name for revolution.[7] Naturally, the petitioner for amnesty presented his case in the most favorable light, yet had Mallory had the opportunity in 1861 to decide fully his political affiliation, he would unquestionably have favored a continuation of the Union. In the United States Senate he had fought strongly for what he considered the rights of the South, but he held firmly to the opinion that the South should seek remedies within the Union for the ills of which it complained. The accusations that his acts in 1861 were tainted with political ambition and bad faith were unfounded, despite his lukewarm support of secession. With Davis, Benjamin, and others, Mallory in January, 1861, feared that Florida forces would attack Fort Pickens and precipitate a civil war. They telegraphed Governor Madison Perry, earnestly asking him not to attack the fort, as the fort was not worth the spilling of a drop of blood, and bloodshed might prove fatal to the South's cause.[8] Mallory continued his efforts, not only to prevent an attack on the fort, but to persuade President James Buchanan not to send reinforcements to it. He was sincere in his desire to avoid war after disunion; his intentions, however, were misunderstood. The belief that his support of independence was lukewarm persisted, and largely explains the continued opposition to him as Secretary of the Navy.

Mallory's appointment gave the Confederacy an experienced student of naval affairs for the direction of its Navy Department. *Harper's Weekly* believed he would be of service if the South

[5] *Charleston Mercury*, March 6, 1861.

[6] *Ibid.*, March 8, 1861.

[7] Mallory to Andrew Johnson, June 21, 1865, in *Official Records*, Ser. II, Vol. VIII, 662–63.

[8] Slidell, Benjamin, Alfred Iverson, John Hemphill, Wigfall, Clay, Benjamin Fitzpatrick, Davis, and Mallory to Perry, January 18, 1861, *ibid.*, Ser. I, Vol. I, 445.

should ever have a navy.[9] The *St. Augustine Examiner* of April 6, 1861, congratulated the people of Florida on the selection of an able son for an important post. In a longer editorial, the *Floridian and Journal,* on March 9, 1861, warmly approved his appointment, expressing its belief that no man in the South was so conversant with naval affairs or so well endowed with executive ability as was Mallory. Florida was entitled to the post, the editorial continued, because of its extended coast line; and its people, notwithstanding statements to the contrary, approved of Jefferson Davis's wise selection for the Navy Department.

Mallory was not a native of Florida. He was born on the island of Trinidad at Port of Spain in 1812 or 1813,[10] son of a Connecticut father and an Irish mother, and was brought to Key West in 1820. There was not much money in the family, and his formal education was limited to brief terms at a school near Mobile and at the Moravian school at Nazareth, Pennsylvania. After some traveling, he entered the customs service at Key West, and studied law in his spare time. He obtained his license to practice law, became interested in politics, and was soon in favor with voters. He was elected to the United States Senate in 1851, by a legislature so badly split that it was necessary to select for the Senate some one whose views were not well known. Six years later he was re-elected in his own right. He was not an outstanding figure in the Senate. He prepared his speeches carefully, but much of their effectiveness was lost because he lacked the gift of oratory. As chairman of the Senate Committee on Naval Affairs he acquainted himself with the more modern methods of naval warfare. He did not advocate a big navy, but he did demand that the United States navy be modernized and that experiments with ironclad ships be made. He resigned his seat in the Senate in 1861, stating that he wished to retire from public life.[11] Mallory, however, loved companionship of the type to be found in official centers, and when Davis offered him a Cabinet post in the Confederacy he could not resist the opportunity to take part in the newly formed government.

He found himself at the head of a Navy Department that

[9] *Harper's Weekly,* June 1, 1861.

[10] Clubbs, "Stephen Russell Mallory," 5.

[11] There is no published biography of Mallory. The best source for his life is Clubbs, "Stephen Russell Mallory."

boasted few ships. The South was almost wholly deficient in means and materials for the construction of naval vessels. The Confederacy abounded in forests and this caused the uninformed to believe the establishment of a navy was only a matter of cutting trees and fitting timbers together; but there was little seasoned timber in the South. Nor was hemp for rope available, and the number of iron and rolling mills was inadequate to the needs of a shipbuilding program. The department, moreover, at first had only one navy yard, and it was made useless by the Federal guns at Fort Pickens. When Virginia joined the Confederacy the partly damaged Gosport Navy Yard came under Mallory's control for a brief period. There were comparatively few ships' carpenters or engineers in the South. All in all, the outlook for a Confederate navy was indeed dismal.

It was hopeless to expect that the Confederacy could compete with the United States in naval matters. The most optimistic of Southern nationalists never entertained the thought that the Confederacy could keep pace with the North in the construction of ships. Nor were the chances of creating a navy by purchase abroad any brighter, for the United States was equally willing, and better able than the South, to buy available foreign craft. The construction of vessels laid down in foreign countries would have to await formal recognition of the Confederacy, or else must depend upon a willingness of alien governments to wink at such an infraction of neutrality. If the South was to have an effective navy, it would have to be one composed of a new and powerful type of naval vessel. This was a fact plain to Mallory.

The Secretary of the Navy was a politician who possessed a keen mind. His most signal achievement as Secretary was in obtaining men, not ships, for the navy. He had a wide acquaintance among officers of the United States navy and made notable appointments from the commissioned personnel. More than three hundred former officers of the United States navy—less than half of the number of Southerners who held commissions in it —had followed the action of their respective states in renouncing allegiance to the Union. Some of the more outstanding of these were Matthew Fontaine Maury, John M. Brooke, John Luke Porter, French Forrest, William P. Williamson, Hunter Davidson, Franklin Buchanan, and Raphael Semmes. These men, acting together, worked out the Confederate naval policy.

Mallory's distinction as Secretary of the Navy lay in his acceptance of recent trends in naval construction and in building vessels peculiarly suited for defensive warfare. It was due to him that ironclad floating batteries to augment the guns of forts, and ironclad rams to break the blockade, became important factors in the Confederacy's fighting forces on the water. The department also conducted experiments with torpedoes, rifled cannon, banded guns, mines, and submarines. Trim speedy cruisers were planned to prey upon Northern commerce. Mallory and his advisers wished to armorplate all their ships with iron, but unfortunately for their plans the South's supply of iron was inadequate.

Mallory hoped to increase the Confederacy's limited naval resources with the aid of foreign countries. Experienced men were sent to the United States and to Canada to buy available vessels, but the opening of hostilities prevented purchases from these two sources. James Dunwoody Bulloch was sent to England on May 9, 1861, authorized to purchase or contract for six propeller-type steamers.[12] The department desired vessels that combined speed with power, so that they could be used against Northern commerce. Eight days later Lieutenant James H. North was sent to France with instructions to procure the ironclad warship *Gloire* from France.[13] In the event that he was unable to obtain a ship by purchase, he was to contract for the construction of two war vessels, one to be built in France, the other in England. The vessels to be contracted for were to be constructed along the general plans of the *Gloire*, pride of the French ironclads, and the *Warrior*, an armored British vessel then building. Mallory instructed his agents to obtain only eight ships, for his buying program was restricted by a parsimonious Congress and limited funds. The South had to be careful not to rush the market in neutral countries lest its chances of obtaining additional ships in the future should be endangered. A single French ironclad, Mallory rightly believed, would play havoc with the wooden ships of the United States navy. The repeated

[12] *Naval Records,* Ser. II, Vol. II, 64–65.   [13] *Ibid.,* 70–72, 122–23.

attempts to purchase vessels of the *Gloire* or *Warrior* class in foreign countries were not successful.

Confederate agents did secure agreements with English and French firms for the construction of armored warships. On May 20, 1862, Lieutenant North signed a contract with the Glasgow shipbuilders, James and George Thompson, for a 3,200-ton ironclad.[14] Bulloch persuaded the Lairds to construct two ironclad rams, the Birkenhead rams,[15] and George T. Sinclair contracted for a 3,000-ton iron ship.[16] The English government never allowed any of these ships to be used by the Confederacy.[17] In the meanwhile Slidell was working diligently to secure the consent of Napoleon III for the construction of vessels in France. By October 28, 1862, Napoleon appeared willing to aid the Confederacy.[18] The agents of Mallory not only transferred their seat of activity from England to France but also attempted, though unsuccessfully, to move to France the ships contracted for in England. Bulloch contracted for four corvettes and two armored warships with the French shipbuilder L. Arman.[19] The six ships were sold on the order of Napoleon, who feared the possibility of war with the United States in 1864.[20] One of the rams, later commissioned the *Stonewall*, was not accepted by the purchaser because of Arman's failure to deliver her on the contractual date. He then delivered the vessel to Bulloch. The *Stonewall* arrived in Havana near the close of the war, was surrendered to the United States, and eventually sold to Japan for $400,000.[21]

Early rebuffs in foreign countries did not cause Mallory to cease his efforts to obtain warships. In 1863 he wrote Bulloch: "We want ironclads, ironclads, ironclads. . . ."[22] Mallory clung

[14] *Ibid.*, 193–99.   [15] *Ibid.*, 222–26.

[16] Herbert H. Todd, *The Building of the Confederate States Navy in Europe* (Nashville, 1941), 15.

[17] For a detailed account of England's seizure of the Confederate ships, see Owsley, *King Cotton Diplomacy*, 421–37.

[18] Slidell to Mason, October 28, 1862, in Pickett Papers; Owsley, *King Cotton Diplomacy*, 437.

[19] Todd, *The Confederate States Navy*, 22.

[20] *Naval Records*, Ser. II, Vol. II, 665–68; Owsley, *King Cotton Diplomacy*, 448–49; Todd, *The Confederate States Navy*, 23–24.

[21] Gideon Welles, *Diary of Gideon Welles, Secretary of the Navy Under Lincoln and Johnson* (New York, 1911), II, 305–307, 335, III, 97, 99, 365, 513.

[22] Mallory to Bulloch, June 6, 1863, in *Naval Records*, Ser. II, Vol. II, 435.

to the hope of foreign aid for his shipbuilding program until the summer of 1864.

Plans were made at the outset for domestic construction of naval vessels and equipment. The navy yard at Norfolk had not been seriously damaged by the retreating Federals, and it was soon in operation. The Secretary expected to produce all the needed guns and ammunition for the navy at this yard, and he bought equipment to enable its machine shops to construct steam engines. The *Merrimac* was raised, and five hundred men were set to work repairing her partly burned hull. The plans called for a three-inch iron plate to sheathe her wooden body, for it was certain she would be comparatively useless unless armored. Mallory realized the impossibility of constructing iron battleships in the Confederacy, and pushed the work of armor-plating wooden ships. The *Merrimac,* renamed the *Virginia,* was the first to be completed, and the destruction she wrought among enemy warships stirred Southern hopes. At the same time, a contract was made with John Hughes and Company of New Orleans for the construction of a million-dollar ironclad, and Mallory's old friend, Asa Tift, was charged with the supervision of another ironclad.

Armored ships were Mallory's pet scheme. His opinions as to their great value were given in his report to Congress on May 10, 1861, when, after reviewing the history of individual and national experiments with them, he wrote:

I regard the possession of an iron-armored ship as a matter of the first necessity. Such a vessel at this time could traverse the entire coast of the United States, prevent all blockades, and encounter, with a fair prospect of success their entire Navy. . . . Naval engagements between wooden frigates, as they are now built, and armed, will prove to be the forlorn hopes of the sea, simply contests in which the question, not of victory, but of who shall go to the bottom first, is to be solved.[23]

This faith in the new type of ship Mallory continued to hold throughout his term as secretary.

With the nucleus of a few ships that state governments turned

[23] *Id.* to Charles M. Conrad, May 10, 1861, *ibid.,* 69.

over, the Navy Department acquired an amazing number of vessels by construction, purchase, and capture. At one time or another there were, in all, at least one hundred and ninety-nine vessels in the Confederate navy.[24] Most of these were constructed in the South, and whenever the metal was available they were plated with iron. Small navy yards dotted the Confederacy. In Richmond and Norfolk, Virginia; Charlotte and Wilmington, North Carolina; Charleston and Columbia, South Carolina; Atlanta, Savannah, and Columbus, Georgia; and Mobile and Selma, Alabama, ships and naval supplies were turned out. The Roanoke, Neuse, Peedee, and Red rivers afforded available sites for construction. With the exception of that at Norfolk, all establishments were small. By distributing the yards throughout the country, Mallory took advantage of the local labor supply, and also guarded against the disabling of the entire department by a quick thrust from the enemy.

Experiments with mines, torpedoes, and submarines engaged the department from time to time. Submarines were developed to high efficiency so far as ability to submerge was concerned. They sank easily to the floor of the ocean and remained there. One submarine did succeed in blowing up a Federal ship, but was blown up itself in the operation. The experience with mines was more successful. Torpedoes, most successful of all, were a constant and formidable threat to a blockading squadron. The torpedo was not, as now, released and self-propelled to its target. A crude percussion-type torpedo was attached to a small vessel by an extending arm, by which the force of the explosion could be directed at a point on the enemy vessel just below the water line. It was an effective defensive weapon against warships lying in protected waters; it was also extremely dangerous work for those aboard the torpedo boat. The torpedo not only accounted for almost as many enemy vessels as were sunk or captured by all other means combined, but it forced blockading squadrons to stand off at a distance from ports, thereby facilitating blockade-running. The experimental branches of the Confederate navy contributed creditably to the service.

In another field, Mallory used a time-honored weapon to prey

24 *Ibid.*, Vol. I, 247–72.

upon the commerce of the North. After war became a certainty, one of President Davis's first acts was to provide for licensing privateers. Individuals and companies rushed to arm vessels in the hope of gaining fame and fortune. From New Orleans and Charleston the privateers *Calhoun, Savannah,* and *Jefferson Davis* searched for and captured prizes.[25] Others followed, but after 1861 the privateer virtually disappeared. Privateering died with the Confederacy.[26]

Mallory was more interested in another type of marauding vessel, the Confederate cruiser. The cruisers, in contrast to the privately owned privateer, were ships of the Confederate navy, manned and officered by navy personnel, and under control of the Navy Department. They were the offensive vessels of the Southern navy. Mallory hoped they would drive enemy ships from the seas, increase marine insurance rates, force the sale of ships to foreign owners, bring the war home to Northern men of wealth, and relieve blockaded Southern ports by drawing off battleships to search for the elusive raiders. Captain Raphael Semmes began his notable career as commander of an old passenger boat which as the *Sumter* was equipped and put into service in June of 1861. When the *Sumter* ended her marauding career at Gibraltar, Captain Semmes went on to new fame as commander of the *Alabama.*[27] The *Florida,* the *Tallahassee,* the *Shenandoah,* and others roamed the seas in the course of the war.[28] Out of touch with the Confederate authorities for long periods, the success of their depredations depended on the initiative and skill of their commanders. Northern newspapers characterized these raiders as pirate ships. However deplorable this type of sea warfare appeared to the North, the ships' crews were disciplined bodies, and their prisoners were treated with consideration. After the war an effort to prosecute their commanders

25 William M. Robinson, Jr., *The Confederate Privateers* (New Haven, 1928), chapters III–V.

26 Robinson, above, has an excellent account of the privateers. At times, however, he fails to distinguish properly between the privateer and the cruiser.

27 The *Alabama* was contracted for by Bulloch and built by the Lairds. Other Confederate cruisers secured in England were the *Florida,* built by contract by Miller and Sons of Liverpool, the *Georgia* and *Rappahannock* bought by M. F. Maury, and the *Shenandoah* bought by Bulloch.

28 Only two of the cruisers operated for more than a year, the *Alabama* and the *Florida,* before capture or conversion to some other use.

was dropped for lack of evidence to substantiate the charges of piracy and cruel treatment of captives. While the damage they inflicted upon the commerce of the United States can only be estimated,[29] they accomplished virtually all that the optimistic Mallory had hoped they would. Yet, in the main, they damaged the enemy more than they helped the Confederacy. Undoubtedly, they caused the United States warships to suspend blockade duty while they searched for the raiders, although some Southerners asserted that the very rumor of the presence of a cruiser at a port caused the blockade to be tightened.

It was impossible for Mallory to control the operations of the cruisers, and as Secretary he seldom attempted to direct the strategy of naval commanders. One of these infrequent occasions occurred in April, 1862, when Flag-officer George N. Hollis, fearing that his vessels on the Mississippi would be useless against the heavier enemy craft that had passed Island Number 10, suggested that his ships might render service at the mouth of the river.[30] Mallory telegraphed the commander not to entertain the thought, but to cooperate with the land forces and to resist any attempt by the enemy to descend the river. Hollis said that this order was "A dispatch exposing the ignorance of the Navy Department."[31] He was already at New Orleans and did not obey the order, and his ships neither served the army nor did they play any important part in the defense of New Orleans. Mallory's belief that Hollis could have supported the land forces was correct, but he was mistaken in his judgment that a fleet descending the Mississippi was a greater menace to New Orleans than David G. Farragut's fleet in the Gulf. In extenuation of Mallory's faulty judgment, it should be said that it was one of but few attempts to interfere with naval commanders. The Secretary had received warning that ironclads were being constructed at St. Louis for the Federals, and the spies he sent there reported that the United States intended to build an enormous

---

[29] The Confederate cruisers destroyed approximately $30,000,000 of Northern property. This actual destruction was of less importance than the losses sustained by increased marine insurance rates, the forced sale of ships at depressed prices, and the transfer of a large part of the United States merchant marine to foreign countries. Owsley, *King Cotton Diplomacy*, 575.

[30] Hollis to Mallory, April 9, 1862, in *Naval Records*, Ser. I, Vol. XXII, 839.

[31] Endorsement by Hollis, Mallory to Hollis, April 10, 1862, *ibid.*, 840.

fleet for the purpose of attacking New Orleans from upstream. The department had received full reports of the danger from the fleet in the Gulf, but Mallory believed Farragut could not pass the forts below New Orleans.

The fall of New Orleans in 1862 was a bitter blow to Mallory. "His friends say he is overwhelmed with grief and gout at the loss . . . ," the *Charleston Mercury* reported. The *Mercury* added, "his enemies say he keeps to bed because he loves it, and because he finds the seclusion of the sheets very comfortable." [32] The even-tempered Secretary did indeed feel the defeat keenly and he expected criticism. On his part, however, he had the inner satisfaction that he had pushed to the utmost the construction of the ironclads *Mississippi* and *Louisiana*. The *Mercury* correspondent admitted that Mallory had made every effort to rush preparations for the city's naval defenses, but added spitefully, "No doubt he did all that a man in a permanent trance could do." [33] The *Wilmington Journal* made the belittling comment: "It is said that at first, the Montgomery Government resolved to ignore a navy. Thinking they need have no navy, they naturally thought nobody was needed as Naval Secretary, and so, to be consistent they choose Mr. Mallory," [34] The House of Representatives on August 20, 1862, instructed the Committee on Naval Affairs to inquire into the expediency of abolishing the Navy Department and investing the powers and duties of the Secretary of the Navy in the Secretary of War.[35] A week later the House appointed a special committee to investigate the administration of the Navy Department, and the Senate provided for joint investigation. The joint committee was made up of both friends and foes of Mallory, and was not, therefore, appointed for "whitewashing" purposes.

For a year and a half the administration of the department was under scrutiny of the investigating committee. The evidence the committee collected presented conflicting views. Charles Conrad, chairman of the House Committee on Naval Affairs, charged that the Secretary had retarded the construction of vessels by refusing to order night and Sunday work on

32 *Charleston Mercury*, May 7, 1862.   33 *Ibid.*, May 1, 1862.
34 *Wilmington Daily Journal*, April 30, 1862.   35 *Journal of Congress*, V, 303.

them; he said that as chairman he felt it his duty to proclaim publicly his "conviction of the incapacity or inefficiency of the Secretary of the Navy." [36] Nelson Tift, a naval supervisor, however, stated that Sunday and night work were done whenever it was possible to obtain workmen, and that construction work was never suspended except on the occasions when, over the objections of the department officials, men were called for military parades.[37] Mallory was completely exonerated from charges of inefficient management, and the report of the joint committee praised him for remarkable accomplishments. "We have no navy," said the *Richmond Enquirer,* "but this is no indication of want of capacity or energy or skill." [38]

The report of the investigating committee called attention to the handicaps under which the Navy Department labored. Among them was its inability to obtain supplies of seasoned lumber, rope, iron, and machinery. A notable weakness of Southern-built vessels was the inferior quality of their power equipment, the engines used in them being poorly constructed or rebuilt ones which often failed at crucial times. Some of them were hardly equal to propelling a ship against the force of an average river current.

Another problem was that of obtaining the services of able seamen. Conscription, as applied by recruiting agents, did not benefit the navy, for the agents pushed most of the drafted men into the land forces. Mallory applied to Secretary of War Benjamin, begging his aid in obtaining the release of soldiers for naval duty. Benjamin ordered commanders to ascertain the number of trained seamen in the ranks who were willing to be transferred to the navy. This order placed the responsibility of reducing their own forces on the army officers who themselves were continually calling for additional recruits. Mallory wrote that no dependence could be placed on such methods to strengthen materially naval personnel.[39] The Secretary of War, a warm personal friend, tried to comply with Mallory's wishes, but he was himself circumvented by the generals.

36 *Official Records,* Ser. I, Vol. VI, 622–24.   37 *Ibid.,* 625–28.
38 *Daily Richmond Enquirer,* February 18, 1864. The evidence taken by the joint committee is found in *Naval Records,* Ser. II, Vol. I, 431–809.
39 Mallory to Benjamin, January 10, 1862, *ibid.,* 127.

When Randolph succeeded Benjamin in the War Department, Mallory's difficulties continued. Randolph at first detailed men to the navy, but in the early summer of 1862 he grew tired of Mallory's importunities and refused to send his applications for details to army commanders. Mallory agreed that the army had greater need of men during the defense of Richmond, but late in the summer he renewed requests for men.

Randolph coöperated with the Navy Department to a greater extent than did his successor, Seddon. Mallory informed the President in 1863 that the department had insufficient men at Savannah, Mobile, Charleston, and Wilmington to man the ships or even the guns on board, and suggested that men be transferred to those ships from near-by land forces. The President approved the suggestion and sent the Secretary's letter to Seddon for prompt attention and action. Seddon in August replied that application should be made for specified men from armies with which the vessels were coöperating, since distant commanders, "not appreciating the exigency for seamen, present every obstacle to the transfer of their tried soldiers." [40] Mallory quickly replied that he had long since placed a specific request for six hundred seamen, giving their names, companies and regiments, all of whom had applied to the Navy Department for service. The Act of Congress of May 1, 1863, compelled the transfer of all men for whom application had been made, and Mallory declared that he recognized no rule other than that laid down by law and had applied for men in regiments stationed near the ships to be manned.[41] The navy finally, with Presidential support, obtained the transfer of some of the men desired.

Another pressing need of the Navy Department was for skilled workmen. This problem was never solved. There were few shipbuilders, machinists, and naval technicians in the agrarian South. Those who were trained in these trades volunteered for army service, and the army made little effort to find or release such men to the naval branch of the military service. Lack of skilled workmen prevented the fitting out of a naval force on the Cum-

---

[40] Seddon to Mallory, August 7, 1863, in *Official Records*, Ser. IV, Vol. II, 697.
[41] Mallory to Seddon, *ibid.*, 705–706.

berland River and seriously delayed the construction of the
Tennessee and the *Arkansas*.[42] Mallory made repeated appeals
to the War Department; he received courteous answers, but few
men. Seddon undoubtedly could have acted more vigorously to
meet the Navy Department's need, but even his mild efforts were
stubbornly resisted by army commanders. In 1864 Mallory presented to the President evidence that naval ordnance work was
being curtailed for want of mechanics. The Selma, Alabama,
yard, that was making only one gun a week, could make three
with adequate man power, and could produce shot and shell for
the entire navy if provided with sufficient workmen, but with
its skeleton force, had been able to supply only a few ships. The
works at Charlotte and Atlanta were operated under similar
handicaps. Mallory suggested, as a remedial measure, the appointment of a board composed of army and navy officers to
survey the Navy Department's needs and to fill them by details
from the army or from conscript camps.[43] Action on this request
was prevented by the pressing necessity of utilizing all available
men to oppose the advance of Grant's forces. The *Richmond
Enquirer*, in October, 1864, berated the Navy Department for
not revoking all its details for sixty days to meet the emergency. The newspaper apologized for its criticism four days
later upon learning that the naval employees for months had
been organized into a fighting body ready for instant call, and
that the number of men detailed to that department was very
small.[44]

At first glance, the War Department would seem to deserve
condemnation for its niggardly supply of men to the navy. It
should be borne in mind, however, that the armed forces of the
Confederacy were depleted by desertions and casualties in 1864,
and were pressed by an enemy greatly superior in numbers. Not
a single man from the army could be spared by any district in the
country. After the first waves of patriotic fervor in 1861 and
1862, men wanted to get out of the service, not in it. Examination of army returns gives convincing proof of the inadequacy of

[42] Report of the Secretary of the Navy, August 16, 1862, in *Naval Records*, Ser.
II, Vol. II, 244.

[43] Mallory to Davis, July 1, 1864, in *Official Records*, Ser. IV, Vol. III, 520–21.

[44] *Daily Richmond Enquirer*, October 17, 1864.

the Confederacy's forces to meet the invader on anything like equal terms. In addition to the requests for men from the naval and other departments, government contractors urgently presented the need for men to be detailed as workmen in their plants. Although many of these requests were denied, the Secretary of War faced a stream of complaints from military men against what they regarded as excessive withdrawals of men from army duty. Many soldiers regarded a permit to transfer to another branch of the service as the first step toward eventual desertion. Serious as was its need, the Navy Department's need for sailors was no greater than that of the army for soldiers.

The army and navy were at odds with each other over various problems. General Braxton Bragg demanded control of the naval craft in Mobile Bay in December, 1861. Naval vessels, he reported, stood idly by when their help was needed. In disgust at the inactivity of one vessel, the General declared: "It would be economy to give her away and discharge the crew." [45] Benjamin forwarded Bragg's report to Mallory and requested that control of harbor defenses be given to the commanding army. The Secretary of the Navy explained the action of his subordinates and, while agreeing that harmony of action should exist between the branches of the service, refused to consent to a military commander's controlling naval forces.[46] He held consistently to this position, but gave orders for the naval forces to cooperate with the army.

Mallory had more cause to complain of a non-cooperative spirit in the War Department than that department had of the navy. When the ironclad *Richmond* was completed the Secretary asked Randolph to order the removal of the obstructions in the James River to allow the ship to pass down, but the engineering bureau advised against making a break in the barrier placed against enemy ships.[47] Mallory renewed his request in April, 1863, and again the engineering bureau reported unfavorably on it, stating that the machinery and speed of the *Richmond*

[45] Bragg to Samuel Cooper, December 29, 1861, in *Naval Records*, Ser. I, Vol. XVII, 16.

[46] Mallory to Benjamin, January 9, 1862, *ibid.*, 16–17.

[47] *Id.* to Seddon, May 24, 1864, in *Official Records*, Ser. I, Vol. XXXVI, Pt. III, 829–30.

were so defective as to render her valueless.[48] Mallory admitted
that the *Richmond*'s machinery was defective and that her speed
was only four miles an hour, but he believed the ship was little
inferior to the enemy monitors. The presence of the *Richmond*
below the James River obstructions, in his opinion, would have
prevented the enemy from sounding and dragging the river in
rowboats under the protection of wooden warships, enabling the
Federals to capture the submarine batteries that had taken the
Confederates two years to build. The *Richmond* could not have
been destroyed except by the use of ironclads, and Confederate
torpedoes could have been used effectively against them.[49] Once
more on January 2, 1864, Mallory requested that the James be
opened, only to be informed that this would be done whenever
the *Richmond* and the *Fredericksburg* were ready to move.[50]

Even more disheartening to the Secretary than the enforced
idleness of his ships, was the repeated destruction of vessels that
were either completed or partly completed. The firing of craft
under construction was often necessitated by successful inroads
of the enemy, but Mallory complained bitterly to Davis about
the ill-timed zeal of army officers in burning Confederate ships.
General Samuel Jones, the commander at Pensacola, the Secretary wrote, had ordered two boats destroyed when there was no
danger that they would be captured by the enemy.[51] One of these
vessels had been completed, the other was in condition to be
moved up the Escambia River had an attack on the city been
made. Destruction of warships continued, much to the chagrin
of the naval officials. Mallory enjoyed showing the wonders of his
ironclads to his friends. On one such occasion when the tour of
inspection had ended, he said to a party of young women: "Well,
ladies, I have shown you everything about them." "Everything
but one," Miss Maggie Howell replied demurely; and at the Secretary's unspoken question, she added, "the place where you
blow them up." [52]

It was no joke to the conscientious Secretary that the ships on
which his department laid great hopes should be destroyed by the

[48] *Ibid.*   [49] *Ibid.*
[50] *Ibid.*
[51] Mallory to Davis, April 12, 1862, in *Official Records*, Ser. I, Vol. VI, 893–94.
[52] DeLeon, *Belles, Beaux and Brains of the 60's*, 415–16.

Confederacy's own forces. He took his disappointment philosophically, however, and planned to continue building naval works at points more distant from the enemy. The abandonment of Norfolk in 1862 was the most severe blow he had yet suffered. The *Virginia* and other vessels under construction there were destroyed, but more serious than the loss of that weakened ship was the forced abandonment of the Confederacy's only yard with shipbuilding facilities, munition works, and machine shops. Much of the machinery and naval equipment was saved, and land was purchased in Charlotte and shops set up to produce projectiles, gun carriages, and laboratory stores.[53] The establishment of naval shops hundreds of miles inland caused derisive comments on the wisdom of a landlocked navy yard. The establishment of the naval works at Charlotte, nevertheless, was a wise move. Similarly, the equipment saved at New Orleans was set up in Atlanta. The works at Charlotte, Atlanta, Columbia, Lynchburg, and other places produced guns, machinery, munitions, and stores for ships constructed at seacoast or river ports.

Mallory had difficulties with the Treasury Department as well as with the War Department. Memminger had been obliged, because of the urgent necessity to sell Confederate bonds, to demand that the bonds be used by those departments which made large purchases. Mallory in his letters of instructions to foreign agents directed them to pay for ships and munitions in Confederate securities whenever possible. The agents, however, found it almost impossible to dispose of the bonds even at high discounts. Mallory pointed out that the failure of the Navy Department to maintain its credit in the domestic field was not the department's fault. His requisitions on the Treasury, he said, at times were met entirely in drafts for Confederate bonds. Agents of the navy had made as many contracts as possible providing for payment in these securities, "but the Treasury . . . deems it proper to send bonds when not required and when we cannot use them, and embarrassment to the Department and losses to creditors inevitably follow."[54] Mallory did not blame Memminger for the

[53] George Minor to Mallory, August 15, 1862, in *Naval Records*, Ser. II, Vol. II, 250–51.
[54] Mallory to Davis, March 8, 1862, in *Official Records*, Ser. I, Vol. VI, 845.

delays and the methods used; he believed the Secretary was doing the best anyone could do under the circumstances.

When the Erlanger loan was arranged in 1863 the War and
Navy departments expected to split the proceeds between them.
Memminger admitted as much, but he informed Mallory that
the money from the loan would be paid out as a mercantile transaction in order to present the cotton account in a true light. He
proposed to take the pound sterling at a fair rate of exchange,
not the "exorbitant and exaggerated" rates of 1863, and he requested the Secretary to place a requisition for $400,000 if he de-
sired 30,000 pounds sterling.[55] This did not meet Mallory's approval, as the House of Representatives had recently appropriated something in excess of $5,000,000 for the navy. If figured
on Memminger's basis, the navy would get only $1,666,666,
whereas the entire appropriation in currency equal to sterling
was needed.[56] Mallory wrote to Albert Gallatin Brown, chairman of the Senate naval committee, requesting that the House
appropriations bill be so amended as to ensure full payment
without deduction for exchange. Senator Brown could not locate
the bill until someone in the Navy Department informed him
that it had passed both houses of Congress and had been signed
by the President. Mallory's worries were needless, for the Erlanger loan in the end amounted to only 40 per cent of its face
value.[57] The amount allotted to the navy was invested chiefly in
English and French contracts for ships that never reached the
Confederacy.

In addition to the annoyances caused by his colleagues, Mallory was the victim of a piece of mendacious journalism. The
New York Sun on December 15, 1863, printed two documents
which were asserted to be those of Confederate department secretaries; one was a genuine report by Secretary Memminger; the
other, a spurious one attributed to Secretary Mallory. The spurious report was addressed to the Speaker of the House, instead of
to the President, and mentioned efforts made by the Confederate
Navy Department to release Confederate prisoners of war by or-

[55] Memminger to Mallory, April 11, 1863, in Naval Records, Ser. II, Vol. II, 400.
[56] Mallory to Memminger, April 13, 1863, ibid., 403–404.
[57] Id. to Bulloch, July 20, 1863, ibid., 467.

ganizing raiding parties from Canada. It also referred to the failure of Mallory's agents to obtain five ironclads in England and three in France.[58] The purpose of the fictitious report was to prove true a contention by the United States that the Confederacy was behind the efforts to build war vessels in England. Secretary of State Seward accepted the report in good faith, and Charles Francis Adams, although expressing doubts as to its genuineness, laid it before the British government as an authentic document.[59] Matthew Fontaine Maury wrote a letter to the *London Herald* branding the report a hoax, but three weeks later Her Majesty's Attorney General successfully defended the seizure of the Birkenhead rams by quoting from the forged report.[60] Mallory on March 10 denounced the report as a contemptible forgery and accused the United States Navy Department of being a party to it.[61] The spurious document eventually reacted against the United States, but not before Mallory had been abused for stupidity in writing it.

In Davis the Secretary of the Navy found a bulwark against the criticisms directed against him by enemies at home and abroad. The President had selected Mallory on the basis of his worth and ability. His conviction that he had picked the best man in the Confederacy to head the Navy Department grew as his association with Mallory progressed. The Secretary had several times indicated his wish to relinquish the cares of office. In the summer of 1861, and again in February, 1862, he urged Davis to release him from his post.[62] The President was convinced that Mallory had no greed for office. What Davis did not know was that Mallory had no intention of resigning. Had he wished to do so, it would have been easy for him to leave the Cabinet. But he was a seasoned political war horse who loved the scent of office. He had won the confidence and esteem of the President by his work and by his tact. Mallory could offer to resign, knowing that his offer would not be accepted.

---

[58] Earnest Balwin, "The 'Mallory Report' and Its Consequences," *National Magazine*, IX (1899), 556.

[59] *Ibid.*, 557–58.   [60] *Ibid.*, 558–59.

[61] Mallory to Benjamin, March 10, 1864; *id.* to Roundell Palmer, March 10, 1864, in *Naval Records*, Ser. II, Vol. II, 596, 601.

[62] *Id.*, Diary, July 26, September 1, 1861, June 24, 1862.

The Secretary of the Navy was the Beau Brummell of the Cabinet. He found happiness in society and in congenial companionship. Mallory never missed an opportunity to flatter even the lowliest member of society. He once described a friend's sister as a sunbeam, "whom Heaven, in pity, has bestowed upon one man only to prevent her from being the death of man." [63] Mallory was more than a flatterer, however; he was a good conversationalist, with a store of interesting anecdotes and a ready wit. Above all, he could listen attentively and appreciatively to the opinions and stories of others. Endowed with a rare understanding of human nature and clever enough to use his gifts to his advantage, the Secretary of the Navy was not troubled by the jealousies of subordinates or by interference of the President.

Whenever Davis intervened in the affairs of the Navy Department it was to support the Secretary. A notable example of Presidential support was the controversy that raged over the value of Confederate cruisers in 1864. In September, General Lee, at the request of Brigadier General William Henry Chase Whiting, commander at Wilmington, protested against the use of the port by cruisers. [64] In the opinion of Whiting these vessels did little more than destroy Federal fishing smacks. Their use of Wilmington as a base for cruisers attracted Federal ships, thereby making it more difficult for ships to run the blockade. Seddon replied to Lee that Mallory's cruisers were doing good service, but he agreed with General Lee's opinion that Charleston should be used by the commerce raiders as a base. [65] Seddon discussed the question with Mallory, who stated his willingness to send the ships at Wilmington to sea, on condition that Whiting aid them by impressing for them one day's supply of coal from each blockade-runner in exchange for an equal amount of North Carolina coal. [66] Whiting thought the use of the poor quality North Carolina coal, because of its dense smoke-producing nature, would endanger the blockade-runners, and he refused to impress the

[63] *Id.* to Virginia C. Clay, June 1, 1864, in Clay Papers.

[64] Jones, *Diary*, II, 291, 314.

[65] Seddon to Lee, September 23, 1864, in *Official Records*, Ser. I, Vol. LI, Pt. II, 1041.

[66] Mallory to Seddon, October 1, 1864, *ibid.*, 1042.

superior coal used by the blockade-runners unless ordered to do so by the President.[67]

Governor Zebulon B. Vance in October joined the controversy with the assertion that the cruisers performed no real service for the Confederacy, and demanded that the *Tallahassee* and the *Chickamauga* be taken out of service. The President requested information of Mallory for an answer to Governor Vance, and Mallory pointed out that the *Tallahassee* had captured thirty-one vessels. The vessel's service, he continued, could not be measured solely by the prizes taken, for her operations made the coastwise commerce of the United States insecure, forced ships to delay their sailings from enemy ports, increased marine insurance rates, and compelled the withdrawal from Wilmington of the warships blockading that port.[68] Mallory's defense of his ship convinced the President that the Secretary should have a free hand in directing the Confederate cruisers. Despite the objections of Governor Vance, General Lee, and two Cabinet members, Benjamin and George Davis, President Davis sustained the Secretary of the Navy.[69] Governor Vance persisted in his attacks on Mallory, but they failed to alienate the President's support of the Secretary.

Mallory appreciated the President's confidence and reciprocated it. During the early months of the government in Richmond he was a frequent guest at the Davis table. He met the President's guests at the station and helped to entertain them at the Spottswood Hotel. When the government executives were established in their homes, Mallory's visits to the Davis home became less frequent. Mallory's wife, the former Angela S. Moreno, of a distinguished Spanish family, did not care greatly for Mrs. Davis, but the lack of cordial relations between their wives did not affect the friendship between Secretary and President. Mallory complained in the summer of 1861 that the Secretary of War would not discuss military projects in Cabinet meetings, and he threatened to resign. He also desired that the

---

[67] Whiting to *id.*, September 20, October 5, 1864, *ibid.*, 1042, 1046–47.
[68] Mallory to Davis, October 22, 1864, in *Naval Records*, Ser. I, Vol. X, 793–94.
[69] Samuel Person to Davis, November 12, 1864, in *Davis Papers*.

Cabinet meet more frequently and that the various military appointments be discussed by the secretaries in council.[70] His criticism was unjustified, for all important military plans and the major appointments were thoroughly discussed in Cabinet sessions. To have considered minor plans of the several departments would have been a waste of time. Except for this controversy, the Secretary of the Navy seemed to be one of the most contented members of the administration.

Mallory needed the President's sympathetic support, for the newspaper editors of the Confederacy severely criticized the Secretary. The press opposition was based, for the most part, on what the newspapers called his lack of aggressiveness in getting ships under construction. The *New Orleans Crescent* believed the entire nation was dissatisfied with his conduct of the Navy Department and was clamoring for his removal for inefficiency. Had he been a capable executive, the newspaper declared, the Confederacy would have had a fleet capable of competing with the enemy gunboats late in 1861.[71] The *Charleston Mercury* was severe in its judgment of the Secretary, saying "D———n that fellow! He's gone to sleep again." [72] An editorial in Rhett's paper accused Mallory of having failed to make use of the admittedly poor facilities that the South possessed. Charleston, according to this newspaper, had shipyards, trained men, foundries and workshops capable of producing engines, machinery, and iron plates, but Mallory refused to consider bids for work from the city's various companies.[73] It was not until late in January, 1862, the *Mercury* asserted, that orders were given to Charleston concerns for materials. Mallory was stirring from his lethargy, Mrs. Chesnut remarked in March, 1862, and was ordering ships built regardless of cost.[74]

There was some justification for the criticism of the Secretary on the score of delayed action. In the early months of the war he based his hope for a Confederate navy on securing warships from abroad. It was nearly summer before he became convinced that he could expect but little aid in Europe for the Confeder-

70 Mallory, Diary, July 26, September 1, 1861, June 24, 1862.
71 *Charleston Mercury*, February 28, 1862, quoting the *New Orleans Crescent*.
72 *Charleston Mercury*, March 26, 1862.   73 *Ibid.*, March 6, 1862.
74 Chesnut, *Diary*, 147.

acy. He then lost further time by haggling over prices with contractors in the Confederacy. By a lavish use of funds, the Navy Department could have made an earlier start at home. By November, 1861, however, Mallory had eighty-seven vessels afloat in the service of the Confederacy.[75] He had actually begun work on the *Merrimac* before Congress appropriated funds for the project. Considering the difficulties under which he labored, his early record was not one to be scorned.

Mallory was doing his utmost in March, 1862, to speed up the activities of the Navy Department. Repeatedly he urged Flag-officer French Forrest, in command of the navy yard at Norfolk, to increase construction work there and to make daily reports of progress. These reports were not such as to satisfy Mallory, and he assigned Captain Sidney Smith Lee to the yard. He instructed Lee to work every available man at top speed and to report any subordinate who fell below the standard in capacity, energy, and industry, so that his place might be filled by another.[76] When Captain Lee objected to night work in the yard because of the danger of fire, Mallory replied that the risks attending night work had been duly considered before the order was given.[77] It was made plain to the highest and lowest subordinates in the Navy Department that speed was essential and that delays would not be tolerated. The immediate danger to Richmond was so great as to make it imperative that work on the ironclads *Virginia* (*Merrimac*) and *Richmond* be completed.

The satisfying demonstration of the *Virginia* against the wooden ships of the enemy was Mallory's reward. The news of the ironclad's victory was to Mrs. Chesnut like a gleam of light illuminating a dark scene. It revived hope in the momentarily dispirited Virginians, and assured Mallory's confirmation as a member of the Cabinet of the permanent government in 1862. ". . . will Mallory be saved from the deluge by making an ark of the *Merrimac?*" William Henry Trescot asked William Porcher Miles.[78] The feeling that Mallory was a lukewarm seces-

[75] John Thomas Scharf, *History of the Confederate States Navy from Its Organization to the Surrender of Its Last Vessel* (New York, 1887), 47.
[76] Mallory to Lee, March 24, 1862, in *Naval Records,* Ser. I, Vol. VII, 749.
[77] *Id.* to *id.,* April 24, 1862, *ibid.,* 773–74.
[78] Trescot to Miles, March 10, 1862, in Miles Papers.

sionist and that he had been lax in naval preparations was still held against him, but after the *Virginia's* victories he was confirmed by the Senate by a safe margin of votes.

When New Orleans fell, a fresh wave of criticism broke upon the Secretary of the Navy. The *Richmond Examiner,* expressing regret at the failure of Congress to vote a resolution of no confidence in Mallory, recalled that the gentlemanly Walker resigned as soon as the country manifested dissatisfaction with his management. Mallory, the newspaper commented, came from Florida, home of the alligator, and he seemed to be as fond of ease and as thick-skinned as the native amphibian. The Secretary would remain in the Cabinet, the *Examiner* continued, since he belonged to the class of persons of whom Jefferson might say, "few die, none resign." [79]

Some of Mallory's critics found fault with him on slightly different grounds. George Fitzhugh thought the Secretary had been unjustly censured for doing too little, when the exact opposite was too true. In his opinion, Mallory was an earnest, energetic, foolish man, the type of person the most mischievous and troublesome in the world. He tried to do the impossible; hence he diverted Confederate strength from tried forms of defense to useless projects. The Secretary, Fitzhugh said, built many vessels, hoping "to take Yankees by surprise, or failing in that, to blow themselves up, in a most extraordinary and heroic way." [80] Mallory, in fact, had a vivid imagination. He suggested that the ironclad *Virginia* steam to New York, attack, and burn the city. He really believed that the *Virginia* could accomplish this feat, and that peace would immediately follow.[81] Subordinates convinced him that the ship was neither seaworthy nor powered to navigate the ocean. The Secretary also experimented with rifled cannon and wrought-iron shot for use against the *Monitor.* He had visions of expeditions to the Great Lakes, destroying shipping and canals; he also contemplated sending men to St. Louis to capture ships under construction, and to add them to the

[79] *Daily Richmond Examiner,* August 29, 1862.
[80] George Fitzhugh in the *Richmond Daily Dispatch,* October 14, 1862.
[81] Mallory to Franklin Buchanan, March 7, 1862, in *Naval Records,* Ser. I, Vol. VI, 780–81.

Confederacy's fleet. Many of his schemes were fanciful, but some of his plans were concrete and workable.

Mallory's feelings were lacerated by bitter criticism, but he was possessed of friends whose praise soothed his hurts. Benjamin did much to help him forget the unkind words spoken to him. Reagan in later life referred to Mallory as a genius who revolutionized naval warfare.[82] Benjamin H. Hill told his constituents that no part of the government was conducted with more industry than the Navy Department.[83] The friendship of Watts, Trenholm, and President Davis was also a comfort to the Secretary of the Navy.

Nor did Mallory lack friends among the press. The *Richmond Enquirer* and the *Richmond Sentinel* both came to his defense. In several editorials the *Enquirer,* reviewing the difficulties under which the department labored, protested against the unfairness of placing the responsibility for the destruction of ships upon Mallory. This newspaper found him to be a hard-working and sensible executive who consulted freely with his commanders and won the approval of such officers as Admiral Franklin Buchanan, Captains Lawrence Rousseau and John M. Brooke, and Commander Arthur Sinclair.[84] The *Sentinel* resented the flippant criticism by witlings whose sole contribution to public service consisted in assailing those who were manfully at work.[85] Expressing its belief that his critics objected to Mallory because he was too fat, the newspaper wished this allegation were in fact true, for "it would be quite a luxury to look at a fat man in these famine times." "We are glad," the editorial continued, "they do not prefer the charge of leanness against the President or Secretary of War; for had they done so, we could not have put in a word of defense." [86] Mallory's navy, the *Sentinel* considered, had won equal distinction with the army. The defense of Mallory by the editor of *De Bow's Review* came nearer the truth than the criticism of any contemporary. It was De Bow's judgment

[82] Reagan, *Memoirs,* 156.
[83] Speech before the Georgia Legislature, December 11, 1862, quoted in Hill, *Benjamin H. Hill,* 257–58.
[84] *Daily Richmond Enquirer,* August 28, September 4, 1862.
[85] *Richmond Sentinel,* February 15, 1864.   [86] *Ibid.,* July 29, 1864.

that, while the Secretary had made mistakes earlier in the war, he had done as well, if not better, than any other man could have done under identical circumstances.[87]

In the late years of the war newspaper criticism of the Secretary became less frequent. A few editors were convinced that Mallory had amended what they had at one time considered his negligent ways. Most of them, however, withheld criticism of the Secretary of the Navy because they saw better opportunities to attack Benjamin, Seddon, and Memminger. The importance of the navy declined as more and more ports of the Confederacy fell to the enemy and attention was centered on the military situation.

Until April 3, 1865, Mallory continued to plan for the development of the navy. By that time the few ships around Richmond had been destroyed, and the sailors and hopeful naval cadets [88] had joined the land forces or were guarding the remaining government funds in the flight of the administration southward. Mallory stayed with the Presidential party until it reached Washington, Georgia. Then, convinced that further resistance was hopeless, he had penned his letter of resignation as Secretary of the Navy at Abbeville, South Carolina. In it he expressed his gratitude for the President's past kindness and consideration and offered to follow his chief, if necessary.[89] In his reply, Davis recalled with regret the trials of the war and the embarrassments caused by a lack of cooperation on the part of Congress. "For the zeal, ability and integrity with which you have so long and so constantly labored," the President wrote, "permit him who had the best opportunity to judge, to offer testimonial and in the name of our country and its sacred cause to return thanks." [90]. In closing his letter, Davis again thanked Mallory for his unwavering friendship and his counsel upon all important measures, counsel that had been a most valuable support to the administration.

Truly, Mallory had made an extraordinarily able Secretary of the Navy. His temperament enabled him to work in harmony

---

[87] "Editorial," De Bow's Review, XXXIV (1864), 102.
[88] Mallory had established a naval training school at Richmond in 1862.
[89] Mallory to Davis, May 2, 1865, in Rowland (ed.), Davis, VI, 586.
[90] Davis to Mallory, May 4, 1865, ibid., 586–87.

with the President, and generally with his fellow Cabinet members and with naval commanders. He had imagination and the initiative to strike out on new paths. He was industrious and kept the business of his department well in hand. He never overworked for, though he loved office, he enjoyed an easygoing existence. Before the war he was an average politician with no extraordinary attainments; after it he retired to a life of comparative ease. But for four years fraught with almost insuperable difficulties he directed the Navy Department of the Confederacy brilliantly.

VIII

Man of Mail

THE Davis administration fully realized the difficulties that it faced in the organization and direction of a postal system for the Confederacy. The people of the South had been well served by the United States postal system, but this service had been performed at the cost of heavy deficits. The fathers of the Confederacy believed the deficits were incurred, in large measure, by Federal grants to Northern business. To prevent such diversion of public money for private gain the Constitution of the Confederacy provided that the Post Office Department should pay its expenses out of its own revenue after March 1, 1863. This provision gave the department two years of grace in which to gather maps, let mail routes, make contracts with railroads, appoint postmasters, obtain paper and stamps, and attend to miscellaneous details. At the end of this time the department had to live within its own income and be self-supporting.

The Confederacy covered an extensive area, much of which was sparsely settled. The United States had furnished postal service to many semi-isolated sections at a tremendous cost. Unless the new government continued this accustomed service, general public dissatisfaction would be the result.

If war came, which was highly probable in March, 1861, the difficulties confronting the Confederacy's postal service would be measurably increased. The Southern states had no railway system equal to the strain of transporting war materials; and in a choice between the needs of the postal service and of the army, the latter would certainly get preference. Moreover, in the event that the Confederacy's coasts were blockaded, there would be increased difficulty in making arrangements for foreign mails. Invasion, which had to be considered as a possibility, might cut off mail routes and disorganize the best-laid plans for a system. In any event, a war would create the need for numerous branch offices to take care of the soldiers' mail; with every change in army locations, routes and offices would have to be shifted. The organization of an efficient postal system would have been a difficult task even in time of peace; in a period of war, it was almost impossible.

Despite the difficulties of the task, there were several alleviating features. First among these was the prospect of assembling a personnel without too much delay. Many Southern men had held office in the United States Post Office Department and, if they could be induced to cast their fortunes with the Confederacy, the department would have a skeleton force of experienced men around which the service could be expanded. The organization of a postal system would be greatly simplified if information could readily be obtained as to postal routes, maps, contractors, post offices, and postmasters from Federal authorities. The fact that the quantity of mail to be handled would be greatly increased by war, with a consequent increase in postal revenue, was another cheering factor. Then, too, the franking privilege had been abolished, and the increased business and the higher postal rates that the provisional Congress had provided would go far toward making it possible to keep the income of the department in balance with its expenses.

Under these extraordinary conditions an able executive would be needed for the difficult task of organizing the postal service. In casting about for the right man, Davis turned to an old friend, Henry T. Ellet, a prominent lawyer and politician in Mississippi, who had been elected to fill out Davis's unexpired term when the latter resigned his seat in Congress in 1846 to enter the Mexican War. Ellet had returned to his law practice in 1848, and in the ensuing years served two years in the Mississippi State Senate, worked on the state code of 1857, and was a leader in the old Democratic party in the Mississippi convention of 1861. The President on February 25, 1861, nominated his friend for Postmaster General and the provisional Congress immediately confirmed the appointment.[1] The appointment evidently was made

---

[1] *Journal of Congress*, I, 85.

without consulting Ellet; he had no desire for office, and he declined the honor on the plea of private duties.[2] Davis was disappointed that his friend would not accept a place in the Cabinet, and offered the post office appointment to Wirt Adams, a member of a prominent Mississippi family. Adams also refused it.[3] After two weeks the President had found no man who was either free or willing to undertake the organization and direction of the Confederate Post Office Department.

JOHN HENNINGER REAGAN

A large, rugged Texan, whom President Davis had known as a member of Congress, had called on Davis to congratulate him upon his election to the presidency. The caller, John Henninger Reagan, frankly told Davis that, had he arrived in Montgomery in time to vote, he would not have voted for Davis as President; not, he explained tactfully, because he distrusted Davis's fitness for the place, but because he favored the former United States Secretary of War for the post of commander in chief of the Confederate army.[4] This adroit flattery pleased the President, who admitted that the military position would have been more to his liking than the presidency.

Reagan was suggested for the postmaster-generalship by his colleagues of the Texas delegation; and the more Davis considered the suggestion, the more he believed that Reagan would be a good selection for the place. He knew Reagan's reputation for honesty and ability, that he had a wide knowledge of the territory embraced by the Confederacy, and that he had served as a member of the postal committee in the United States House of Representatives. He decided to offer the Cabinet post to Reagan.

The tender was made to the Texan on March 6. Reagan, however, was not too receptive and repeatedly declined the appointment. His unwillingness to accept it, he explained, was because he feared that no man in a short time could provide as good a

---

[2] *Charleston Daily Courier,* March 7, 1861.

[3] Reagan, *Memoirs,* 109; *id.,* "An Account of the Organization and Operations of the Postoffice Department of the Confederate States of America, 1861 to 1865," Southern History Association, *Publications,* VI (1902), 314.

[4] *Id., Memoirs,* 109.

postal service as the people had become accustomed to under the old government. In their dissatisfaction, the public, Reagan thought, would attribute the shortcomings of the postal system to the incompetence of the Postmaster General. He desired to serve the Confederacy, but he had no yearning to be a scapegoat. Under persuasion by the President, members of the Cabinet and of Congress, who promised to defend him against unjust criticism, Reagan finally accepted the appointment, but under no illusion that the office would be a sinecure. On the contrary, he felt that before long he would be condemned by the public as incompetent.[5] What little attention the appointment received was favorable. The Texas delegation unanimously endorsed their colleague, and the provisional Congress confirmed the nomination without question.[6] The *Charleston Mercury* did not doubt that Judge Reagan would show that his administrative ability was equal to the talent he had shown as a legislator in the halls of Congress.[7]

John Henninger Reagan was a self-made man. He had had little opportunity for education in his youth. Born in Sevier County, Tennessee, on October 8, 1818, the son of Timothy and Elizabeth Lusk Reagan, he received his primary education at Nancy Academy at Sevierville, and in his spare time, worked in his father's tanyard and on a farm. By the time he reached sixteen years of age he had saved enough money to enable him to attend Boyd Creek Academy. After a further period of work he studied for two sessions at Maryville Seminary, now Maryville College. This was the extent of his formal education. After leaving school, he wandered southwestward, working at various times as a bookkeeper, a tutor, and a plantation overseer. The last-named job paid well, but he gave it up because the men under his supervision did not get enough to eat. He found himself in Texas in May, 1839, and became in quick succession an Indian fighter, a surveyor, and a married man. Two years later, after he had become the owner of a small farm, his wife died. He studied law and obtained a license to practice his profession in Palestine, Texas. At the age of twenty-nine years, he was in a

[5] *Ibid.*, 110.   [6] *Charleston Daily Courier*, March 9, 1861.
[7] *Charleston Mercury*, March 7, 1861.

position rapidly to increase his wealth and standing in the community.

His election to the state legislature in 1847 was the beginning of a long political career. He was elected district judge in 1852, and soon made a reputation by clearing his district of gamblers. In the same year he married Edwina Moss Nelms, who bore him six children before her death in Richmond eleven years later. Reagan became a member of the United States House of Representatives in 1857, but resigned his seat in 1861 to follow his state out of the Union. He served in the Texas secession convention, and in the Montgomery convention that established the Confederate States of America.[8]

Reagan was not a "fire-eating" Southern nationalist. He had on every occasion defended the rights of his section, but had never advocated secession per se. After the election of Lincoln to the presidency, he saw no hope for the maintenance of Southern rights under the prevailing interpretation of the Constitution. He foresaw the triumph of a Republican regime, and advocated the calling of a Southern convention for the purpose of obtaining guaranties and reaffirming constitutional rights.[9] When it became evident that a solution of the question by this means was impossible, he came out strongly for secession. He had little fear that war would result from disunion, for he believed the domestic commercial and manufacturing interests would oppose a conflict. Even should the United States be so foolhardy as to attempt war, he believed that commercial interests in Europe would force foreign intervention. He had cause to regret his confidence during the succeeding four years.

Once he had accepted the postmaster-generalship, Reagan lost no time in attacking the formidable task of providing an administrative department for the postal system he was to establish. H. P. Brewster was sent to Washington immediately to get key men in the Federal postal system to assist in building the Confederate postal system. These men were: Henry St. George Offut, chief clerk in the office of the sixth auditor; Benjamin Clements,

[8] The account of Reagan's life is based on Reagan, *Memoirs,* and Walter F. McCabel, "John H. Reagan," Texas State Historical Association, *Quarterly,* IX (1905–1906), 41–51.

[9] Francis Richard Lubbock, *Six Decades in Texas,* . . . (Austin, 1900), 299.

chief clerk to the Postmaster General; Joseph Lewis, head of the bond division of the Post Office Department; Captain Gustav A. Schwartzman, head of the Dead Letter Office; McNair, of the Finance Bureau; and Hobly, third assistant Postmaster General. Brewster offered them positions in the Confederate government and requested them to bring with them the last annual report of the Postmaster General, samples of every blank form then used in the postal service, and postal maps of the Southern states. All but Hobly accepted the offer and brought most of the information requested.[10] After the more important positions were assigned to experienced men, other appointments were made. It was soon found that there was a dearth of men capable of handling the office details, so a departmental school was organized to train clerks for postal service, the trained men acting as instructors. By the time the necessary record books were acquired, the department had a partially trained force ready for work; and the names of postmasters, special agents, and star route contractors, with the salaries to be paid them, were entered on the records. When the special session of Congress convened, Reagan reported that his department was fully organized.

The Confederacy, however, still depended upon the United States postal service. On May 13, Reagan issued a proclamation setting June 1 as the date when the Confederate postal system would begin to function; until May 31, 1861, regular accounts would be made from the South to the Post Office Department in Washington.[11] On that date a final accounting was made and all property of the United States government, except mail sacks and locks, were to be returned to it. It was believed that this evidence of a willingness to pay the United States for services rendered would result in a continuation of the service to Confederate territory. Postmaster General Montgomery Blair responded with a proclamation suspending United States service in the Southern states from June 1 forward.[12] For some time there was the unique situation of a country providing postal facilities for its foe. This was in line with Lincoln's contention

10 Reagan, *Memoirs*, 125.

11 Frank Moore (comp.), *The Rebellion Record: . . .* (New York, 1861–1863, 1864–1868), I, 325; Reagan, *Memoirs*, 131.

12 *Naval Records*, Ser. I, Vol. IV, 356; Reagan, *Memoirs*, 132.

that a combination of people which was too strong for the regular court machinery to suppress was in rebellion against the legal government. As long as service could be maintained, the United States Post Office Department would continue to function in the South.

In the meantime, Reagan used these weeks of grace to obtain supplies for his department. Draughtsmen were obtained to make postal maps; blank forms were prepared; and the department advertised for bids to supply mail bags, paper, blank forms, twine, sealing wax, envelopes, and stamps. Congress was asked for and granted the power to retain in office postmasters and contractors who had been in the Federal service. The department lacked postal supplies, but felt ready nevertheless to take over the direction of mail service on June 1, 1861.

Less than three weeks later complaints of poor service began coming in from the section around Bull Run,[13] and from then on they increased steadily until 1862. Thereafter they declined in number and varied in intensity. At no time in the life of the Confederate postal service, however, was there a period when the newspapers and individuals did not denounce the service for inefficiency. The *Richmond Examiner* on August 10, 1861, complained of the poor service of the Richmond post office and declared that the fault was due to false economy and the lack of clerks to handle a threefold increase in the quantity of mail. ". . . we trust that the Postmaster-General," the editorial continued, "with regard to serious public interests, as well as to the exigencies of official economy, will be prompt to amend the present unsatisfactory and crippled condition of the Richmond office." The newspaper again, on September 6, complained of the fatal policy of economy. It happily announced a few months later that enough new clerks had been appointed to ensure efficient service. The *Charleston Courier* was willing to give odds of ten to one that if the Richmond mails arrived in Charleston one morning, no mail would get to Charleston from Richmond the next day.[14] The *Petersburg Express* favored turning over the

13 L. R. Garrison, "Administrative Problems of the Confederate Post Office Department," *Southwestern Historical Quarterly*, XIX (1915–1916), 115.
14 *Charleston Daily Courier*, October 3, 1861.

mail deliveries to the express carriers unless the service were improved. Two out of three letters passing between Richmond and Montgomery were lost in transit, the *Montgomery Mail* reported.[15] From Virginia to Texas the newspapers commented on the failure of the mails.

An efficient postal service was of special interest to the newspapers, but there were accusations of faulty service from private persons also. A friend wrote Alexander H. Stephens: "If I send this letter by mail I shall be compelled to frank it and let you pay postage. The rule, I fear at our post office here is on all paid letters to receive the money and throw the letters in the fire." [16] "Complaints are increasing," a constituent in North Carolina reported to his congressman, and he added: "Our Postmaster General must be a very slow coach. . . ." [17]

Secretary Seddon wrote to Governor Vance that the latter's letter of July 5 was not received until July 23; but Seddon explained that there had been an interruption of transportation facilities.[18] References to delays in mail deliveries at various times are found in the correspondence of other Cabinet members.

While the Confederate postal service was undoubtedly poor in comparison with that formerly given by the United States, it was not a total failure. The numerous complaints may mislead one who fails to remember that the postal service was rarely mentioned except when one complained because of the failure to receive a letter or paper promptly. For every lost piece of mail there were thousands that reached their destinations safely. For every instance of delay or interruption there were hundreds of pieces of mail that left and arrived on schedule.

Continued criticism became almost unbearable to the Postmaster General. Because of the illness of his wife he did not ar-

[15] *Daily Richmond Examiner,* September 30, 1861, quoting the *Montgomery Mail.*

[16] Thomas W. Thomas to Stephens, October 10, 1861, in Phillips (ed.), *Correspondence of Toombs, Stephens, and Cobb,* 580–81.

The use of the word "frank" in the above is misleading. The franking privilege or free use of the mails by any official was not allowed in the Confederacy. Letters could be sent prepaid or C.O.D.

[17] Henry Guin to T. D. McDowell, August 3, 1861, in John M. McDowell Papers, University of North Carolina.

[18] Seddon to Vance, July 23, 1864, in *Official Records,* Ser. IV, Vol. III, 555.

rive in Richmond until over a month after the removal of the capital from Montgomery.[19] Worried over family affairs and dismayed by the complaints of inefficient postal service, Reagan determined to leave the Cabinet at the expiration of the provisional government. The *Charleston Mercury* was willing to have him start raising a military command, for it was evident that he had "great talent for some sort of out-door business." [20] The *Tennessee Fayetteville Observer* found a growing desire for the resignation of the Postmaster General.[21] Other newspapers joined in the demand for his resignation. Reagan was ready to join the army, and early in 1862 he handed in his resignation. The President and members of the Cabinet induced him to withdraw it, representing to him that his retirement might be interpreted as dissatisfaction with the administration.[22] Reagan never again seriously considered leaving the Cabinet.

In the meantime, newspapers had come to the defense of the department. A correspondent sent by the *Charleston Courier* to investigate the management of the postal service found the officials most courteous and keenly aware of the delays attending the inauguration of mail service. The officials explained that the war had upset the system. Again, hardly had postal arrangements been completed for the seven states originally composing the Confederacy when four more entered and the department had been thrown into confusion. Many contractors had refused to renew their contracts after June 1, 1861. For instance, the firm of Sawyer and Risher, which was responsible for routes in Texas at a cost of $130,000 a year, had declined to consider a renewal of the contract. The same was true of the agents in Arkansas, who had stopped their work on July 1. On May 13, Reagan had called upon all postmasters, contractors, special and route agents to forward their names to the department so

19 Reagan was absent from his office from May 25, 1861, to July 13, 1861, Post Office Department of the Confederate States of America, Record of letters and other communications from March 7, 1861, to October 12, 1863, Manuscripts Division, Library of Congress, 156–69. Cited hereafter as Letter Book, Post Office Department.

20 *Charleston Mercury*, October 10, 1861.

21 *Daily Richmond Examiner*, October 3, 1861, quoting the *Tennessee Fayetteville Observer*.

22 Reagan, *Memoirs*, 150.

that new commissions might be issued, but by October only a small percentage of the number had been heard from. The railroad executives had also added to the difficulties of the department, for the postal authorities had no way of forcing them to live up to their contracts. Few trains ran on time and the roads often changed their schedules without having given the postal authorities advance notice. The Postmaster General had called a conference of railway superintendents with the hope of regulating schedules, but only one executive had answered the call. Troop transportations, too, were continually throwing the whole arrangement of the service out of order. The *Courier's* correspondent was convinced that the department was doing its best to give the public regular postal service.[23] The *New Orleans Picayune* thought Reagan one of the most energetic men in the government, and that, despite great difficulties, he was bringing order out of chaos; [24] and the *New Orleans Crescent* agreed that he had done all that any man could be expected to do.[25] When the provisional government came to an end, the newspapers were generally agreed that, while the postal service was poor, they doubted that any other man could better it under the existing circumstances. Hence there was little demand for Reagan's resignation in March, 1862. The President believed the Postmaster General had accomplished much under trying and unusual difficulties, and without hesitation he renominated him for the post in the permanent government. The appointment was quickly confirmed by the Senate.

Economy was the dominant note in Reagan's management of his department. His desire for economy was behind most of the causes, other than those created by the war, of inefficient mail service. Repeatedly, the shrewd editor of the *Richmond Examiner* pointed out that innumerable troubles were caused by this false idea. Many newspapers were of the opinion that there was an urgent need to pare the extensive mail service that had been operated before secession. The *Shreveport Southwestern* compared the United States Postmaster General to the frog that

23 *Charleston Daily Courier*, October 7, 1861. The *Daily Richmond Enquirer* of December 5, 1861, carried a similar vindication.

24 *New Orleans Daily Picayune*, October 19, 1861.

25 *Charleston Mercury*, February 28, 1862, quoting the *New Orleans Crescent*.

tried to puff himself up to the size of an ox. Under his administration mail routes had been lavishly extended, stage lines had been thrown across the desert, and post offices had sprung up as thick as mushrooms. Under these conditions, the newspaper said, Reagan had applied the pruning knife to lop off the superfluous limbs and suckers which had retarded the prosperity of the whole service; he had had no alternative but to reduce unnecessary post offices and mail routes. These eliminations, the *Southwestern's* editor concluded, had caused the attacks upon the Post Office Department.[26]

Reagan considered it his primary duty to keep the department to the letter of the constitutional provision that the expenses of the postal department must be met out of his own revenue after March 1, 1863; furthermore, he believed that it was a wise provision. The postal expenditures of the United States for the states forming the Confederacy were $2,897,530.97 in 1860, and the receipts, $938,105.34.[27] The Confederacy hoped to overcome this deficit of nearly $2,000,000 by increasing postage on letters to five cents per one-half ounce up to five hundred miles, and to ten cents above that distance; by discontinuing unprofitable routes and minor post offices; and by reducing daily to triweekly service on many routes. When he had become familiar with the postal arrangements, Reagan saw an additional opportunity to cut expenses in railroad transportation. He called together the executives of the principal carrier systems and they agreed to reduce their transportation charges by one half. Post offices and routes were eliminated wholesale. Reagan's attempt to force the adoption of the star routes met with resistance, however, for contractors refused to carry the mails for less than they had received under the old system.[28] The Postmaster General made new contracts but, despite success in pruning expenses, the postal system ran up sizeable deficits. An increase in postage rates seemed to be the only solution. There was much justification

26 *Daily Richmond Enquirer,* November 25, 1861, quoting the *Shreveport Southwestern.*

27 Reagan, *Memoirs,* 133.

28 Reagan to Williamson Simpson Oldham, September 5, 1861, in Letter Book, Post Office Department, 190–91.

for such increase, as currency depreciation had added to the expenses of the department. Congress therefore provided for the department by doubling the postage rates on letters, effective July 1, 1862.[29] The rate for carrying a one-half ounce letter five hundred miles was increased to ten cents, but this did not begin to take care of the deficit in the operation of the service.

Late in 1862, Reagan became convinced that the only hope of wiping out the deficit lay in another increase in postal rates. Newspapers suggested that this objective might be brought about by a decrease in rates which might augment the volume of mail handled, but the President agreed with the Postmaster General and, on September 30, 1862, he asked Congress to make some provision enabling the Post Office Department to raise sufficient operating revenue. Davis in his communication indicated that it would be satisfactory to him if Congress should pass an appropriation to make up the postal deficit.[30] The request for increased rates was premature, for it had been made before time to appraise the results of the increase already effective on July 1 had elapsed.

Two unconsidered factors were working in the meantime to aid Reagan in his struggle to operate his department within the constitutional provision. The first was that postage stamps were being used in place of petty cash, because the Treasury Department had issued no paper money in denominations smaller than a dollar and small coins had virtually disappeared from circulation. The other favoring circumstance was a sudden reduction in the cost of operating mail routes. Where there had once been haggling over compensation for servicing star routes, bids now poured in for the competitive routes at rates as low as one mill

[29] *Daily Richmond Examiner,* June 21, 1862.

[30] Davis wrote to the Congress: "If in your opinion, the clause of the Constitution above referred to merely directs that Congress shall pass such laws as may be best calculated to make the postal service self-sustaining, and does not prohibit the appropriation of money to meet deficiencies, the question is one of easy solution. But if, on the contrary, you should consider that the constitutional provision is a positive and unqualified prohibition against any appropriation from the Treasury to aid the operations of the Post Office Department, it is for you to determine whether the difficulty can be overcome by a further increase of the rates of postage or by other constitutional means." Richardson (ed.), *Messages and Papers,* I, 252.

per mile. They came from those who desired to escape being
drafted into military service and who were eager to obtain exemption through service in the postal department. These two
fortuitous circumstances, together with less important aids, enabled Reagan to solve his great problem. The department late
in 1863 was able to report a surplus of $675,048.34.[31] The sur-
plus grew, and Reagan in his *Memoirs* proudly recalled that the
Confederate Post Office operated at a profit during the entire
war.[32]

What he considered a great achievement was of little real sig-
nificance. It is impossible to say whether or not Reagan could
have operated the service within its income in normal times. The
postal department was the beneficiary of very high postal rates
at the same time that the currency was steadily depreciating.
Against the excessively high-priced materials—paper, for instance, was $1.00 a pound in 1863—were the absurdly low sal-
aries of postal workers and reduced railway charges. Any attempt
to compute a balance for the Confederacy's postal system would
have to take into account an estimate of the stamps purchased
for currency uses. The solution of one problem would only lead
to the creation of many others. The important need of the Confederacy, after all, was a reliable and efficient mail service rather
than a crippling economy.

The very fact that Reagan was able to pile up large surpluses
in his department indicates a weakness in his conduct of it. Although it is inconceivable that any man could have given perfect
mail service to the Confederacy ravaged by war, it is plain that
the department would have rendered better service had all its
income been used for improving the service. The undue emphasis put upon economy led to some incongruous situations.
A special act of April, 1863, provided for a postage rate of fifty
cents on half-ounce letters on special routes across the Mississippi

31 *Ibid.*, 378–79.

32 Reagan, *Memoirs*, 134. Reagan mistakenly declared that the Post Office Department was self-sustaining from the beginning to the end of the Confederacy.
The deficit for the first month's operations (June, 1861) was estimated at $108,553.30.
Letter Book, Post Office Department, 248. The deficit for the second year of
operation was nearly one and a half million. *Daily Richmond Examiner*, March
17, 1863. Over the four-year period the profits of the last years more than offset
the losses of the first.

River.[33] Less than two weeks later authorization was given for the establishment of a fast mail service for government letters and dispatches at a rate of one dollar per half-ounce for a distance of five hundred miles. Thus the government charged itself for postal service.

Moreover, newspaper reports indicate that economy continued throughout the war to be placed above service. The *Richmond Examiner* pointed out that no provision was made for transporting mail beyond points of breakage in railroads while they were being repaired,[34] and this newspaper repeatedly reminded the department that false economy promoted inefficiency in the service. A Georgia newspaper, which collected and reprinted the criticisms of the department by newspapers in the Confederacy, reported that a ton of letters was held up in the Lynchburg post office and 100,000 letters in that of Charleston.[35] The *Petersburg Express* reported that it took as long for a Richmond paper to reach Petersburg as it did for a New York newspaper to come through the blockade, and that frequently it required three days for a letter to go twenty to thirty miles. The management of the post office, said the *Augusta Chronicle*, was in truth as bad as, if not worse than, that of the Treasury. "It is one of the results of a picayune, narrow-minded management," the newspaper declared. "If things keep progressing, we shall soon be as far advanced in postal facilities, as were the nations of the fourteenth century." [36] A Postmaster General, the *Chronicle* concluded, who desired a surplus revenue must either desire to annoy the public or else he lacked common sense to know the true uses of the department. These severe criticisms, however, were made by newspapers unfriendly to the administration, and obviously they exaggerated conditions. Nevertheless, the emphasis placed on economy was an important cause of poor postal service.

To what extent Reagan could have increased the efficiency of the system had he used all the available sums of his department

[33] *Public Laws of the Confederate States of America*, 1 Cong., 3 Sess. (Richmond, 1862–1864), 108.
[34] *Daily Richmond Examiner*, February 4, 1864.
[35] *Augusta Daily Chronicle and Sentinel*, June 24, August 17, 1864.
[36] *Ibid.*, August 17, 1864.

can only be estimated. Judging from the report of December 18, 1863, the service could have been bettered by more than 25 per cent. While such an estimate is based on the dubious assumption that ample revenue could have assured a truly efficient postal service, it is undoubtedly true that a willingness to spend more freely would have removed many serious delays and avoided much of the difficulty with the railroads.

All the blame of a policy of economy at any price cannot fairly be laid to Reagan. The policy was but the expression of a general desire. Before the department had demonstrated its ability to operate on a self-sustaining basis, the House of Representatives was considering the advisability of abolishing the entire postal service.[37] A resolution had been passed authorizing an inquiry into the expediency of reducing the expenses of the Post Office Department to a point within its income by abolishing the department, or by allowing express companies to carry mailable matter on which postage was prepaid. The resolution received little consideration, but it was symptomatic of the widespread demand for economy in the conduct of the postal system.

This penny-pinching urge led to what was perhaps the most acrimonious dispute in the Cabinet during its entire existence. To pick up the thread of the story it is necessary to go back to the early operation of the Post Office Department. Reagan had placed advertisements inviting bids to furnish stamps for the department and acceptable responses had been received from concerns in the United States. Meanwhile, the war had cut off this source of supply. New contracts for the stamps made with Southern firms had not been fulfilled or had been unduly delayed because of the firms' lack of materials, tools, and skilled men.[38] Consequently, the sender or receiver of mail had to pay

---

[37] *Journal of Congress*, VI, 74–75.

[38] The first stamps were placed on sale October 16, 1861. *Daily Richmond Examiner*, October 16, 1861. Not until months later did the supply of stamps equal the demand. Because of pressing demands, individual postmasters had printed their own stamps. Those of Postmaster Bass of Petersburg were a simple square design of flowers with "five cents" in the center. *Petersburg Daily Express*, September 23, 1861. These local stamps were gladly received but added to the confusion of the service. The fact that postmasters were able to print stamps before the Post Office Department did, was not an indication of Reagan's neglect of duty. The

for postage in specie. Even after a satisfactory supply of stamps had been obtained by the department, small purchases had to be paid for in specie. From time to time deposits of specie were made in the Treasury, supposedly to the credit of the Post Office Department. In June, 1863, Reagan asked for $50,000 in current exchange for specie, the money to be placed on deposit in England to the credit of the Post Office Department to be expended for postal supplies which Reagan contemplated buying. The Comptroller of the Treasury, Lewis Cruger, refused to comply with the request, stating that the Post Office Department had no specie to its credit, and that Reagan should have asked for $145,000, the currency equivalent of $50,000 in specie. The frugal Postmaster General felt that to follow this advice would mean the loss of $95,000 to his department, which he estimated had more than $50,000 in specie deposited to its credit in the Treasury. His attempt to obtain this coin led to a heated controversy with Secretary Memminger, who contended that the small amount of gold in the Confederate Treasury, no matter what was its original source, belonged to the government and should be used to meet the urgent necessities of the War Department. Reagan wrote Memminger that the money belonged solely to his department, and that technically it had never been out of his control. Memminger replied that postal funds had not been kept in a separate account prior to October 15, 1861, and that there was no way of telling the amount of postal deposits in the Treasury. The Postmaster General by this time was thoroughly angry. He wrote heatedly that the funds should have been kept separate, and he threatened that if the Treasurer, Edward D. Elmore, persisted in his refusal to deliver the money to him he would report him to the President for removal on the grounds that he was acting in violation of the law.[39]

Memminger refused to allow the specie to leave the Treasury and the controversy was referred to the President on June 30, 1863. Reagan's position was based on three points: that the

---

local stamps were poorly done and easily counterfeited. For a detailed account of the problem of securing stamps, see Garrison, "Administrative Problems of the Confederate Post Office Department," *loc. cit.*, 111–42, 232–51.

[39] *Ibid.*, 233.

Treasurer was prohibited by law from exchanging specie for other funds, or exchanging funds of greater value for those of less value; that the law required the Treasurer to keep separate and distinct accounts of money deposited in the Treasury by the Post Office Department; and that the Postmaster General had full control of the funds of his department.[40] The Secretary of the Treasury, Reagan asserted, had, on other occasions, interfered with the department in regard to accounts.[41]

I will add if it be true that the Treasurer can receive specie without keeping a separate account of it, and at his direction pay out treasury notes or other depreciated currency in lieu of it, this would offer the strongest possible temptation to unlawful and dishonest speculations in the public moneys, which are the evils the legislation herein referred to was designed to prevent.[42]

The controversy was discussed in Cabinet meeting and referred for decision to Attorney General Watts; his opinion completely upheld Reagan's contentions.

Memminger was not disposed to accept the Attorney General's opinion as closing the matter. He desired to renew the correspondence, stating that he had no way of ascertaining the amount to which the Post Office Department was entitled. Furthermore, the Postmaster General was only one of many creditors of the Treasury Department, and it would be unfair to pay his department in coin and the others in notes. In fact, Memminger wrote, the Post Office Department was not justified in claiming payment in coin because as early as September 30, 1861, it had overdrawn its account, and since then two deficiency appropriations had been made, for which Congress had provided treasury notes only.[43] Besides, he said, the only coin in the Treasury was that taken from the Louisiana banks. Reagan replied that, if the last statement were true, there had been dishonesty somewhere.

[40] Reagan to Davis, June 30, 1863, in Letter Book, Post Office Department, 721.
[41] A dispute had occurred in the summer of 1862. At this time Memminger agreed that the Postmaster General was correct in his contention, recognized his control over funds, and ordered the payment of a requisition demanded. Letters from Secretaries, Comptroller's Office, Confederate States of America, January 10, 1862–June 11, 1863, p. 49, National Archives.
[42] Reagan to Davis, June 30, 1863, in Letter Book, Post Office Department, 722.
[43] Garrison, "Administrative Problems of the Confederate Post Office Department," loc. cit., 234.

It was October before Reagan won his fight. After the President had received from him a formal complaint against the Treasurer, Davis enclosed Watts's opinion, stated that the only grounds upon which the Treasury Department could refuse to honor the requisition of the Post Office Department was a lack of funds to its credit, and ordered the Treasurer to pay the money as Reagan directed.[44] Thus, after three months of official squabbling the Post Office Department obtained the $50,000 in specie that it had demanded. From a legalistic standpoint, Reagan was right, but Memminger's stand had more of common sense to commend it. There would have been no occasion for the dispute had it not been for a depreciated currency and Reagan's firm conviction that the postal service should be self-supporting. The way by which the controversy was settled was perhaps the most significant thing about it. When the two disputants were unable to come to an agreement, the matter was referred to the President, who brought it up in Cabinet meeting and referred it to the Attorney General, whose decision finally was forced upon Memminger. Disputes of this kind were rare. This one shows that the President allowed his advisers a great deal of freedom of action in settling their own differences.

Reagan was not so successful in controversies with the War Department as he was in his disputes with Memminger. Because of military necessities, the various secretaries of war and army officers interfered at times with civil matters. Before the passage of the Conscription Act, Reagan protested that the recruiting of postal employees by state military authorities was seriously hampering the service. Such action, he believed, would disorganize the government, for military authorities had "as much right to compel the President and Heads of Departments and members of Congress to enter the Service as they have to compel postmasters and their clerks." [45] The Postmaster General wrote many letters to Secretary of War Randolph concerning interference by the military with train schedules, and the seizure of postal property and telegraph lines. Randolph in most instances was conciliatory and made amends whenever possible.

[44] Davis to Treasurer of the Confederate States, October 5, 1863, in Rowland (ed.), *Davis,* VI, 56.
[45] Reagan to Davis, March 17, 1862, in Letter Book, Post Office Department, 409.

After Seddon became Secretary of War a real difficulty occurred. Congress, at first, had provided exemption from military service for postal employees but, after October, 1862, all postmasters and contractors who were within the age limit, and who had not been nominated by the President and confirmed by the Senate, became liable to military duty. This necessitated making new appointments and contracts by the Post Office Department. Reagan found that the decrease in the number of persons eligible for contracts resulted in the receipt of bids equal to only about one eighth of the necessary mail routes. He became convinced that unless exemptions were obtained the postal service must be discontinued. The President rather reluctantly supported Reagan's demands for special legislation, and Congress granted exemptions for contractors and mail route agents, but with many exceptions. Reagan seems to have kept to the letter of the law, but he charged that conscription officers disregarded both the law and decisions of the courts.[46]

In a spirit of cooperation, the Postmaster General organized his departmental men into a military reserve, to which newspapers gave the name "Reagan Rangers," or "Reagan Rifles." As the army continued to draft contractors who, Reagan thought, were legally exempt, the Postmaster General advised them to obtain writs of habeas corpus, and then, in order to instill a little respect for the law and the rights of others into military men, to sue them for false arrest. The dispute grew more serious month by month. Secretary Seddon charged that men enrolled in the army were obtaining postal contracts by low bids in order to leave army service, and he asserted that the Post Office Department in advertising for contractors emphasized that as employees in the postal service they would be exempt from army duty.[47] Reagan replied that he had tried to avoid awarding contracts in such cases where evidence indicated that the bid had been made chiefly to escape service in the army.

[46] Garrison, "Administrative Problems of the Confederate Post Office Department," loc. cit., 129.

[47] Seddon to Reagan, February 3, 1864, in Official Records, Ser. IV, Vol. III, 70–74. Reagan could turn the tables on Seddon. The Postmaster General, feeling himself mistreated by a commissary agent named Witson, wrote Seddon that the man was able-bodied and should be in the army. Jones, Diary, II, 319.

Early in 1864 the correspondence between the two departments grew heated. Reagan wrote the Secretary of War that two of his letters had been ignored. In one of them he had accused an army captain of evicting the postmaster at Ivor, Virginia, and using the post office as a combination dance hall and saloon. Since the Secretary of War had answered none of his recent letters, thus preventing further communication between the two departments without the loss of his self-respect, Reagan threatened to submit the matter to the President.[48] Seddon then replied that Reagan's complaints against military officers were being investigated. On his part, Seddon complained that the Post Office Department had not played fair in rejecting contractors' bids, and in setting forth the advantage of military exemption in its advertising for lower bids. This policy, he said, had resulted in the department's acceptance of bids by persons who agreed to take over a mail route for compensation of one cent a year. With these contracts as evidence of their right to exemption, Seddon wrote, soldiers had obtained release from army duty.[49] Reagan admitted that 147 out of 1,253 bids were of nominal value, but he imagined that the War Department had as many able-bodied men exempt from army service as the Post Office Department.[50] Seddon replied that, as there seemed to be a difference between them which no amount of discussion could remove, he saw no reason for further correspondence.[51]

The controversy dragged on with diminished intensity. In September, 1864, Reagan admitted that his department had made contracts for 252 routes at nominal compensations, but he did not believe there were 500 persons in the postal service who would be liable for military duty. As the mail service was extremely important to Confederate morale, he believed that a diminution of the deliveries of letters would increase desertions from the army. He stated his willingness to leave the final decision of the question to the Cabinet and the President, and if they demanded it, he would conduct the postal system without benefit of exemption. Meanwhile, General Lee complained that

[48] Reagan to Seddon, January 23, 1864, in *Official Records*, Ser. IV, Vol. III, 52–53.
[49] Seddon to Reagan, February 3, 1864, *ibid.*, 70–74.
[50] Reagan to Seddon, February 15, 1864, *ibid.*, 121–25.
[51] Seddon to Reagan, February 17, 1864, *ibid.*, 126.

exemption of postal employees was a severe drain on his army. He denounced one Leftwich, who resided and carried on a business in Richmond, but who had obtained release from the army by contracting for a mail route in Alabama.[52] Reagan by now was tired of fighting a losing battle to obtain the necessary personnel for his department, and as the Confederacy was rapidly crumbling he dropped the controversy.

In retrospect, the difference between the two departments seems to have been wholly unnecessary. An efficient mail service was needed to bolster the morale of soldiers and civilians. It appears that the number of men liable for military duty who were employed in the postal service was comparatively small. The War Department, despite the numerous demands for details which weakened the army, should have recognized the indispensable need of men to carry the mails. The number of soldiers thus lost to the army was negligible, but these men were invaluable to the Post Office Department. Reagan, nevertheless, was partly at fault. His department was showing a profit at the time. It was quite true that contractors were actually paying up to $6,000 a year to obtain men, who were undoubtedly not liable to military service, to carry the mails for them. While the contractor himself was paid as little as one cent a year by the Post Office Department, he was thereby enabled to qualify as exempt from military service. Had Reagan been willing to pay more for service rendered he could have obtained the mail carriers he needed and the controversy would have been avoided.

Reagan had his difficulties with private business also, especially with the railroad and express companies. At first the railroads showed willingness to cooperate wholeheartedly with the Post Office Department as a patriotic duty. As time passed the Postmaster General was disappointed to see the carriers fail to live up to their agreements. The railway executives, on their part, felt that their sacrifices were not appreciated and many of them had little inclination to extend themselves to serve the Post Office Department.[53] At bottom, most disputes of the kind

[52] Lee to Seddon, September 10, 1864, *ibid.*, 660.
[53] Garrison, "Administrative Problems of the Confederate Post Office Department," *loc. cit.*, 237.

had their origin in Reagan's all-pervading wish to conduct operations with the greatest possible economy. Had his primary emphasis been on service, his relations with the railroads would have run a smoother course. Although the situation was somewhat different, the same held true of the disputes with the express companies.

Whatever the nature or merit of the dispute, Reagan seldom acted beyond his legal rights; although he stretched the concept of the law, he never violated it. The rugged and gruff Texan, who had lived and fought on the frontier, was at heart the Judge Reagan of the bench. He was as faithful to legal forms as he was to a friend. He would fight for either to the bitter end with all the weapons at his command.

Davis was fortunate to have had Reagan as an adviser. The Postmaster General's controversies with Memminger and the secretaries of war bear out Reagan's claim to being the most aggressive member of the Cabinet.[54] He often found himself dissenting from the majority opinion in the official meetings. Early in 1861 he was for sending troops to Kentucky. In 1863 he objected vigorously to sending General Lee into Pennsylvania and proposed that a united effort be made to capture General Grant's army.[55] The Cabinet opposed him, but he asked that they reconsider their decision and they consented to do so. It was about this time that Reagan renewed his frequent objections to the policy of the government and suggested that he would resign from the Cabinet if the President thought Reagan's intransigent course objectionable. The President, however, refused to consider the offer, as the clear-cut ideas and forthright expression of this adviser pleased him. Instead, he complimented the Texan for acting as any good Cabinet member should.[56]

When he accepted the appointment as Postmaster General, Reagan had been assured by the President that he would have his support against unjustified attacks. Davis fulfilled his pledge. In his messages to Congress, Davis explained the difficulties under which the Post Office Department operated, and asked for aid for the department. The President's acquaintance with the

[54] Reagan, *Memoirs*, 162. [55] *Ibid.*, 151–53.
[56] *Ibid.*, 162.

conduct of the department was such that he had no hesitancy in characterizing its directing head as a man of zeal, industry, and ability, who spared no effort in the task entrusted to him.[57] There was never any interference by the President with Reagan's work or plans for his department.

In return, Reagan gave Davis unflagging devotion. The self-made frontiersman and one-time Indian fighter, with perhaps less polish than any of his colleagues in the Cabinet, was second only to Benjamin in his possession of tact in his personal relationships. Additionally, his sincerity carried conviction. He handled the President tactfully; he believed in his worth and ability. Of all the Cabinet members, Reagan was the only one who remained with the President to the very end. The Federal cavalry that took Jefferson Davis prisoner found the Postmaster General at his side.

Davis knew that Reagan, although unsuccessful in satisfying the public's demand for an efficient mail service, had done his best. The Post Office Department was conducted in a remarkably business-like manner and its routine affairs were handled with dispatch. Reagan's absences from his office exceeded those of any other secretary,[58] but, like Mallory, he chose capable men as assistants, to whom he gave trust and freedom of action. He was not above giving personal assurance to a valued subordinate. His letters to a special agent, G. G. Lynch, were most tactful, reassuring, and encouraging.[59] The relatively low salaries paid clerks in the postal service were a source of worry to his sympathetic nature. The clerks in the Richmond post office, who were paid as little as sixty dollars a month in a period when prices had advanced 500 per cent, went on strike on the night of August 20, 1863. The *Richmond Examiner* demanded an immediate suppression of the evil combination of workers, declaring:

Nothing can justify a combination either of employees or employers, to force terms which should depend solely upon supply and demand.

[57] Richardson (ed.), *Messages and Papers,* I, 138–39.
[58] Reagan often visited his children and his sick wife in Atlanta, Georgia.
[59] Reagan to Lynch, October 30, 1863, G. G. Lynch Papers, University of North Carolina. A number of Reagan's letters in this collection bear testimony of his executive ability.

It is fighting with disloyal weapons; playing with cogged dice. It is unfair and subversive of the whole system of free labor.

. . . The course they have adopted is wholly indefensible and unless the Postmaster General is both a fool and a coward, he cannot yield to them.[60]

The *Examiner* urged that the clerks be forced to work at their existing salaries, or else put in the army. Reagan was neither "fool" nor "coward" enough to follow the newspaper's advice. Instead, he admitted that the employees' grievances were real, told them of his own wish for better salaries for them, and showed them that the power to better their condition lay with Congress, not with him. He promised, and faithfully fulfilled his pledge, to do all in his power to obtain increases for them from Congress. Thereupon the clerks returned to work on August 23.[61]

The Postmaster General was alive to the shortcomings of the postal service. When defects were reported, he was quick to send an agent to investigate the causes of delay. Despite his best efforts the mails were interfered with, and delays in deliveries were daily occurrences. The postmaster at Richmond explained that he had lost more than one third of his workers within nine months, that his regular force had been called out for local defense, and that, as a result of a constantly changing personnel, there was inefficiency of operation.[62] Similar experiences could have been related by numerous other postmasters. When the fall of Vicksburg cut the Confederacy in two, it became necessary to arrange an entirely new system with secret convoys across the Mississippi. Every time Southern territory was occupied, either permanently or temporarily, different lines of mail communication had to be established. It was impossible to avoid a measure of confusion for the postal facilities of the Confederacy.

To keep foreign routes of communication open was an even more difficult problem than that of maintaining domestic service. Every steamer that ran the blockade carried government and private dispatches to foreign lands. Attempts were made, but

[60] *Daily Richmond Examiner,* August 21, 1863.   [61] *Ibid.,* August 24, 1863.
[62] *Ibid.,* December 23, 1864.

unsuccessfully, to form regular service by the way of Mexico and the islands of the Caribbean. Mail was sneaked into the Confederacy through Northern ports by trusted agents.[63] Sometimes, but not often, dispatches were sent out under the seals of foreign consuls. In anticipation of peace, plans were considered for the inauguration of a line of steamships to carry the mails between Norfolk and Queenstown, Ireland, but Reagan rejected the suggestion for reasons of economy. He estimated that the service, even with a postage rate of twenty cents a letter, would cost the Confederacy more than half a million dollars a year in subsidies. As subsidies were anathema to the South, having been one of its grievances against the North, Reagan thought the government should fix a rate of postage for overseas mail and let the steamships take it at that price or leave it.[64]

Criticism of the Postmaster General subsided, though it never ceased entirely, as time went on. The death of his wife in 1863 perhaps helped to soften the critics' harshness. Reagan's own attitude served to convince many that he was a sincere and earnest official. The *Richmond Sentinel* said of him that he was, for a short time, a favorite mark for detractors, but "His character was firm and as pure as thrice refined steel,"[65] and he possessed a moral firmness which set at defiance all attempts to disturb his equanimity. With the passage of time the people of the Confederacy became dissatisfied with almost every branch in the government, but respect for the Postmaster General increased.[66] It was the highest compliment that could have been paid the sincere Texan.

President Davis could not reasonably have asked more of Reagan than he gave as a Cabinet adviser. Stable and sensible in counsel, he could advance his ideas forcefully and pertina-

---

[63] An interesting account of the difficulties encountered by Confederate mail runners is found in Absalom Carlisle Grimes, *Absalom Grimes, Confederate Mail Runner,* . . . (New Haven, 1926).

[64] Reagan to Davis, March 14, 1863, in Letter Book, Post Office Department, 665–69.

[65] *Richmond Sentinel,* July 29, 1864.

[66] Reagan was serenaded on Saturday evening, November 9, 1863. The *Sentinel* reported the event and complimented Reagan. ". . . by his uniform urbanity, and his able and assiduous discharge of the duties of his office, he has elicited the regard and esteem of all who have business relations with him, or who have met him in society." *Richmond Sentinel,* November 10, 1863.

ciously, or when overborne, accept the will of the majority and
strive with equal zeal to obtain results by following the path
considered by the Cabinet to be the best. Having preserved to
the end his friendship and devotion to his President, Reagan
could forget the years of fruitless struggle for the Confederacy
and, under an old and honored flag, carve out for himself a new
career of usefulness in another field.

IX

Men of Justice

THOMAS BRAGG

WHEN Judah P. Benjamin assumed temporary charge of the War Department in September, 1861, he retained his official status as Attorney General. He had had considerable leisure time in the Department of Justice, but the direction of the War Department occupied all of his time, and the actual conduct of the Attorney General's office fell to Wade Keyes, his assistant. Although Benjamin continued to exercise a technical jurisdiction, Keyes conducted the business of the office and rendered opinions requested by the President and secretaries, delivering six in the space of about two months.[1]

As the period of Benjamin's *ad interim* service in the War Department lengthened and as his direction of the department gave satisfaction, it became evident that he would receive a permanent appointment which would make necessary the appointment of his successor in the Attorney General's office. Keyes would have filled the position competently, and his appointment would have gratified Alabama, since that state had no representation in the Cabinet after the resignation of Walker. North Carolina, Tennessee, or Arkansas, however, had more valid claims than Alabama to a Cabinet post, if Davis intended to continue his policy of spreading the patronage to include all the states in the Confederacy. The *North Carolina Standard* suggested that North Carolina had been too modest in advancing its claim to an important place in the administration; no state in the Confederacy, however, had surpassed it in the number of men or the amount of supplies given to the nation. The

---

[1] A summary of the work of Wade Keyes is given on pp. 310–12.

attorney-generalship, the newspaper thought, by right should go
to a North Carolina man, and the names of George Badger, William Alexander Graham, and Thomas Bragg, among others,
were suggested for the appointment.[2] The President settled on
Bragg and the provisional Congress unanimously confirmed
the nomination.[3]

The *Standard* regarded the appointment as a compliment to
North Carolina as well as a recognition of Bragg's ability and
worth; the journal was especially pleased that the office was
given to a former conservative who had been ignored by those
who claimed to have started the war.[4] The President, in the
opinion of another North Carolina newspaper, could not have
made a more suitable appointment than that of the eminent jurist and patriot, Thomas Bragg.[5] Other newspapers scattered
throughout the South expressed approval of the North Carolinian's selection.

Bragg was born at Warrenton, North Carolina, on November
9, 1810. He was educated at a local school and at the Norwich
Military Academy, Middletown, Connecticut. He studied law
with Judge John Hall, of Warrenton, Associate Justice of the
Supreme Court of North Carolina, and began his career as a
lawyer at Jackson, in Northhampton County, with a total capital
of fifty dollars. He built up a remunerative practice in his community and was elected to the North Carolina legislature in
1844, but failed of re-election. Ten years after his election to the
legislature, he was elected Governor of North Carolina. He was
re-elected and, after the completion of his second term, was sent
to the United States Senate, in which he served until he resigned
when North Carolina seceded from the Union.[6]

[2] *North Carolina Semiweekly Standard*, November 2, 1861.

[3] What or who influenced Davis to appoint Bragg is not known. The records
relating to Bragg's appointment, work, and resignation are meager. Perhaps
Davis acted on the advice of North Carolina's representatives in the provisional
Congress. Only two of them, A. W. Venable and George Davis, however, arrived
in Richmond to vote for confirmation of Bragg's appointment.

[4] *North Carolina Semiweekly Standard*, November 23, 1861.

[5] *Raleigh State Journal*, November 20, 1861.

[6] Sketches of Bragg's life are found in Pulaski Cowper, *Sketch of the Life of
Governor Thomas Bragg* (Raleigh, 1891), and Samuel A'Court Ashe, *Biographical
History of North Carolina from Colonial Times to the Present* (Raleigh, 1905–
1917), VI, 95–98.

Davis believed that the selection of Bragg, who represented the political views on secession of the majority of North Carolinians, would do much to bring political factions in that state to the support of the Confederate administration. Bragg had believed that a settlement of the differences between North and South could be accomplished within the Union and he had advised his state against secession. He believed that leaders in the South had mistaken fervor for harmony, and he feared that united action by the South would not be forthcoming should severe sacrifices be called for to repel invaders. When it became evident that North Carolina must either fight with or against its neighbor states in the South, Bragg became a secessionist and gave his wholehearted support to the Confederacy. In appointing Bragg, therefore, Davis honored one whose influence might operate to heal old political wounds in his state.

The newly appointed Attorney General left Raleigh for Richmond on November 19, 1861, before the provisional Congress had confirmed his nomination. He entered upon the duties of his office immediately, one of his first official acts being to advise Benjamin on the government's responsibility for private property impressed by order of a Confederate official. Interpreting the law strictly, Bragg concluded that the government was responsible for all property taken or destroyed by order of the military department. The only exception he noted to this responsibility was in case of a slave, a peculiar type of property having reasoning powers, who might cause his own injury or death.[7] The Attorney General in the ensuing months gave six other opinions on questions referred to him: two each to Mallory and Benjamin, one to the President, and one to William M. Browne. Bragg's opinions were rendered in language less clear and vigorous than that of his predecessor. He invariably held to what he considered the letter of the law in interpreting Congressional acts referred to him for opinions. For the greater part, the questions asked the Attorney General concerned such trivialities as the salary of a clerk in the Navy Department, the payment to be made for the return of a fugitive slave, the dis-

[7] Bragg to Benjamin, November 25, 1861, "Records of the Confederate Attorneys-General," New York Public Library, *Bulletin*, I (1897), 341–42.

tribution of prize money for the capture of a ship, and pardons. In an opinion of more importance than the foregoing, Bragg held that the Treasury Department should honor requisitions approved by the War Department without investigating their legality, since it was the responsibility of the War Department to observe the provisions of the law in making its accounts.[8]

Answering correspondence constituted the greater part of the Attorney General's duties. Many citizens seemed to regard the Secretary as a bureau of information, and letters poured into his office requesting his opinion as to the constitutionality of various laws. The act of Congress, authorizing the Department of Justice, stated that it was the duty of the Attorney General to advise the President and heads of departments at their request; Bragg and his successor, therefore, quite properly refused to set themselves up as judges for the people on the validity of acts of Congress. Bragg answered such inquiries courteously, but informed the writers that he had no right to give them an opinion on law. Congress from time to time provided for the filing of claims against the government, and it fell to the Attorney General to weigh evidence and allow or disallow compensation in such cases. Claims against the United States by citizens of the Confederacy were also filed in the department, but the law specified that they were not to be presented to Congress until after the war should have ended. Bragg presented a report on the work of his department on claims at each session of Congress.

In his brief term of office Bragg made only one report for the information of the President and Congress. It was a concise document of some six pages in which he gave an account of departmental operations and recommended that Congress fulfill the intent of the permanent Constitution by establishing a Supreme Court.[9] The President heartily concurred in this recommendation.

Davis and Bragg worked in harmony. The Attorney General was a man of commanding presence, quiet in demeanor, and of simple and unpretentious dignity.[10] He was not one either to

[8] Bragg to Benjamin, January 7, 1862, in Opinion Book, 37–40.
[9] *Richmond Daily Dispatch*, March 11, 1862.
[10] Ashe, *Biographical History of North Carolina*, VI, 97.

truckle to a superior or to attempt to interfere in matters outside his province. Possessing a strong intellect and a logical mind,
his advice was unequivocal but conservative and unimaginative.
He was abreast of current public questions and Davis never had
cause to question the Attorney General's ability as a lawyer. The
two men had known each other slightly before secession; they
teamed together in shaping Confederate policy, and when they
parted, it was on friendly terms.

Bragg resigned from the Cabinet in March, 1862, but the
reason for his retirement remains a mystery. Unquestionably
he had his personal reasons for requesting that he not be renominated in the permanent government. He may, perhaps,
have accepted the appointment on condition that it was only
for the duration of the provisional government. Or, again, it is
possible that his health did not permit his continuing in an office, the duties of which, while not overburdening, were trying.[11] After his retirement on March 18, 1862, he remained
closer to the President than any other North Carolinian, and his
return to his home may have been with the thought that he
could render more service to the Confederate cause in his state
than in Richmond.[12]

Bragg continued to serve the administration after his withdrawal from the Cabinet, working for reconciliation and cooperation when the differences between the Confederacy and
Governor Vance arose. To combat the growing peace sentiment
in North Carolina, he headed a committee in Raleigh to buy
the *State Journal,* rename it "The Confederate," and publish it
in the interest of Southern independence.[13] In March, 1864, he
accepted the task of investigating the cases of persons arrested by
the military authority in North Carolina and reporting his findings to Secretary Seddon. At the close of the war the former
Attorney General accepted reunion in good faith and resumed
the practice of law in Raleigh.

[11] The *Petersburg Daily Express,* September 12, 1861, spoke of the "continued
ill health," of Bragg.

[12] Ashe, *Biographical History of North Carolina,* VI, 98. Ashe suggested that
Davis had appointed men of the Democratic party and desired a representative
of the old Union-Whig party. The appointment of Thomas Hill Watts, a former
leader of the Whig party, to succeed Bragg supports Ashe's theory.

[13] *North Carolina Semiweekly Standard,* April 20, 1864.

THOMAS HILL WATTS

President Davis on March 17, 1862, nominated Thomas Hill Watts of Alabama as Attorney General, without having consulted him, and the Senate on the following day unanimously confirmed the nomination. "A Union man *par excellence*" had been appointed, in the opinion of Mrs. Chesnut.[14] The *North Carolina Standard* quickly pointed out that Watts was not a representative of the Union group that appeared to be proscribed from Cabinet positions, for he had become an ardent secessionist after Lincoln's election.[15] The *Standard* was more nearly correct in its opinion than was Mrs. Chesnut in hers.

Thomas Hill Watts was born on the frontier in Butler County, Alabama, on January 3, 1819, and attended the local log-house school, the Airy Mount Academy in Dallas County, and the University of Virginia. He was graduated from the University in 1840, and after obtaining his license to practice law, he represented Butler County in the state legislature from 1842 to 1845. He moved to Montgomery two years later and continued to serve as a representative and later as a senator in the legislature. He was active in support of the Whig party in the 1840's, and in 1850 he ran for Congress as the candidate of the Know-Nothing party, but was defeated.[16] In the crucial election of 1860 he was a Bell-Everett elector, but declared that in the event of Lincoln's election he would favor immediate secession.[17] When that event took place, he opposed further delay in Alabama's withdrawal from the Union where "the black flag of abolition dominion" would rule. To the advocates of cooperative secession he said: "The co-operation to be desired is not co-operation before, but co-operation after secession." [18] His attitude won him a place in the Alabama convention where he took his stand with William L. Yancey as a straight-out secessionist. In selecting Watts for a

[14] Chesnut, *Diary*, 147.

[15] *North Carolina Semiweekly Standard*, April 2, 1862.

[16] The account of Watts's life is based on Emma Beall Culver, "Thomas Hill Watts, A Statesman of the Old Regime," Alabama Historical Society, *Transactions*, IV (1899–1903), 415–39.

[17] Charles Phillips Denman, *The Secession Movement in Alabama* (Montgomery, 1933), 83.

[18] Culver, "Thomas Hill Watts, A Statesman of the Old Regime," *loc. cit.*, 431–32.

Cabinet position, Jefferson Davis appointed a former Whig who, in 1860, had become as uncompromising a secessionist as any "fire-eating" Southern Democrat.

Watts predicted that war would result from disunion, but he was confident of foreign aid; and, too, he overestimated the South's military power. He organized the Seventeenth Alabama Infantry Regiment and served as its colonel at Pensacola and Corinth. He was commanding his regiment in Tennessee when he received the call to go to Richmond. Some three weeks later, April 9, Watts entered upon his duties as Attorney General.

Powerful of frame, with a massive head, and features that bespoke a resolute character, the Alabamian pleased the Richmond public from its first glimpse of him. The *Charleston Courier* correspondent described him as "Tall, corpulent, jocund, his equilibrium never destroyed, his soul beaming from his eye, his heart in his hand. . . ." [19] From his war experience Watts had amassed a store of anecdotes which he enjoyed telling, and his cordial hatred of Yankees and his buoyant optimism added zest to the telling of his tales.

The Attorney General gradually took over the direction of the department from his assistant, Wade Keyes. Watts's predecessor, Bragg, had made the necessary appointments of judges, marshals, and attorneys for the district courts, so Watts had little to do except to exercise a general supervision of the courts' proceedings and to audit their accounts. The patent and printing offices and other departmental bureaus continued their work undisturbed. Much of the Attorney General's time was occupied in hearing claims against the government, for Watts took the responsibility of his office seriously and wanted to have a firsthand knowledge of all the claims he approved or dismissed. He was considerate of the claimant and inclined to give him the benefit of the doubt.

The demands of citizens made heavy inroads on his time.[20]

---

[19] "Sigma," *Charleston Courier*, March 22, 1861.

[20] "When he went to Richmond to enter the cabinet of Mr. Davis he made of course a formal call on the different public bureaus. He found red tape splurging on stilts and swelling swimmingly; he saw with indignant disgust honest and polite visitors to the departments met by squirting attaches with curt incivility, and he saw a world of fancy airs put on, and pompously put on under the shelter of a very 'little brief authority.' Of course he had to open an office of his own,

Fellow Alabamians called on him for favors in obtaining positions in his department, and also for help in obtaining the appointment, transfer, promotion, or release of friends in the army. One such petitioner, apologizing for bothering the Cabinet officer, explained that both the men and officers in the army regarded Watts as the soldiers' friend who would cheerfully aid the enlisted men.[21] From all parts of the Confederacy he received requests for his opinion as to the constitutionality of various laws. He had no objection to answering these inquiries, but he pointed out that whatever he might say in answer to them would be valueless.

Most of his work consisted of digesting requests from departmental heads and writing opinions for them on the interpretation of various laws. Benjamin and Bragg, his predecessors in the department, had submitted thirteen and seven opinions, respectively, but Watts wrote one hundred. Many of these were short, but others ran to more than eight pages of closely written legal-size sheets. Watts, unlike his predecessors, supported his interpretations by citing precedents set by cases in the history of the United States. His opinions were clearly stated, although frequently running to verbosity.

Study of the opinions rendered by Watts affords an insight upon the work of other Cabinet members. During his short term of office, Secretary of War Randolph called on the Attorney General for opinions twenty-seven times. No matter how trivial the occasion, Randolph appeared either incapable of proceeding, or unwilling to do so, without requesting legal support. When Watts's interpretation went against him, Randolph wished to disregard the Attorney General's opinion but the President refused to allow him to do so. The Secretary of War occasionally

---

and when he did so, he gave it as a law unto his clerks, usherers, etc., that the penalty of incivility to even a beggar, in his department would be a kicking down stairs. Urbanity being one of the canons of his nature, he made it a statute to regulate his department. In the hospitals at Richmond he was found at morning's early dawn and at evening's holy hour at the bed-side of the dying soldier receiving his nuncupative bequest, writing his will, administering to his every earthly want, and pouring into his sad soul the consultation of religion." Newspaper clipping, in Thomas Hill Watts Papers, Alabama Department of Archives and History.

21 J. W. A. Sanford to Watts, March 19, 1863, in Henry Semple Papers, University of North Carolina.

repeated his request, on which occasions Watts would rather curtly refer him to an opinion already given. Seddon, who held office much longer than Randolph, requested legal advice only eighteen times. Next in order of the number of requests for legal opinions came Memminger with seventeen; President Davis, sixteen; Mallory, thirteen; and Reagan, four. Five other Confederate officials sought legal advice from the Attorney General.

The most important of the Attorney General's opinions were those he wrote for the War Department. The Conscription Act and the exemptions connected with it created many legal problems. Questions concerning the reorganization of regiments and the appointment of officers frequently arose. Watts, in August, 1862, reversed an opinion given by Benjamin relative to the appointment of officers to command troops furnished by states in response to requisitions by the Confederate government. The former Attorney General had held that there were two classes of troops in the army, Confederate and state, and that governors had the right to make appointments or fill vacancies in the ranks of the state troops. Watts's opinion held that all troops received into the service of the Confederacy were under the direction of the President. This was a reasonable interpretation which was welcome to the War Department. In other opinions the Attorney General held that foreigners who possessed property in the South and who had not given evidence of returning to their native countries, were subject to conscription.[22] Watts interpreted the law rigidly in his opinions for the War Department.

The Presidential requests for legal advice concerned the relations between the Confederacy and the states, the constitutionality of Congressional legislation, proclamations, and pardons. Watts informed the President that the Conscription Act was constitutional, as complete power had been given the central government to provide for the nation's defense; hence Congress had the right to enact laws to make this possible.[23] On other occasions he was quick to point out errors in the wording of proclamations, and the President always agreed to the altera-

22 Watts to Randolph, May 3, June 1, 1862, in Opinion Book, 50–52, 68.
23 Id. to Davis, May 16, 1862, ibid., 58–62.

tions suggested. The Attorney General believed that martial law should interfere as little as possible with the civil jurisdiction of the courts, for the people of the South were jealous of their liberty as contrasted with the "vandal tyranny of the North." [24] Watts was at all times willing to advise the President and he took advantage of opportunities to go beyond the immediate bounds of the President's requests for opinions.

At times the Attorney General expressed his views on the nature of the Confederacy and upbraided Congress for not carrying out the intent of the Constitution. Writing to Mallory, he argued for a rigid interpretation of the Constitution: "A strict construction . . . is not only demanded by the nature of our federal system logically considered, but it is enforced by the dear bought experience of the past, and by every consideration of the future welfare and greatness of the Confederate States." [25] The failure of Congress to establish a Supreme Court stirred Watts deeply, for the intent of the Constitution was clear to him. He held that, in the absence of such court, a litigant had the right to have a decision of the District Court stayed until a Supreme Court should have been established and his case brought before it for review.[26]

Every Attorney General of the Confederacy regarded the establishment of a Supreme Court as of first importance. President Davis, in his first message to Congress, reminded the legislators of their duty to set up a Supreme Court in obedience to the mandate of the Constitution.[27] Although he never again specifically referred to the need for this tribunal, he gave general approval to the recommendations of the Attorneys General for its establishment. Notwithstanding persistent demands for the court, Congress failed to agree on an act for its establishment. Bills were introduced in both houses providing for the setting up

24 *Id* to *id.*, April 25, 1862, *ibid.*, 44–46.
25 *Id.* to Mallory, May 6, 1862, *ibid.*, 53–54.
26 *Id.* to Davis, June 15, 1863, *ibid.*, 176–78.
27 Richardson (ed.), *Messages and Papers*, I, 191. William Alexander Montgomery, one-time Justice of the North Carolina Supreme Court, in his unpublished manuscript on the Confederacy, says that Davis never really desired a Supreme Court. Montgomery points out that the President failed to take the opportunity to appoint justices under the act of the provisional Congress of March 16, 1861, which provided for the establishment of a Supreme Court, and also quickly approved the act of July 31, 1861, repealing the former law.

of a Supreme Court, but all were either tabled or allowed to die. The dangerous military situation was responsible in many cases for the failure to act on the bills. There was also bitter difference of opinion as to the powers to be given the court, especially as to whether it should have appellate jurisdiction over state courts.[28] Finally, there was the personal factor. A few congressmen objected to a court, the appointment of whose justices might be influenced by Benjamin, while others feared the tribunal might be used by the President to increase his power.[29]

The Confederate government was not greatly affected one way or the other by the lack of a Supreme Court. Decisions of state courts adverse to the government were of course embarrassing to it, but these were often disregarded, or reversals of the decisions were obtained. An unfavorable opinion by the court of one state was never considered by Confederate officials as a precedent which should bind them in their course in another state. If obliged to, they obeyed the command of a court within the specific state, but elsewhere they continued to interpret the laws to their liking. Had there been a Supreme Court, it is entirely possible that its decisions would more often have run counter to the administration policy than did the occasional adverse decisions of the state courts. In the absence of a court of last resort, the Attorneys General of the Confederacy on occasion passed on the constitutionality of laws, and their decisions were accepted as final by the administration, which thereby was assured of having a favorable interpretation of laws for the prosecution of the war.

Aside from his disappointment at the refusal of Congress to provide for a Supreme Court, Watts was happy in his office. He irritated Seddon by his refusal to withdraw legal proceedings in the district court of Alabama against Ford, Hurd and Company for trading with the enemy.[30] The genial Alabamian had no serious differences with other members of the Cabinet. He delighted especially in the companionship of Mallory, whom he regarded as the best, but worst abused, member of the Cabinet.

28 An excellent account of the Supreme Court controversy is found in Robinson, *Justice in Grey,* 420–91.
29 *Daily Richmond Examiner,* December 17, 1863.
30 Jones, *Diary,* I, 376.

Watts and Mallory were men of congenial tastes and habits; each loved social contacts and well-told tales, and each found the time to relax in gentlemanly ease. Watts's attitude toward the President was respectful but not subservient. He would be at great pains to advise the Executive on legal matters, but the nature of the Attorney General's office did not bring him into contact with the President as often as other department heads. Watts was convinced of the President's devotion to the country's good and he developed a high personal regard for the Confederacy's head. The Attorney General's spirit of cooperation and his ebullient confidence in the eventual success of the Confederacy were refreshing to the President, and he sincerely regretted Watts's resignation in the fall of 1863.[31]

Early in the spring of 1863, Watts's friends in Alabama had begun to persuade him to become a candidate for governor. Watts had been perplexed as to what course he should follow. He was "content to hold the honorable and responsible position so generously and gracefully tendered" by the President, but he felt that he was more closely tied to his native state than to the central government.[32] The attorney-generalship, although a pleasant and worthwhile office, was not a colorful one. As governor of his sovereign state, Watts would be in the public's notice. In the end he decided to allow his friends to advocate his candidacy for that office. In June, 1863, he wrote the people of Alabama that, believing high offices were public trusts created for the public, he would not in the midst of the war canvass or scramble for office, but would accept the governorship of his state if the people so desired.[33] In August he was elected, and on September 8 he submitted his resignation as Attorney General. The President accepted it ten days later, but Watts continued to hold office until October 1, 1863.

Watts's resignation, following his election to the governorship of Alabama, gave rise to rumors that he was leaving the Cabinet because of dislike for the President and as a protest against the continuation of the war. In refutation of this, he wrote:

[31] Davis to Watts, September 18, 1863, in Rowland (ed.), *Davis*, VI, 41.
[32] Watts to L. W. Lawler, March 21, 1863, in *Richmond Sentinel*, May 16, 1863.
[33] "To the People of Alabama," June 8, 1863, *ibid.*, June 27, 1863.

He who is now, deliberately or otherwise in favor of "reconstruction" with the states under Lincoln's dominion is a traitor in his heart to the State, and deserves a traitor's doom. If I had the power, I would build up a wall of fire between Yankeedom and the Confederate States, there to burn for ages, as a monument to the folly, wickedness, and vandalism of the puritanic race. No sir! rather than re-unite with such a people, I would see the Confederate States desolated with fire and sword.[34]

He paid glowing tribute to Davis in speeches delivered in Alabama in October and November. In his judgment, Davis was "the right man in the right place," one whose patriotism and justice were unsurpassed, whose ability to administer the government was not exceeded by any other man's. Watts declared that he withdrew from the Cabinet with a far higher appreciation of the President's virtues than he had when he entered it.[35] In his inaugural address Governor Watts called for a generous support of the President and those associated with him.

Unfortunately for the Richmond administration, Watts was soon in conflict with the War Department over the conscription of Alabama troops. The former Attorney General, however, did not break with his one-time colleagues, for in 1864 the President and his aides renewed old ties of friendship as guests of the Governor in Montgomery.

WADE KEYES

When Watts was elected to the governorship of Alabama the *Charleston Mercury* advised the President to use the opportunity thus presented for a general reconstruction of the Cabinet. It was

[34] Watts to Ira Foster (Quartermaster General of Georgia), September 12, 1863, in *Sumter Republican*, September 25, 1863.

The former Alabama Unionist was carried away by his patriotism. He continued: "Let the patriot sires, whose children have bared their breasts to the Yankee bullets, and welcomed glorious deaths, in this struggle for self-government, rebuke the foul spirit which even whispers 'reconstruction.' Let the noble mothers, whose sons have made sacred with their blood so many fields consecrated to Freedom, rebuke the fell heresy! Let our blood-stained banners now unfurled 'to the battle and the breeze,' rebuke the cowardice and cupidity which suggests 'reconstruction.' The spirit of our heroic dead—the martyrs to our sacred cause, rebuke—a thousand times rebuke, 'reconstruction'! . . . In any and every event let us prefer death, to a life of cowardly shame."

[35] *Richmond Sentinel*, October 31, November 2, 1863.

the *Mercury* editor's belief that the opinion was general that the Cabinet was neither equal to the emergency, nor was it consulted and permitted to have a voice in the administration. The President had called for prayer and self-examination, wrote the editor; he should examine himself and, if convinced that the Cabinet was the wisest obtainable and that he had availed himself of all the wisdom it possessed, he should then invoke superhuman aid.[36] The President was not moved by this appeal; he appointed the dependable Wade Keyes as Attorney General *ad interim*.

No man was better equipped than Keyes to take over the office. He had held second place in the Attorney General's office from the organization of the department. He had seen three Attorneys General come and go, and had himself become the steadying influence in the department. By his past training in law he was qualified to write opinions more erudite than those of any of the Attorneys General. He had been the actual director of the office at intervals, once for two months in the fall of 1861, again during the Christmas holidays of the same year while Thomas Bragg was absent, in October and November in 1862, and in August, 1863, when Watts had left the department in his charge. During these periods and in a succeeding one in September and October, 1864, when the last Attorney General, George Davis, was on vacation, Keyes had entire charge of the office. He wrote twenty-three opinions for the President and the secretaries. The opinions often ran to detailed accounts of Keyes's reasoning process and quoted from United States court cases to support his conclusions.

Keyes was born of wealthy parents at Mooresville, Alabama, and received his education at LaGrange College and the University of Virginia. After studying law he made an extended tour of Europe to widen his horizon, then settled down in Tallahassee, Florida, where he engaged in writing a work on the legal aspects of property rights. He moved to Montgomery, Alabama, in 1861, and two years later the state legislature elected him chancellor of the southern division of the state, a position he retained for six years.[37] Keyes was an able jurist, a profound scholar, and

[36] *Charleston Mercury*, August 17, 1863.
[37] Evans (ed.), *Confederate Military History*, I, 602–603.

an astute business man, but was not essentially a politician. Had he been a more important figure politically, the President would have given him the permanent appointment as Attorney General. Davis liked the quiet, unassuming man in the Attorney General's office, whose advice in council was dependable and who steadily performed his duties. On the other hand, had Keyes desired the appointment, he probably could have obtained the support of men with sufficient influence to assure that the office would be offered him. But he seemed well content to see others outrank him while he remained the work horse of the department. The President could be sure of the continued attachment of Wade Keyes, and he thought it best to offer the permanent Cabinet position to another man.

GEORGE DAVIS

During the last three months of 1863 the President sought some one of ability and with the proper political affiliation to head the Department of Justice. All the states except Tennessee and Arkansas had been represented in the Cabinet at one time or another.[38] These two states were largely controlled by the enemy, and besides, were relatively unimportant as far as political considerations were concerned. Nevertheless, the administration had been ably supported by Senator Gustavus A. Henry of Tennessee, and Davis offered him the appointment.[39] Henry declined, however, and the problem of finding a suitable man for the post remained. There seemed to be more disaffection with the administration and a greater peace sentiment in Georgia and North Carolina than in any of the other states. Of the two, Georgia was more important to the Confederacy; and, according to the *Charleston Mercury,* the vacant Cabinet office was offered to a Georgia man, Judge Charles Jones Jenkins of the Georgia Supreme Court, who also refused the honor.

The President at length turned to a North Carolinian, Senator George Davis, who had been friendly to the administration

[38] Kentucky and Missouri, recognized by the Confederacy as members of the Southern union, had had no citizen in the Cabinet. In 1865, John C. Breckinridge, a Kentuckian, was appointed to a Cabinet post.

[39] *Charleston Mercury,* November 2, 1863; *Augusta Daily Chronicle and Sentinel,* November 3, 1863.

in Congress, although he had not supported it consistently. The selection of a former leader of the Whig party was gratifying to the *Richmond Whig,* which accepted the President's act as indicative of a desire to harmonize old political differences and soothe irritated sensibilities. If the President should continue to be guided by such motives, the newspaper was certain that he would bring discontent to an end and at the same time recover the confidence and affection of the people.[40]

The *North Carolina Standard* took issue with its Richmond contemporary, asserting that, while he had at one time been a conservative Whig, George Davis had become a thoroughgoing secessionist in 1861. The North Carolinian was elected Confederate Senator in 1862 because he was a "Destructive." The legislature of his state declined on that account to re-elect him in 1864, naming instead William Alexander Graham, a tried conservative. The President appointed George Davis Attorney General, the *Standard's* editor concluded, because he had been rejected by the conservative state legislature.[41] Replying to the *Standard's* attack, the *Charlotte Democrat* said that the President chose George Davis for his ability and because his appointment had been requested by Graham and other important men of both parties in North Carolina, including almost every member of the legislature.[42] The appointment was lauded by three Richmond papers, the *Enquirer,* the *Sentinel,* and the *Dispatch,* but an Alabama newspaper classed George Davis as a respectable gentleman of fair, but neither brilliant nor powerful, intellect.[43] Generally, the appointment met with approval. It pleased the members of the Confederate Senate, who unanimously confirmed the nomination.[44]

[40] *North Carolina Weekly Standard,* January 13, 1864, quoting the *Richmond Daily Whig.*

[41] *Ibid.,* January 13, 1864.

[42] *Richmond Sentinel,* January 16, 1864, quoting the *Charlotte Democrat* from the *Wilmington Daily Journal.*

[43] *Mobile Advertiser and Register,* January 16, 1864. Perhaps the *Advertiser* was piqued because Wade Keyes was not appointed.

[44] Louis T. Wigfall wrote Clement C. Clay, who failed to be re-elected to the Senate, and to whom President Davis offered a place on a military court: "Had you been the President and [Jefferson] Davis a defeated Senator, do you think you would have filled a place in your Cabinet with a stranger, and offered him a Judgeship on the Military Court?" Wigfall to Clay, April 12, 1864, in Clay Papers.

The new Attorney General was unique among his fellow Cabinet members in that he had held no political office prior to 1861. He was born in Wilmington, North Carolina, on March 1, 1820, to a family whose ancestors were among the first settlers of South Carolina, and was reared in the best Southern tradition. He was graduated with highest honors from the University of North Carolina at the age of eighteen years. Three years later he was admitted to the bar. He soon gained a reputation as a lawyer and a brilliant orator; but as a consistent Whig in a Democratic district, he had won no chance to demonstrate his oratorical powers in legislative halls.[45] He was appointed a delegate to the Peace Convention at Washington in 1861, and returned from the convention convinced that the South could not hope for justice at the hands of "Black Republicans," [46] although up until that time, he had opposed secession. When North Carolina withdrew from the Union, Davis became a delegate of his state in the provisional Congress, and when the permanent government was organized he entered the Senate and served there for two years.

In the Confederate Congress, George Davis had taken an active, though not a colorful, part. In his quiet manner he had supported or opposed the administration according to his convictions. In the main, he was in accord with the President's ideas, and the former North Carolina Whig was wholeheartedly devoted to the cause of Southern independence. In appointing him the President had been influenced by political considerations, but he was also convinced of the North Carolinian's patriotism and ability.

George Davis took office in January, 1864, the fourth man to serve as Attorney General of the Confederacy. Many of his duties consisted of routine affairs, such as supervision of bureaus, hearing evidence in claims against the government, directing the prosecution of cases in the district courts, selecting men to fill vacancies, and answering the many inquiries that came with every mail. He performed these duties with dispatch and satis-

[45] The account of Davis's life is based on James Sprunt, *George Davis* (Raleigh, 1919), and Samuel A'Court Ashe, *George Davis, Attorney General of the Confederate States* (Raleigh, 1916).
[46] *Daily Wilmington Herald*, March 4, 1861.

faction; more important were his services to other members of the Cabinet and to the President.

During his term in office he wrote seventy-four opinions.[47] His decisions were phrased with less formality than those of his predecessors. At times he followed the form Benjamin had used; he restated the problem, developed his argument, and gave his answer. In other instances he stated his conclusions immediately after reviewing the question, then gave the reasons for his opinion. He often used the pronoun "I" and the phrase "I think not." Most of his opinions were very brief, some running to less than half a page.

Although George Davis was inconsistent at times, his opinions expressed many ideas of merit. Twice he declared state laws forbidding the manufacture of whiskey unconstitutional because they were in conflict with a law of the Confederate Congress.[48] On May 3, 1864, he gave his opinion that a section of the Congressional act enacted on April 4 preceding, taxing the salaries of Confederate judges, was unconstitutional and illegal. But in October, he became convinced that he had no right to deliver an opinion against the constitutionality of an act of Congress once the President had approved it. The time to have questioned the legality of a bill was in Cabinet meeting when the President asked for advice; once a bill became a law, it was the duty of the secretaries to enforce it, whether constitutional or not, until the question of its constitutionality should be passed on by the courts.[49] The problem of the constitutionality of laws, Davis realized, demonstrated the need for a Supreme Court. Commenting on an opinion the Attorney General gave Seddon, the war

[47] George Davis's opinions were for the following: 21 for Trenholm, 13 for Seddon, 13 for Jefferson Davis, 11 for Mallory, 8 for Memminger, 3 for Breckinridge, 2 for Reagan, 1 for Benjamin, and 2 for non-Cabinet members.
[48] Various states, to conserve food, had prohibited distilleries, but Confederate law allowed the production of whiskey for use in the army and navy. On December 18, 1863, Wade Keyes ruled that the State of Virginia had no right to prevent one of her citizens, who had a contract to supply the Confederate government, from producing whiskey. On March 7, 1864, Davis followed the reasoning of Keyes in declaring a law of South Carolina unconstitutional. The weight of the Attorney General's opinion did not keep Virginia from interfering and on November 30, 1864, Davis, while declaring the state law unconstitutional, advised that the problem be laid before the legislature and governor of the state.
[49] George Davis to Trenholm, October 4, 1864, in Opinion Book, 317.

clerk Jones said: "In other words, the cabinet ministers must 'see that the laws be faithfully executed,' even should they be clearly and expressly unconstitutional. Is not the Constitution the law? Have they not sworn to support it, etc.?" [50] The diarist thought that Davis's theory was unsound, and feared that its effect would be to make the President absolute. As a matter of fact, the Attorney General's stand was logical and gave the Executive no more power to rule autocratically than it gave to Congress the power to pass unconstitutional laws.

The Attorney General held to a rigid compliance with the law. At times, however, he was contemptuous of the legal phraseology of Congressional enactments, one of which he characterized as "This very obscure Act." [51] Despite his strict constructionism, he had the common sense to disregard law when necessary. After the fall of Richmond he advised the President to divide the hard money in the Confederate Treasury among the faithful soldiers,[52] and in April, 1865, he thought Jefferson Davis should ignore his constitutional limitations and surrender the shattered Confederacy to the victorious Sherman.

George Davis has no claim to greatness as a lawyer, but he possessed a delightful personality. Of medium height, he carried himself with poise under all circumstances, but was never affected in manner. Friendly, kind, and gentle, he had a genius for winning friends and he was sincere in his devotion to humanity. Though a man of decided opinions, he was neither dogmatic nor intolerant of the opinions of either friend or foe. A devout but unobtrusive Christian, he was the soul of honor. Cosmopolitan in tastes and in learning, his quick mind and vast store of information made him a charming and delightful companion. The President's wife wrote of him: "He was one of the most exquisitely proportioned of men. His mind dominated his body, but his heart drew him near to all that was honorable and tender, as well as patriotic and faithful in mankind." [53] Tolerant

[50] Jones, *Diary*, II, 322.
[51] George Davis to the Secretary of the Treasury, March 24, 1865, "Records of the Confederate Attorneys-General," New York Public Library, *Bulletin*, II (1898), 199.
[52] DeLeon, *Belles, Beaux and Brains of the 6o's*, 96.
[53] Sprunt, *George Davis*, 17.

of human infirmities but quick to denounce meanness, George Davis was "a polished gentleman, loyal and steadfast in his friendships, with high ideals and lofty purposes." [54] Not a word of slander or detraction had been directed toward the Attorney General, said the *Richmond Sentinel,* and even the critical *North Carolina Standard* paid tribute to him for his refined but unaffected manners. [55] George Davis approximated the ideal of a Southern gentleman of the old school, one who loved life and knew how to live graciously.

As an adviser to the President and in the deliberations of the Cabinet his services were extremely valuable. The President and his Attorney General did not always see eye to eye, Jefferson Davis told his wife, but more often than not the Chief Executive found the advice of his counselor right in the end. The President had little time to give to the affairs of the Department of Justice, but he had confidence in the competency of the Attorney General and a most sincere friendship for him. On his part, George Davis's respect for the President grew as the two men came into more intimate contact. The occasions when they met on official business were most often when pardons were under discussion, for every decision of a military court referred to the President was sent by him to the Department of Justice for review. George Davis was of a kindly nature, but he had difficulty in keeping the President from pardoning every offender. The Attorney General regarded Jefferson Davis as an able and considerate executive in Cabinet meetings, as well as in other particulars of administration. At every opportunity he encouraged the President, and by his faith in Confederate victory aided the morale of the administration.

George Davis's hope for the South's ability to repel its foe continued until General Grant's forces drew close to Richmond, but when defeat came he accepted it courageously. When General Lee surrendered, the Attorney General became convinced that independence was no longer possible and he advised the President to end the war by accepting the best terms he could

---

[54] Ashe, *Biographical History of North Carolina,* II, 74.
[55] *Richmond Sentinel,* July 29, 1861; *North Carolina Weekly Standard,* September 18, 1861.

obtain. The North Carolinian was the first member of the Cabinet to resign his office after the surrender, but he did so only when he was assured that he could no longer be of assistance to the Southern cause or to the President. The defeat of the Confederacy was a hard blow to George Davis, for his political career began and ended with it. As he said after the war, his "ambition went down with the banner of the South, and, like it, never rose again." [56]

[56] Sprunt, *George Davis*, 20.

X

Court Life at the Confederate Capitals

MONTGOMERY

Montgomery lacked many of the things a national capital should have. Its drab streets and general dullness reminded William Howard Russell, the *London Times* correspondent, of a small somnolent town in the interior of Russia, and in his judgment the city had little claim to the dignity of a seat of government. Other observers were no more favorably impressed by the city's physical aspects. One wrote that the city's cobbled main street, ascending gradually from the Alabama River to the colonnaded capitol, and the other streets running from the main artery appeared to have been "laid out before the surveyor's compass was in use. . . ." Its sidewalks of irregular and fantastic construction, and the prevalence of holes and mounds convinced him that "there must be a wide field for so much of the practice of law as relates to the suit for damages." Furthermore, this sarcastic reporter advised the visitor to consult *Appleton's Guide* while traversing Montgomery's streets, in order to avoid "missing land marks and fetching up in Georgia and Mississippi." [1]

Yet the city was not wholly devoid of comeliness. Its private residences, standing back from the street in their setting of gardens fragrant with the perfume of magnolias, were homes of stateliness and beauty. Kindlier observers could excuse Montgomery's urban shortcomings and even see an element of attractiveness in them. The city was not commercially important, for its cotton trade had been declining for years. Even before the establishment of the Confederacy its main business had been government. Young though it was, Montgomery gave the appear-

[1] "Sigma," *Charleston Daily Courier*, February 5, 1861.

ance of a city that was old and static, bearing "an air of solid dilapidation, that would never quite topple into decay, an air of changeless repose." [2]

The disappointment aroused by the appearance and decay of Montgomery was mitigated by the qualities of its people. Their cordial welcome to the officials of the Confederacy and their wives made the new arrivals feel at home at the outset. Sharing was the dominant note of the hour. A round of social affairs began even before the government officials had been established in homes. The President's wife held her first levee at the Exchange Hotel in early March. The presence of outstanding men and women from all parts of the South lent attraction even to official receptions. Guests, drawn to Mrs. Davis's levee by curiosity and an eagerness to get a glimpse of the President's wife, often went away admiring her as a worthy representative of Southern womanhood. This opening levee was followed by a succession of parties given by the wives of high officials in the government. At Mrs. Robert Toombs's reception one saw, among other statesmen, the cadaverous Alexander H. Stephens, discussing in accents of doom the dangers that lay ahead of the Confederacy, and voicing his fear of the outcome.[3] Jefferson Davis was affable to all those who surrounded him. Mrs. Davis frequently entertained the women of the government set at luncheon, where the table talk wontedly was of their men and their South. They agreed that Montgomery's hotels were sadly wanting and that their deficiencies would probably cause the city the loss of the capital, for statesmen loved their ease.[4] While the conversation at these luncheons customarily turned to serious topics, the atmosphere was by no means somber and there were frequent intervals of relief. On the whole, social life in the capital at that time was marked by pleasing simplicity. Personal animosities had not developed, cliques had not had time to form, and a democratic temper prevailed.

On the last day of April, Mrs. Davis held a public levee at the "White House," the first of a series of Tuesday receptions. William Howard Russell, who attended one of these functions, wrote

2 Tate, *Jefferson Davis*, 16.   3 Chesnut, *Diary*, 49.
4 *Ibid.*, 55.

a description of it for his paper.[5] The guests on arrival were
ushered into the moderately sized parlor by a Negro servant; if
the visitor did not chance to know Mrs. Davis, he was formally
presented to her and, in turn, to the other guests. There was an
absence of ceremony or constraint among the small company of
ladies and gentlemen, the former simply attired and wearing
bonnets, the latter in morning dress à la midi. Mrs. Davis, a
great favorite among her guests, some of whom called her "Queen
Varina," was a comely, vivacious woman of good figure, well
dressed, gracious in manner, and clever in conversation. There
was an atmosphere of friendliness about these affairs, and the talk
among the guests was sprightly and informal. Although the President seldom appeared, members of his Cabinet frequently took
time from their duties to attend and pay their respects to Mrs.
Davis.

Some of the guests were drawn to these afternoon receptions
by curiosity to see the interior of the President's residence, for
which an enormous rental was paid. The house was an unpretentious villa, semiclassic in architecture, painted white and
standing in a small garden, entered through an open gate. The
President was not hedged about by pomp and circumstance; it
required no formality for even a stranger to gain admittance to
his presence. The *Examiner*'s correspondent noted with pleasure
that no armed sentries stood guard over the President, waking
or sleeping. He went about unattended and, except for official
routine, led the life of any gentleman in private station in Montgomery. He had no fear of unwelcome intrusion or of any vio-
lence to his person, and he and his family felt secure in their
small but homelike "mansion." In its simplicity the government
at Montgomery approached the republican ideal of the fathers,
in contrast, as one reporter saw it, with "the vulgar pretension,
coward fears and Pretorian bands which surround the northern
usurper at Washington." [6]

Cabinet members were not so fortunate as was their chief in
the matter of housing. Until they could obtain homes, they
stayed at the Exchange Hotel or rented rooms in private homes,

5 Russell, *My Diary North and South*, 71.
6 "Ariel," *Daily Richmond Examiner*, May 13, 1861.

as did Vice-President Stephens. Later, some of them obtained
residences of a none too satisfactory nature. At the Exchange
Hotel the rooms were dirty, the service poor, and the accommo-
dations inadequate. At times four persons were crowded into
one room, and "Had it not been for the flies, the fleas would have
been intolerable, but one nuisance neutralized the other." [7] For
food, one had to go to a near-by restaurant where, in spite of
soiled linen and half-washed dishes, a good meal was obtainable.

Montgomery grew steadily in disfavor as the site of the capital,
and the need for a change in location increasingly formed the
subject of conversation among officials. There were various reasons advanced in support of the arguments for a change. For one,
the city lacked buildings which could readily be reconditioned
for use as government offices. Buildings for the purpose could
have been constructed, of course, had secession not been attended
by war; but the needs of the army were now paramount. Again,
Montgomery's two small hotels were unequal to the task of ac-
commodating the number of visitors necessarily drawn to the
capital. Besides, the hotels were unkempt and poorly managed.
"Mosquitos, and a want of neatness," Mrs. Chesnut wrote, "and
a want of good things to eat, drove us away." [8] Montgomery had
at least one defender in the *Charleston Courier*. That journal,
recognizing the effort being made to remove the capital to Richmond, held that there were no solid reasons for leaving Montgomery, but that a move to Richmond would be interpreted as
preliminary to the occupancy of Washington.[9]

It was regarded as a certainty in Montgomery that the United
States intended to invade Virginia. Furthermore, there were
some among the officials who doubted that state's loyalty to the
Confederacy. D. G. Duncan, whom the Secretary of War, Leroy
Pope Walker, sent to Richmond on a mission of observation
which amounted almost to a spying assignment, reported that
Davis alone could save Virginia to the Confederacy. "Intelligent
and distinguished men believe Virginia on the very brink of be-

[7] Russell, *My Diary North and South*, 66.   [8] Chesnut, *Diary*, 79.
[9] *Charleston Daily Courier*, May 7, 1861.

ing carried back," Duncan wrote on May 7, 1861, "and say no man but President Davis can save her. The people will rally around him; they universally call for his presence. There is disappointment that he does not assume entire direction of affairs here." [10] While there is no evidence that Hunter's friends colored the picture for this emissary, the Virginian was an astute politician and he ardently desired the removal of the seat of government to Richmond.

The newspapers generally also encouraged Davis's preference for Richmond as the logical place for the capital because it was the locale of the important military operations. The *Charleston Courier* waged a losing fight against the mounting sentiment for removal of the capital, warning that the transfer of the seat of government to Richmond would intensify the war between the states. Granting that the President and the military command should be in Richmond, that newspaper was unable to see any wisdom in having Congress and the departments moved there, arguing that the presence of Congress could not be of aid to military operations. Indeed, the *Courier*'s editor feared that the removal of the capital to Richmond would be construed as a threat to take Washington; he believed it would be folly to do anything to encourage the prevailing delusion of the Northern people that Washington would be attacked, that the flag of the Confederacy would supplant the Stars and Stripes over the dome of the Capitol, and that in expectation of this outcome President Davis had retained his church pew in Washington.[11] The *Courier,* along with several other newspapers, protested in vain. Richmond became the capital of the Confederacy in May, 1861.

Montgomery lapsed into its wonted calm, shorn of its shortlived honor, almost desolated. No more were its shabby and winding streets thronged with gayly dressed visitors, the flower of Southern civilization. It was no longer the heart of the Confederacy, where momentous questions of state were weighed and decided, where the high strategy of military campaigns was planned and directed, and where the workings of the machinery

---

[10] Duncan to Walker, May 7, 1861, in *Official Records,* Ser. I, Vol. LI, Pt. II, 71.
[11] *Charleston Daily Courier,* May 27, 1861.

of government gave the little community a national importance.[12]

RICHMOND

In addition to being a city with a population of 40,000, a status
to which Montgomery really had no valid claim, the new capital
had other undoubted advantages over the quondam seat of government. Besides having buildings suitable for government offices, Richmond's hotels were of a character to satisfy the comfort-
loving Southern statesmen and their friends. The prospect
afforded by the city itself, seen from a vantage point, was pleasing. From a distance one saw its buildings stretching along a
range of hills overlooking the James River, and in the center,
dominating the picture, the gleaming bulk of the state capitol.
Richmond was a center of social activity, and had long attracted
the first families of the state, who either lived in the city or visited
it during the season. Many wealthy planters and lawyers maintained homes in the city as well as on their ancestral lands. Others
during the winter months would take up their residence in the
Richmond hotels or visit friends. It was an urbane community
of Virginians who took pride in their history and in a traditional
culture. They believed that in no other section of the South
could the suave polished manners of a Virginia gentleman be
matched or even approximated. History and importance considered, the Confederate capital by all rights belonged in Virginia. Yet the coming of the Confederate officials to Richmond
was the cause of misgivings to many old residents of the new
capital.

Their fears soon were realized. Within a few weeks of the
transfer of the seat of government, Richmond became a changed
city. Tents in increasing numbers dotted the surrounding hill-
sides. The city's normal population was more than doubled by
a floating population. In the throngs that swarmed its streets
were types representative of all sections of the South: the shaggy
ranger from Texas; heavily bearded Marylanders of courtly bearing; river boatmen, red-shirted and uncouth; sallow turpentine-
makers from North Carolina; scarlet-trousered Zouaves from

12 *Charleston Mercury*, May 30, 1861.

New Orleans; complacent South Carolinians, distinguishable by
the inevitable sprigs of palmetto stuck in their hats; [13] soldiers
on leave and invalided, camp followers, government clerks,
tradesmen, place-hunters, speculators, and countless nonde-
scripts—human rubbish, the detritus of a nation at war.

The capital was aflame with military enthusiasm. Shop clerks
who had never been near a battlefield, at night lounged around
the hotel lobbies, resplendent in the uniforms and insignia belonging to the rank of major. They brushed elbows with many
a man of self-admitted importance who had journeyed to Richmond to advise the President and his Cabinet, had tarried to
apply for some office in the government and, being refused, became "sure that Jefferson Davis was a despot, and that the Southern Confederacy was fast going to the devil." [14] In all this bustle
and excitement hardly any place except the government bore
any semblance of order or business method.

The sudden increase in population brought in its train crimi-
nal and troublesome elements. By October, 1861, Richmond was
declared to be a conquered city "in the possession of gamblers
and prostitutes." [15] Streetwalkers frequently paraded the city's
thoroughfares in "indecent" masquerade of male attire. The
gamblers, in semimilitary dress, loafed on street corners, ogling
women or enticing young men into their gambling dens. These
parasites operated boldly, unchecked by the seedy and undis-
ciplined police, whose activities were directed mainly toward
frightening Negroes and petty offenders.[16] The county jail soon
became overcrowded, and an abandoned part of it was remodeled
to house the overflow of prisoners. At the mayor's court, scene
of many interesting and sometimes diverting cases, justice was
not uniformly evenhanded. There was the case of a husband, one
Mike, charged with beating his wife, who won the sympathy of
the court by his counter-accusation of her. "It was yersilf that up
wid a basin and struck me over the face." But another defendant
who had thrashed the man who beat his wife was bound over

---

[13] Felix Gregory De Fontaine, *Marginalia; or Gleanings from an Army Note-Book* (Columbia, 1864), 44.

[14] An English Combatant, *Battlefields of the South, . . .* (New York, 1864), 115.

[15] *Daily Richmond Examiner*, October 30, 1861.

[16] *Ibid.*

for trial in a higher court. A never-ending procession of drunks passed through the city's courts, thence to a temporary sojourn in jail. The nimble fingers of pickpockets were busy wherever crowds congregated; burglars and murderers were at large in unprecedented numbers. In the demoralization of war Richmond grew unkempt, dirty, dissolute.

Away from the principal business streets a healthier atmosphere prevailed. There, life was less fevered, more quiet and orderly. Children played their games, among which that of soldier was favorite. The more daring among the younger boys, the "Sidney Cats" and the "Shockoe Cats," met at the old plank road on afternoons for a battle royal. The older boys, the "Butcher Cats" and the "Hill Cats," fought on Navy Hill nearly every evening in contests something like a class war, in which the casualties were many and frequent. Then at the close of the battle the wounded mimic soldier, forgetting his role, would run home to the comforting arms of his mother. The mother herself lived in daily dread of news that a member of her family, a father or a brother, had been killed or wounded in battle, and toward the end she had to worry about the next day's supply of food for her "little soldier."

As the war went on, food became scarcer. Time was when the lusty cries of the street vender could be heard in every Richmond street. But they grew less frequent and then ceased altogether. In the latter years of the war many a housewife would have welcomed the watermelon hawker's chant of "Got 'em, got 'em, got 'em nice; got 'em sweet; got 'em fine; got 'em fresh from the livin' vine." It was in the side streets and back alleys, the districts of the poor, that the tragic results of a long war were most in evidence. The rich, of course, suffered too, but the alternate phases of hope and despair of the Confederacy experienced by all its people were more strikingly reflected among the poor during the years of bitter struggle.

Privations common to the poor of Richmond were unknown to the members of its upper strata of society. True, men and women of rank and wealth in time were obliged to forego little luxuries of food, but they rarely faced starvation. The women had to wear old and outmoded dresses, but they seldom lacked for clothing enough to keep them warm. There were gay parties, or thrilling excursions to the points of the city's defense. A visit to the capital, with its gayety, variety, and the presence of many unattached officers, was an experience many a provincial girl in the Confederacy welcomed. Life there was at a little faster tempo than usual; love-making more impetuous, marriage more hasty, and death more sudden. Through all the vicissitudes of war Richmond society kept its poise and showed a brave front.

Richmond's highest society gave an immediate and cordial welcome to the Confederate officials and their families. Jefferson Davis was received with great enthusiasm upon his arrival on May 20. Until a suitable house could be obtained for them, a suite in the Spottswood Hotel was provided for the President and his family. Here Mrs. Davis held her court and entertained her women friends at tea. Occasionally the President visited with intimate friends, men and women. His easy manner and sound ideas impressed most of those who met him. He laughed at the boast that one Southerner was equal to three Northerners, but added that he needed to be equal to twelve. While he had faith in his countrymen's courage and patriotism, he foresaw a long war. "He said only fools doubted the courage of the Yankees, or their willingness to fight when they saw fit." [17]

Women were not included in the company at state occasions such as the receptions for the members of the Virginia convention. At these functions, visitors entered the parlors of the President's apartment by a private entrance and were presented to the chief of the Confederacy and his Cabinet. This ceremony over, the President moved freely among the guests, complimenting one, exchanging reminiscences with another, passing a pleasant word here and there, and in general acting as a gracious host. He was at his best among a company of his admirers. "You look, you listen, and you talk. Magnetized by one of the most irresistible smiles in the world, charmed with his language, and yet, involuntarily drawn into the expression of your own sentiments, you soon forget that you are talking with the President of the Southern union, and remember the man." [18] The members of his Cabinet, too, moved through the company, making new ac-

[17] Chesnut, *Diary*, 71.   [18] *Charleston Daily Courier*, June 21, 1861.

quaintances, renewing old friendships. The austere Christopher G. Memminger would recall for a listener a prior visit to Richmond and the efforts made to convince Virginia men that co-operative secession was the only course for the South. Robert Toombs would bustle about, endeavoring to make himself the center of interest, and Stephen Mallory would hold a guest's amused attention with many a well-told anecdote. The formality of the occasion was a little relieved by the presence of the President's two small children, Maggie and Jeff. It was a purely social gathering; no speeches were made, although the *Charleston Courier* reporter noted the presence of some politicians whose oratorical guns were loaded and primed to discharge a few remarks on a moment's notice.

The President often entertained at meals men and women of importance whose conversation usually turned to the all-absorbing topic of the conduct of the war. The large Presidential group included General and Mrs. James B. Chesnut, Judah P. Benjamin, and Stephen R. Mallory. At one of these dinners the story that the Secretary of War had refused the offer of twenty thousand well-armed North Carolina troops amused the officials. The President remarked that, so eager was the War Department for accessions to the Confederacy's military forces, it would not have refused to accept a single recruit, let alone twenty thousand.[19] These dinners never lacked for sparkling conversation, and the occasional outsider admitted to the brilliant inner circle found the time too fleeting and the dinner ending all too soon. It was while they were living at the Spottswood Hotel that the President and his family made their most favorable impression upon the Richmond public. He and the members of his Cabinet were often seen in the hotel lobby or in the main dining hall in a section only partly screened from the other hotel guests. But such a manner of living was rather too trying on a man burdened with official cares and it was further considered that the dignity of the nation required that its chief be housed in his own private mansion.

Accordingly the Brockenbrough home, then the residence of James A. Seddon, today the Confederate Museum, was obtained for the new Presidential residence. The city of Richmond had

[19] Chesnut, *Diary*, 73.

bought it for presentation to the President, but Congress purchased it from the municipality, believing that the whole nation, and not one city, should provide the Chief Executive's residence. The house was situated on the southeast corner of Clay and Twelfth streets, on the crest of a hill overlooking a green valley traversed by a winding stream which flowed into the James River. It faced north on Clay Street and, from the street level, steps led up to a small open portico. The simple entrance opened upon a large foyer, from which through a doorway on the right could be seen the circular stairway leading to the bedrooms on the second and third floors. From the high-ceilinged dining room, study, and parlor on the first floor French windows opened upon the south porch with its massive columns. The residence became known as the Grey House, in contradistinction, an English visitor supposed, to the White House in Washington.[20]

Under Mrs. Davis's touch the spacious old mansion was soon transformed into a home. Callers sometimes found it difficult to gain admittance to the family, for Spencer, an officious household servant, would invariably deny that the President was at home. If the caller persisted, Spencer would lose patience and declare, "I tell you, sir, Marse Jeff 'clines to see you." Fortunately, some other servant or member of the family usually intervened and the embarrassed guest would be made welcome. Mrs. Davis, a tactful, accomplished hostess, was ably assisted in her social duties by her sister, Margaret Howell, in years hardly beyond the debutante stage, a girl of bubbling spirits and unconstrained manners. Mrs. Davis's devotion to her husband and children was notable. On his part, the busy President always gave his family at least an hour each day; and a visitor during the early evening hours would find him in the company of Mrs. Davis and their children, to whom he was unvaryingly tender and kind. The spirit pervading this home was manifest to the visitor on more intimate terms of acquaintance with the family, when at times could be seen a little lad in night clothes, repeating at his father's knee his evening prayer of thankfulness and supplication. It was an example of a simple God-fearing household which had no

[20] An English Officer, "A Month's Visit to the Confederate Headquarters," *Blackwood's Edinburgh Magazine*, XCIII (1863), 9.

critic save only the editor of the *Richmond Examiner,* a man embittered against the Yankees, the Southern leader, and even against God.

Mrs. Davis held a court of her own, at which the wives of the President's aides and others of her friends attended. Although she was always at home to visitors, who received from her a cordial welcome, she asserted her position as the wife of the President and was insistent that the President and she return no calls. While she was usually gracious, either as hostess or guest, she could give her critics blow for blow and with her wit and irony could scathe those who had displeased her.[21] It was perhaps this ability to hold her own against the unfriendly that prompted Edward A. Pollard's characterization of her as a brawny, able-bodied woman who lacked feminine grace and whose manner was loud and coarse.[22] This prejudiced critic thought her complexion in hue like that of a mulatto, and berated her because of her liveried servants and elegant horses and carriage.

Mrs. Davis had been accepted by the leaders of Richmond society, who were glad to have her as a guest in their homes and happy to be received by her at the Grey House. As factions developed among the political leaders, however, bickerings and animosities arose among their women-folk and spiteful comment and gossip spared neither Mrs. Davis nor the ladies of her little court. Behind backs it was whispered that her ladies were neither young nor pretty, and their taste in clothes was derided. Mrs. Louis T. Wigfall referred to the President's wife as a "coarse Western woman." Mrs. Joseph E. Johnston, who at first had called the President's wife "a western belle," revised the complimentary reference by substituting "woman" for "belle." [23] Mrs. Robert Toombs declared that a Presidential reception was such a failure that even Mrs. John H. Reagan could have done better.[24] Mrs. Stephen R. Mallory, herself the wife of a social favorite, became more than merely irked at Mrs. Davis's request that the wives of Cabinet secretaries visit her regularly.

As division grew wider and criticism more bitter and unre-

---

21 DeLeon, *Belles, Beaux and Brains of the 60's,* 67; Morgan, *Recollections of a Rebel Reefer,* 221.

22 Pollard, *Jefferson Davis,* 154.   23 Chesnut, *Diary,* 101–102.
24 *Ibid.,* 112.

strained, Mrs. Davis increasingly withdrew herself into the more congenial company of tried friends. With them she was frank and kind, sharing with them delicacies from her luncheon table and partaking of theirs in turn. Yet the changed atmosphere of official society could not make her shirk her duty as the wife of the Confederacy's head. Nor did she meet these obligations perfunctorily. There were times, as when she went to tell some one of the death of a husband, that her sympathetic nature was evidenced by the pallor of her features, bespeaking the grief in her heart. She loved the Confederacy and she willingly sacrificed herself for it, maintaining a gallant front in the face of much hurtful criticism. That she was unable to count many of the leaders of haughty Richmond society among her real friends was due rather to their caste prejudices than to any fault of hers. Her father, William Burr Howell, was reputed to be of humble origin, and this damning fact was sufficient to debar her from the intimacy or favor of those of "high birth," even though of less exalted station.[25] At Montgomery, Mrs. Davis would have been esteemed as the wife of the President of the Confederacy and as a social queen in her own right. In Richmond she was the President's wife.

It was Mrs. Davis's intention originally to entertain guests at a series of formal dinners. Only a few such dinners were attempted, however, for it seemed that invariably they were clouded by the arrival of news of the death of a friend or of some fresh military disaster. As Davis suffered from nervous dyspepsia and became very ill if obliged to continue a meal in a state of excitement, he concluded that he must either give up entertaining at dinner or relinquish his office. The alternative to be adopted was clear. Hence all official formal dinners were discontinued except on rare occasions. Cabinet members and congressmen, however, were his guests occasionally at breakfasts where the chat was intimate. They, and other friends of the President, were invited to informal dinners, from which the President felt free to excuse himself in the event that disturbing news was received. These informal dinners and breakfasts necessarily were infrequent, depending as they did on the President's health, and this moved the *Richmond Examiner* to inveigh

---

[25] Jones, *Diary*, II, 453.

against what it regarded as the parsimony of the Executive and to accuse him of hoarding his salary and becoming rich while his people grew poor. Had there been more frequent social contact of the President with Confederate leaders, undoubtedly greater harmony might have resulted. If those who opposed him could have met and talked with the quiet, unassuming man who headed the government, many animosities might have given way to understanding.

President and Mrs. Davis inaugurated a series of weekly public receptions at the Grey House, but after a trial the scheduled levees were changed to fortnightly occasions. At the beginning of each year a public reception was held which lasted throughout most of the afternoon. These annual receptions were attended by throngs, all eager to greet the President and to extend to him and his lady the compliments of the season.[26] Davis on these occasions would pass through the great company, unfailingly courteous and kindly in his greetings, sometimes pausing briefly to chat with a guest personally known to him. On these occasions his manner was grave, giving one the impression that upon his frail shoulders God had placed an undue share of the sorrows of the world. Yet for all his gravity and obvious sense of the responsibilities of his office, he was unvaryingly gracious, at times even playful in his complimentary teasing of the younger ladies.

The regularly fortnightly levee was usually held from eight to ten o'clock in the evening. The President's custom was to make the rounds of the parlors, extending to each guest the greeting, "I am glad to meet you here tonight." [27]

Everyone of importance, unless in deep mourning, came to these receptions. Mrs. Davis conducted her salon with her accustomed grace and conversational ease. Even her wonted equanimity must have been gravely threatened with upset, however, when on one such occasion the hats of sixty-four guests were stolen by some light-fingered opportunist. At times of grave crisis these regular levees were omitted. The *Richmond Enquirer* on January 18, 1864, announced that a levee would be held between eight and ten o'clock on every Tuesday evening following, but a month later the diarist Jones noted that the

---

[26] *Petersburg Daily Express*, January 2, 1862.   [27] Jones, *Diary*, II, 136.

President had discontinued his Tuesday evening receptions.[28]
How regularly the President received is not known, but Mrs.
Davis made every effort to give both the residents of Richmond
and provincial citizens of the Confederacy opportunity to meet
him.

The style of living of most of the members of the Cabinet was
not such as to bring upon them the charges of parsimony directed
against their chief. The Mallory home was a favorite with distinguished visitors in Richmond, as well as with the leaders in
its society. Mallory and his Spanish wife were little known in
Richmond prior to 1861, but his wit, his powers as a raconteur,
his genial manners and frank courtesy soon won general esteem.[29]
Both he and his wife possessed in high degree the social graces
which put guests at ease immediately upon entering their home.
Mallory was somewhat of a gourmet and Mrs. Mallory was adept
at preparing salads. Her husband was famous for his skill at
mixing mint juleps with which even those of a Kentucky colonel
could not compare, and his stories were as good as his juleps. He
was known as the most adroit flatterer in Richmond and expressed his compliments in neatly turned phrases. To Mrs.
Clement C. Clay he wrote: ". . . come to the front, where
security, sympathy, mint juleps and brandy smashes, and admiring audiences, the freshest gossip and the most unselfish regard,
all combine with the boom and flash of the guns to welcome your
coming." [30] The Mallory home was the rendezvous of Cabinet
officers who frequently went there to consult the Secretary of the
Navy.[31]

George Wythe Randolph, too, and his wife, the former Mrs.
Pope of Mobile, nee Adams of Mississippi, were accomplished
hosts. Mrs. Randolph, a beauty of Oriental type, because of her
great wealth would entertain on a lavish scale. During her husband's incumbency as Secretary of War her prestige as a hostess
made their home the most popular among those of government
officials in Richmond. President Davis and all the members of
the Cabinet attended the charades which were a feature of her

[28] *Ibid.*, 152.   [29] DeLeon, *Belles, Beaux and Brains of the 60's,* 85.

[30] Mallory to Virginia C. Clay, August 1, 1864, in Clay Papers.

[31] "The Brave Wife of Stephen Mallory," *New Orleans Daily Picayune,* January
12, 1898, quoted in Clubbs, "Stephen Russell Mallory," 305.

parties, and at one of these they saw General J. E. B. Stuart act
and were greatly amused when he accidentally let a young lady
fall on the stage. The Randolphs between them possessed a combination ideal for success in society: he had a family background
of distinguished Virginia ancestry; she had money, beauty, and
talent. Their reign in the society of the capital was short-lived,
however, for Randolph lost his executive position and, through
his mismanagement, a considerable part of his wife's fortune.
Before the war ended they left Richmond and went to Europe
to reside.

The vacancy in the official social life was filled by the George
A. Trenholms in 1864. Upon her arrival in Richmond, Mrs.
Trenholm, in compliance with custom called on Mrs. Davis and
the wives of Cabinet members. As related by one who subsequently became her son-in-law, Mrs. Trenholm, being desirous
of observing all the official amenities, included on her list of
calls one at the Stephens's residence. At the home of the Vice-
President the eyes of the old darky servant fairly bulged in their
sockets when the caller inquired if Mrs. Stephens were at home.
"Mam," he told her earnestly, "Mr. Stephens ain't married. My
God! Did you ever see him?" [32]

Although Mrs. Trenholm had known few people in Richmond
prior to living there, her home soon became the scene of many
delightful parties. Her Saturday evenings especially were attractive to distinguished men and women, who enjoyed the
sparkle of witty conversation and, not less, the hospitality of a
table renowned for its bounteous food. For the wealthy Secretary
of the Treasury, with his fleet of blockade-runners, was able to
supply his larder with many desired luxuries at a time when other
households could only with great difficulty obtain the necessities
of life. The Trenholm cellar was stocked with fine old Madeira
which was the envy and delight of war-weary Richmond society.
An invitation to dine at the Trenholms' was rarely declined.
The attraction for guests, however, was not all in the bounteous
table for which the ménage was noted. For in addition to the

[32] Morgan, *Recollections of a Rebel Reefer*, 203. There could be no truth to this
tale. Stephens had no residence in Richmond; besides, he and his servant were in
Georgia when the Trenholms came to Richmond.

pleasant picture of family life to which his wife and daughters contributed, Trenholm was of a genuinely hospitable nature, and the charm of his conversation, enhanced by a delightful wit, was equaled only by that of Judah P. Benjamin.

In the social life of Richmond the Reagans did not occupy a very high place. Reagan was generally regarded as an uncouth frontiersman whom circumstances had thrust into a cultured society to which he was not accustomed. Mrs. Reagan, who had been in poor health, died in the midst of the war, but Reagan kept his Richmond home and lived there with his children. There he had as his guest Francis Richard Lubbock, former governor of Texas, who shared the government rations, the only fare his host could offer him. For breakfast and supper the family had black coffee, sorghum, and biscuits made of flour, salt, and water. The menu for dinner was a little more elaborate, for as added dishes there were meat and rice. Even for the poor sorghum they had paid as high as $150 a gallon. The Reagan fare, however, was somewhat less frugal on one occasion when the Texan entertained his fellow Cabinet members at dinner. Among the dishes was a platter of ham and eggs and Reagan was perplexed, perhaps obviously so, as to the propriety of offering them to Benjamin. The latter, however, sensing his host's dilemma, resolved his doubts as to his own attitude toward Jewish dietary laws by remarking casually that a thief had broken into his smokehouse the night before and had stolen all his fine hams.[33]

Among all the members of Davis's Cabinet, Benjamin was the most socially acceptable. As his Catholic wife lived in Paris, except for one short and unsatisfactory interlude in Richmond, he kept only a modest residence on Main Street, which from time to time many Louisiana congressmen shared with him. There were few homes, indeed, whether those of officials or of persons in private life, whether in a company of old or young, at the informal hour or the most formal dinner, at the small intimate party or a large reception, where this versatile man was not at all times welcome. On his part, he was markedly social-minded, always ready to respond to any request for his company. He was of a cosmopolitan make-up, a blend of racial character-

[33] Reagan, *Memoirs*, 163.

istics, Jewish in blood, English in tenacity of grasp and purpose, French in delicacy and discriminating taste.[34] He was master of the art of conversation, to which a pleasing voice lent added charm, and his talk always contained substance which made it worth hearing. While his conversation was listened to for its own brilliance, his hearers, mindful of his close association with President Davis, were ever hopeful that he might divulge some hint of an important state secret or other matter of official news. Benjamin was not promiscuous in his social contacts, but ". . . moved into and through the most elegant or simplest assemblages on rubber-tired and well-oiled bearings, a smile of recognition for the mere acquaintance, a reminiscent word for the intimate, and a general diffusion of placid bonhomme." [35]

Benjamin was happiest at the small dinner party. He was a frequent dinner guest of Mrs. Davis and of Mrs. Barton Haxall, a prominent Richmond hostess. Fastidious though he was in his food preferences, neither religious scruples nor lack of relish for a dish on his host's table would ever cause him to refuse to partake of the food. With a generous slice of bread spread with anchovy paste, a glass of McHenry sherry and some English walnuts, he once remarked to Mrs. Davis, a man's patriotism became rampant.[36] Certainly, while there was any supply for entertainment left in Richmond the shadow of this accomplished diner-out never would have grown less. Whatever criticism there was of him as an official, he was generally acclaimed as a wholly delightful person socially.

Little record exists to show the impression made upon Richmond society by the other Cabinet secretaries. Mrs. Leroy Pope Walker, wife of the first Secretary of War, was a social failure measured by the standards of Richmond society. A beauty, an heiress, and one of the best dressed women of the Confederacy, she had been a belle in Alabama, but she did not repeat her triumph in the capital and her husband's failure as Secretary of War made her unhappy and dissatisfied. John C. Breckinridge, the handsome former Vice-President of the United States, was a striking figure in any company of ladies and gentlemen. He wel-

[34] DeLeon, *Belles, Beaux and Brains of the 60's,* 92–93.
[35] *Ibid.,* 91.   [36] V. Davis, *Jefferson Davis,* II, 207.

comed every occasion that offered the opportunity for congenial companionship and the pledging of convivial toasts. Seddon lived quietly in a Richmond hotel, but his vivacious wife, Sally, spent little time in the city. Christopher G. Memminger, prim and austere, cared little for the gay atmosphere of society, but was happy in the companionship of his intimates and in the indulgence of his hobby of collecting books on religious subjects. George Davis, thanks to the circumstance that his wife was of Virginia birth, was acceptable to Richmond society, but its attitude toward the Thomas Hill Wattses at first was somewhat cool because of their reputation as one-time Alabama Unionists. But no Cabinet officer or member of his family was ever left uninvited to a formal party given by the socially elect of Richmond.

There was considerable social intercourse between members of the Cabinet, who frequently went on various excursions or met for a meal at the home of one of their number. Well-fed officials caused envious comment by Jones, understandably perhaps, because his own household economy was so reduced that on one occasion he was glad to make use of a partly eaten chicken the cat had brought into the yard. Seeing an invitation to Seddon and Trenholm to have "pea soup" at Mallory's, the hungry diarist wrote that the "pea soup" would be oysters, champagne, and every delicacy of the epicure.[37] Jones deprecated what he viewed as feasting and enjoyment while brave men languished sorely wounded and the very pillars of government crumbled under the enemy's assault. His criticisms were not wholly justified, for the Cabinet members worked diligently at their official duties, although they did not labor from morning until midnight, as some writers have indicated. They were ever ready to avail themselves of the entertainment offered either within their own circle or by Richmond friends.

There was, indeed, no lack of such entertainment, for Richmond society was enlivened by a ceaseless round of dinners, parties, and receptions. Mrs. Thomas Jenkins Semmes, wife of the Louisiana Senator, entertained so lavishly that in the last year of the war the running expenses of her household amounted

37 Jones, *Diary*, II, 290.

to thirty thousand dollars.[38] Her charade parties, at one of which
the President and Mrs. Davis proudly watched their little
daughter Maggie act parts, were among the most notable given
in Richmond. At the home of Mrs. Robert Standard, dark-eyed
widow of wealth and exotic beauty, whose brilliant mental qualities and great attraction for men aided her in realizing the French
ideal of a salon more successfully than any other hostess in the
capital, Judah P. Benjamin delighted in telling his unique tales,
to give his dramatic recitations of scrap verse, and to comment
in clever phrases on men, women, and books.[39] Even the recluse
Stephens, on occasions, emerged from his seclusion to pay his
respects to the mistress of this hospitable home.

Private theatricals were much the vogue in Richmond of the
war years, and the audiences included high officials of the Confederacy whose generous applause heartened the amateur players.
When at one of the theatricals at Mrs. J. C. Ives's home the
audience seemed unresponsive, Mrs. Clay, one of the cast, sent
out an appeal to friends in the audience for some show of appreciation that would encourage the players. General Breckinridge gallantly complied with the request, and thereafter applause greeted the players at every opportunity. After the play,
Mrs. Chesnut has recorded, General Breckinridge complimented
Mrs. Clay on her mass of beautiful hair, "And all my own," the
lady told him in acknowledging his praise. Mrs. Clay's answer
was a true but disingenuous one. She afterwards admitted that
she had been unable to obtain enough false hair for the requirements of her towering coiffure and had placed on her head a
pair of black satin boots which were then covered with her own
tresses.[40]

There was one discordant note in all this record of gayety. It
was sounded by the members of the little court that paid homage
to Mrs. Joseph E. Johnston, of the distinguished McLane family
of Baltimore. They disputed the social leadership of the Grey
House and the coterie of official families, and grew ever more
antagonistic toward the administration group.

[38] "Hon. Thomas J. Semmes," New Orleans Daily Picayune, January 23, 1898,
reprinted in Southern Historical Society, Papers, XXV (1897), 326.
[39] Mrs. Burton Harrison, Recollections Grave and Gay (New York, 1911), 160.
[40] Chesnut, Diary, 285.

For every elaborate reception and amateur theatrical given in Richmond, there were hundreds of less ambitious parties. The return of any popular young soldier on furlough, or the visit of a well-known officer, was invariably the occasion for entertaining. Eager as the soldiers might be to see Richmond's lovely women, their feminine admirers were much the more eager to see the soldiers. War led to love-making. An acquaintance of Mrs. Chesnut stated that "soldiers do more courting here in a day than they would do at home, without a war, in ten years." [41] Life then was gay and heedless, for death lurked near-by in the background.

These small parties were really more enjoyable than the expensive receptions where guests were served with tasty suppers of oysters, chicken salads, ice cream, and champagne. There was more spontaneous gayety at the "starvation parties," with their dancing, simple music, and easy informality than at the formal gatherings. As the war dragged on, the "starvation social" was adopted into even the higher reaches of Richmond society. The women's costumes were simple and jewels were rarely worn; young girls appeared at balls in old gowns that had belonged to their mothers or grandmothers, made over to suit their more youthful lines; resourceful debutantes made themselves alluring by a skillful adaptation of the living room draperies to the purpose of a dress frock. The soldiers' uniforms were faded and patched, but sartorial deficiencies were ignored and the soldiers could be sure of a welcome in polite company. The men and women of the South in their devotion to the Confederacy counted these deprivations as nothing, or at least as small sacrifices they gladly made to the cause of Southern independence. Even with the sound of cannon booming in their ears, they laughed and danced and were gallantly happy in their enjoyment of the moment.

Despite the war, life in Richmond was never dull, at least for its young people. A round of varied amusements—parties arranged to enjoy strawberries and ice cream at Pizzini's, the locally famous caterer, band concerts, serenades in the evenings by sentimental youths, expeditions to Drewey's Bluff in the company of

41 *Ibid.*, 288.

convalescent officers—for the moment dispelled the ever-present
gloom of the war period. The blockaded ironclads of Secretary
Mallory received a due share of admiring attention. Military
parades at the fair grounds brought out all elements of the population, old and young, rich and poor, and on at least one occasion
provided a serio-comic incident for its delectation. This was in
August of 1861 when the dashing Brigadier General Toombs,
mounted on a spirited horse, performed perhaps too recklessly
before the crowd and was thrown with his foot still in the stirrup.
Before he could disengage his foot, Toombs was dragged up to
the wheels of a near-by carriage. Looking down at the welter of
flailing hoofs and the prostrate rider, Mrs. Chesnut saw an up-
turned face purple and distorted with rage.[42] To the admiration
of the ladies, the flushed and discomfited officer succeeded in
extricating his foot from the stirrup and vaulted into the saddle.

The diversions of capital society, however innocent, did not
escape criticism. "You have heard of some things," the correspondent of a Mobile newspaper told his readers, ". . . but you
have not heard that the living statues of young ladies had their
feet naked and chalked to imitate marble more closely." [43]
Women of irreproachable respectability wore Swiss costumes that
fell only slightly below the knees, and not only on the stage but
in the parlor after the tableaux. At masked balls many ladies
wore shirts as part of their costume; one, more daring than her
sisters, even arrayed herself in full masculine attire. In an effort
to give realism to her borrowed identity, she took such liberties
with other young women that, to save herself from punishment
by an enraged gentleman, she had to unmask and shake out her
curls to convince him of her sex. "It grieves me to say it," the
shocked correspondent wrote in conclusion, "but we are in
danger of re[e]nacting the license of the French Revolution." [44]
Much of what a mid-Victorian age regarded as social laxness grew
directly out of incidents of the war. "Legs" simply could not be
kept out of the conversation, try as the ladies would, Mrs. Chesnut reported. Yet, despite a scandalized older generation, society

[42] *Ibid.*, 97.   [43] *Mobile Advertiser and Register*, January 16, 1864.
[44] *Ibid.*

in the war-torn capital could be said to possess a character of well-bred propriety and its conduct was circumspect.

Some remarkable pen pictures of the personalites at the wedding of Colonel William B. Tabb and Miss Emily Rutherford in the winter of 1864–1865 have been left by John S. Wise.[45] President Davis, wontedly clean-looking and with the manners of a dignified gentleman accustomed to good society, was there and laughingly claimed the privilege of kissing the bride. It was observed that he seemed thin and careworn, that his hair and beard were whitening rapidly, and that an appearance of emaciation was given him by his bloodless cheeks and slender nose. Yet his eyes were clear and keen, his smile winning, and his manner affable and most attractive. By his side, Mrs. Davis, his opposite in physique, appeared large and well-nourished. She made no effort to conceal her pride in her husband, and was perhaps too ready to show her resentment toward those who did not share her enthusiasm over his qualities. After the Davises, Secretary Benjamin glided into the room, his keglike form and too-deferential manner suggesting a prosperous, ingratiating shop-keeper. Next came Mallory, old, bluff, and hearty in manner, one of the most popular members of the President's official family. After him came the massive-framed Postmaster General Reagan, ill at ease in a social gathering and looking like a farmer fresh from his fields and yoke of oxen, but withal a man of extraordinary common sense. It is easy to believe that in the midst of all the celebrities present the poor bride felt like an insignificant guest at her own wedding.

Too often, war marriages had a sad ending. A gay company of Richmond society witnessed the marriage on January 19, 1865, of beautiful Hetty Cary to the popular John Pegram. Three weeks later a sorrowing party of friends saw his flag-draped coffin occupying the space where he had stood to claim his bride. There were few households that death had not visited, and on April 30, 1864, the President was brought face to face with a tragedy in his own family. It was on that date that his little son, Joe, died as the result of injuries suffered in a fall from the north

[45] Wise, *The End of an Era*, 400–402.

porch of the Grey House to the brick pavement below. Many
visitors called at the mansion to express their sympathy with the
family. Overcome with grief, the President withdrew and went
to the family living quarters upstairs. The slow tramp of his
footsteps as he paced the room sounded loud in the stilled home.
All through the night the unceasing tread of the sorrowing father
was heard.[46] Sympathetic crowds went to the funeral, and it
seemed that every child in Richmond had brought flowers and
green leaves to lay at the bier of their President's little son. The
child's body was laid to rest in the cemetery, the little mound
above it covered with flowers, crosses, and evergreens. Quickly
the crowd dispersed, for death was an all too-familiar visitant.
Jefferson Davis returned to the work of his station, the lines on
his face a little deeper, the military set of his shoulders a little
less rigid.

But Richmond was more accustomed to another kind of
funeral, the military. Although death now was never unexpected,
it seemed to strike with dramatic swiftness the most beloved
personalities in society. General J. E. B. Stuart was among the
gayest spirited guests at one of Mrs. Ives's parties when he was
called to duty in the field. He left the home smiling at some jest,
and wearing a flower pinned to his lapel by some pretty girl. Next
day came the news of his death; fallen in battle. Then soldiers
bore his body down a street of the capital, his horse, with empty
saddle and stirrups reversed, at the head of the little cortege.
Behind the coffin bearers marched a small military band playing
"Maryland, My Maryland." Only a few days before the gay-
hearted General had amused others by singing "Old Joe Hooker,
Will You Come Out of the Wilderness." Presently the funeral
procession came to a halt before the St. James Church, the
metallic coffin, blanketed with white flowers and a cross of evergreens interspersed with lilies of the valley and sprigs of laurel,
was carried into the church and placed just below the pulpit.
The President and Cabinet were there, and behind them, seated
in the central aisles, were the members of Congress. The short
funeral service of the Episcopal Church was read, and the procession moved on to Hollywood Cemetery where the soldier was

[46] Chesnut, *Diary*, 305-306.

buried. No military escort accompanied Stuart's body to his grave, for the Confederacy, struggling desperately for its life, needed every fighting man at the front.

When the end came for the gay life of Richmond no funeral was held for it, for its passing had long been known to be inevitable by the well-informed in the capital. The people of the beleaguered city had been courageous during the long drawn-out war. They had put on a good show for the soldier weary of life in the field and eager for some respite from it. There had been fear among the citizens, but it had been masked by laughter and gayety, spontaneous and unforced. Hardworking and worried officials found in the congenial atmosphere of social commingling the opportunity to relax and to revive morale. The waning confidence in ultimate victory was revived under the stimuli of happy parties and visiting with friends. For a spell, at least, the thunder of the enemy's guns was muted for them and they could shut out thoughts of their nation's peril.

There had been a time, in 1862, when husbands, believing the fall of the capital to be imminent, had sent their families from the capital. When these fears had not been realized, society in Richmond resumed where it had left off. By March, 1865, hope for the successful defense of the capital had been abandoned. Once more officials bethought themselves for the safety of their wives and families, who were sent from Richmond to places to the south and southwest, there to await the coming of their husbands and fathers. By April the exodus was well under way. The old order gave place to the new.

"Yes, the social life in Richmond during the war was very beautiful, and characterized by that old-time grace and hospitality for which the South was famous. It was, indeed, the last chapter in the history of that olden life." [47]

47 "Hon. Thomas J. Semmes," *loc. cit.,* 326.

XI

The Fugitives

SUNDAY, April 2, 1865, was a clear, smiling day in Richmond. Idlers in the capitol square basked in the morning sun, enjoying to the full the annual miracle of spring, delighting their senses with the sights and scents of newly growing things about them. Only an occasional rumbling in the distance disturbed the quiet of the scene. There was a rumor that the Confederate defense had suffered a severe reverse near Petersburg; but there had been similar rumors from time to time, and the great mass of the people were not seriously disturbed by this latest one. As the church bells intoned their summons to worship, loungers in the square could see the spare figure of President Davis entering St. Paul's for the morning services. In all the scene there was promise of the usual quiet Sunday for the Confederacy's capital.[1]

Yet the officials of the administration knew that this was to be perhaps their last Sabbath in Richmond. General Lee had informed the War Department the night before that he had little hope of being able to hold his weakened lines against the assaults of Grant's army. Sunday morning, word had come that Lee would retire, and Reagan brought word of the General's decision to Jefferson Davis before the President had arrived at St. Paul's Church.[2] The news caused no panic among the government officials; as far back as 1862, plans had been discussed as to the method of abandoning the capital should the necessity arise. In May, 1864, preparations had been made for the retreat of the officials by way of the Danville railroad in the event of Lee's defeat.[3] When that seemed imminent nearly a year later, hurried

1 Based on Stephen R. Mallory, "Last Days of the Confederate Government," *loc. cit.*, 100.
2 Reagan, *Memoirs*, 196.   3 Jones, *Diary*, II, 207.

but orderly abandonment of Richmond had begun as early as March; archives of the Confederacy had been packed in boxes and shipped out of the capital.[4] The families of government officials had gradually left the city for destinations farther south. Despite the news that Reagan now brought, the President saw no need for undue haste and proceeded to church.

As the Reverend Dr. Charles Minnigerode was delivering the sermon an official messenger came down the aisle to Jefferson Davis's pew and gave him a message. Calmly the President read it, then followed the messenger out of the church. Lee's situation evidently was most desperate and the need for hasty departure from the capital more urgent than it was at first believed to be. When the President left St. Paul's he hastened to his office, from which he sent word to the Cabinet members to meet him there. Governor John Letcher and Joseph Mayo, the mayor of Richmond, were present when the Cabinet met.[5] There was no confusion or excitement among those present at the meeting.[6] One of the important matters discussed was the disposition of government records that had not already been sent out of the city. Many of them were now destroyed, and the more important documents were prepared for shipment that night. Richmond must be abandoned, but it was hoped that the seat of government might be established in a city farther south. A union of the forces of Generals Lee and Johnston might succeed in defeating Sherman. If so, the cause of the Confederacy was far from being lost. Jefferson Davis and his secretaries were not preparing for flight, but for a strategic retreat. The President said as much in a cheering proclamation issued several days later. The best

[4] *Ibid.*, II, 441–42, 445.

[5] Reagan, *Memoirs,* 197. George Davis was not present at the Cabinet meeting. George Davis to W. T. Walthall, September 4, 1877, in Southern Historical Society, *Papers,* V (1878), **124.**

[6] *Ibid.,* 124–25; Jones, *Diary,* II, 465; Mallory, "Last Days of the Confederate Government," *loc. cit.,* 102. Mallory wrote: "Mr. Benjamin having completed his plain and unexceptional toilet, and scanned the latest foreign papers, pursued his way from his residence on Main Street beyond Adams Street to the State Department, with his usual happy, jaunty air; his pleasant smile, his mild Havanna, and the very twirl of his slender, gold-headed cane contributing to give, to casual observers, expression to that careless confidence of the last man outside of the ark, who assured Noah of his belief that 'it would not be such a h—— of a shower, after all.' " *Ibid.,* 101.

method of continuing the struggle for independence, and of assuring their safe departure from the city, engaged the thoughts of the administrative officials. Preparations were made with these purposes in mind.

Sunday afternoon was spent in attending to the final official duties and personal affairs. George Davis, who had not received notification in time to attend the Cabinet meeting, reported later to the President, whom he found alone, calm and composed.[7] The President had given his orders and there was little for him to do but wait. Perhaps, after the Attorney General had left him, Jefferson Davis wondered why this disaster had to happen. What had he done that should not have been done, or what left undone that should have been done? His recollections of the last four years could not have been pleasant to this sensitive man who had led a gallant people in a losing fight. His thoughts perhaps reverted to that agonized night when the body of a little child lay in dreamless sleep in a stilled house, when the world had seemed so far away, an inscrutable God so near. But now, as then, the responsibility of leadership lay upon him. In other parts of the city his assistants busied themselves giving last minute orders. Secretary Mallory, who often had been obliged to suffer the destruction of his ships at the hands of the Confederacy itself because of military necessity, now sent orders to Rear Admiral Raphael Semmes to blow up the James River squadron to prevent its capture by the enemy.[8] Early in the evening, after the necessary orders and directions had been given, the secretaries went to the railway station.

It had been planned for the train to leave Richmond for Danville promptly at eight o'clock. The work of loading the baggage, however, required more time than had been expected, and while the party awaited the train's departure, one observed Postmaster General Reagan intently whittling a stick, chewing all the while, and meditating in evident perplexity.[9] Within the station and around it was a crowd of excited or agitated persons, some were bidding friends Godspeed, others vainly trying to

---

[7] George Davis to Walthall, September 4, 1877, in Southern Historical Society, *Papers*, V (1878), 125.

[8] *Naval Records*, Ser. I, Vol. XII, 191.

[9] Mallory, "Last Days of the Confederate Government," *loc. cit.*, 104.

obtain the right to leave Richmond with the administration party. At length the train was ready to begin the journey southward. The train crew awaited the signal to start, but nothing happened; the hissing engine and its coaches remained motionless on the rails. The impatient passengers at first were puzzled, then became worried. The President and Secretary Breckinridge were responsible for the delay. They hoped to hear better news from General Lee at the last moment, but none arrived, and they boarded the train. Soon a decrepit engine was slowly pulling the old cars out of the station over treacherous rails. The Confederate administration was in flight.

When the party arrived in Danville, preparations were made to set up the government, and orders were given that fortifications be thrown up for the city's defense. Meanwhile, word from General Lee was anxiously awaited. Available places were examined with the view of continuing the work of government as soon as army protection should arrive. On Saturday, April 8, a messenger brought word that General Lee would be forced to surrender. In the afternoon of the following Monday came the news that the shattered army had capitulated. By midnight, April 10, the Cabinet had left Danville and was on its way to Greensboro, North Carolina.

En route the official party narrowly escaped falling into the hands of a roving troop of Federal cavalry, but this did not serve to abate the flagrant unfriendliness of Greensboro's citizens. Only after much difficulty were lodgings obtained for the President and Secretary Trenholm, who was now ill. The other members of the Cabinet and officials of the party lived in a railroad coach, the "cabinet car." A Negro boy cooked for them, and Mallory reports that the officials were far from being unhappy. The following is his description of one of their meals:

Here was the astute "Minister of Justice," a grave and most exemplary gentleman, with a piece of half-broiled "middling" in one hand and a hoe-cake in the other, his face beaming unmistakable evidence of the condition of the bacon. There was the clever Secretary of State busily dividing his attention between a bucket of stewed dried apples and a haversack of hard boiled eggs. Here was a Postmaster-General sternly and energetically running his bowie knife through a ham as if it were the chief business of life; and there was the Secretary of the Navy courteously swallowing his coffee scalding hot that he might not keep the venerable Adjutant-General waiting too long for the coveted tin cup; . . . state sovereignty, secession, foreign intervention and recognition, finance and independence, the ever recurring and fruitful themes of discussion gave place to the more pressing and practical questions of dinner or no dinner, and how, when, and where it was to be had, and to schemes and devices for enabling a man six feet tall to sleep upon a car seat four feet long.[10]

Despite anxiety and the open hostility of Greensboro's citizens, there was a feeling of relief among the officials at their freedom from routine duties. Nevertheless, a series of Cabinet meetings was held during the stay in the unfriendly city. On the twelfth the President called the secretaries to a session at which Generals Johnston and Beauregard were present.[11] It was, Reagan thought, the most solemnly funereal meeting that he had ever attended.[12] The President opened the discussions with the remark that, while the recent disasters were terrible, they were not necessarily fatal. General Johnston was firmly of the opinion that the people were tired of war and would not respond to further calls to sacrifice for a cause they believed to be doomed. His small force, he said, was a mere bagatelle in comparison with Sherman's, and the deserters from his army far outnumbered recruits. General Beauregard concurred in his fellow officer's opinion that continued resistance would be foolish; the only practical course was to obtain peace on the best possible terms. The President reminded them that he had tried to make peace but that the United States had never consented to treat with him. In the present circumstance, he was convinced, the enemy would refuse to negotiate with him even on the basis of surrender. The meeting was adjourned without any decision having been reached.

It was resumed on the thirteenth, with Secretary of War Breckinridge also in attendance.[13] He, Mallory, Reagan, and George

10 *Ibid.*, 239.
11 Trenholm and Breckinridge were absent: the former was ill and the latter did not leave Richmond with the Cabinet but traveled on horseback, arriving in Greensboro a short time later.
12 Reagan, *Memoirs*, 129.
13 James Elliott Walmsley, "The Last Meeting of the Confederate Cabinet," *Mississippi Valley Historical Review*, VI (1920), 339.

Davis argued that the only move possible to the Confederacy was one looking to the termination of the war; Benjamin advocated continuing the struggle.[14] General Johnston suggested that he be authorized to treat with Sherman as one military commander with another, and his suggestion was accepted by the President and a majority of the Cabinet. Johnston was provided with a letter containing the general principles by which he should be guided in his negotiations with General Sherman. The Confederacy would disband its military force and would recognize the authority of the United States, on condition that existing state governments be preserved, that all political and property rights of the people of the Confederacy be respected, and that there be no persecutions or penalties inflicted on them for their participation in the war. Pending the satisfactory conclusion of the agreement, all hostilities should be suspended. General Johnston agreed to present these proposals to the Union General and to obtain the best terms possible.

The next day the President and his departmental secretaries resumed their journey southward. Their way led through Lexington, Salisbury, and Concord to Charlotte, which they reached on April 19. When the party had covered approximately half the distance between Greensboro and Charlotte a telegram arrived from General Johnston requesting the assistance of Cabinet members in the parleys with General Sherman. Secretaries Breckinridge and Reagan turned back and rode without stopping from ten o'clock one night to twelve o'clock the next night in order to be present at the conference between the two generals. As a result of the negotiations the Johnston-Sherman convention was drawn. Although Sherman refused to concede the liberal terms proposed by the Confederate Cabinet, he consented to make an agreement similar to that made by Grant at Appomattox, which he believed would be satisfactory to his government. Hostilities were suspended pending confirmation of the convention.

In the meantime the fugitives had been kindly received at Charlotte, where Cabinet meetings were held in the offices of Drewey's Branch of the Bank of North Carolina. The officials retained the hope that peace and a reconstruction of the Union

14 Reagan, *Memoirs*, 200; Johnston, *Narrative of Military Operations*, 399.

could be accomplished to the satisfaction and benefit of both North and South. It was at Charlotte that news of the assassination of President Lincoln came to the Cabinet. When Secretaries Breckinridge and Reagan returned to Charlotte with the terms of the Johnston-Sherman convention, considerable dissatisfaction was expressed because Sherman had rejected the Confederate proposals. President Davis called for written expressions from all the Cabinet members, requesting them to state their opinions as to whether or not he should ratify the convention, and, if so, in what way he should comply with its terms. He realized that there was no alternative to acceptance of the convention, but he was unwilling even in this crisis to exceed the limits of his constitutional powers, which did not include authority to surrender territory and dissolve the Confederacy.

Five secretaries submitted written replies between April 22 and 24. All of them favored acceptance of the terms of the convention. They pointed out that the Confederacy had no forces with which to continue the war, no materials and no opportunity to obtain them, and no money; that the North, on the contrary, possessed the strongest military forces in the world, with unlimited supplies, and ample reserves of man power. Even a concentration of Confederate forces west of the Mississippi would only temporarily check the power of the United States; the struggle could be continued only as an undesirable guerilla warfare. "Seeing no reasonable hope of our ability to conquer our independence; admitting the undeniable fact that we have been vanquished in the war; it is my opinion," Benjamin's reply concluded, "that these terms should be accepted, being as favorable as any that we, as the defeated belligerent, have reason to expect or can hope to secure. . . ." [15] Mallory believed that the people were weary of the conflict and that guerilla warfare between peoples of common origin, language, and institutions would never be successful.[16] Breckinridge, Reagan, and George Davis concurred in the opinions expressed by Benjamin and Mallory.[17]

A majority of the Cabinet members advised the President to

[15] Benjamin to Davis, April 22, 1865, in Rowland (ed.), *Davis*, VI, 571.

[16] Mallory to *id.*, April 24, 1865, *ibid.*, 574–75.

[17] Breckinridge to *id.*, April 23, 1865, George Davis to *id.*, April 22, 1865, Reagan to *id.*, April 22, 1865, *ibid.*, 572–73, 577–79, 579–85.

accept the terms offered by Sherman and to recommend that the individual states ratify the convention, after which he should resign. The states, they thought, could ratify the convention either in special conventions or through their regular governments. Mallory agreed with Jefferson Davis's view that the Constitution gave the President no power to dissolve the Confederacy, but he urged him not to stand on constitutional grounds. Benjamin was of the opinion that by a general peace Jefferson Davis could obtain for the seceding states rights and advantages they would not obtain by separate action. He believed the President of the Confederacy had the constitutional power as commander in chief of the army to ratify an agreement entered into by a subordinate and could recommend to the states that they accept such agreement. Reagan urged that the President, in accepting the convention, insist on the payment of the Confederate debt along with that of the United States, on the ground that war was forced on a peaceful South. George Davis wrote:

There are circumstances so desperate as to override all constitutional theories, and such are those which are pressing upon us now. The Government of the Confederate States is no longer potent for good. Exhausted by war in all its resources, to such a degree that it can no longer offer a respectable show of resistance to its enemies, it is already virtually destroyed. And the chief duty left for you to perform, is to provide as far as possible for the speedy delivery of the people from the horrors of war and anarchy.[18]

Jefferson Davis telegraphed his acceptance of the terms to General Johnston on the afternoon of April 24.[19] Within an hour General Sherman reported the refusal of his government to ratify the convention, and he gave notice that his army would renew hostilities within forty-eight hours. When President Davis received news of this latest development he and his Cabinet, including Trenholm who was still ill, met to consider their future course. Postmaster General Reagan in submitting his opinion on the advisability of accepting the Johnston-Sherman convention had qualified his declaration in favor of it.

18 George Davis to id., April 22, 1865, ibid., 579.
19 Johnston, Narrative of Military Operations, 410.

But, if the terms of this agreement should be rejected, or so modified by the government of the United States, as to refuse a recognition of the right of local self-government, and our political rights and rights of person and property, or as to refuse amnesty for past participation in this war; then, it will be our duty to continue the struggle as best we can, however unequal it may be; as it would be better and more honorable to waste our lives and substance in such a contest than to yield both to the mercy of a remorseless conqueror.[20]

This was now evidently the sentiment of the Cabinet. Orders were sent to General Johnston to disband his infantry, after instructing them to meet again at another place. His cavalry and the available light ordnance should be sent on to the administration party. General Johnston realized the folly of obeying these orders, and immediately surrendered his forces to General Sherman.

When the fleeing government officials learned of the refusal of the United States government to ratify the Johnston-Sherman convention, they prepared to continue the journey southward with a military escort of about 2,000 men. George Davis asked to be relieved of his official duties and his request was granted. His home in Wilmington was in the hands of the Federals, his wife was dead, and his children were with friends near-by, but were without means of support. He asked his fellow fugitives whether they thought he should go on with them or not. The President and his colleagues in the Cabinet advised him to remain behind with his children, as there now was little service he could render the Confederacy.[21] Secretary Trenholm, who had not recovered from his illness, made an effort to continue the journey with the party, but found his strength unequal to it, and he resigned soon after leaving Charlotte. Reagan received the *ad interim* appointment as Secretary of the Treasury, which led Benjamin to remark jokingly that he believed it unconstitutional for a man to head two departments at the same time. The President, however, felt that the sturdy Texan would be equal to the duties of both offices. In truth, little remained for any of the party to do except to seek food and shelter. Reagan, however, as

20 Reagan to Davis, April 22, 1865, in Rowland, *Davis*, VI, 585.
21 Reagan, *Memoirs*, 208.

acting secretary kept accurate accounts of the party's disbursements. Eventually the Confederate treasury notes were burned, most of the gold and silver was divided among troops or officials, and the remainder given into the custody of trusted men to deliver to the order of the Confederacy at some point outside the United States.[22]

After leaving Charlotte the Presidential party headed toward Abbeville, South Carolina. On the way Davis and the Cabinet members mingled and talked freely with the soldiers of their escort. Breckinridge, a gallant figure in the saddle, rode one of the few good horses left, but most of the other officials rode in open or partly covered wagons. Benjamin, of all the Cabinet members, was of most interest to the common soldiers; they had heard all sorts of rumors about him as the evil genius of the administration, but he surprised the men by his good spirits and vivacity. The general opinion among the troops was that Breckinridge, Reagan, and the President could escape if they wanted to. But all considered it certain—and they regretted it, for he was now a favorite with them—that Benjamin would be captured.[23] The President's family traveled ahead of the administrative group. According to Burton H. Harrison, the family's escort, the teamsters were instructed to say nothing about the presence of Mrs. Davis and her children in the little caravan. It amused him to hear the replies of drivers and old soldiers to queries of inquisitive countrymen along the way. "Who is that lady?" would be asked. "Mrs. Jones," was the laconic answer. "Where did you come from?" "Up the road." "Where are you going?" "Down the road a bit."[24]

The oddly assorted body of soldiers in tattered uniforms, guarding distinguished men in flight, reached Abbeville on May 2, 1865. The South Carolinians welcomed their visitors most cordially. Jefferson Davis was a guest of Major Armistead Burt, at whose home a meeting was held, with Breckinridge and the military commanders in attendance. The warmth of the re-

[22] A detailed account of the disposition of the Confederate money is given in Alfred Jackson Hanna's *Flight Into Oblivion* (Richmond, 1938), chapters II and III.

[23] Basil Wilson Duke, "Last Days of the Confederacy," in Johnson and Buel (eds.), *Battles and Leaders of the Civil War*, IV, 764.

[24] Harrison, "Narrative," in Rowland (ed.), *Davis*, VII, 8–9.

ception Abbeville gave him heartened the President and he was in excellent spirits. Pleading against defeatism, he said he believed that when the panic that had seized the people had subsided they would rally to the Confederacy.[25] The commanders, however, saw no hope of continuing the struggle and told the President they were willing to remain with him only until he was safely out of the country. But Davis refused to listen to any suggestions that concerned only his personal safety. When his eloquent appeal failed to move the officers, the President rose and "walked so feebly as he proceeded to leave the room that General Breckinridge stepped hastily up and offered his arm."[26]

It has often been said that Jefferson Davis showed unreasoning optimism and hope for the ultimate victory of the Confederacy after the fall of Richmond. His proclamations, his belief that Johnston could fight Sherman on even terms if the people of the Confederacy would rally to his support, and his project to set up the government in the trans-Mississippi, all seem to testify to buoyant optimism. On the other hand, the evidence may cover his hidden purposes and actual beliefs about the situation. The President's decisions after the fall of Richmond were those reached by the Cabinet members or concurred in by them. At the Greensboro conference he had not been averse to negotiations, if it were possible to enter upon them. When a plausible method of treating for peace had been arranged, he had consented. When the Johnston-Sherman convention was made, he had asked for written opinions from the secretaries as to acceptance of the agreement and he had concurred in the Cabinet's opinion. When the United States government refused to sanction the convention, the Confederate President and his advisers saw only one course open to them. They knew the Confederacy had been destroyed beyond all hope of reviving it, but their sense of duty to the Confederate Constitution, no less than consideration of their own personal dignity, forbade that they should forthwith declare the Confederacy extinct and seek safety in flight.

Jefferson Davis's seeming optimism after Appomattox is not to

25 Duke, "Last Days of the Confederacy," in Johnson and Buel (eds.), *Battles and Leaders of the Civil War*, IV, 764.

26 *Ibid.*, 765.

be explained on the theory that he sincerely believed that it was still possible for the Confederacy to triumph. He had read the reports of the War Department and he knew that the country had exhausted all its available resources of men and materials. Above all, he knew that the people of the South had wearied of the war and craved peace, for he had led, almost forced, the country to continued resistance in the face of repeated reverses. During the flight from Richmond, there had been a show of loyalty to the cause, and praise and adulation of the President; but for every such manifestation of devotion there had been evidences of enmity and defeatism. Jefferson Davis was not a fatuous optimist. He knew that the Confederacy had become a lost cause.

The reason for his expressed hope of victory even in this dark hour must be sought for in the long-developed traits of his character. First of all, he had a responsibility to the Confederacy; he must be true to the purpose for which he was elected chief of the nation; there was no warrant in the Constitution for him to declare the Confederacy at an end. Secondly, the President had a strong sense of soldierly honor. As a military man he was constrained from fleeing to some hiding place. To do so would mean the loss of honor; but he could be captured in line of duty and retain his prestige. It was no disgrace for one who had fought valiantly against great odds and who had striven to the utmost for victory to be taken prisoner. The soldier-President would remain true to his duty and his ideals until the very last. Finally, in exploring the reasons that motivated him, it should be remembered that Jefferson Davis was a man of sensitive nature, jealous of the opinion of his contemporaries, desirous of the approbation of posterity. How else can one explain his extraordinary request for written opinions on the Johnston-Sherman convention? To obtain the ideas of that closely associated party of fugitives it was not necessary that they should submit their opinions in writing. Decisions of even greater importance had been reached before in the Cabinet when the President had not called for written memoranda from the secretaries. The circumstances were different now. The President was acting in a moment that history would record as momentous, and it was but justice to the actor that the historian should have full evidence of the necessity for surrender. Thus, after leaving Charlotte, Davis planned to retreat to the trans-Mississippi.

In fact, the hegira was more a "running wait" for capture, than a flight. He had fought the losing fight long enough. Even if he eluded the roving Federal cavalry patrols and reached Cuba, what then? Consistency would require that he go immediately to Texas and make a show of continuing the struggle. Had Jefferson Davis really desired to escape, there can be little doubt that he would have succeeded.[27] Three members of his Cabinet and a former Secretary were able to escape. While of course a greater effort would be made by the Federals to capture the President, Southerners would have given more aid to him in efforts to escape than they gave to subordinate officials of the administration. The conclusion is inevitable that the President of the Confederacy was made prisoner because, under the circumstances, he preferred capture to escape.

After the conference at Abbeville on May 2, the Presidential party decided to push on toward Georgia. It was impossible to conceal the presence of the Confederacy's administrative officers in so large a party. Benjamin, who desired above all to escape falling into Federal hands, soon realized that such a large party of men was bound to attract attention. After they crossed the Savannah River he parted with the President. When Reagan asked him his destination, Benjamin told him, "To the farthest place from the United States . . . if it takes me to the middle of China." [28] The rest of the party continued, and arrived at Washington, Georgia, on May 3. Mallory was willing to accompany the President if he desired to escape by way of Florida but, believing that any attempt to continue the war would be an unwise policy, submitted his resignation from his official position.

[27] Basil W. Duke, a member of the party, in recalling the flight, said: "I have never believed, however, that Mr. Davis really meant or desired to escape after he became convinced that all was lost. . . . He and his party were admirably mounted, and could easily have outridden the pursuit of any party they were not strong enough to fight. Therefore, why he deliberately procrastinated as he did, when the fact of his presence in that vicinity was so public, and in the face of the effort that would certainly be made by the Federal forces to secure his person, I can only believe that he had resolved not to escape." *Ibid.*, 766.

[28] Reagan, *Memoirs*, 211.

His resignation as Secretary of the Navy was accepted and he left the party to join his family at La Grange, Georgia, saying that he had no intention of attempting to escape. The President, Postmaster General Reagan, and Secretary of War Breckinridge spent a day in disposing of the Confederate treasury notes, distributing the coin, and providing for the safe removal of the bullion. Toombs, long in opposition to the administration, now generously offered to do anything in his power to aid the President to escape. Reagan and Breckinridge suggested that Davis dress in the uniform of a common soldier and, accompanied by one companion, attempt to reach the Florida coast, and thence take passage to Cuba; once there, he could make his way to the Rio Grande. In the meantime, the two secretaries would try to take troops overland to Texas. To their suggestions, the President replied, "I shall not leave Confederate soil while a Confederate regiment is on it." [29] Ostensibly, he hoped to reach General Kirby Smith with sufficient troops to augment the General's forces to 60,000 men.

Eventually the President was prevailed on to start with an escort of ten men. Breckinridge and Reagan, after disposing of some unfinished business in Washington, were to rejoin their chief. Reagan did follow and succeeded in overtaking the President's party. Within the next few days they caught up with the President's wife and children on their flight southward. Mrs. Davis, however, refused to endanger her husband's safety by remaining with his party and slowing up its progress. She and the children continued their journey under the escort of Burton H. Harrison. The President followed the course southward planned for him, but there were disquieting rumors that his wife was in danger, and in the end he turned to her assistance. He reached her on the evening of May 9, and the two small parties camped near a wooded creek about a mile from Irwinville, Georgia.[30]

The next morning a troop of Federal cavalry commanded by Lieutenant B. D. Pritchard surprised the little camp. Davis attempted to escape even when the camp was surrounded by the

29 *Ibid.,* 212.
30 *Official Records,* Ser. I, Vol. XLIX, Pt. I, 530–32; Hanna, *Flight Into Oblivion,* 95.

Federals. In his haste he picked up his wife's raincoat and Mrs. Davis threw a shawl over his head and his shoulders. He was not disguised in woman's dress, as was later asserted. When the troops closed on the camp, Davis and the entire group of Confederates were placed under arrest and sent to Macon, Georgia, under escort of Federal soldiers.

With the capture of Jefferson Davis any lingering hope for the survival of the Confederacy vanished. The scattered members of his party and some others among those who had been closely associated with him now began to lead hunted lives.

After the President left Washington, Breckinridge decided that the chances for escape would be bettered if the fugitives gave the Federal cavalry several trails to follow. When the former Vice-President of the United States learned of Davis's capture he changed his course and succeeded in reaching Madison, Florida. Below Madison he was joined by Colonel John Taylor Wood, who had eluded the Federal cavalry when the President's party was captured. The adventures of Breckinridge and Wood were such as to shame the inventiveness of a writer of fiction. From Madison the two men journeyed southeast to the Suwanee River, where they took the old St. Augustine road. They followed a route south to a point below Ocala, then turned left and reached the St. John's River at Fort Butler a short distance below Lake George. Continuing up the river toward its source, and overland to the Indian River, they followed an inland waterway southward. After leaving the protection of the river, the two men hugged the Florida coast, made an unsuccessful attempt to cross to the Bahamas, and at length reached Cardenas, Cuba, on June 11.[31]

Breckinridge had been continually on the move for more than a month, his flight taking him through sparsely settled districts and mosquito-infested swamplands. At times his only food was that obtained by searching the sands for turtle eggs. Once he forced some frightened deserters to trade their seaworthy boat for his smaller one. His life was one of harrowing adventure,

[31] A detailed account of Breckinridge's escape is given in Hanna, *Flight Into Oblivion*, chapters VII and VIII.

but the reception accorded him in Cuba compensated for the many hardships he endured as a fugitive in Florida.

The Spanish Governor General of Cuba provided a special railway car to bring Breckinridge to Havana.[32] In the Cuban capital the former official of a fallen government received a hearty welcome. Breckinridge, after a stay in Havana, traveled to England, and from there to Toronto, Canada, where his wife and two of his children joined him. In 1869 he returned to his native Kentucky.

Toombs, one-time Secretary of State of the Confederacy, knowing that the United States government considered him one of the ring-leaders of the Confederacy, determined never to be captured alive. A squad of Federal soldiers arrived at his residence in Washington, Georgia, on the night of May 12, to arrest him. While Mrs. Toombs delayed them at the front of the house, the old general escaped by way of a back door to a farm near-by. There he mounted a horse brought him by a friend and began his travels which eventually led him to safety. He wandered around Georgia for months. In August his wife inquired if her husband would be paroled if he surrendered to the military authorities, but President Andrew Johnson ordered that he be imprisoned if captured.[33] Evidently Toombs heard of this order, for he made his way to Mobile, Alabama, where on November 4 he took passage on a ship bound for Cuba. From that island he went to Paris, France, thence returned to the United States by way of Canada. In the national capital he called on President Johnson, but neither then nor afterward did he petition for restoration of his citizenship. When asked on one occasion why he had never sought a pardon from Congress, Toombs replied, "Pardon for what? I have not pardoned you all yet."[34]

After Benjamin had taken leave of the President and members of the Cabinet at the Savannah River, he affected a simple disguise, knowing that his features were easily recognizable. A

---

[32] John Taylor Wood, "Escape of the Confederate Secretary of War," *Century Magazine*, XLVIII (1893), 123.

[33] James B. Steedman to Edwin M. Stanton, August 5, 1865, Stanton to Steedman, August 11, 1865, in *Official Records*, Ser. II, Vol. VIII, 714, 716.

[34] Stovall, *Robert Toombs*, 314.

friend saw him on May 11, traveling in a light wagon as a French gentleman. He had let his beard grow, his flashing black eyes were hidden by goggles, and a large cloak concealed the outlines of his roly-poly figure. No one would have recognized the former Confederate Secretary, Colonel John Taylor Wood believed, but Benjamin himself realized that his disguise was likely to attract more than usual attention, with possibly disastrous results to his freedom. He soon exchanged it for the dress of a farmer and let it be known that he was traveling in search of land in Florida. Having obtained a horse and rig, the former Secretary of State drove over little-used roads to north central Florida, thence to Sarasota Bay. After a long delay, he obtained a boat and engaged the services of two men for the trip down the west coast of Florida. The little party left the bay in a yawl on June 23, hugged the coast, and after narrowly escaping capture by a Federal gunboat, reached the Bimini Islands off the eastern tip of Florida on July 10. After engaging passage on a small sloop for Nassau, Benjamin felt comparatively safe, but the vessel foundered and Benjamin was rescued from the water by a British ship which brought him back to the Bimini Islands on July 15. Benjamin now chartered a more seaworthy vessel, which made the hundred-mile voyage to Nassau in six days. From that point it was comparatively easy to reach Havana, whence he sailed to England, there to carve out a new career for himself.[35]

The courtly George Davis, who had resigned from the Cabinet just before the President left Charlotte, North Carolina, had no doubt that he would soon be a Federal prisoner unless he left "Union-infested" North Carolina. He went to his brother's residence in Camden, South Carolina, and from there set out southward on horseback.[36] By June 3 he had reached the plantation of a cousin in north central Florida, going on from there to Gainesville and Ocala. He wandered for nearly three months

[35] Benjamin describes his escape in letters to his sister, dated July 22, August 1, and September 29, 1865, in Butler, *Benjamin*, 363–73. The best account of Benjamin's trials and difficulties in reaching safety is found in Hanna, *Flight Into Oblivion*, chapter X.

[36] George Davis tells of his flight in a letter to his son, Junius Davis, on November 14, 1865, in Ashe, *George Davis, Attorney General of the Confederate States*, 19–20. For an interesting account of Davis, see Hanna, *Flight Into Oblivion*, chapter XI.

in Sumter County just below Ocala, which was on "the very
verge of civilization." Hearing that a boat was to leave New
Smyrna for Nassau, he hurried to the town and engaged to work
out his passage on the vessel. The boat was too small and unsea-
worthy to breast the heavy seas to Nassau; instead, it was steered
down the coast line to safe harbor in Key West on October 18,
1865. Here the former Attorney General could have obtained
passage to a foreign land, but he learned that several of the
Confederate Cabinet members had been released from prison
and he decided to surrender. While awaiting an opportunity to
sail North he was recognized and arrested. Although he did not
know what was to be his destination, he was relieved to have left
behind him his life as a homeless wanderer and fugitive. For
some reason "known only to God and the Republican party,"
George Davis was sent a prisoner to New York, and was confined
in Fort LaFayette, although most of the other members of the
Confederate administration had been freed. He was released
on January 1, 1866, and returned to his home in Wilmington,
North Carolina.

After Trenholm, because of ill-health, left the fleeing Confederate Cabinet below Charlotte, he continued to Abbeville, South
Carolina, where he arrived after the town had been occupied by
Union troops. No attempt was made to arrest him, however, and
he and his family moved to Columbia. There he was placed under constructive arrest, and freedom was given him to report at
Charleston, where after temporary confinement in the city jail
he was sent to Hilton Head, South Carolina.[37] In consideration
of Trenholm's feeble health and his many acts of kindness to
Union prisoners, Major General Quincy Adams Gillmore paroled him to the corporate limits of Columbia,[38] instead of sending him prisoner to Fort Pulaski. For this generous act General
Gillmore was censured and Trenholm was rearrested and sent
to Fort Pulaski.[39]

Secretary of the Navy Mallory, after leaving the President at
Washington, Georgia, visited Atlanta and then went to join his

[37] John P. Hatch to Quincy A. Gillmore, in *Official Records,* Ser. I, Vol. XLVIII,
Pt. III, 647-48.
[38] Gillmore to Lorenzo Thomas, June 21, 1865, *ibid.,* Ser. II, Vol. VIII, 664.
[39] *Ibid.,* 694, 701, 723-24.

family at La Grange. As chief of the Confederate naval service he was held responsible by the North for the "piratical outrages" of the Southern cruisers, and it was thought possible to find evidence to convict him and perhaps inflict the death penalty on him. Some twenty soldiers came late in the night of May 20, 1865, to arrest Mallory and former Senator Hill. Neither man offered resistance or made any attempt to escape, but the troops were taking no chances with their prisoners who were hurried off without having had an opportunity to don proper clothing. Eventually both men were confined in Fort LaFayette, New York.[40]

After the collapse of the Confederacy two former members of the Cabinet remained in Virginia. At first it appeared probable that Hunter and Seddon would escape imprisonment. Both General Grant and General Halleck thought it best not to molest Hunter, who had quietly retired to his home and was advising everyone to accept the defeat of the Confederacy as final and to make his submission to the Union. By special order of Secretary Stanton, however, Hunter was arrested on May 1, and a week later Seddon was ordered to be confined in Libby prison. Both former secretaries were later transferred to a gunboat in the James River and on June 1, they were sent to Fort Pulaski for an indefinite term of imprisonment.[41]

Postmaster General Reagan was captured with President Davis and his escort on May 10. Davis and Reagan were sent to Savannah by way of Macon, Atlanta, and Augusta. On the way to Savannah, Stephens, who had been seized at his home on May 11, was added to the captive party. Jefferson Davis was sent from Savannah to Fortress Monroe, and Reagan and Stephens to Fort Warren in Boston Harbor.

Several of the former Confederate officials had the good fortune after the fall of their government not to be molested by the Federal authorities. There is no clear explanation why some of the Confederate Cabinet members were imprisoned and others were not. Generally, the United States government desired to punish all those who had resigned Federal offices to join their lots with the Confederacy. Reagan, Benjamin, Breckinridge,

[40] *Ibid.*, 577, 640, 652, 723–24.   [41] *Ibid.*, 576, 583, 674.

Toombs, Hunter, Bragg, and Mallory, all of whom were in the category, would have been listed for imprisonment. Bragg, perhaps because he had held only a minor office for a short time, was not arrested. The members of the Cabinet who were in office at the time of the Confederacy's fall were on the official list for condign punishment. Trenholm and Davis would thus be among the number for such treatment. Seddon was not an official when the collapse came, but he had been Secretary of War for a long period and he was listed for punishment on the ground that in in his executive position he had been responsible for the mistreatment of Northern prisoners of war. Of the four other members of the Davis Cabinet, Randolph was abroad, and Memminger, Watts, and Walker were never imprisoned. In all, five of the fourteen men who were at one time in the Cabinet were not molested, and three escaped from the country.

The moderation shown by the victors in the punishment of the vanquished was astonishing. Many of the administration leaders themselves expected drastic punishment, if not death; only six of the executive secretaries were held in prison for any length of time, the terms running from three months to ten months. Furthermore, they were treated with much leniency as prisoners. A few suffered the indignity of brief solitary confinement, but this harsh treatment was soon abandoned. Most of the political prisoners were confined in what had been the officers' quarters in the United States forts, and they were allowed considerable freedom within the bounds of the various military strongholds. Those held at Fort Pulaski, for instance, had the freedom of the island during the daytime and of the main walks at all hours.[42] When Seddon and Trenholm, who were prisoners there, learned that the commander of the fort, Major William C. Manning, was to be transferred, they wrote him thanking him for his considerate treatment of them.[43] Imprisonment, in the view of proud men who believed their past course of action to be right and honorable, was a disgrace, cruel and unjust. Yet the suffering of the Confederate President and members of his Cabinet in prison came mostly from their own mental anguish, not from the harshness of vengeful jailers. Of all the former of-

[42] *Ibid.*, 723–24.   [43] *Ibid.*, 761–62.

ficials of the Confederacy, only Jefferson Davis was submitted to harsh and degrading treatment. For a time he was chained in his cell like a common murderer, but as the period of his imprisonment lengthened the indignities inflicted upon him abated. In later life, the Confederate chief must have been grateful for that brief period when he was shackled. In the end his chains helped to restore him to his deserved place in the affections of those faithful to the lost cause.

The wives, families, and friends of the captives perhaps suffered as much or even more than the officials of the fallen Confederacy. They had to endure the gnawing fear and uncertainty as to the eventual fate of the prisoners. They had to stifle their pride and bend in supplication to the victors in behalf of husbands or friends. In a sense, all loyal Southerners experienced vicarious imprisonment with their leaders; the indignities in confinement were not so much those inflicted on men as upon a righteous and glorious cause. It does not require much imagination to realize the anguish of Mrs. Davis at Savannah, Georgia.[44] At night she heard the prayers of her children Jeff and Billy, offered for their father's safety. During the day soldiers and playmates of Jeff told the boy his father had stolen eight million dollars, and the two-year-old Billy was bribed to sing in his childish voice, "We'll Hang Jeff Davis on a Sour Apple-Tree." Two women from Maine even contemplated whipping the youngster on learning that he was the son of the former President of the Confederacy.[45]

The Confederate executives not only escaped heavy punishment; they were allowed to retain their property. They had not profited from the war; they had suffered heavily in their private fortunes, although none of them was destitute. Their property had been seized by Federal forces or agencies and their material wealth had been reduced to virtually nothing in comparison with their former possessions. Several of them, however, were comparatively wealthy men at the end of the war. Memminger, Trenholm, Benjamin, and perhaps several others, quite certainly

[44] Mrs. Davis's account of her experiences in Savannah, Georgia, is found in her letter to John J. Craven, October 10, 1865, in Rowland (ed.), *Davis*, VII, 44–48.
[45] *Ibid.*, 47.

would have come under President Johnson's ban against those whose property was valued at more than twenty thousand dollars. All of them had fairly extensive holdings of land or town property. A direct tax was collected after the conflict, but the Federal government did nothing to confiscate the property of Confederate officials.

Of the Confederate Cabinet members who fled to foreign lands, Judah P. Benjamin never again set foot on United States soil. The others returned from exile to pass active and useful lives in their changed and changing South. The former secretaries perhaps had thought, as had others, of establishing a Southern colony in South America, but if they had indeed contemplated self-imposed exile, they never acted upon the impulse. Jefferson Davis did not want to have his followers leave the South. *"The night may seem long,"* he wrote, *"but it is the part of fidelity to watch and wait for morning."* [46]

The curtain had fallen on the last act of a great tragedy. The South lay prostrate and exhausted, its leaders overpowered and dispersed. The Confederacy became enshrined in the hearts of Southerners as the Lost Cause.

In the years that have passed, both its friends and its foes have sought to determine why the South failed in its struggle for independence. The answers to the question have been legion. A recent student of the Confederacy's civil government, Burton J. Hendrick, has concluded that the central reason for the South's failure is that "It produced no statesmen, such as the South had produced in the revolutionary crisis of 1776 and afterward." [47] Other historians have singled out as major causes for the defeat of the South the internal weakness of the Confederacy, its loss of morale, or the superiority of the United States.

Can the collapse of the Confederacy justly be attributed to defects of the Southern civil administration? The answer is emphatically no. The Confederate Cabinet was composed of the ablest men in Southern public life; all of them were men of education, of experience in government, and all were patriotic and zealous in the performance of duty. The members of Jeffer-

---

[46] Davis to V. Davis, March 13, 1866, *ibid.*, 69.
[47] Hendrick, *Statesmen of the Lost Cause*, 11.

son Davis's Cabinet stood head and shoulders above the average of their contemporaries in ability, tenacity of purpose, and the will to achieve the independence of the South. True, they were not supermen, for with their strength they also had their weaknesses. Among them were a few who were miscast for the parts they were called on to play, but they were soon weeded out of the administration. In Benjamin, Seddon, Memminger, Mallory, Reagan, and Watts, the Confederacy possessed a group of excellent administrators who compare favorably with the Cabinet members of the United States, during the war and at other times.

The members of the Confederate Cabinet were not spineless yes men; Jefferson Davis did not require of his secretaries an unquestioning conformity as a condition of their remaining in the Cabinet. At the same time, a secretary who thought to dominate the government from his office in the State Department, or any other department, was bound to be disabused of the idea; but it did not follow that the secretary was to be ruled, or dictated to, by the President. Davis wanted their counsel and encouraged them to present their views freely. A democratic atmosphere pervaded the meetings of the Cabinet, and the plans that took shape at them matured slowly after ample discussion and full consideration. The occasions when the President overruled the majority opinion of his Cabinet were rare. There were differences between him and them, as there were among the members themselves, but an amicable agreement was the rule rather than the exception. Davis was especially interested in the conduct of the War Department, for, as Robert S. Henry has said, the Confederacy "was war." [48] Often he was his own Secretary of War, but he was eager to have as his military advisers Lee and Bragg, and he leaned heavily on competent secretaries such as Benjamin and Seddon. In the conduct of the other departments, the secretaries were free to formulate their own lines of policy, confident that they could count on the President's support. At the same time, the final authority resided in Davis, as did the ultimate responsibility, and he adroitly guided into cooperative effort the sometimes divergent tendencies of forceful personalities in the Cabinet.

[48] Robert Selph Henry, *The Story of the Confederacy* (Indianapolis, 1936), 11.

The President in selecting the members of his administration consciously sought to give each state in the Confederacy representation in the Cabinet. He was severely criticized for this spreading of patronage, yet the fact that he drew from nearly all the states for the Cabinet personnel did not of itself imply that he had selected inferior men; the South's supply of able men was not concentrated in any one state, or small group of states. Davis's policy in this respect undoubtedly worked out to the national advantage. It obtained for the administration needed support in Congress, and, too, it helped to iron out the conflicts between the states and the central government.

The members of the Confederate Cabinet were representative of a cross-section of the ruling class in the South. Among the secretaries were some from old, aristocratic families, and others of less distinguished antecedents who by their own efforts had carved a place for themselves in the established society of the well-born. Ten of the secretaries would fall, more or less, in the first named category; four of them, Benjamin, Memminger, Mallory, and Reagan, belonging in the second. Those secretaries who had risen to distinction in their own generation, as a rule made better civil officers than did those who were members of old established families. There were men from the upper South and the lower South in the Confederate Cabinet. Of the fourteen men who served in the group of Presidential advisers, seven were from the states of Virginia, North Carolina, South Carolina, and Georgia, and the combined length of their terms in the Cabinet was approximately ten years. The border states and the states of the lower South were represented by seven men also, who served, in all, fourteen years. They were representative men all, and they served their country faithfully and well.

The one great failure of the Cabinet was the Confederacy's defeat. The South's unavailing effort against great odds to win its independence has blinded the unthinking to the real merits, the ability, and high-mindedness of the men in the Davis administration, just as whatever of excellence the Confederacy itself possessed has been beclouded by its ultimate failure. There was not enough of romanticism or glory in the part played by a Cabinet member in the Confederacy's drama to make him a heroic figure in defeat. The world glorifies success, and it avails little to adduce evidence that the ability of the Confederate secretaries outweighs their shortcomings or mistakes. In the face of their failure to achieve their great objective, their deficiencies will be singled out and their excellences forgotten or belittled.

However, to the deeper student of things less superficial than mere success or failure, a study of Davis and his Cabinet is well worth while. Around their efforts for a cause that was lost glistens halo-like a "glory of the vanquished," pale and less effulgent than the light of victory, but none the less glorious. They did not achieve ultimate success, yet failing to win they left their impress on history—these leaders of the Lost Cause.

Bibliography

CONTEMPORARY SOURCES

I. Manuscripts

Badham, William, Jr., Papers, Duke University. Five letters of Thomas Bragg on North Carolina politics and secession, 1860–1861 in this collection.

Beatty, Taylor, Diary, Southern Collection, University of North Carolina.

Benjamin, Judah P.; Bragg, Braxton; and Walker, Leroy Pope, Papers, Alabama Department of Archives and History.

Bragg, Thomas, Papers, Duke University. Forty-five letters written in 1843–1845, 1856, and after 1869.

Buchanan, Screven, Papers, University of North Carolina. Typewritten copies of letters that include many from Stephen Russell Mallory.

Clay, Clement Claiborne, Papers, Duke University. A large and valuable collection.

Davis, Jefferson, Papers, Duke University. A collection of over five hundred letters, a few of which pertain to the Confederate period.

Graham, William Alexander, Papers, University of North Carolina. A tremendous collection, but meager for the war period.

Letter Book of Official Correspondence, War Department, Confederate States of America, February 21–September 15, 1861, Manuscripts Division, Library of Congress.

Letters from Secretaries, Comptroller's Office, Confederate States of America, January 10, 1862–June 11, 1863, National Archives. Letters from the Treasury, War, Navy, and Justice Departments as well as miscellaneous correspondence.

Lynch, G. G., Papers, University of North Carolina. The letters of a special post-office agent that contain information about the Confederate Post Office Department.

McDowell, John M., Papers, University of North Carolina. A number of letters that include applications for postal positions and suggestions in regard to the postal service.

Mallory, Stephen R., Diary, University of North Carolina.

Mason, James M., Papers, Manuscripts Division, Library of Congress.

Memminger, Christopher G., Papers, University of North Carolina. Special and official reports of the Secretary of the Treasury and personal letters.

Miles, William Porcher, Papers, University of North Carolina. Valuable for the politics of the war period. A tremendous collection that includes letters of William Henry Trescot, William Gilmore Simms, Robert Edward Lee, and William Henry Gregory, as well as members of the Cabinet.

Milton, John, Papers, Florida Historical Society. Copies of letters from Cabinet officials and especially valuable for Stephen Russell Mallory's letters to the governor of his state.

Opinion Book, Opinions of the Confederate Attorneys-General, 1861–1865, New York Public Library.

Pickett, Col. John T., Papers, Manuscripts Division, Library of Congress.

Post Office Department of the Confederate States of America, Record of letters and other communications from March 7, 1861, to October 12, 1863, Manuscripts Division, Library of Congress. Reports of the Postmaster General, letters to the President and secretaries, and telegrams.

Randolph, George Wythe, Papers, Confederate Museum, Richmond. Two letters written by Randolph to Major J. T. Brown, describing the state of his health and his happiness to be out of the War Department, in this collection.

Seddon, James A., Papers, Duke University. Three letters dealing with routine matters of the War Department.

Semmes, Thomas Jenkins, Papers, Duke University. A large collection that includes letters of Memminger, Mallory, and Stephens.

Semple, Henry, Papers, University of North Carolina.

Smith, Gustavus W., Papers, Duke University. Letters on army matters.

Stephens, Alexander Hamilton, Papers, Duke University. A collection of twenty letters, a few of which are very valuable for this study.

Stovall, Marcellus, Scrapbook, Southern Collection, University of North Carolina.

Toombs, Robert, Papers, Duke University. Three letters, of which one written to Davis is of value.

Treasury Department, Confederate States of America, Miscellaneous Letter Books, September 17 to November 28, 1864; January 22 to April 2, 1865, Confederate Museum, Richmond.

Treasury Department, Confederate States of America, Telegrams, February 27, 1861, to July 30, 1864, National Archives.

Trenholm, George A., Papers, 1853–1866, 1867–1897, Manuscripts Division, Library of Congress.

Turner, Josiah, Papers, University of North Carolina. Letters, 1861–1865, illustrate the Southern attitude toward the government.

Walker, Leroy Pope, Papers, Duke University. Letters on routine affairs of the War Department.

Watts, Thomas Hill, Papers, Alabama Department of Archives and History.

Williams-Chesnut-Manning, Papers, University of North Carolina. A collection that includes letters of Robert Barnwell, Jefferson Davis, a criticism of Leroy Pope Walker, and considerable material on the social life of officials at Richmond.

Yancey, William L., Papers, Alabama Department of Archives and History.

II. Official Records and Documents

Calendar of Virginia State Papers and Other Manuscripts from January 1, 1836, to April 15, 1869, 11 vols., William P. Palmer, H. W. Flournoy, and Sherwin McRae (eds.), Richmond, 1893.

Candler, Allen D. (ed.), *The Confederate Records of the State of Georgia,* 6 vols., Atlanta, 1909–1911.

Correspondence Between Governor Brown and President Davis, On the Constitutionality of the Conscription Act, Atlanta, 1862.

Journal of the Congress of the Confederate States of America, 7 vols., Washington, 1904–1905.

Matthews, James M. (ed.), *Statutes at Large of the Provisional Government of the Confederate States of America,* Richmond, 1864.

Official Records of the Union and Confederate Navies in the War of the Rebellion, 30 vols., Washington, 1894–1927.

Papers Relating to the Alabama Claims, 2 vols., Washington, 1871.

Public Laws of the Confederate States of America, 1–4 Sessions, First Congress, First Session, Second Congress, Richmond, 1862–1864.

Report of the Roanoke Island Investigating Committee, Richmond, 1862.

Report of the Secretary of War, January 3, 1863, Richmond, 1863.

Richardson, James D. (ed.), *A Compilation of the Messages and Papers of the Confederacy, Including the Diplomatic Correspondence, 1861–1865,* 2 vols., Nashville, 1905.

The War of the Rebellion: A Compilation of the Official Records of the Union and Confederate Armies, 128 vols., Washington, 1880–1901.

Thion, R. P. (ed.), *Reports and Correspondence of the Treasury Department, Confederate States of America,* Richmond, 1862–1864.

III. Collected Source Materials

Ambler, Charles Henry (ed.), *Correspondence of Robert M. T. Hunter, 1826–1876,* American Historical Association, *Annual Report,* 1916, Vol. II, Washington, 1918.

Dumond, Dwight Lowell (ed.), *Southern Editorials on Secession,* New York, 1931.

Hamilton, Joseph Grégoire de Roulhac (ed.), *The Correspondence of Jonathan Worth,* 2 vols., Raleigh, 1909.

——, *The Papers of Randolph Abbott Shotwell,* 3 vols., Raleigh, 1929–1936.

——, *The Papers of Thomas Ruffin,* 4 vols., Raleigh, 1918–1920.

Moore, Frank (comp.), *The Rebellion Record: A Diary of American Events, with Documents, Narratives, Illustrative Incidents, Poetry, etc.,* 11 vols., New York, 1861–1863, 1864–1868.

McPherson, Edward (comp.), *The Political History of the United States of America, During the Great Rebellion from November 6, 1860, to July 4, 1864,* New York, 1864.

Phillips, Ulrich Bonnell (ed.), *The Correspondence of Robert Toombs, Alexander H. Stephens, and Howell Cobb,* American Historical Association, *Annual Report,* 1911, Vol. II, Washington, 1913.

Pollard, Edward A. (comp.), *Echoes from the South: Comprising the Most Important Speeches, Proclamations, and Public Acts Emanating from the South During the Late War,* New York, 1866.

Rowland, Dunbar (ed.), *Jefferson Davis, Constitutionalist. His Letters, Papers, and Speeches,* 10 vols., Jackson, 1923.

The American Annual Cyclopaedia and Register of Important Events, . . . Embracing Political, Civil, Military, and Social Affairs; Public Documents; Biography, Statistics, Commerce, Finance, Literature, Science, Agriculture and Mechanical Industry, 15 vols., New York, 1864–1875.

IV. Pamphlets

Breckinridge and Lane Campaign Documents Number 8, Washington, 1860.

De Bow, James Dunwoody Brownson, *The Interest in Slavery of the Southern Non-Slaveholder,* Charleston, 1860.

Green, Duff, *Facts and Suggestions on the Subjects of Currency and Direct Trade,* Macon, 1861.

——, *Facts and Suggestions Relating to Finance and Currency Addressed to the President of the Confederate States,* Augusta, 1864.

Lemmonds, Cyrus Q., *Speech on the Convention Bill Delivered in the House of Commons, on Thursday, January 17, 1861,* Raleigh, 1861.

Pollard, Edward A., *The Two Nations: A Key to the History of the American War,* Richmond, 1864.

Pryor, Roger Atkinson, *Speech on the Resolution Reported by the Committee of Thirty-Three, Independence of the South,* Washington, 1861.

Townsend, John, *The Doom of Slavery in the Union: Its Safety Out of It,* Charleston, 1860.

————, *The South Alone Should Govern the South and African Slavery Should Be Controlled by Those Only Who Are Friendly to It,* Charleston, 1860.

Troup [Isaac William Hayne], *To the People of the South, Senator Hammond and the Tribune* (extract of the Speech of Hon. James H. Hammond delivered in the Senate of the United States, March 4, 1858), Charleston, 1860.

V. Contemporary Books and Diaries

Abrams, A. S., *President Davis and His Administration, Being a Review of the Rival Administration Lately Published in Richmond, and Written by E. A. Pollard, Author of the First and Second Years of the War,* Atlanta, 1864.

An English Combatant, *Battlefields of the South, From Bull Run to Fredericksburg; With Sketches of Confederate Commanders, and Gossip of the Camps,* New York, 1864.

An English Merchant, *Two Months in the Confederate States Including a Visit to New Orleans Under the Domination of General Butler,* London, 1863.

Avary, Myrta Lockett (ed.), *Recollections of Alexander H. Stephens: His Diary Kept When a Prisoner at Fort Warren, Boston Harbour, 1865: Giving Incidents and Reflections of His Prison Life and Some Letters and Reminiscences,* New York, 1910.

Booth, Edwin Gilliam, *In War Time—Two Years in the Confederacy and Two Years North—with Many Reminiscences of the Days Long Before the War,* Philadelphia, 1885.

Chesnut, Mary Boykin, *A Diary from Dixie, as Written by Mary Boykin Chesnut, wife of James Chesnut, Jr., United States Senator from South Carolina, 1859–1861: and Afterwards an Aide to Jefferson Davis and a Brigadier-General in the Confederate Army,* Isabella D. Martin and Myrta Lockett Avary (eds.), New York, 1929.

Craven, John J., *Prison Life of Jefferson Davis, Embracing Details and Incidents in His Captivity, Particulars Concerning His*

Health and Habits, Together with Many Conversations on Topics of Great Public Interests, New York, 1866.

Day, Samuel Phillips, *Down South or An Englishman's Experience at the Seat of the American War,* 2 vols., London, 1862.

De Fontaine, Felix G., *Marginalia; or Gleanings from an Army Note-Book,* Columbia, 1864.

———, *Army Letters 1861–1865,* Columbia, 1896.

Freemantle, Arthur James Lyons, *Three Months in the Southern States: April–June 1863,* New York, 1864.

Jones, John Beauchamp, *A Rebel War Clerk's Diary at the Confederate States Capital,* 2 vols., Howard Swiggett (ed.), New York, 1935.

Kirke, Edmund (James Roberts Gilmore), *Down in Tennessee and Back by Way of Richmond,* New York, 1864.

Malet, William Wyndam, *An Errand to the South in the Summer of 1862,* London, 1863.

Pollard, Edward A., *The Rival Administrations: Richmond and Washington in December, 1863,* Richmond, 1864.

Ross, Fitzgerald, *A Visit to the Cities and Camps of the Confederate States,* London, 1865.

Russell, William Howard, *My Diary North and South,* New York, 1863.

———, *Pictures of Southern Life, Social, Political and Military,* New York, 1861.

Scott, John, *Letters to an Officer in the Army: Proposing Constitutional Reform in the Confederate Government after Close of the Present War,* Richmond, 1864.

Welles, Gideon, *Diary of Gideon Welles, Secretary of the Navy Under Lincoln and Johnson,* 3 vols., New York, 1911.

VI. Newspapers and Periodicals

Augusta Daily Chronicle and Sentinel, 1861–1865.

Charleston Daily Courier, 1861–1865.

Charleston Mercury, 1861–1865.

Daily Richmond Enquirer, 1861–1865.

Daily Richmond Examiner, 1861–1865.

Daily South Carolinian (Columbia), 1864.

Daily Wilmington Herald, January 1, 1861–May 1, 1861.

Floridian and Journal (Tallahassee), 1861–1862.

Harper's Weekly, 1861–1865.

London Index, May 1, 1862–August 12, 1865.

Mobile Advertiser and Register, September 5, 1862–December 31, 1862.

Montgomery Daily Advertiser, 1861–1865.

Montgomery Daily Mail, 1861–1865.

Montgomery Daily Post, 1861.

Montgomery Weekly Advertiser, 1861–1865.

Montgomery Weekly Mail, 1861–1865.

New Orleans Daily Picayune, January, 1861–May, 1862.

North Carolina Semiweekly Standard, 1861–1862.

North Carolina Weekly Standard, 1860–1865.

Petersburg Daily Express, May 25, 1861–May, 1862.

Raleigh State Journal, December 4, 1861–January 7, 1863.

Richmond Daily Dispatch, 1861–1865.

Richmond Sentinel, March 11, 1863–April 1, 1865.

Southern Illustrated News (Richmond), September, 1862–September, 1864.

Sumter Republican (Americus, Ga.), January, 1862–June, 1865.

Wilmington Daily Journal, 1861–1865.

NON-CONTEMPORARY SOURCES

I. Articles in Periodicals

Allenben, A. E., "A Pro-Slavery Statesman," *National Magazine*, XVI (1891), 299–311.

Anderson, D. R., "Robert Mercer Taliaferro Hunter," *John P. Branch Historical Papers of Randolph Macon College*, II (1905–1906), No. 2, 4–77.

An English Officer, "A Month's Visit to the Confederate Headquarters," *Blackwood's Edinburgh Magazine*, XCIII (1863), 1–29.

Balwin, Earnest, "The 'Mallory Report' and Its Consequences," *National Magazine*, IX (1899), 555–61.

Benjamin, Judah P.; and Butler, B. F., "Two Witnesses on the 'Treatment of Prisoners,' " Southern Historical Society, *Papers*, VI (1878), 183–89.

Bobbitt, B. Boisseau, "Our Last Capital," Southern Historical Society, *Papers*, XXXI (1903), 334–39.

Bradford, Gamaliel, "Blunders of the Confederate Government," *De Bow's Review*, After War Series, V (1868), 471–89; 643–57.

Chase, W. H., "The Secession of the Cotton States: Its Status, Its Advantages and Its Power," *De Bow's Review*, XXX (1861), 93–101.

Clay-Clopton, Mrs. Virginia, "Clement Claiborne Clay," Alabama Historical Society, *Transactions*, II (1897–1898), 74–82.

Cleland, Robert Glass, "Jefferson Davis and the Confederate Congress," *Southwestern Historical Quarterly*, XIX (1916), 215–31.

Confederate Veteran, XX, 170–72; XXV, 257–59; XXVI, 334–36; XXXIV, 327; XXXV, 374–76, 420–23; XXXVII, 210–12; XXXVIII, 426–28; XXXIX, 178–82, 251–54.

Culver, Emma Beall, "Thomas Hill Watts, A Statesman of the Old Regime," Alabama Historical Society, *Transactions,* IV (1899–1903), 415–39.

Dorris, Jonathan T., "Pardoning the Leaders of the Confederacy," *Mississippi Valley Historical Review,* XV (1928–1929), 3–21.

DuBose, John Witherspoon, "Confederate Diplomacy," Southern Historical Society, *Papers,* XXXII (1904), 102–16.

Duncan, George W., "Hon. Archibald Campbell," Alabama Historical Society, *Publications,* V (1904), 107–51.

"Editorials," *De Bow's Review,* XXX (1861), 251–56; XXXIII (1864), 81–96; XXXIV (1864), 97–104.

"Editorials," *Southern Literary Messenger,* XXXI (1860), 468–74; XXXII (1861), 71–76, 240; XXXIII (1861), 465–67; XXXIV–XXXVI (1862), 192–98, 396–97, 689–90.

Ezekiel, H. T., "Judah P. Benjamin," Southern Historical Society, *Papers,* XXV (1897), 297–302.

Fitzhugh, George, "Cuba: The March of Empire and the Course of Trade," *De Bow's Review,* XXX (1861), 30–42.

———, "Disunion Within the Union," *De Bow's Review,* XXVIII (1860), 1–7.

———, "The Message, the Constitution, and the Times," *De Bow's Review,* XXX (1861), 156–67.

"From the Autobiography of Herschel V. Johnson, 1856–1867," *American Historical Review,* XXX (1924–1925), 311–36.

Garrison, L. R., "Administrative Problems of the Confederate Post Office Department," *Southwestern Historical Quarterly,* XIX (1915–1916), 111–42, 232–51.

Gipson, Lawrence H., "The Collapse of the Confederacy," *Mississippi Valley Historical Review,* IV (1917–1918), 437–58.

Glassell, W. T., "Reminiscences of Torpedo Service in Charleston Harbor," Southern Historical Society, *Papers,* IV (1877), 225–35.

Goode, John, "The Confederate Congress," *Conservative Review,* IV (1900), 97–113.

Hamilton, Joseph Grégoire de Roulhac, "The State Courts and the Confederate Constitution," *Journal of Southern History,* IV (1938), 425–48.

Hardy, Sallie Marshall, "Some Virginia Lawyers of the Past and Present," *Green Bag,* X (1898), 149–61.

Hart, Albert Bushnell, "Why the South Was Defeated in the Civil War," *New England Magazine,* V (1891–1892), 363–76.

Hay, Thomas Robson, "The Davis-Hood-Johnston Controversy of 1864," *Mississippi Valley Historical Review,* XI (1924–1925), 54–84.

———, "The South and the Arming of the Slaves," *Mississippi Valley Historical Review,* VI (1919–1920), 34–73.

Henderson, Archibald, "Jeff Davis Determined to Continue Flight Even After Armistice Signed," *Greensboro Daily News,* September 1, 1935.

Henry, C. S., "Kenner's Mission to Europe," *William and Mary Quarterly,* XXV (1917), 9–12.

Holcombe, Wm. H., "The Alternative: A Separate Nationality, or the Africanization of the South," *Southern Literary Messenger,* XXXII (1861), 81–88.

"Hon. Thomas J. Semmes," Southern Historical Society, *Papers,* XXV (1897), 317–33.

Hull, A. L. (ed.), "Correspondence of Thomas Reade Rootes Cobb, 1860–1862," Southern History Association, *Publications,* XI (1907), 147–85, 233–60, 312–28.

———, "The Making of the Confederate Constitution," Southern History Association, *Publications,* IX (1905), 272–92.

"If We Had the Money," Southern Historical Society, *Papers,* XXXV (1907), 201–203.

James, Alfred P., "General Joseph Eggleston Johnston, Storm Center of the Confederate Army," *Mississippi Valley Historical Review,* XIV (1927–1928), 342–59.

Johnson, Bradley T.; Wright, John V.; Orr, J. A.; and Washington, L. Q., "Why the Confederate States of America Had No Supreme Court," Southern History Association, *Publications,* IV (1900), 81–101.

Kohler, Max J., "J. P. Benjamin, Statesman and Jurist," American Jewish Historical Society, *Publications,* XII (1904), 63–85.

"Letter from the Hon. George Davis, late Attorney-General of the Confederate States," Southern Historical Society, *Papers,* V (1878), 124–26.

"Letter of Stephen R. Mallory, 1861," *American Historical Review,* XII (1906), 103–108.

"Letter to a Peace Democrat," *Atlantic Monthly,* XII (1863), 776–89.

McCabel, Walter F., "The Organization of the Post-Office Department of the Confederacy," *American Historical Review,* XII (1906–1907), 66–74.

———, "John H. Reagan," Texas State Historical Association, *Quarterly,* IX (1905–1906), 41–51.

Mallory, Stephen R., "Last Days of the Confederate Government," *McClure's Magazine,* XVI (1900–1901), 99–107, 239–48.

Meade, Robert Douthat, "The Relations Between Judah P. Benjamin and Jefferson Davis," *Journal of Southern History,* V (1939), 468–78.

"Our Danger and Our Duty," *De Bow's Review,* XXXIII (1862), 43–51.

Owsley, Frank Lawrence, "Local Defense and the Overthrow of the

Confederacy, A Study in States Rights," *Mississippi Valley Historical Review*, XI (1924–1925), 490–525.

Phillips, Ulrich Bonnell, "The Central Theme of Southern History," *American Historical Review*, XXIV (1928–1929), 30–43.

"Political Portraits with Pen Pictures—James A. Seddon, of Virginia," *United States Magazine and Democratic Review*, XXVI (1850), 459–68.

Pollard, Edward Albert, "The Confederate Congress," *Galaxy*, VI (1868), 749–58.

Pollock, Baron, "Reminiscences of Judah P. Benjamin," *Green Bag*, X (1898), 396–401.

Ramsdell, Charles W., "The Confederate Government and the Railroads," *American Historical Review*, XXII (1917), 794–810.

Randall, James G., "The Newspaper Problem in Its Bearing upon Military Secrecy During the Civil War," *American Historical Review*, XXIII (1918), 303–23.

Reagan, John H., "An Account of the Organization and Operations of the Postoffice Department of the Confederate States of America, 1861 to 1865," Southern History Association, *Publications*, VI (1902), 314–27.

———, "Southern Political Views, 1865," Southern History Association, *Publications*, VI (1902), 132–42, 210–19.

"Records of the Confederate Attorneys-General," New York Public Library, *Bulletin*, I (1897), 341–42; II (1898), 196–98.

Redpath, James, "Neither Traitor nor Rebel," *Commonwealth*, II (1890), 385–92.

Robinson, William M., Jr., "Legal System of the Confederate States," *Journal of Southern History*, II (1936), 453–67.

Ruffin, Edmund, "Extracts from the Diary of Edmund Ruffin," *William and Mary Quarterly*, XIV–XXIII (1905–1915), *passim*.

Ruffin, F. B., "A Chapter of Confederate History," *North American Review*, CXXXIV (1882), 97–110.

Schwab, John Christopher, "Prices in the Confederate States, 1861–1865," *Political Science Quarterly*, XIV (1899), 281–304.

———, "The Confederate Foreign Loan: An Episode in the Financial History of the Civil War," *Yale Review*, I (1892), 175–86.

———, "The Financier of the Confederate States," *Yale Review*, II (1893), 288–301.

"Southern Trade," *De Bow's Review*, XXX (1861), 567–70.

"Southern Wealth and Northern Profits," *De Bow's Review*, XXIX (1860), 197–215.

Stephenson, N. W., "A Theory of Jefferson Davis," *American Historical Review*, XXI (1915–1916), 73–90.

———, "The Question of Arming the Slaves," *American Historical Review*, XVIII (1912–1913), 295–308.

Sumner, John O., "Materials for the History of the Government of the Southern Confederacy," *American Historical Association, Papers,* IV (1890), 5–19.

Swallon, W. H., "Retreat of the Confederate Government from Richmond to the Gulf," *Magazine of American History,* XV (1896), 596–608.

"The Future of Our Confederation," *De Bow's Review,* XXXI (1861), 35–41.

"The South, In the Union or Out of It," *De Bow's Review,* XXIX (1860), 448–65.

"The South's Power of Self-Protection," *De Bow's Review,* XXIX (1860), 545–61.

"The Times and the War," *De Bow's Review,* XXXI (1861), 1–13.

Tompkins, Henry Clay, "Judah Phillips Benjamin," *Sewanee Review,* V (1897), 129–45.

Trexler, Harrison A., "Jefferson Davis and the Confederate Patronage," *South Atlantic Quarterly,* XXVIII (1929), 45–58.

Walmsley, James Elliott, "The Last Meeting of the Confederate Cabinet," *Mississippi Valley Historical Review,* VI (1919–1920), 336–49.

Washington, L. Q., "Confederate States State Department," *Southern Historical Society, Papers,* XXIX (1901), 341–49.

Wood, John Taylor, "Escape of the Confederate Secretary of War," *Century Magazine,* XLVII (1893), 110–23.

Woodbury, Charles J., "Toombs," *Overland Monthly,* New Series, VII (1886), 125–28.

II. Autobiographies, Memoirs, and Reminiscences

Alexander, Edward Porter, *Military Memoirs of a Confederate: A Critical Narrative,* New York, 1907.

Campbell, John A. *Reminiscences and Documents Relating to the Civil War During the Year 1865,* Baltimore, 1887.

Clay-Clopton, Mrs. Virginia, *A Belle of the Fifties: Memoirs of Mrs. Clay of Alabama Covering Social and Political Life in Washington and the South, 1853–1866, Put into Narrative Form by Ada Sterling,* New York, 1905.

Davis, Jefferson, *The Rise and Fall of the Confederate Government,* 2 vols., New York, 1881.

———, *A Short History of the Confederate States of America,* New York, 1890.

Davis, Varina Howell, *Jefferson Davis, Ex-President of the Confederate States of America, A Memoir by His Wife,* 2 vols., New York, 1890.

DeLeon, Thomas Cooper, *Belles, Beaux and Brains of the 60's,* New York, 1909.

——, *Four Years in Rebel Capitals: An Inside View of Life in the Southern Confederacy, from Birth to Death; from Original Notes Collated in the Years 1861 to 1865,* Mobile, 1892.

Duke, Basil Wilson, *Reminiscences of General Basil W. Duke, C.S.A.,* New York, 1911.

Early, Jubal Anderson, *Autobiographical Sketch and Narrative of the War Between the States,* R. H. Early (ed.), Philadelphia, 1912.

Eggleston, George Cary, *A Rebel's Recollections,* New York, 1905.

Foote, Henry S., *Casket of Reminiscences,* Washington, 1874.

——, *War of the Rebellion; or Scylla and Charybdis, Consisting of Observations Upon the Causes, Course, and Consequences of the Late Civil War in the United States,* New York, 1866.

Gay, Mary Ann Harris, *Life in Dixie during the War, 1861–1865,* Atlanta, 1894.

Gordon, John B., *Reminiscences of the Civil War,* New York, 1903.

Gramp, William Edgar Hughes, *The Journal of a Grandfather,* St. Louis, 1912.

Harrison, Mrs. Burton, *Recollections Grave and Gay,* New York, 1911.

Johnson, R. U.; and Buel, C. C. (eds.), *Battles and Leaders of the Civil War, Being for the Most Part Contributions by Union and Confederate Officers . . . ,* 4 vols., New York, 1887–1888.

Johnston, Joseph E., *Narrative of Military Operations, Directed, During the Late War Between the States,* New York, 1874.

Longstreet, James, *From Manassas to Appomattox, Memoirs of the Civil War in America,* Philadelphia, 1896.

Lubbock, Francis Richard, *Six Decades in Texas, or Memoirs of Francis Richard Lubbock, Governor of Texas in War Times, 1861–1863: A Personal Experience in Business, War, and Politics,* C. W. Raines (ed.), Austin, 1900.

Morgan, James Morris, *Recollections of a Rebel Reefer,* Boston, 1917.

Pryor, Mrs. Roger A., *My Day: Reminiscences of a Long Life,* New York, 1909.

——, *Reminiscences of Peace and War,* New York, 1905.

Putnam, Sallie A., *Richmond During the War; Four Years of Personal Observation,* New York, 1867.

Reagan, John H., *Memoirs with Special Reference to Secession and the Civil War,* Walter F. McCabel (ed.), New York, 1906.

Smith, Gustavus W., *Confederate War Papers: Fairfax Court House, New Orleans, Seven Pines, Richmond and North Carolina,* New York, 1884.

Stephens, Alexander Hamilton, *A Constitutional View of the Late War Between the States: Its Causes, Character, Conduct and Re-*

sults Presented in a Series of Colloquies at Liberty Hall, 2 vols., Philadelphia, 1868.

Wise, John S., *The End of an Era,* Boston, 1900.

Wright, Mrs. Giraud D. (Louise Wigfall), *A Southern Girl in '61: The War-Time Memories of a Confederate Senator's Daughter,* New York, 1905.

III. Biographies

Alfriend, Frank H., *The Life of Jefferson Davis,* Cincinnati, 1868.

A Memorial of the Hon. George Davis, Wilmington, 1896.

Ashe, Samuel A'Court (ed.), *Biographical History of North Carolina from Colonial Times to the Present,* 10 vols., Greensboro, 1905–1917.

———, *George Davis, Attorney-General of the Confederate States,* Raleigh, 1916.

Bradford, Gamaliel, *Confederate Portraits,* Boston, 1914.

Butler, Pierce, *Judah P. Benjamin,* Philadelphia, 1907.

Capers, Henry D., *The Life and Times of C. G. Memminger,* Richmond, 1893.

Carson, James Petigru, *Life, Letters and Speeches of James Louis Petigru: The Union Man of South Carolina,* Washington, 1920.

Cleveland, Henry, *Alexander H. Stephens, in Public and Private, with Letters and Speeches, Before, During, and Since the War,* Philadelphia, 1866.

Clubbs, Occie, "Stephen Russell Mallory, the Elder," unpublished Master's Thesis, University of Florida, 1936.

Connor, Henry Graves, *John Archibald Campbell, Associate Justice of the United States Supreme Court 1853–1861,* Boston, 1920.

Cowper, Pulaski, *Sketch of the Life of Governor Thomas Bragg,* Raleigh, 1891.

Craven, Avery, *Edmund Ruffin, Southerner: A Study in Secession,* New York, 1932.

Cutting, Elizabeth Brown, *Jefferson Davis, Political Soldier,* New York, 1930.

Daniel, John W. (ed.), *Life and Reminiscences of Jefferson Davis, by Distinguished Men of His Time,* Baltimore, 1890.

Dodd, William E., *Jefferson Davis,* Philadelphia, 1907.

Dowd, Clement, *Life of Zebulon B. Vance,* Charlotte, 1897.

DuBose, John Witherspoon, *The Life and Times of William Lowndes Yancey, A History of Political Parties in the United States, From 1834 to 1864; Especially as to the Origin of the Confederate States,* Birmingham, 1892.

Eckenrode, Hamilton J., *Jefferson Davis: President of the South,* New York, 1923.

Freeman, Douglas Southall, *R. E. Lee, A Biography,* 4 vols., New York, 1934–1936.

———, *Lee's Lieutenants: A Study in Command,* 2 vols., New York, 1943.

Gordon, Armistead, *Jefferson Davis,* New York, 1918.

Grayson, William John, *James Louis Petigru,* New York, 1886.

Henderson, G. F. R., *Stonewall Jackson and the American Civil War,* New York, 1934.

Hill, Benjamin Harvey, Jr., *Senator Benjamin H. Hill of Georgia. His Life, Speeches and Writings,* Atlanta, 1893.

Hodgson, Joseph, *The Cradle of the Confederacy; or, The Times of Troup, Quitman, and Yancey. A Sketch of Southwestern Political History from the Formation of the Federal Government to A.D. 1861,* Mobile, 1876.

Johnson, Allen; and Malone, Dumas (eds.), *Dictionary of American Biography,* 20 vols., New York, 1928–1936.

Johnston, Richard Malcolm; and Browne, William Hand, *Life of Alexander H. Stephens,* Philadelphia, 1878.

Jones, Charles C., *Brigadier-General Robert Toombs* (an address delivered before the Confederate Survivors Association, April 26, 1886), Augusta, 1886.

McElroy, Robert, *Jefferson Davis the Unreal and the Real,* 2 vols., New York, 1937.

Mason, Virginia, *The Public Life and Diplomatic Correspondence of James M. Mason with Some Personal History by Virginia Mason (His Daughter),* New York, 1906.

Mayes, Edward, *Lucius Q. C. Lamar: His Life, Times, and Speeches 1825–1893,* Nashville, 1896.

Meade, Robert Douthat, *Judah P. Benjamin: Confederate Statesman,* New York, 1943.

Owen, Thomas M., *History of Alabama and Dictionary of Alabama Biography,* 4 vols., Chicago, 1921.

Pearce, Haywood J., Jr., *Benjamin H. Hill: Secession and Reconstruction,* Chicago, 1928.

Pendleton, Louis, *Alexander H. Stephens,* Philadelphia, 1908.

Phillips, Ulrich Bonnell, *The Life of Robert Toombs,* New York, 1913.

Pollard, Edward A., *Life of Jefferson Davis with a Secret History of the Southern Confederacy gathered "Behind the Scenes in Richmond . . . ,"* Atlanta, 1869.

Roman, Alfred, *The Military Operations of General Beauregard in the War Between the States, 1861 to 1865, including a Brief Sketch and a Narrative of His Services in the War with Mexico, 1846–8,* 2 vols., New York, 1884.

Rowland, Dunbar, *Encyclopedia of Mississippi History Comprising*

Sketches of Counties, Towns, Events, Institutions and Persons, 2 vols., Madison, 1907.

Rowland, Eron, *Varina Howell, Wife of Jefferson Davis*, 2 vols., New York, 1927.

Schaff, Morris, *Jefferson Davis, His Life and Personality*, Boston, 1922.

Sears, Louis Martin, *John Slidell*, Durham, 1925.

Simms, Henry Harrison, *Life of Robert M. T. Hunter, A Study in Sectionalism and Secession*, Richmond, 1935.

Sprunt, James, *George Davis*, Raleigh, 1919.

Stillwell, Lucille, *John Cabell Breckinridge: Born to Be a Statesman*, Caldwell, 1936.

Stovall, Pleasant A., *Robert Toombs, Statesman, Speaker, Soldier, Sage—His Career in Congress and on the Hustings—His Work in the Courts—His Record with the Army—His Life at Home*, New York, 1892.

Tate, Allen, *Jefferson Davis: His Rise and Fall. A Biographical Narrative*, New York, 1929.

Trent, William Peterfield, *Southern Statesmen of the Old Regime*, New York, 1897.

Washington, L. Q., *A Memoir of Robert M. T. Hunter by Martha T. Hunter (His Daughter) with an Address on His Life*, Washington, 1903.

Winston, Robert Watson, *High Stakes and Hair Trigger. The Life of Jefferson Davis*, New York, 1930.

White, Laura Amanda, *Robert Barnwell Rhett: Father of Secession*, New York, 1931.

Willson, Beckles, *John Slidell and the Confederates in Paris (1862–65)*, New York, 1932.

IV. General Works and Special Studies

Alexander, Violet G., *The Confederate States Navy Yard at Charlotte, N.C., 1862–1865*, Charlotte, 1914.

Annals of the War, Written by Leading Participants North and South, Philadelphia, 1879.

Blythe, Vernon, *A History of the Civil War in the United States*, New York, 1914.

Bonham, Milledge Louis, Jr., *Studies in History, Economics and Public Law, Vol. XLIII, No. 3, The British Consuls in the Confederacy*, New York, 1911.

Bradford, Gamaliel, *Wives*, New York, 1925.

Brantley, Rabun Lee, *Georgia Journalism of the Civil War Period*, Nashville, 1929.

Brooks, Robert Preston, *Conscription in the Confederate States of America 1862–1865*, Athens, 1917.

Bulloch, James Dunwoody, *The Secret Service of the Confederate States in Europe; or How the Confederate Cruisers Were Equipped*, 2 vols., New York, 1883.

Cable, George Washington, and others (eds.), *Famous Adventures and Prison Escapes of the Civil War*, London, 1894.

Callahan, James Morton, *The Diplomatic History of the Southern Confederacy*, Baltimore, 1901.

Carpenter, Jesse Thomas, *The South as a Conscious Minority: A Study in Political Thought*, New York, 1930.

Chadwick, French Ensor, *The American Nation: A History, Volume 19, Causes of the Civil War, 1859–1861*, New York, 1906.

Chandler, Julian Alvin Carroll, et al. (eds.), *The South in the Building of the Nation. A History of the Southern States Designed to Record the South's Part in the Making of the American Nation; to Portray the Character and Genius, to Chronicle the Achievements and Progress and to Illustrate the Life and Traditions of the Southern People*, 12 vols., Richmond, 1909.

Claiborne, John Herbert, *Seventy-Five Years in Old Virginia, with Some Account of the Life of the Author and Some History of the People Amongst Whom His Lot Was Cast; Their Character, Their Condition, and Their Conduct Before the War, During the War and After the War*, New York, 1904.

Crawford, Samuel Wylie, *The Genesis of the Civil War, The Story of Fort Sumter, 1860–1861*, New York, 1887.

Curry, Jabez Lamar Monroe, *Civil History of the Government of the Confederate States, with Some Personal Reminiscences*, Richmond, 1900.

Denman, Clarence Phillips, *The Secession Movement in Alabama*, Montgomery, 1933.

Derry, Joseph Tyrone, *Story of the Confederate States; or History of the War for Southern Independence, Embracing a Brief But Comprehensive Sketch of the Early Settlement of the Country, Trouble with the Indians, the French, Revolutionary and Mexican Wars, and a Full, Complete and Graphic Account of the Great Four Years' War Between the North and the South, Its Causes, Effects, Etc.*, Richmond, 1895.

Dumond, Dwight Lowell, *The Secession Movement 1860–1861*, New York, 1931.

Eggleston, George Cary, *The History of the Confederate War: Its Causes and Its Conduct. A Narrative and Critical History*, 2 vols., New York, 1910.

Evans, Clement Anselm (ed.), *Confederate Military History: A Li-*

brary of Confederate States History . . . *Written by Distinguished Men of the South,* . . . , 12 vols., Atlanta, 1899.

Fish, Carl Russell, *The American Civil War: An Interpretation,* edited by William Ernest Smith, New York, 1937.

Fleming, Walter Lynwood, *Civil War and Reconstruction in Alabama,* New York, 1915.

Grimes, Absalom Carlisle, *Absalom Grimes, Confederate Mail Runner, Edited from Captain Grimes' Own Story by M. M. Quaife,* New Haven, 1926.

Hanna, A. J., *Flight Into Oblivion,* Richmond, 1938.

Hendrick, Burton J., *Statesmen of the Lost Cause: Jefferson Davis and His Cabinet,* New York, 1939.

Henry, Robert Selph, *The Story of the Confederacy,* Indianapolis, 1936.

Hesseltine, William Best, *Civil War Prisons: A Study in War Psychology,* Columbus, 1930.

Hill, Louise B., *State Socialism in the Confederate States of America,* Charlottesville, 1936.

Hilliard, Henry W., *Politics and Pen Pictures at Home and Abroad,* New York, 1892.

Hosmer, James K., *The Appeal to Arms, 1861–1863,* New York, 1907.

———, *The American Nation: A History, Volume 21, The Outcome of the Civil War, 1863–1865,* New York, 1907.

Huse, Caleb, *The Supplies for the Confederate Army: How They Were Obtained in Europe and How Paid for: Personal Reminiscences and Unpublished History,* Boston, 1904.

Kettell, Thomas Prentice, *Southern Wealth and Northern Profits; Showing the Necessity of Union to the Future Prosperity and Welfare of the Republic,* New York, 1860.

Kilpatrick, Emmett, *Le Departement Exécutif des États Confédérés d'Amérique (1861–1865),* Paris, 1924.

LaBree, Ben (ed.), *The Confederate Soldier in the Civil War, 1861–1865,* Louisville, 1895.

Lee, Guy Carleton, *The True History of the Civil War,* Philadelphia, 1903.

Lonn, Ella, *Desertion During the Civil War,* New York, 1928.

McHenry, George, *The Cotton Trade: Its Bearing upon the Prosperity of Great Britain and Commerce of the American Republics Considered in Connection with the System of Negro Slavery in the Confederate State,* London, 1863.

McKim, Randolph H., *A Soldier's Recollections: Leaves from the Diary of a Young Confederate, with an Oration on the Motives and Aims of the Soldiers of the South, with a History of the 15th Alabama Regiment and the Forty-eight Battles in Which It Was Engaged* . . . , New York, 1910.

Maurice, Sir Frederick Barton, *Statesmen and Soldiers of the Civil War, A Study of the Conduct of the War,* Boston, 1926.

Miller, Francis Trevelyan (ed.), *The Photographic History of the Civil War,* 10 vols., New York, 1911.

Moore, Albert Burton, *Conscription and Conflict in the Confederacy,* New York, 1924.

Oates, William Calvin, *The War Between the Union and the Confederacy and Its Lost Opportunities,* New York, 1905.

Owen, Thomas McAdory, *Annals of Alabama, 1819–1900,* Birmingham, 1900.

Owsley, Frank Lawrence, *King Cotton Diplomacy. Foreign Relations of the Confederate States of America,* Chicago, 1931.

————, *State Rights in the Confederacy,* Chicago, 1931.

Pollard, Edward A., *The Lost Cause: A New Southern History of the Confederates Comprising a Full and Authentic Account of the Rise and Progress of the Late Southern Confederacy—the Campaigns, Battles, Incidents, and Adventures of the Most Gigantic Struggle of the World's History . . . ,* New York, 1866.

————, *Southern History of the War, Two Volumes in One,* New York, 1866.

Rainwater, Percy Lee, *Mississippi, Storm Center of Secession, 1856–1861,* Baton Rouge, 1938.

Randall, James Garfield, *The Civil War and Reconstruction,* Boston, 1937.

Reed, John Calvin, *The Brothers War,* Boston, 1906.

Rhodes, James Ford, *History of the Civil War, 1861–1865,* New York, 1919.

Robinson, William M., Jr., *The Confederate Privateers,* New Haven, 1928.

————, *Justice in Grey: A History of the Judicial System of the Confederate States of America,* Cambridge, 1941.

Ruffin, Edmund, *Anticipations of the Future to serve as lessons for the Present Time. in the form of Extracts of letters from an English Resident in the United States, to the London Times, from 1864 to 1870,* Richmond, 1870.

Russel, Robert Royal, *Economic Aspects of Southern Sectionalism, 1840–1861,* Urbana, 1924.

Scharf, John Thomas, *History of the Confederate States Navy from Its Organization to the Surrender of Its Last Vessel. Its Stupendous Struggle with the Great Navy of the United States; the Engagements Fought in the Rivers and Harbors of the South, and upon the High Seas; Blockade-running, First Use of Iron-Clads and Torpedoes, and Privateer History,* New York, 1887.

Schouler, James, *History of the United States of America Under the Constitution,* 7 vols., New York, 1894–1913.

Schwab, John Christopher, *The Confederate States of America, 1861–1865; A Financial and Industrial History of the South During the Civil War,* New York, 1901.

Shanks, Henry Thomas, *The Secession Movement in Virginia, 1847–1861,* Richmond, 1934.

Simkins, Francis Butler; and Patton, James Welch, *The Women of the Confederacy,* Richmond, 1936.

Smith, Ashton Earnest, *The History of the Confederate Treasury,* Richmond, 1901.

Stanard, Mary Newton, *Richmond, Its People and Its Story,* Philadelphia, 1928.

Stephenson, N. W., *The Day of the Confederacy; A Chronicle of the Embattled South,* New Haven, 1920.

Studies in Southern History and Politics, Inscribed to William Archibald Dunning, Ph.D., LL.D., Lieber Professor of History and Political Philosophy in Columbia University by His Former Pupils the Authors, New York, 1914.

Tansill, Robert, *Free and Impartial Exposition of the Causes which Led to the Failure of the Confederate States to Establish Their Independence,* Washington, 1865.

Tatum, Georgia Lee, *Disloyalty in the Confederacy,* Chapel Hill, 1934.

Thompson, Samuel Bernard, *Confederate Purchasing Operations Abroad,* Chapel Hill, 1935.

Todd, Herbert H., *The Building of the Confederate States Navy in Europe,* Nashville, 1941.

Wesley, Charles Harris, *The Collapse of the Confederacy,* Washington, 1937.

Index